Original illisible
NF Z 43-120-10

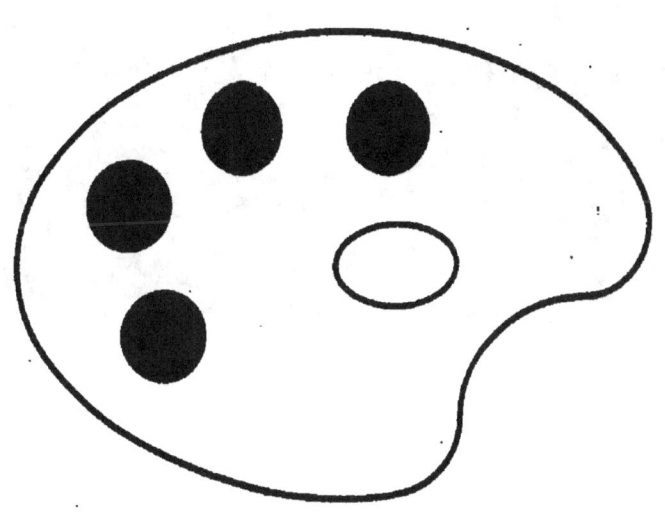

Original en couleur
NF Z 43-120-8

"VALABLE POUR TOUT OU PARTIE
DU DOCUMENT REPRODUIT".

THE COLUMN OF JULY (HISTORY REPEATS ITSELF)

PARIS

UNDER THE COMMUNE:

OR,

THE SEVENTY-THREE DAYS OF THE SECOND SIEGE.

WITH NUMEROUS ILLUSTRATIONS, SKETCHES TAKEN ON THE SPOT, AND PORTRAITS (FROM THE ORIGINAL PHOTOGRAPHS).

By JOHN LEIGHTON, F.S.A.,

&c.

LONDON:
BRADBURY, EVANS, & CO., 10, BOUVERIE ST.
1871.

[All Rights reserved.]

Socialism, or the Red Republic, is all one; for it would tear down the tricolour and set up the red flag. It would make penny pieces out of the Column Vendôme. It would knock down the statue of Napoleon and raise up that of Marat in its stead. It would suppress the Académie, the École Polytechnique, and the Legion of Honour. To the grand device Liberty, Equality, and Fraternity, it would add "Ou la mort." It would bring about a general bankruptcy. It would ruin the rich without enriching the poor. It would destroy labour, which gives to each one his bread. It would abolish property and family. It would march about with the heads of the proscribed on pikes, fill the prisons with the suspected, and empty them by massacres. It would convert France into the country of gloom. It would strangle liberty, stifle the arts, silence thought, and deny God. It would bring into action these two fatal machines, one of which never works without the other—the assignat press and the guillotine. In a word, it would do in cold blood what the men of 1793 did in fever, and after the grand horrors which our fathers saw, we should have the horrible in all that was low and small.

(Victor Hugo, 1848.)

BRADBURY, EVANS, AND CO., PRINTERS, WHITEFRIARS.

PREFACE.

EARLY in June of the present year I was making notes and sketches, without the least idea of what I should do with them. I was at the Mont-Parnasse Station of the Western Railway, awaiting a train from Paris to St. Cloud. Our fellow passengers, as we discovered afterwards, were principally prisoners for Versailles; the guards, soldiers; and the line, for two miles at least, appeared desolation and ruin.

The façade of the station, a very large one, was pockmarked all over by Federal bullets, whilst cannon balls had cut holes through the stone wall as if it had been cheese, and gone down the line, towards Cherbourg or Brest! The restaurant below was nearly annihilated, the counters, tables, and chairs being reduced to a confused heap. But there was a book-stall! and on that book-stall reposed a little work, entitled the "Bataille des Sept Jours," a brochure which a friend bought and gave to me, saying, "*Voilà la texte de vos croquis.*" From seven days my ideas naturally wandered to seventy-three—the duration of the reign of the Commune—and then again to two hundred and twenty days—that included the Commune of 1871 and its antecedents. Hence this volume, which I liken to a French château, to which I have added a second storey and wings.

And now that the house is finished, I must render my obligations to M. Mendès and numerous French friends, for their kind assistance and valuable aid, including my confrères of "*The Graphic,*" who have allowed me to enliven the walls with pictures from their stores; and last, and not least, my best thanks are due to an English Peer, who placed at my disposal his unique collection of prints and journals of the period bearing upon the subject—a subject I am pretty familiar with. Powder has done its work, the smell of petroleum has passed away, the house that called me master has vanished from the face of the earth, and my concierge and his wife are reported *fusillés* by the Versaillais; and to add to the disaster, my rent was paid in advance, having been deposited with a *notaire* prior to the First Siege. . . . . But my neighbours, where are they? In my immediate neighbourhood six houses were entirely destroyed, and as many more half ruined. I can only speak of one friend, an amiable and able architect, who, alas! remonstrated in person, and received a ball from a revolver through the back of his neck. His head is bowed for life. He has lost his pleasure and his treasure, a valuable museum of art,—happily they could not burn his reputation, or the monument of his life—a range of goodly folio volumes that exist "*pour tous.*"

L.

LONDON, 1871.

CONTENTS.

	PAGE
PREFACE	v
CONTENTS	vii
LIST OF PLATES AND ILLUSTRATIONS	xiii

INTRODUCTORY CHAPTER—The 30th October, 1870—The Hôtel de Ville invaded—Governor Trochu resigns—A Revolt attempted—Meetings, Place de la Bastille—The Prussians enter Paris—Hostility of the National Guard 1

    I. The Memorable 18th of March—Line and Nationals Fraternise—Discipline at a Discount 27

    II. Assassination of Generals Lecomte and Clément Thomas 31

    III. Proclamation of M. Picard—The Government retires to Versailles 33

    IV. The New Regime Proclaimed—Obscurity of New Masters 37

    V. Paris Hesitates—Small Sympathy with Versailles . . 43

    VI. The Buttes Montmartre 45

    VII. An Issue Possible—An Approved Proclamation . . 47

    VIII. Demonstration of the Friends of Order 50

    IX. The Drama of the Rue de la Paix—Victims to Order . 53

    X. A Wedding 56

    XI. The Bourse and Belleville 57

    XII. Watching and Waiting 60

    XIII. A Timid but Prudent Person 61

    XIV. Some Federal Opinions 64

		PAGE
XV.	Proclamation of Admiral Saisset—Paris Satisfied	66
XVI.	A Widow	69
XVII.	The Central Committee Triumphs	70
XVIII.	Paris Elections	73
XIX.	The Commune a Fact—A Motley Assembly	75
XX.	Proclamation of the Elections	77
XXI.	A Batch of Official Decrees—Landlord and Tenant	79
XXII.	Requisitions and Feasts	83
XXIII.	Removals and Retirements	84
XXIV.	A General Flight	85
XXV.	An Envoy to Garibaldi	88
XXVI.	Commencement of Civil War—Beyond the Arc de Triomphe	91
XXVII.	Mont Valérien opens on the Federals—Contradictory News	98
XXVIII.	Death of General Duval—Able Administration	103
XXIX.	Antipathy to the Church—The Archbishop Interrogated	108
XXX.	The Accomplices of Versailles	111
XXXI.	Death of Colonel Flourens	113
XXXII.	The Cross and the Red Flag	117
XXXIII.	Colonel Assy of Creuzot—Disgrace of Lullier	118
XXXIV.	Fighting goes on	123
XXXV.	Federal Funerals	125
XXXVI.	Prudent Counsel	126
XXXVII.	Suppression of Newspapers	128
XXXVIII.	The Second Bombardment—Avenue de la Grande Armée—Reckless Aim of the Versaillais	130
XXXIX.	The Plan of Bergeret	143
XL.	Another General!—Police and Pressgang—A Citizen of the World	147
XLI.	Women and Children	152
XLII.	Why is Conciliation Impossible?	154
XLIII.	The Portable Guillotine	156

CONTENTS.

		PAGE
XLIV.	The Common Grave	158
XLV.	Idle Paris	159
XLVI.	The Press	161
XLVII.	Day follows Day	163
XLVIII.	The Condemned Column—Model Decrees	164
XLIX.	Thiers and Conciliation—Paris and France	170
L.	Communist Caricatures—Political Satire	174
LI.	Gustave Courbet—Federation of Art—Courbet, President	179
LII.	Camp, Place Vendôme	183
LIII.	Elections of the 16th of April	185
LIV.	The "Change" under the Commune	188
LV.	Elections sans Electors—Farce of Universal Suffrage	190
LVI.	À la Mode de Londres	194
LVII.	The Little Sisters of the Poor	196
LVIII.	Bécon and Asnières taken—Declaration to the French People—Federation of Communes—The Commune or the Deluge	198
LIX.	A Court-Martial	210
LX.	A Heroic Gamin	211
LXI.	Killing the Dead	212
LXII.	The Truce at Neuilly—Porte-Maillot destroyed—Neuilly in Ruins	212
LXIII.	Masonic Mediation—The Envoy of Peace—Citizens and Brothers—A White Flag on Porte-Maillot	219
LXIV.	Prudent Monsieur Pyat	227
LXV.	Resources of the Commune—The Royal Road to Riches	231
LXVI.	The Prophecy of Proudhon	234
LXVII.	Revolutionary Balloons	236
LXVIII.	A Confession of Conscience	238
LXIX.	Communist Journalism—Sensation Articles	238
LXX.	Fort Issy falls	248
LXXI.	Cluseret arrested	250
LXXII.	The Executive Commission—Committee of Public Safety	253

		PAGE
LXXIII.	A Competent Tribunal	256
LXXIV.	The Password betrayed	256
LXXV.	The Condemned Chapel	259
LXXVI.	Restitution is Robbery	261
LXXVII.	The Nuns of Picpus	263
LXXVIII.	Rossel resigns—The Semblance of a Government	264
LXXIX.	Want of Funds—The Sinews of War	271
LXXX.	Passwords—The Chariot of Apollo—Refractories	273
LXXXI.	Sacrilege—Clubs in the Churches	279
LXXXII.	Refractories in Danger	284
LXXXIII.	The Home of M. Thiers, Demolition and Removal	287
LXXXIV.	Filial Love	291
LXXXV.	Communal Secessionists—Save himself who can	293
LXXXVI.	The Failing Cause—The Column Vendôme falls	296
LXXXVII.	A Concert at the Tuileries	299
LXXXVIII.	Cartridge Magazine Explosion	302
LXXXIX.	The Advent of Action—Paris ceases to smile	305
XC.	The Troops enter—Street Fortifications—Insurgents at home	308
XCI.	Arrests and Murders	324
XCII.	Fire and Sword	325
XCIII.	Barricade at the Place de Clichy	327
XCIV.	Rack and Ruin	329
XCV.	Bloodshed and Brigandage	331
XCVI.	Hôtel de Ville on Fire—A Furnace	335
XCVII.	Pétroleurs and Pétroleuses	338
XCVIII.	Streets of Paris	340
XCIX.	The Expiring Demons—The Hostages—Reprisals—Cemeteries	340
C.	Sewers and Catacombs	347
CI.	Mourning and Sadness	350

APPENDIX.

	PAGE
Chronology of the Commune	353
Memoir of Rochefort	357
The 18th of March	360
The Prussians and the Commune	362
Memoir of Gambon	363
Memoir of Lullier	364
Memoir of Protot	366
Translation from Victor Hugo	366
Note of Jourde	367
Last Proclamations of the Commune	367
Note of Férré	369
The Hostages—Gendarmes, &c.	368
President Bonjean	371
Note of Urbain	373
Devastations of Paris	374
Official Report of General Ladmirault	386
Ammunition expended on Second Siege of Paris	387
List of Monuments and Buildings destroyed	389
Index to Plan—Damages by Fires, &c.	396

LIST OF ILLUSTRATIONS.

* Separate Plates on tinted paper.

	PAGE
* FRONTISPIECE :—THE COLUMN OF JULY (HISTORY REPEATS ITSELF)	
PORTRAIT OF M. THIERS, PRESIDENT OF THE FRENCH REPUBLIC	1
*THE STATE OF PARTY—PICTURED BY THEMSELVES. ALLEGORICAL PAGE—ROCHEFORT, CLÉMENT THOMAS, &C. (*facsimile.*)	2
COLUMN OF JULY—PLACE DE LA BASTILLE	13
THE BUTTES MONTMARTRE—FEDERAL ARTILLERY PARKED THERE	19
MONTMARTRE—FIRST LINE OF SENTINELS	20
THE RED FLAG ON THE COLUMN OF JULY	26
* PURIFICATION OF THE CHAMPS ÉLYSÉES AFTER THE DEPARTURE OF THE PRUSSIANS — CONSTRUCTION OF THE FIRST BARRICADE, 18TH MARCH	27
DEFENCE OF THE HOTEL DE VILLE	33
SENTINELS, BOULEVARD SAINT-MICHEL	34
BEHIND A BARRICADE—THE DÉJEUNER	46
PORTRAIT OF GAMBON, MEMBER OF THE COMMUNE	88
BEHIND A BARRICADE—THE EVENING MEAL	92
PLACE DE LA CONCORDE—FEDERALS GOING OUT	94
PORTRAIT OF GENERAL BERGERET	98
PORTRAIT OF ABBÉ DEGUERRY, CURÉ OF THE MADELEINE	109
PORTRAIT OF RAOUL RIGAULT, PROCUREUR OF THE COMMUNE	110
PORTRAIT OF MONSEIGNEUR DARBOY, ARCHBISHOP OF PARIS	*ib.*
PORTRAIT OF COLONEL FLOURENS	114
PORTRAIT OF COLONEL ASSY, GOVERNOR OF THE HOTEL DE VILLE	118
THE RED FLAG ON THE PANTHEON	118

LIST OF ILLUSTRATIONS.

	PAGE
PORTRAIT OF GENERAL CLUSERET	123
THE ARC DE TRIOMPHE DE L'ÉTOILE	134
HORSE CHASSEUR ACTING AS COMMUNIST ARTILLERYMAN	137
MARINE GUNNER AND STREET BOY	142
THE CORPS LÉGISLATIF—HEAD QUARTERS OF GENERAL BERGERET	145
PORTRAIT OF GENERAL DOMBROWSKI	147
* BURNING THE GUILLOTINE IN THE PLACE VOLTAIRE	158
COLONNE VENDÔME	165
* CARICATURE DURING THE COMMUNE—LITTLE PARIS AND HIS PLAYTHINGS (*facsimile*)	178
* THE MODERN "EROSTRATE"—COURBET AND THE DEBRIS OF THE VENDÔME COLUMN	180
* FEDERAL VISIT TO THE LITTLE SISTERS OF THE POOR	197
PORTRAIT OF VERMOREL, DELEGATE OF THE EXECUTIVE COMMISSION	200
FEMALE CURIOSITY AT PORTE MAILLOT	213
PORTE MAILLOT AND CHAPEL OF ST. FERDINAND	214
ARMISTICE—INHABITANTS OF NEUILLY ENTERING PARIS	214
WATCHING FOR THE FIRST SHOT FROM FORT VALERIEN	217
FEMALE IMPERTURBABILITY AFTER THE ARMISTICE	218
PORTRAIT OF PROTOT, DELEGATE OF JUSTICE	220
PORTRAIT OF FÉLIX PYAT, MEMBER OF THE COMMITTEE OF PUBLIC SAFETY	222
FREEMASONS AT THE RAMPARTS	226
PORTRAIT OF VERMESCH, EDITOR OF THE "PÈRE DUCHESNE"	239
PORTRAIT OF PASCHAL GROUSSET, DELEGATE OF FOREIGN AFFAIRS	241
PORTRAIT OF DUPONT, COMMISSIONER OF TRADE AND COMMERCE	255
CHAPELLE EXPIATOIRE (CONDEMNED BY THE COMMUNE)	260
* CARICATURE DURING THE COMMUNE—PARIS EATS A GENERAL A-DAY (*facsimile*)	264
PORTRAIT OF DELESCLUZE, DELEGATE OF WAR	266
PORTRAIT OF FONTAINE, DIRECTOR OF PUBLIC DOMAINS AND REGISTRATION	272
RÉFRACTAIRES ESCAPING FROM THE CITY BY NIGHT	276
PORTRAIT OF GENERAL LA CÉCILIA	280
CHURCH OF ST. EUSTACHE (EXTERIOR)	281

LIST OF ILLUSTRATIONS.

	PAGE
INTERIOR OF ST. EUSTACHE, USED AS A RED CLUB	282
HOUSE OF M. THIERS IN THE PLACE ST. GEORGES	288
HOUSE DURING DEMOLITION—AFTER ITS SACK	290
PORTRAIT OF COURNET, PREFECT OF POLICE	292
PORTRAIT OF ARTHUR ARNOULD, COMMISSIONER OF FOREIGN AFFAIRS	294
* THE SEINE: FOUNDERED GUN-BOATS—PORTE MAILLOT, DESOLATION AND DESTRUCTION	295
BARRICADE OF THE RUE CASTIGLIONE FROM THE PLACE VENDÔME	297
PALACE OF THE TUILERIES	300
PORTRAIT OF BAZOUA, GOVERNOR OF THE MILITARY SCHOOL	303
* CAFÉ LIFE UNDER THE COMMUNE—A SLIGHT INTERRUPTION—PLAY-BILLS AND BURNT-OFFERINGS—"SPECTACLES DE PARIS"	309
* PLACE DE LA CONCORDE—STATUES OF LILLE AND STRASBOURG	312
* FIRE AND WATER—THE EFFECT OF FIRE ON THE FOUNTAINS OF THE PLACE DE LA CONCORDE AND THE CHÂTEAU D'EAU—HIRONDELLES DE PARIS	313
PORTRAIT OF JULES VALLÈS, DELEGATE OF FOREIGN AFFAIRS AND OF PUBLIC INSTRUCTION	317
BARRICADE CLOSING THE RUE DE RIVOLI FROM THE PLACE DE LA CONCORDE	319
* BULLET MARKS "EN FACE" AND "EN PROFIL"—THE TREES AND LAMPS	321
RUE ROYALE, LOOKING FROM THE MADELEINE TO THE PLACE DE LA CONCORDE	330
* A WARM CORNER OF THE TUILERIES	330
PORTRAIT OF MILLIÈRE, EX-DEPUTY, MEMBER OF THE COMMUNE	332
PALAIS DE JUSTICE	333
* POLICE OF PARIS—MINISTRY OF FINANCE, RUE DE RIVOLI	335
PORTRAIT OF FERRÉ, PREFECT OF POLICE	335
PALACE OF THE LUXEMBOURG (AMBULANCE HOSPITAL OF THE COMMUNE)	338
* PÉTROLEURS AND PÉTROLEUSES	338
* THE THEATRE OF THE PORTE ST.-MARTIN—ALL THAT REMAINS OF THE HOME OF SENSATION DRAMA	342
CELL OF THE ARCHBISHOP OF PARIS IN THE PRISON OF LA ROQUETTE	343

LIST OF ILLUSTRATIONS.

	PAGE
YARD OF LA ROQUETTE WHERE THE ARCHBISHOP AND HOSTAGES WERE SHOT	344
* MY NEIGHBOUR OPPOSITE, BUSINESS CARRIED ON AS USUAL—MY NEIGHBOUR NEXT DOOR, HE THINKS HIMSELF FORTUNATE	346
PARIS UNDERGROUND (SEWERS AND CATACOMBS)	348
* THE ENEMIES OF PROGRESS (LES ARISTOCRATES ENCORE)—CORPS DE GARDE DE L'ARMÉE DE VERSAILLES	348
* THE PUBLIC PROMENADES—A CAMP IN THE LUXEMBOURG—THE NEW MASTERS—PROCLAMATION OVER PROCLAMATION	350
THE LUXEMBOURG (PRESENT TOWN HALL OF PARIS, 1871)	351
PORTRAIT OF MARSHAL MACMAHON, DUKE OF MAGENTA	352
* LIGHT AND AIR ONCE MORE—THE FOSSE COMMUNE (THE END)	353

APPENDIX.

MUSÉE OF THE LOUVRE, FROM THE PLACE DU CARROUSEL	378
PALAIS ROYAL	379
HOTEL DE VILLE	381
FOREIGN OFFICE	382
PALACE OF THE LEGION OF HONOUR	384

MAP OF PARIS, WITH INDICATIONS OF ALL THE PARTS DAMAGED OR DESTROYED.

M. THIERS,

Voted Chief of the Executive Power, Feb. 18, 1871,
and President of the Republic, Sept. 1871.

PARIS UNDER THE COMMUNE.

INTRODUCTORY.

LATE in the day of the 30th October, 1870, the agitation was great in Paris; the news had spread that the village of Le Bourget had been retaken by the Prussians. The military report had done what it could to render the pill less bitter by saying that *"this village did not form part of the system of defence,"* but the people though kept in ignorance perceived instinctively that there must be weakness on the part of the chiefs. After so much French blood had been shed in taking the place, men of brave will would not have been wanting to occupy it. We admit that Le Bourget may not have been important from a military point of view, but as regarding its moral effect its loss was much to be regretted.

The irritation felt by the population of Paris was changed into exasperation, when on the following day the news of the reduction of Metz appeared in the *Official Journal:*

"The Government has just been acquainted with the sad intelligence of the capitulation of Metz. Marshal Bazaine and his army were compelled to surrender, after heroic efforts, which the want of food and ammunition alone rendered impossible to maintain. They have been made prisoners of war."

And after this the Government talks of an armistice! What! Strasburg, Toul, Metz, and so many other towns have resisted to the last dire extremity, and Paris, who expects succour from the provinces, is to capitulate, while a single effort is left untried? Has she no more bread? No more powder? Have her citizens no more blood in their veins? No, no! No armistice!

In the morning, a deputation, formed of officers of the National Guards, went to the Hôtel de Ville to learn from the Government what were its intentions. They were received by M. Etienne Arago, who promised them that the decision should be made known to them about two o'clock.

The rappel was beaten at the time mentioned; battalions of the National Guards poured into the Place, some armed, many without arms.

Over the sea of heads the eye was attracted by banners, and enormous placards bearing the inscriptions—

"Vive la République!   "Vive la Commune!
 "No Armistice!"   or else   "Death to Cowards!"

Rochefort,* with several other members of the Government, shows himself at the principal gate, which is guarded by a company of Mobiles. General Trochu appears in undress; he is received with cries of "*Vive la République! La levée en masse!* No Armistice! The National Guards, who demand the *levée en masse*, would but cause a slaughter. We must have cannon first; we will have them." Alas! it had been far better to have had none whatever, as what follows will prove. While some cry, "Vive Trochu!" others shout, "Down with Trochu!" Before long the Hôtel de Ville is invaded; the courts, the saloons, the galleries, all are filled. Each one offers his advice, but certain groups insist positively on the resignation of the Government. Lists of names are passed from hand to hand; among the names are those of Dorian (president), Schœlcher, Delescluze, Ledru Rollin, Félix Pyat.

* Memoir, see Appendix I.

Cries are raised that if the Government refuse to resign, its members will be arrested.

"Yes! yes! seize them!" And an officer springs forward to make them prisoners as they sit in council.

"Excuse me, Monsieur, but what warrant have you for so doing?" asks one of the members.

"I have nothing to do with warrants. I act in the name of the people!"

"Have you consulted the people? Those assembled here do not constitute the people."

The officer was disconcerted. Not long afterwards, however, the crowd is informed that the members of the Government are arrested.

The principal scene took place in the cabinet of the ex-prefect. Citizen Blanqui approaches the table; addressing the people, he requests them to evacuate the room so as to allow the commission to deliberate. The commission! What commission? Where does it spring from? No one knew anything of it, so the members must evidently have named themselves. Monsieur Blanqui had seen to that, no doubt. During this time the adjoining room is the theatre of the most extraordinary excitement; the men of the 106th Battalion, who were on guard in the interior of the Hôtel de Ville, are compelled to use their arms to prevent any one else entering. After some tumult and struggling, but without any spilling of blood, some National Guards of this battalion manage to fight their way through to the room in which the members of the Government are prisoners, and succeed in delivering them.

At about two o'clock in the morning, the 106th Battalion had completely cleared the Hôtel de Ville of the crowds. No violence had been done, and General Trochu was reviewing a body of men ranged in battle order, which extended from the Place de l'Hôtel de Ville to the Place de la Concorde. An hour later, quiet was completely restored.

The members of the Government, who had been incarcerated

during several hours, now wished to show their authority; they felt that their power had been shaken, and saw the necessity of strengthening it.

What can a Government do in such a case ? Call for a plébiscite. But this time Paris alone was consulted, and for a good reason. Thus, on the 1st November, the people of Paris were enjoined to express their wishes by answering yes or no to this simple question :—

"Do the people of Paris recognise the authority of the Government for the National Defence ?"

This was clear, positive, and free from all ambiguity.

The partizans of the Commune declared vehemently that those who voted in the affirmative were reactionists. "Give us the Commune of '93-!" shouted those who thought they knew a little more about the matter than the rest. They were generally rather badly received. It is no use speaking of '93 ! Replace your Blanquis, your Félix Pyats, your Flourens by men like those of the grand revolution, and then we shall be glad to hear what you have to say on the subject.

The inhabitants of Montmartre, La-Chapelle, Belleville, behaved like good citizens, keeping a brave heart in the hour of misfortune.

However it came about, the Government was maintained by a majority of 557,995 votes against 62,638.

Well, Messieurs of the Commune, try again, or, still better, remain quiet.

During the night of the 21st of January the members of the National Defence and the chief officers of the army were assembled around the table in the council-room. They were still under the mournful impression left by the fatal day of the nineteenth, on which hundreds of citizens had fallen at Montretout, at Garches, and at Buzenval. Thanks to the want of foresight of the Government, the people of Paris were rationed to 300 grammes of detestable black bread a day for each person. All representations made to them had been in vain. Ration our bread by degrees, had been said, we should thus accustom ourselves to privation, and be prepared insensibly for greater sufferings, while the duration of our provisions would be lengthened. But the answer always was: "Bread? We shall have enough, and to spare." When the great crisis was seen approaching, the public feeling showed itself by violent agitation. It was not surprising, therefore, that all the faces of these gentlemen at the council-table bore marks of great depression. The Governor of Paris offered his resignation, as he was in the habit of doing after every rather stormy sitting; but his colleagues refused to accept it, as they had before. What was to be done? Had not the Governor of Paris sworn never to capitulate? After a night spent in discussing the question, the members of Government decided on the following plan of action. You will see that it was as simple as it was innocent! The following announcement was placarded on all the walls:—

"The Government for the National Defence has decided that the chief commandment of the army of Paris shall in future be separate from the presidency of the Government.

"General Vinoy is named Commandant-in-Chief of the army of Paris.

"The title and functions of the Governor of Paris are suppressed."

The trick is played: if they capitulate now, it will no longer be the act of the Governor of Paris. How ingenious this would have been, if it had not been pitiful!

"General Trochu retains the presidency of the Government."

By the side of this placard was the proclamation of General Thomas.

"TO THE NATIONAL GUARD.

"Last night, a handful of insurgents forced open the prison of Mazas, and delivered several of the prisoners, amongst whom was M. Flourens. The same men attempted to occupy the *mairie* of the 20th arrondissement (Belleville), and to instal the chiefs of the insurrection there; your commander-in-chief relies on your patriotism to repress this shameful sedition.

"The safety of Paris is at stake.

"While the enemy is bombarding our forts, the factions within our walls use all their efforts to paralyse the defence.

"In the name of the public good, in the name of law, and of the high and sacred duty that commands you all to unite in the defence of Paris, hold yourselves ready to frustrate this most criminal attempt; at the first call, let the National Guard rise to a man, and the perturbators will be struck powerless.

"The Commander-in-Chief of the National Guard,
"CLÉMENT THOMAS.

"A true copy.
"Minister of the Interior ad interim,
"JULES FAVRE.

"Paris, 22nd January, 1871."

In the morning, large groups of people assembled from mere curiosity, appeared on the Place of the Hôtel de Ville, which however wore a peaceful aspect.

At about half-past two in the afternoon, a detachment of a hundred and fifty armed National Guards issued from the Rue du Temple, and stationed themselves before the Hôtel de Ville, crying, "Down with Trochu!" "Long live the Commune!" A short colloquy was then held between several of the National Guards and some officers of the Mobiles, who spoke with perfect calmness. Suddenly, a shot is fired, and at the same moment, as in the grand scene of a melodrama, the windows and the great door are flung open, and two lines of Mobile Guards are seen, the front rank kneeling, the second standing, and all levelling their muskets and prepared to fire. Then came a volley which spread terror amidst the crowds of people in the Place, who precipitated themselves in all directions, uttering cries and shrieks. In another moment the Place is cleared. Ah! those famous chassepots can work miracles.

The insurgents, during this mad flight of men, women, and children, had answered the attack, some aiming from the shelter of angles and posts, others discharging their rifles from the windows of neighbouring houses.

Then the order to cease firing is heard, and a train of litter-bearers, waving their handkerchiefs as flags, approach from the Avenue Victoria. At the Hôtel de Ville one officer only is wounded, but on the Place lie a dozen victims, two of whom are women.

At four o'clock the 117th Battalion of the National Guard takes up its position before the municipal palace. They are reinforced by a detachment of *gendarmes*, mounted and on foot, and by companies of Mobiles, under the command of General Carréard.

General Clément Thomas hastens to address a few words to the 117th; later, he paid with his life for thus appearing on the side of order. Finally, General Vinoy arrives, followed by his staff, to take measures against any renewed acts of aggression. Mitrailleuses and cannon are stationed before the Hôtel de Ville; the drums beat the *rappel* throughout the town, and a great number of battalions of National Guards assemble in the Rue de Rivoli, at the Louvre, and on the Place de la Concorde; others bivouac before the Palais de l'Industrie, while on the other side of the Champs Elysées regiments of cavalry, infantry, and mobiles, are drawn out. The agitators have disappeared, calm is restored, within the city be it understood, for all this did not interrupt the animated interchange of shells between the French and Prussian batteries, and a great number of Parisians, who had twice helped to disperse the insurgents of October and January, thought involuntarily of the Commune of the 10th of August, 1793, which headed the revolution, and said to themselves that there were perhaps some amongst the present insurgents who, like the former, would rise up to deliver them from the Prussians. For these agitators have some appearance of truth on their side : " You are weak and timorous," they cry to those in power ; "you seem awaiting a defeat rather than expecting a victory. Give place to the energetic, obscure though they may be ; for the men of the great Commune, of our first glorious revolution, they also were for the greater part unknown. We have confidence in the army of Paris, and we will break the iron circle of invasion."

Though the Communists have since then shown bravery, and sometimes heroism, in their struggle against the Versailles troops, we are very doubtful, now that we have seen their chiefs in action, whether the efforts they talked of would have been crowned with success. Their object was power, and, having nothing to risk and all to gain, they would have forthwith disposed of public property in order to procure themselves enjoyment and honours. The few right-minded men who at first committed themselves, proved this by the fact of their giving in their resignation a few days after the Commune had established itself.

Tranquillity had returned. In the morning of the 25th, guards patrolled the Place de la Bastille, the Place du Château d'Eau, the Boulevard Magenta, and the outer boulevards. Paris started as if she had been aroused from some fearful dream, and the waking thought of the enemy at her gates stirred up all her energies once more.

The Communists had been defeated for the second time; but they were soon to take a terrible revenge.

The vow made by the Governor of Paris had been repeated by the majority of the Parisians, and all parties seemed to have rallied round him under the same device : vanquish or die. After the forts, the barricades, and as a last resource, the burning of the city. Who knows? Perhaps the fanatics of resistance had already made out the plan of destruction which served later for the Commune. It has been proved that nothing in this work of ruin was impromptu.

The news of the convention of the 28th of January, the preliminary of the capitulation of Paris, was thus very badly received, and M. Gambetta, by exhorting the people, in his celebrated circular of the 31st of January, to resist to the death, sowed the seeds of civil war :—

"CITIZENS,—

"The enemy has just inflicted upon France the most cruel insult that she has yet had to endure in this accursed war, the too-heavy punishment of the errors and weaknesses of a great people.

"Paris, the impregnable, vanquished by famine, is no longer able to hold in respect the German hordes. On the 28th of January, the capital succumbed, her forts surrendered to the enemy. The city still remains intact, wresting, as it were, by her own power and moral grandeur, a last homage from barbarity.

"But in falling, Paris leaves us the glorious legacy of her heroic sacrifices. During five months of privation and suffering, she has given to France the time to collect herself, to call her children together, to find arms, to compose armies, young as yet, but valiant and determined, and to whom is wanting only that solidity which can be obtained but by experience. Thanks to Paris, we hold in our hands, if we are but resolute and patriotic, all that is needed to revenge, and set ourselves free once more.

"But, as though evil fortune had resolved to overwhelm us, something even more terrible and more fraught with anguish than the fall of Paris, was awaiting us.

"Without our knowledge, without either warning us or consulting us, an armistice, the culpable weakness of which was known to us too late, has been signed, which delivers into the hands of the Prussians the departments occupied by our soldiers, and which obliges us to wait for three weeks, in the midst of the disastrous circumstances in which the country is plunged, before a national assembly can be assembled.

"We sent to Paris for some explanation, and then awaited in silence the promised arrival of a member of the government, to whom we were determined to resign our office. As delegates of government, we desired to obey, and thereby prove to all, friends and dissidents, by setting an example of moderation and respect of duty, that democracy is not only the greatest of all political principles, but also the most scrupulous of governments.

"However, no one has arrived from Paris, and it is necessary to act, come what may; the perfidious machinations of the enemies of France must be frustrated.

"Prussia relies upon the armistice to enervate and dissolve our armies; she hopes that the Assembly, meeting after so long a succession of disasters, and under the impression of the terrible fall of Paris, will be timid and weak, and ready to submit to a shameful peace.

"It is for us to upset these calculations, and to turn the very instruments which are prepared to crush the spirit of resistance, into spurs that shall arouse and excite it.

"Let us make this same armistice into a code of instruction for our young troops; let us employ the three coming weeks in pushing on the organization of the defence and of the war more ardently than ever.

"Instead of the meeting of cowardly reactionists that our enemies expect, let us form an assembly that shall be veritably national and republican, desirous of peace, if peace can ensure the honour, the rank, and the integrity of our country, but capable of voting for war rather than aiding in the assassination of France.

"FRENCHMEN,

"Remember that our fathers left us France, whole and indivisible; let us not be traitors to our history; let us not deliver up our traditional domains into the hands of barbarians. Who then will sign the armistice? Not you, legitimists, who fought so valiantly under the flag of the Republic, in the defence of the ancient kingdom of France; nor you, sons of the bourgeois of 1789, whose work was to unite the old provinces in a pact of indissoluble union; nor you, workmen of the towns, whose intelligence and generous patriotism represent France in all her strength and grandeur, the leader of modern nations; nor you, tillers of the soil, who never have spared your blood in the defence of the Revolution, which gave you the ownership of your land and your title of citizen.

"No! Not one Frenchman will be found to sign this infamous act; the enemy's attempt to mutilate France will be frustrated, for, animated with the same love of the mother country and bearing our reverses with fortitude, we shall become strong once more and drive out the foreign legions.

"To the attainment of this noble end, we must devote our hearts, our wills, our lives, and, a still greater sacrifice perhaps, put aside our preferences.

"We must close our ranks about the Republic, show presence of mind and strength of purpose; and without passion or weakness, swear, like free men, to defend France and the Republic against all and everyone.

"To arms!"

The Government, by obtaining from M. de Bismarck a condition that the National Guards should retain their arms, hoped to win public favour again, as one offers a rattle to a fractious child to keep him quiet; and it published the news on the 3rd of February:

"After the most strenuous efforts on our part, we have obtained, for the National Guard, the condition ratified by the convention of the 28th January."

Three days after, on the 6th of February, Gambetta wrote:

"His conscience would not permit him to remain a member of a government with which he no longer agreed in principle."

The candidates, elected in Paris on the 8th of February, were Louis Blanc, Victor Hugo, Garibaldi, Gambetta, Rochefort, Delescluze, Pyat, Lockroy, Floquet, Millière, Tolain, Malon. The provinces, on the other hand, chose their deputies from among the party of reaction, the members of which have been so well known since under the name of *rurals*.

Loud murmurs arose in the ranks of the National Guard, when the decrees of the 18th and 19th of February, concerning their pay, were published; and later, when an order from headquarters required the marching companies to send in to the state depôt all their campaigning paraphernalia.

On the 18th of February, M. Thiers was named chief of the executive power by a vote of the Assembly.

On Sunday, the 26th of February, the Place de la Bastille, in which manifestations had been held for the last two days in celebration of the revolution of February '48, became as a shrine, to which whole battalions of the National Guard marched to the sound of music, their flags adorned with caps of liberty and cockades. The Column of July was hung with banners and decorated with wreaths of immortelles. Violent harangues, the theme of which was the upholding of the Republic "to the death," were uttered at its foot. One man, of the name of Budaille, pretended that he held proofs of the treachery of the Government for the National Defence, and promised that he would produce them at the proper time and place.

Up to this moment, the demonstrations seemed to have but one result—that of impeding circulation; but they soon gave rise to scenes of tumult and disorder. Towards one o'clock, when perhaps twenty or thirty thousand persons were on the above Place, an individual, accused of being a spy, was dragged by an infuriated mob to the river, and flung, bound hand and foot, into the lock by the Ile Saint Louis, amidst the wild cries and imprecations of the madmen whose prey he had become.

The night of the 26th was very agitated; drums beat to arms, and on the morning of the 27th the Commander-in-Chief of the

National Guard issued a proclamation, in which he appealed to the good citizens of Paris, and confided the care of the city to the

COLUMN OF JULY, PLACE DE LA BASTILLE.

National Guard. This had no effect, however, on the aspect of the Place de la Bastille ; the crowd continued to applaud, frantically, the incendiary speeches of the socialist party, who had sworn to raise Paris at any cost.

On the same day, the 27th of February, the Government informed the people of Paris of the result of the negociations with Prussia, in the following proclamation :

"The Government appeals to your patriotism and your wisdom;

you hold in your hands the future of Paris and of France herself. It is for you to save or to ruin both!

"After a heroic resistance, famine forced you to open your gates to the victorious enemy; the armies that should have come to your aid were driven over the Loire. These incontestable facts have compelled the Government for the National Defence to open negotiations of peace.

"For six days your negotiators have disputed the ground foot by foot; they did all that was humanly possible, to obtain less rigorous conditions. They have signed the preliminaries of peace, which are about to be submitted to the National Assembly.

"During the time necessary for the examination and discussion of these preliminaries, hostilities would have recommenced, and blood would have flowed afresh and uselessly, without a prolongation of the armistice.

"This prolongation could only be obtained on the condition of a partial and very temporary occupation of a portion of Paris: absolutely to be limited to the quarter of the Champs Elysées. Not more than thirty thousand men are to enter the city, and they are to retire as soon as the preliminaries of peace have been ratified, which act can only occupy a few days.

"If this convention were not to be respected the armistice would be at an end: the enemy, already master of the forts, would occupy the whole of Paris by force. Your property, your works of art, your monuments, now guaranteed by the convention, would cease to exist.

"The misfortune would reach the whole of France. The frightful ravages of the war, which have not heretofore passed the Loire, would extend to the Pyrenees.

"It is then absolutely true to say that the salvation of France is at stake. Do not imitate the error of those who would not listen to us when, eight months ago, we abjured them not to undertake a war which must be fatal.

"The French army which defended Paris with so much courage will occupy the left of the Seine, to ensure the loyal execution of the new armistice. It is for the National Guard to lend its aid, by keeping order in the rest of the city.

"Let all good citizens who earned honour as its chiefs, and showed themselves so brave before the enemy, reassume their authority, and the cruel situation of the moment will be terminated by peace and the return of public prosperity."

This clause of the occupation of Paris by the Prussians was regarded by some people as a mere satisfaction of national vanity; but the greater number considered it as an apple of discord thrown by M. de Bismarck, who had every reason to desire that civil war should break out, thus making himself an accomplice of the Socialists and the members of the International.

Confining ourselves simply to the analysis of facts, and to those considerations which may enlighten public opinion respecting the causes of events, we shall not allow ourselves to be carried over the vast field of hypothesis, but preserve the modest character of narrators.

On the night of the 27th of February, the admiral commanding the third section of the fortifications, having noticed the hostile attitude of the National Guard, caused the troops which had been disarmed in accordance with the conditions of the armistice to withdraw into the interior of the city. The men of Belleville profited by the circumstance to pillage the powder magazines which had been entrusted to their charge, and on the following day they went, preceded by drums and trumpets, to the barracks of the Rue de la Pépinière to invite the sailors lodged there to join them in a patriotic manifestation on that night. Believing that the object was to prevent the Prussians entering Paris, a certain number of these brave fellows, who had behaved so admirably during the siege, set out towards the Place de la Bastille; but having been met on their way by some of their officers, they soon separated themselves from the rioters. Thirty of them had been invited to an open-air banquet in the Place de la Bastille; but seeing the probability of some disorder they nearly all retired, and on the following morning only eight of them were missing at the roll-call. Not one of the six thousand marines lodged in the barracks of the Ecole Militaire absented himself.

On the same day, the 28th, a secret society, which we learned later to know and to fear, issued its first circular under the name of the Central Committee of the National Guard; the part since played by this body has been too important for us to omit to insert this proclamation here: its decisions became official acts which overthrew all constituted authority.

"CENTRAL COMMITTEE OF THE NATIONAL GUARD.

"CITIZENS,—

"The general feeling of the population appears to be to offer no opposition to the entry of the Prussians into Paris. The Central Committee, which had emitted contrary advice, declares its intention of adhering to the following resolutions:—

"'All around the quarters occupied by the enemy, barricades shall be raised so as to isolate completely that part of the town. The inhabitants of the circumscribed portion should be required to quit it immediately.

"'The National Guard, in conjunction with the army, shall form an unbroken line along the whole circuit, and take care that the enemy, thus isolated upon ground which is no longer of our city, shall communicate in no manner with any of the other parts of Paris.

"'The Central Committee engages the National Guard to lend its aid for the execution of the necessary measures to bring about this result, and to avoid any aggressive acts which would have the immediate effect of overthrowing the Republic.'"

But here is a little treacherous placard, manuscript and anonymous, which takes a much fairer tone:—

"A convention has permitted the Prussians to occupy the Champs Elysées, from the Seine to the Faubourg St. Honoré, and as far as the Place de la Concorde.

"Be it so! The greater the injury, the more terrible the revenge.

"But, if some panderer dare to pass the circle of our shame, let him be instantly declared traitor, let him become a target for our balls, an object for our petroleum, a mark for our Orsini bombs,* an aim for our daggers!

"Let this be told to all.

"By decision of the Horatii,
"(Signed)   POPULUS."

The effervescence in the minds of the people was so great, that the entry of the Prussians was delayed for forty-eight hours, but on the first of March, at ten in the morning, they had come into the city, and the smoke of their bivouac fires was seen in the Champs Elysées. On the evening of the same day, a telegram from Bordeaux announced that the National Assembly had ratified the preliminaries of peace by a majority of 546 voices against 107. On the following day the ex-Minister of Foreign Affairs left for Versailles, and by nine o'clock in the evening, everything was prepared for the evacuation of the troops, which was effected by eleven, on the third of March. During the short period of their stay, the city was in veritable mourning; the public edifices (even the Bourse) were closed, as were the shops, the warehouses, and the greater part of the cafés. At the windows hung black flags, or the tricolour covered with black crape, and veils of the same material concealed the faces of the statues † on the Place de la Concorde.

All these demonstrations had, however, a pacific character, and the presence of the enemy in Paris gave rise to no serious incident.

---

* The police had seized, some time before, in Paris, ten thousand Orsini bombs, and hundreds of others of a new construction, charged with fulminating mercury.

† The eight gigantic female figures, representing the principal towns of France: Strasbourg, Lille, Metz, &c., &c.

Nevertheless, the agitation of the public mind was not allayed; some attributed this to a plot the Socialists had formed, and which had arrived at maturity. Others believed that the Prussians had left emissaries, creators of disorder, behind them, in revenge for their reception on the Place de la Concorde. In truth, their entry was anything but triumphal; their national airs were received with hisses; their officers were hooted as they promenaded in the Tuileries, and those who attempted to visit the Louvre were compelled to retreat without having satisfied their curiosity.

On the evening of the 3rd of March, a note emanating from the Ministry of the Interior, pointed out in the following terms the danger to be feared from the Central Committee:—

" Incidents of the most regrettable nature have occurred during the last few days, and menace seriously the peace of the capital. Certain National Guards in arms, following the orders, not of their legitimate chiefs, but of an anonymous Central Committee, which could not give them any instructions without committing a crime severely punishable by the law, took possession of a considerable quantity of arms and ammunition of war, under the pretext of saving them from the enemy, whose invasion they pretended to fear. Such acts should at any rate have ceased after the departure of the Prussian army. But such is not the case, for this evening the guard-house at the Gobelins was invaded, and a number of cartridges stolen.

" Those who provoke these disorders draw upon themselves a most terrible responsibility; it is at the very moment that the city of Paris, relieved from contact with the foreigner, desires to reassume its habits of serenity and industry, that these men are sowing trouble and preparing civil war. The Government appeals to all good citizens to aid in stifling in the germ these culpable manifestations.

" Let all who have at heart the honour and the peace of the city arise; let the National Guard, repulsing all perfidious

THE HILL OF MONTMARTRE—WITH THE GUNS OF THE NATIONAL GUARD PARKED THERE.—VIEW TAKEN FROM THE PLACE ST.-PIERRE.

instigations, rally round its officers, and prevent evils of which the consequences will be incalculable. The Government and the Commander-in-Chief (General d'Aurelle de Paladines, nominated on the same day by M. Thiers to the chief command of the National Guard) are determined to do their duty energetically; they will cause the laws to be executed; they count on the patriotism and the devotion of all the inhabitants of Paris."

It was indeed time to put a stop to the existing state of affairs, for already twenty-six guns were in the possession of the insurgents, who had formed a regular park of artillery in the Place d'Italie, and this is the aspect of the Buttes Montmartre on the sixth of March, as described by an eye-witness:—

"The heights have become a veritable camp. Three or four hundred National Guards, belonging partly to the 61st and 168th Battalions, mount guard there day and night, and relieve each other regularly, like old campaigners. They have two drummers and four trumpeters, who beat the rappel or ring out the charge whenever the freak takes them, without any one knowing why or wherefore. The officers, with broad red belts, high boots, and their long swords dragging after them, parade the Place with pipes or cigars in their mouths. They glance disdainfully at the passers-by, and seem almost overpowered with the importance of the high mission they imagine themselves called upon to fulfil.

"This is of what their mission consists: at the moment of the entry of the Prussians into Paris, the National Guard of Montmartre, fearing that the artillery would be taken from them to be delivered to the enemy, assembled and dragged their pieces, about twenty in number, up to the plateau which forms the summit of Montmartre, and then placed them in charge of a special guard. Now that the Prussians have left, they still keep their stronghold, thinking to use it in the defence of the Republic against the attacks of the reactionists.

The guns are pointed towards Paris, and guard is kept without a moment's relaxation. There are four principal

SENTINELS AT MONTMARTRE.

posts, the most important being at the foot of the hill, on the Place Saint Pierre. The guards bivouac in the open air, their muskets piled ready at hand. Sentinels are placed at the corner of each street, most of them lads of sixteen or seventeen; but they are thoroughly in earnest, and treat the passers-by roughly enough.

"All the streets which debouche on the Place Saint-Pierre are closed by barricades of paving-stones. The most important was formed of an overturned cart, filled with huge stones, and with a red flag reared upon the summit. A death-like silence reigned around. There were but few passers-by, none but National Guards with their guns on their shoulders."

The appearance of the Boulevard de Clichy and Boulevard Rochechouart is completely different. The cafés are overflowing with people, the concert-rooms open. Men and women pass tranquilly to and fro, without disturbing themselves about the cannon that are pointed towards them.

The Government, before coming to active measures, appealed to the good sense of the people in a proclamation, dated the 8th of March, saying that this substitution of legal authority by a secret power would retard the evacuation of the enemy, and perhaps expose us to disasters still more complete and terrible.

"Let us look our position calmly in the face. We have been conquered; nearly half of our territory has been in the power of a million of Germans, who have imposed upon us a fine of five milliards. Our only means of discharging this weighty debt is by the strictest economy, the most exemplary conduct and care. We must not lose a moment before putting our hands to work, which is our one and solitary hope. And at this awful moment shall our miserable folly lead us into a civil strife? . . .

"If, while they are meeting to treat with the enemy, our negotiators have sedition to fear, they will break down as they did on the 31st of October, when the events of the Hôtel de Ville authorised the enemy to refuse us an armistice which might have saved us."

This form of reasoning was not illogical, but those who were working in secret for the furtherance of their own ambition, cared little to be convinced, and their myrmidons obeyed them blindly, and gloated over the wild, bombastic language of the demagogic press, which, though they did not understand it, impressed them no less with its inflated phrases.

The Government, perceiving that it would be perhaps necessary to use rigorous measures, gave orders to hasten the arrival of the rest of the Army of the North.

Some few days after the 13th of March, they resolved to deal a decided blow to the Democratic party in suppressing at once the *Vengeur*, the *Mot d'Ordre*, the *Cri du Peuple*, the *Caricature*, the *Père Duchesne*, and the *Bouche de Fer*.

The National Guards had a perfect mania for collecting cannon; after having placed in battery the mitrailleuses and pieces of seven, the produce of patriotic subscriptions, they also seized upon others belonging to the State, and carried them off to the Buttes Montmartre, where they had about a hundred pieces. The retaking of this artillery was the matter in question. While they at Versailles were occupied with the solution of the problem, the National Guards continued their manifestations at the Place de la Bastille, dragging these pieces of artillery in triumph from the Champ de Mars to the Luxembourg, from the park of Montrouge to Notre Dame, from the Place des Vosges to the Place d'Italie, and from the Buttes Montmartre to the Buttes Chaumont.

Before making use of force, the Government desired to make a last effort at conciliation, and on the 17th of March the following proclamation was posted on the walls:—

"INHABITANTS OF PARIS,

"Once more we address ourselves to you, to your reason, and your patriotism, and we hope that you will listen to us.

"Your grand city, which cannot live except with order, is profoundly troubled in some of its quarters, and this trouble, without spreading to other parts, is sufficient nevertheless to prevent the return of industry and comfort.

A CONCILIATORY PROCLAMATION.

"For some time a number of ill-advised men, under the pretext of resisting the Prussians, who are no longer within our walls, have constituted themselves masters of a part of the city, thrown up entrenchments, mounting guard there and forcing you to do the same, all by order of a secret committee, which takes upon itself to command a portion of the National Guard, thus setting aside the authority of General d'Aurelle de Paladines so worthy to be at your head, and would form a government in opposition to that which exists legally, the offspring of universal suffrage.

"These men, who have already caused you so much harm, whom you yourselves dispersed on the 31st of October, are placarding their intention to protect you against the Prussians, who have only made an appearance within our walls, and whose definite departure is retarded by these disorders, and pointing guns, which if fired would only ruin your houses and destroy your wives and yourselves; in fact, compromising the very Republic they pretend to defend; for if it is firmly established in the opinion of France that the Republic is the necessary companion of disorder, the Republic will be lost. Do not place any trust in them, but listen to the truth which we tell you in all sincerity.

"The Government instituted by the whole nation could have retaken before this these stolen guns, which at present only menace your safety, seized these ridiculous entrenchments which hinder nothing but business, and have placed in the hands of justice the criminals who do not hesitate to create civil war immediately after that with the foreigner, but it desired to give those who were misled the time to separate themselves from those who deceived them.

"However, the time allowed for honourable men to separate themselves from the others, and which is deducted from your tranquillity, your welfare, and the welfare of France, cannot be indefinitely prolonged.

"While such a state of things lasts, commerce is arrested, your shops are deserted, orders which would come from all parts are suspended; your arms are idle, credit cannot be recreated, the capital which the Government requires to rid the territory of the presence of the enemy, comes to hand but slowly. In your own interest, in that of your city, as well as in that of France, the Government is resolved to act. The culprits who pretend to institute a Government of their own must be delivered up to justice. The guns stolen from the State must be replaced in the arsenals; and, in order to carry out this act of justice and reason, the Government counts upon your assistance.

"Let all good citizens separate themselves from the bad; let them aid, instead of opposing, the public forces; they will thus hasten the return of comfort to the city, and render service to the Republic itself, which disorder is ruining in the opinion of France.

"Parisians! we use this language to you because we esteem your good sense, your wisdom, your patriotism; but, this warning being given, you will approve of our having resort to force at all costs, and without a day's delay, that order, the only condition of your welfare, be re-established entirely, immediately, and unalterably."

As soon as the party of disorder saw the intentions of the Government of Versailles thus set forth, a chorus of recriminations burst forth:—"They want to put an end to the Republic!"—"They are about to fire on our brothers!"—"They wish to set up a king," &c. The same strain for ever! In order to prevent as far as possible the mischievous effects of this insurrectionary propaganda, the Government issued the following proclamation, which bore date the 18th of March:—

"NATIONAL GUARDS OF PARIS!—

"Absurd rumours are spread abroad that the Government contemplates a *coup d'état*.

"The Government of the Republic has not, and cannot have, any other object but the welfare of the Republic.

"The measures which have been taken were indispensable to

the maintenance of order; it was, and is still, determined to put an end to an insurrectionary committee, the members of which, nearly all unknown to the population of Paris, preach nothing but Communist doctrines, will deliver up Paris to pillage, and bring France into her grave, unless the National Guard and the army do not rise with one accord in the defence of the country and of the Republic."

The Government had many parleys with the insurrectionary National Guards at Montmartre; at one moment there was a rumour that the guns had been given up. It appeared that the guardians of this artillery had manifested some intention of restoring it, horses had even been sent without any military force to create mistrust, but the men declared that they would not deliver the guns, except to the battalions to which they properly belonged. Was there bad faith here? or had those who made the promise undertaken to deliver up the skin before they had killed the bear.

Public opinion shaped itself generally in somewhat the following form:—"If they are tricking each other, that is not very dangerous!"

Many an honest citizen went to bed on the seventeenth of March full of hope. He saw Paris marching with quick steps towards the re-establishment of its business, and the resumption of its usual aspect; the emigrants and foreigners would arrive in crowds, their pockets overflowing with gold to make purchases and put the industry of Paris under contribution; the French and foreign bankers will rival each other to pay the indemnity of five *milliards*.

The dream of good M. Prudhomme* was, however, somewhat clouded by the figure of the Buttes Montmartre bristling with

---

* "Joseph Prudhomme" is the typical representative of the Parisian middle-class (*Bourgeois*); the honest simple father of family, peaceful but patriotic, proud of his country and ready to die for it.

cannon; but the number of guards had become so diminished, and they seemed so tired of the business, that it appeared as if they were about to quit for good. The following chapter will inform you what were the waking thoughts of the Parisians on the morning of the eighteenth of March.

I.

ISTEN! What does that mean? Is it a transient squall or the first gust of a tempest? Is it due to nature or to man's agency; is it an émeute or the advent of a revolution that is to overturn everything?

Such were my reflections when awakened, on the 18th of March, 1871, at about four in the morning, by a noise due to the tramp of many feet. From my window, in the gloomy white fog, I could see detachments of soldiers walking under the walls, proceeding slowly, wrapped in their grey capotes; a soft drizzling rain falling at the time. Half awake, I descended to the street in time to interrogate two soldiers passing in the rear.

"Where are you going?" asked I.—"We do not know," says one; "Report says we are going to Montmartre," adds the other.*

They were really going to Montmartre. At five o'clock in the morning the 88th Regiment of the line occupied the top of the hill and the little streets leading to it, a place doubtless familiar to some of them, who on Sundays and fête days had clambered up the hill-sides in company with apple-faced rustics from the outskirts, and middle-class people of the quarter; taking part in the crowd on the Place Saint-Pierre, with its games and amusements, and "assisting," as they would say, at shooting in a barrel, admiring the ability of some, whilst reviling the stupidity of others; when they had a few sous in their pockets they would try their own skill at throwing big balls into the mouths of fantastic monsters, painted upon a square board, while their country friends nibbled at spice-nuts, and thought them delicious. But on this 18th of March morning there are no women, nor spice-nuts, nor sport on the Place Saint-Pierre: all is slush and dirt, and the poor lines-men are obliged to stand at ease, resting

* Appendix, note 2.

upon their arms, not in the best of humour with the weather or the prospect before them.

Ah! and the guns of the National Guard that frown from their embrasures on the top of the hill, have they been made use of against the Prussians? No! they have made no report during the siege, and were only heard on the days on which they were christened and paid for; elegant things, hardly to be blackened with powder, that it was always hoped would be pacific and never dangerous to the capital. Cruel irony! those guns for which Paris paid, and those American mitrailleuses, made out of the savings of both rich and poor, the farthings of the frugal housewife, and the napoleons of the millionaires; the contributions of the artists who designed, and the poets who pen'd, are ruining Paris instead of protecting it. The brass mouths that ate the bread of humanity are turned upon the nation itself to devour it also.

But, to return to the 88th Regiment of Line, did they take the guns? Yes, but they gave them up again, and to whom? why, to a crowd of women and children; and as to the chiefs, no one seemed to know what had become of them. It is related, however, that General Lecomte had been made a prisoner and led to the Château-Rouge, and that at nine o'clock some Chasseurs d'Afrique charged pretty vigorously in the Place Pigalle a detachment of National Guards, who replied by a volley of bullets. An officer of Chasseurs was shot, and his men ran away, the greater part, it is said, into the wine-shops, where they fraternised with the patriots, who offered them drink. I was told on the spot that General Vinoy, who was on horseback, became encircled in a mob of women, had a stone and a cap* thrown at him, and thought it prudent to escape, leaving the National Guards and linesmen to promenade in good fellowship three abreast, dispersing themselves about the outer boulevards and about Paris. Indeed, I have just seen a drunken couple full of wine and friendship, strongly reminding one of a duel ending in

---

* A mark of insult.

a jolly breakfast. And who is to blame for this? Nobody knows. All agree that it is a bungle,—the fault of maladministration and want of tact.

Certainly the National Guards at Montmartre had no right to hold the cannons belonging to the National Guards, as a body, or to menace the reviving trade and tranquillity of Paris, by means of guns turned against its peaceful citizens and Government officials; but was it necessary to use violence to obtain possession of the cannons? Should not all the means of conciliation be exhausted first, and might we not hope that the citizens at Montmartre would themselves end by abandoning the pieces of artillery* which they hardly protected. In fact, they were encumbered by their own barricades, and they might take upon themselves to repave their streets and return to order.

Monsieur Thiers and his ministers were not of that opinion. They preferred acting, and with vigour. Very well! but when resolutions are formed, one should be sure of fulfilling them, for in circumstances of such importance failure itself makes the attempt an error.†

Well! said the Government, who could imagine that the line

---

* This useless artillery was much ridiculed; jokers said that the notary of General Trochu was working out faithfully the "plan" of his illustrious client in these tardy fortifications.

† How was the Government to act in the presence of these facts; to await events, or to strike a great blow?

Some think that the resistance of the insurgents was strengthened by the measures taken by Government, which ought to have been more diplomatic and skilful. The agitation of these men of Montmartre, at the entry of the Prussians, had calmed down in a few hours; it was now the duty of Government to allay the irritation which had caused the insurgents to form their Montmartre stronghold, and not to follow the advice of infuriated reactionaries, who make no allowance for events and circumstances, neither analysing the elements of that which they are combating, nor weighing the measures they do not even know how to apply with tact.

The guns had not been re-taken, but Paris was very calm. Dissensions had broken out in the Montmartre Committee, some of whose members wished the cannon to be returned (the Committee sat at No. 8 of the Rue des Rosiers, with a court-martial on one hand, and

would throw up the butt ends of their muskets,* or that the Chasseurs, after the loss of a single officer, would turn their backs upon the Nationals, and that their only deeds should be the imbibing of plentiful potations at the cost of the insurgents? But how could it be otherwise? Not many days since the soldiers were wandering idly through the streets with the National

military head-quarters on the other). Danger seemed now to be averted, and the authorities had but one thing to do, to allow all agitation to die out, without listening to blind or treacherous counsellors, who advocated a system of immediate repression. It was said, however, that the greater number of the members of Government were inclined to temporise, but the *provisional* appointment of General Valentin to the direction of the Prefecture of Police, seemed to contradict this assertion.

During this time, the leaders who held Montmartre, spurred on by the ambitious around them, and by those desirous of kindling civil war for the sake of the illicit gains to be obtained from it, were getting up a manifestation, which was to claim for the National Guard the right of electing its commander-in-chief; and the post was to be offered to Menotti Garibaldi. But though the men of Montmartre declared that all who did not sign the manifestos were traitors, yet the addresses remained almost entirely blank. The insurrection had evidently few supporters. According to others, the insurrection of 1871 was the result of a vast conspiracy, planned and nurtured under the influence of a six months' siege. No simple Paris *émeute*, but a grand social movement, organised by the great and universal revolutionary power; the Société Internationale, Garibaldiism, Mazziniism, and Fenianism, have given each other rendezvous in Paris. Cluseret, the American; Frankel, the Prussian; Dombrowski, the Russian; Brunswick, the Lithuanian; Romanelli, the Italian; Okolowitz, the Pole; Spillthorn, the Belgian; and La Cécilia, Wroblewski, Wenzel, Hertzfel, Rozyski, Syneck, Prolowitz, and a hundred others, equally illustrious, brought together from every quarter of the globe; such were these ardent conspirators, all imbued, like their colleagues the Flourens, the Eudes, the Henrys, the Duvals, and *tutti quanti*, with the principles of the French school of democracy and socialism.

This strong and terrible band, we are told, is under the command of a chief who remains hidden and mute, while ostensibly it obeys the Pyats, Delescluzes, and Rocheforts, politicians, who not being generals, never condescend to fight.

In the first days of March all was prepared for a coming explosion, and in spite of the departure of the Prussians, the Socialist party determined that it should take place. (*Guerre des Communeux*, p. 61.)

* A sign that they refused to fight.

Guards; were billeted upon the people, eating their soup and chatting with their wives and daughters, unaccustomed to discipline and the rigour of military organisation; enervated by defeat, having been maintained by their officers in the illusion of their invincibility; annoyed by their uniform, of which they ceased to be proud, the humiliated soldiers sought to escape into the citizen. Were the commanding officers ignorant of the prevailing spirit of the troops? Must we admit that they were grossly deceived, or that they deceived the Government, when the latter might and ought to have been in a position to foresee the result. Possibly the Assembly had the right to coerce, but they had no right to be ignorant of their power. They must have known that 100,000 arms (chassepots, tabatières,* and muskets) were in the hands of disaffected men, clanking on the floors of the dealers in adulterated wines and spirits, and low cabarets. The fact is, the Government took a leap in the dark, and wondered when they found the position difficult.

II.

At three o'clock in the afternoon there was a dense group of linesmen and Nationals in one of the streets bordering on the Elysée-Montmartre. The person who told us this did not recollect the name of the street, but men were eagerly haranguing the crowd, talking of General Lecomte, and his having twice ordered the troops to fire upon the citizen militia.

"And what he did was right," said an old gentleman who was listening.

Words that were no sooner uttered than they provoked a

* A smooth-bore musket arranged as breech-loader, and called a snuff-box, from the manner of opening the breech to adjust the charge.

torrent of curses and imprecations from the by-standers. But he continued observing that General Lecomte had only acted under the orders of his superiors; being commanded to take the guns and to disperse the crowd, his only duty was to obey.

These remarks being received in no friendly spirit, hostility to the stranger increased, when a vivandière approached, and looking the gentleman who had exposed himself to the fury of the mob full in the face, exclaimed, "It is Clément Thomas!" And in truth it was General Clément Thomas; he was not in uniform. A torrent of abuse was poured forth by a hundred voices at once, and the anger of the crowd seemed about to extend itself to violence, when a ruffian cried out: "You defend the rascal Lecomte! Well, we'll put you both together, and a pretty pair you'll be!" and this project being approved of, the General was hurried, not without having to submit to fresh insults, to where General Lecomte had been imprisoned since the morning.

From this moment the narrative I have collected differs but little from that circulated through Paris.

At about four o'clock in the afternoon the two generals were conducted from their prison by a hundred National Guards, the hands of General Lecomte being bound together, whilst those of Clément Thomas were free. In this manner they were escorted to the top of the hill of Montmartre, where they stopped before No. 6 of the Rue des Rosiers: it is a little house I had often seen, a peaceful and comfortable habitation, with a garden in front. What passed within it perhaps will never be known. Was it there that the Central Committee of the National Guard held their sittings in full conclave? or were they represented by a few of its members? Many persons think that the house was not occupied, and that the National Guards conducted their prisoners within its walls to make the crowd believe they were proceeding to a trial, or at least to give the appearance of legality to the execution of premeditated acts. Of one thing there remains little doubt, namely, that soldiers of the line stood round about at the time, and that the trial, if any took place, was not long, the

HOTEL DE VILLE, AS FORTIFIED BY THE NATIONAL GUARD, MARCH, 1871.

The Hôtel de Ville of Paris, which witnessed so many national ceremonies and republican triumphs, was commenced in 1533, and it was finished in 1628. Here the first Bourbon, Henry IV., celebrated his entry into Paris after the siege of 1589, and Bailly the *maire*, on the 17th July, 1789, presented Louis XVI. to the people, wearing a tricolor cockade. Henry IV. became a Catholic in order to enter "his good city of Paris," whilst Louis XVI. wore the democratic insignia in order to keep it. A few days later the 172 commissioners of sections, representing the municipality of Paris, established the Commune. The Hôtel de Ville was the seat of the First Committee of Public Safety, and from the green chamber, Robespierre governed the Convention and France till his fall on the 9th Thermidor. From 1800 to 1830 fêtes held the place of political manifestations. In 1810 Bonaparte received Marie-Louise here; in 1821, the baptism of the Duke of Bordeaux was celebrated here; in 1825 fêtes were given to the Duc d'Angoulême on his return from Spain, and to Charles X., arriving from Rheims. Five years later, from the same balcony where Bailly presented Louis XVI. to the people, Lafayette, standing by the side of Louis Philippe, said, "This is the best of Republics!" It was here, in 1848, that De Lamartine courageously declared to an infuriated mob that, as long as *he* lived, the red flag should *not* be the flag of France. During the fatal days of June, 1848, the Hôtel de Ville was only saved from destruction by the intrepidity of a few brave men. The Queen of England was received here in 1855, and the sovereigns who visited Paris since have been fêted therein. On the 4th of September the bloodless revolution was proclaimed; and on the 31st of October, 1870, and the 22nd of January, 1871, Flourens and Blanqui made a fruitless attempt to substitute the red flag for the tricolor; but their partizans succeeded on the 18th of March, when it was fortified, and became the head-quarters of the Commune of 1871.

condemned being conducted to a walled enclosure at the end of the street.

As soon as they had halted, an officer of the National Guard seized General Clément Thomas by the collar of his coat and shook him violently several times, exclaiming, whilst he held the muzzle of a revolver close to his throat,—"Confess that you have betrayed the Republic." To this Monsieur Clément Thomas only replied by a shrug of his shoulders; upon this the officer retired, leaving the General standing alone in the front of the wall, with a line of soldiers opposite.

Who gave the signal to fire is unknown, but a report of twenty muskets rent the air, and General Clément Thomas fell with his face to the earth.

"It is your turn now," said one of the assassins, addressing General Lecomte, who immediately advanced from the crowd, stepping over the body of Clément Thomas to take his place, awaiting with his back to the wall the fatal moment.

"Fire!" cried the officer, and all was over.

Half an hour after, in the Rue des Acacias, I came across an old woman who wanted three francs for a bullet—a bullet she had extracted from the plaster of a wall at the end of the Rue des Rosiers.

III.

It is ten o'clock in the evening, and if I were not so tired I would go to the Hôtel de Ville, which, I am told, has been taken possession of by the National Guards; the 18th of March is continuing the 31st of October. But the events of this day have made me so weary that I can hardly write all I have seen and heard.

On the outer boulevards the wine shops are crowded with tipsy people, the drunken braggarts who boast they have made a revolution. When a stroke succeeds there are plenty of rascals ready to say: I did it. Drinking, singing, and talking are the order of the day. At every step you come upon "piled arms." At the corner of the Passage de l'Elysée-des-Beaux-Arts I met crowds of

SENTINELS, RUE DU VAL DE GRÂCE AND BOULEVARD ST. MICHEL.

people, some lying on the ground; here a battalion standing at ease but ready to march; and at the entrance of the Rue Blanche and the Rue Fontaine were some stones, ominously posed one on the other, indicating symptoms of a barricade. In the Rue des Abbesses I counted three cannons and a mitrailleuse, menacing the Rue des Martyrs. In the Rue des Acacias, a man had been arrested, and was being conducted by National Guards to the guard-house: I heard he was a thief. Such arrests are characteristic features in a Parisian émeute. Notwithstanding these little scenes the disorder is not excessive, and but for the multitude of men in uniform one might believe it the evening of a popular fête; the victors are amusing themselves.

Among the Federals this evening there are very few linesmen; perhaps they have gone to their barracks to enjoy their meal of soup and bread.

Upon the main boulevards noisy groups are commenting upon the events of the day. At the corner of the Rue Drouot an officer of the 117th Battalion is reading in a loud voice, or rather reciting, for he knows it all by heart, the proclamation of M. Picard, the official poster of the afternoon.

"The Government appeals to you to defend your city, your home, your children, and your property.

"Some frenzied men, commanded by unknown chiefs, direct against Paris the guns defended from the Prussians.

"They oppose force to the National Guard and the army.

"Will you suffer it?

"Will you, under the eyes of the strangers ready to profit by our discord, abandon Paris to sedition?

"If you do not extinguish it in the germ, the Republic and France will be ruined for ever.

"Their destiny is in your hands.

"The Government desires that you should hold your arms energetically to maintain the law and preserve the Republic from anarchy. Gather round your leaders; it is the only means of escaping ruin and the domination of the foreigner.

"The Minister of the Interior,

"ERNEST PICARD."

The crowd listened with attention, shouted two or three times "To arms!" and then dispersed—I thought for an instant, to arm themselves, though in reality it was only to reinforce another group forming on the other side of the way.

This day the Friends of Order have been very apathetic, so much so that Paris is divided between two parties: the one active and the other passive.

To speak truly, I do not know what the population of Paris could have done to resist the insurrection. "Gather round your chiefs," says the proclamation. This is more easily said than done, when we do not know what has become of them. The division caused in the National Guard by the Coup d'Etat of the Central Committee had for its consequence the disorganisation of all command. Who was to distinguish, and where was one to find the officers that had remained faithful to the cause of order?

It is true they sounded the "rappel"* and beat the "générale;"† but who commanded it? Was it the regular Government or the revolutionary Committee?

More than one good citizen was ready to do his duty; but, after having put on his uniform and buckled his belt, he felt very puzzled, afraid of aiding the émeute instead of strengthening the defenders of the law. Therefore the peaceful citizen soldiers regarded not the call of the trumpet and the drum.

It is wise to stay at home when one knows not where to go. Besides, the line has not replied, and bad examples are contagious; moreover, is it fair to demand of fathers of families, of merchants and tradesmen, in fact of soldiers of necessity, an effort before which professional soldiers withdraw? The fact is the Government had fled. Perhaps a few ministers still remained in Paris, but the main body had gone to join the Assembly at Versailles.

* The roll call.
† Muster call in time of danger, which is beaten only by a superior order emanating from the commander-in-chief in a stronghold or garrison town.

I do not blame their somewhat precipitate departure,* perhaps it was necessary; nevertheless it seems to me that their presence would have put an end to irresolution on the part of timid people.

Meanwhile, from the Madeleine to the Gymnase, the cafés overflowed with swells and idlers of both sexes. On the outer boulevards they got drunk, and on the inner tipsy, the only difference being in the quality of the liquors imbibed.

What an extraordinary people are the French!

IV.

Next morning, the 19th of March, I was in haste to know the events of last night, what attitude Paris had assumed after her first surprise. The night, doubtless, had brought counsel, and perhaps settled the discord existing between the Government and the Central Committee.

Early in the morning things appeared much as usual; the streets were peaceful, servants shopping, and the ordinary pas-

---

* The army of Paris was drawn off to Versailles in the night of the 18th of March, and on the 19th, the employés of all the ministries and public offices left Paris for the same destination.

On the 19th of March, as early as eight in the morning, Monsieur Thiers addressed the following circular to the authorities of all the departments:—

"The whole of the Government is assembled at Versailles: the National Assembly will meet there also.

"The army, to the number of forty thousand men, has been assembled there in good order, under the command of General Vinoy. All the chiefs of the army, and all the civil authorities have arrived there.

"The civil and military authorities will execute no other orders but those issued by the legitimate government residing at Versailles, under penalty of dismissal.

"The members of the National Assembly are all requested to hasten their return, so as to be present at the sitting of the 20th of March.

"The present despatch will be made known to the public.
"A. Thiers."

sengers going to and fro. In passing I met a casual acquaintance to whom I had spoken now and then, a man with whom I had served during the siege when we mounted guard on the ramparts. "Well," said I, "good morning, have you any news?"—"News," replied he, "no, not that I know of. Ah! yes, there is a rumour that something took place yesterday at Montmartre." This was told me in the centre of the city, in the Rue de la Grange-Batélière. Truly there are in Paris persons marvellously apathetic and ignorant. I would wager not a little that by searching in the retired quarters, some might be found who believe they are still governed by Napoleon III., and have never heard of the war with Prussia, except as a not improbable eventuality.

On the boulevards there was but little excitement. The newspaper vendors were in plenty. I do not like to depend upon these public sheets for information, for however impartial or sincere a reporter may be, he cannot represent facts otherwise than according to the impression they make upon him, and to value facts by the impression they make upon others is next to impossible.

I directed my steps to the Rue Drouot in search of placards, and plentiful I found them, and white too, showing that Paris was not without a government; for white is the official colour even under a red Republic.*

Taking out a pencil I copied hastily the proclamation of the new masters, and I think that I did well, for we forget very

* No one may use white placards—they are reserved by the government.

The following is an extract from the *Official Journal* of Versailles, bearing the date of the 20th of March, which explains the official form of the announcements made by the Central Committee:—

"Yesterday, 19th March, the offices of the *Official Journal*, in Paris, were broken into, the employés having escaped to Versailles with the documents, to join the Government and the National Assembly. The invaders took possession of the printing machines, the materials, and even the official and non-official articles which had been set up in type, and remained in the composing-rooms. It is thus that they were enabled to give an appearance of regularity to the publication of their decrees, and to deceive the Parisian public by a false *Official Journal*."

quickly both proclamations and persons. Where are they now, the official bills of last year?

> "RÉPUBLIQUE FRANÇAISE.
> "LIBERTÉ, ÉGALITÉ, FRATERNITÉ.
> "*To the People.*
> "CITIZENS,—The people of Paris have shaken off the yoke endeavoured to be imposed upon them."

What yoke, gentlemen—I beg pardon, citizens of the Committee? I assure you, as part of the people, that I have never felt that any one has tried to impose one upon me. I recollect, if my memory serves me, that a few guns were spoken of, but nothing about yokes. Then the expression "People of Paris," is a gross exaggeration. The inhabitants of Montmartre and their neighbours of that industrious suburb are certainly a part of the people, and not the less respectable or worthy of our consideration because they live out of the centre (indeed, I have always preferred a coal man of the Chaussée Clignancourt to a coxcomb of the Rue Taitbout); but for all that, they are not the whole population. Thus, your sentence does not imply anything, and moreover, with all its superannuated metaphor, the rhetoric is out of date. I think it would have been better to say simply—

> "CITIZENS,—The inhabitants of Montmartre and of Belleville have taken their guns and intend to keep them."

But then it would not have the air of a proclamation. Extraordinary fact! you may overturn an entire country, but you must not touch the official style; it is immutable. One may triumph over empires, but must respect red tape. Let us read on:

> "Tranquil, calm in our force, we have awaited without fear as without provocation, the shameless madmen who menaced the Republic."

The Republic? Again an improper expression, it was the cannons they wanted to take.

"This time, our brothers of the army. . . . "

Ah! your brothers of the army! They are your brothers because they fraternised and threw up the butt-ends of their muskets. In your family you acknowledge no brotherhood except those who hold the same opinion.

"This time, our brothers of the army would not raise their hands against the holy ark of our liberty."

Oh! So the guns are a holy ark now. A very holy metaphor for people not greatly enamoured of churchmen.

"Thanks for all; and let Paris and France unite to build a Republic, and accept with acclamations the only government that will close for ever the flood gates of invasion and civil war.

"The state of siege is raised.

"The people of Paris are convoked in their sections to elect a Commune. The safety of all citizens is assured by the body of the National Guard.

"Hôtel de Ville of Paris, the 19th of March, 1871.
   "The Central Committee of the National Guard:
      "Assy, Billioray, Ferrat, Babick, Ed. Moreau, Ch. Dupont, Varlin, Boursier, Mortier, Gouhier, Lavallette, Fr. Jourde, Rousseau, Ch. Lullier, Blanchet, G. Gaillard, Barroud, H. Geresme, Fabre, Pougeret." *

---

* Here is an extract from the *Official Journal* upon the subject (numbers of the 29th March and 1st June):—

"In the insurrection, the momentary triumph of which has crushed Paris beneath so odious and humiliating a yoke, carried the distresses of France to their height, and put civilisation in peril, the International Society has borne a part which has suddenly revealed to all the fatal power of this dangerous association.

"On the 19th of March, the day after the outbreak of the terrible sedition, of which the last horrors will form one of the most frightful pages in history, there appeared upon the walls a placard which made known to Paris the names of its new masters.

"With the exception of one, alone, (Assy), who had acquired a

There is one reproach that the new Parisian Revolution could not be charged with; it is that of having placed at the head men of proved incapacity. Those who dared to assert that each of the persons named above had not more genius than would be required to regenerate two or three nations would greatly astonish me. In a drama of Victor Hugo it is said a parentless child ought to be deemed a gentleman; thus an obscure individual ought, on the same terms, to be considered a man of genius.

But on the walls of the Rue Drouot many more proclamations were to be seen.

"RÉPUBLIQUE FRANÇAISE.

"LIBERTÉ, EGALITÉ, FRATERNITÉ.

"*To the National Guards of Paris.*

"CITIZENS,—You had entrusted us with the charge of organising the defence of Paris and of your rights."

Oh! as to that, no; a thousand times, no! I admit—since you appear to cling to it—that cannon are an ark of strength, but under no pretext whatever will I allow that I entrusted you with the charge of organising anything whatsoever. I know nothing of you; I have never heard you spoken of. There is no one in the world of whom I am more ignorant than Ferrat, Babick, unless it be Gaillard and Pougeret (though I was national guard myself, and caught cold on the ramparts for the King of Prussia* as much as anyone else). I neither know what you wish nor where you are leading those who follow you; and I can prove to you, if you like, that there are at least a hundred thousand

deplorable notoriety, these names were unknown to almost all who read them; they had suddenly emerged from utter obscurity, and people asked themselves with astonishment, with stupor, what unseen power could have given them an influence and a meaning which they did not possess in themselves. This power was the International; these names were those of some of its members."

* *Travailler pour le Roi de Prusse*, "to work for the King of Prussia," is an old French saying, which means to work for nothing, to no purpose.

men who caught cold too, and who, at the present moment, are in exactly the same state of mind concerning you as your humble servant.

"We are aware of having fulfilled our mission."

You are very good to have taken so much trouble, but I have no recollection of having given you a mission to fulfil of any kind whatever!

"Assisted by your courage and presence of mind! . . . ."

Ah, gentlemen, this is flattery!

"We have driven out the government that was betraying you.
"Our mandate has now expired . . ."

Always this same mandate which we gave you, eh?

"We now return it to you, for we do not pretend to take the place of those which the popular breath has overthrown.
"Prepare yourselves, let the Communal election commence forthwith, and give to us the only reward we have ever hoped for—that of seeing the establishment of a true republic. In the meanwhile we retain the Hôtel de Ville in the name of the people.
"Hôtel de Ville, Paris, 19th March, 1871.
"The Central Committee of the National Guards:
"Assy, Billioray, and others."

Placarded up also is another proclamation[*] signed by the citizens Assy, Billioray, and others, announcing that the Communal

---

[*] "THE CENTRAL COMMITTEE OF THE NATIONAL GUARD.
"Inasmuch:—
"That it is most urgent that the Communal administration of the City of Paris shall be formed immediately,
  "Decrees:—
"1st. The elections for the Communal Council of the City of Paris will take place on Wednesday next, the 22nd of March.

elections will take place on Wednesday next, 22nd of March, that is to say in three days.

This then is the result of yesterday's doings, and the revolution of the 18th March can be told in a few words.

There were cannon at Montmartre; the Government wished to take them but was not able, thanks to the fraternal feeling and cowardice of the soldiers of the Line. A secret society, composed of several delegates of several battalions, took advantage of the occasion to assert loudly that they represented the entire population, and commanded the people to elect the Commune of Paris—whether they wished or not.

What will Paris do now between these dictators, sprung from heaven knows where, and the Government fled to Versailles?

V.

PARIS remains inactive, and watches events as one watches running water. What does this indifference spring from? Surprise and the disappearance of the chiefs might yesterday have excused the inaction of Paris, but twenty-four hours have passed over, every man has interrogated his conscience, and been able to listen to its answer. There has been time to reconnoitre, to concert together; there would have been time to act!

"2nd. The electors will vote with lists, and in their own arrondissements.

"Each arrondissement will elect a councillor for each twenty thousand of inhabitants, and an extra one for a surplus of more than ten thousand.

"3rd. The poll will be open from eight in the morning to six in the evening. The result will be made known at once.

"4th. The municipalities of the twenty arrondissements are entrusted with the proper execution of the present decree.

"A placard indicating the number of councillors for each arrondissement will shortly be posted up.

"Hôtel de Ville, Paris, 29th March, 1871."

Why is nothing done? Why has nothing been done yet?

Generals Clément Thomas and Lecomte have been assassinated; this is as incontestable as it is odious. Does all Paris wish to partake with the criminals in the responsibility of this crime? The regular Government has been expelled. Does Paris consent to this expulsion? Men invested with no rights, or, at least, with insufficient rights, have usurped the power. Does Paris so far forget itself as to submit to this usurpation without resistance?

No, most assuredly no. Paris abominates crime, does not approve of the expulsion of the Government, and does not acknowledge the right of the members of the Central Committee to impose its wishes upon us. Why then does Paris remain passive and patient? Does it not fear that it will be said that silence implies consent? How is it that I myself, for example, instead of writing my passing impressions on these pages, do not take my musket to punish the criminals and resist this despotism? It is that we all feel the present situation to be a singularly complicated one. The Government which has withdrawn to Versailles committed so many faults that it would be difficult to side with it without reserve. The weakness and inability the greater part of those who composed it showed during the siege, their obstinacy in remaining deaf to the legitimate wishes of the capital, have ill disposed us for depending on a state of things which it would have been impossible to approve of entirely. In fine, these unknown revolutionists, guilty most certainly, but perhaps sincere, claim for Paris rights that almost the whole of Paris is inclined to demand. It is impossible not to acknowledge that the municipal franchise is wished for and becomes henceforth necessary.

It is for this reason that although aghast at the excesses in perspective and those already committed by the dictators of the 18th March, though revolted at the thought of all the blood spilled and yet to be spilled—this is the reason that we side with no party. The past misdeeds of the legitimate Government of

Versailles damp our enthusiasm for it, while some few laudable ideas put forth by the illegitimate government of the Hôtel de Ville diminish our horror of its crimes, and our apprehensions at its misdoings.

Then—why not dare say it?—Paris, which is so impressionable, so excitable, so romantic, in admiration before all that is bold, has but a moderate sympathy for that which is prudent. We may smile, as I did just now, at the emphatic proclamation of the Central Committee, but that does not prevent us from recognizing that its power is real, and the ferocious elements that it has so suddenly revealed are not without a certain grandeur. It might have been spitefully remarked that more than one patriot in his yesterday evening walk on the outer boulevards and in the environs of the Hôtel de Ville, had taken more *petit vin* than was reasonable in honour of the Republic and of the Commune, but that has not prevented our feeling a surprise akin to admiration at the view of those battalions hastening from all quarters at some invisible signal, and ready at any moment to give up their lives to defend . . . what? Their guns, and these guns were in their eyes the palpable symbols of their rights and liberties. During this time the heroic Assembly was pettifogging at Versailles, and the Government was going to join them. Paris does not follow those who fly.

VI.

The Butte-Montmartre is *en fête*. The weather is charming, and every one goes to see the cannon and inspect the barricades. Men, women, and children mount the hilly streets, and they all appear joyous . . . for what, they cannot say themselves, but who can resist the charm of sunshine? If it rained, the city would be in mourning. Now the citizens have closed their shops and put

BEHIND A BARRICADE: THE MORNING MEAL—THIRTY SOUS A DAY AND NOTHING TO DO.

on their best clothes, and are going to dine at the restaurant. These are the very enemies of disorder, the small shopkeepers and the humble citizens. Strange contradiction! But what would you have? the sun is so bright, the weather is so lovely. Yesterday no work was done because of the insurrection; it was like a Sunday. To-day therefore is the holiday-Monday of the insurrection.

VII.

In the midst of all these troubles, in which every one is borne along, without any knowledge of where he is drifting—with the Central Committee making proclamations on one side, and the Versailles Government training troops on the other, a few men have arisen who have spoken some words of reason. These men may be certain from this moment that they are approved of by Paris, and will be obeyed by Paris—by the honest and intelligent Paris—by the Paris which is ready to favour that side which can prove that it has the most justice in it.

The deputies and maires of Paris have placarded the following proclamation:—

"RÉPUBLIQUE FRANÇAISE.

"Liberté, Egalité, Fraternité.

"Citizens,—Impressed with the absolute necessity of saving Paris and the Republic by the removal of every cause of collision, and convinced that the best means of attaining this grand object is to give satisfaction to the legitimate wishes of the people, we have resolved this very day to demand of the National Assembly the adoption of two measures which we have every hope will contribute to bring back tranquillity to the public mind.

"These two measures are: The election of all the officers of the National Guard, without exception, and the establishment of a municipal council, elected by the whole of the citizens.

"What we desire, and what the public welfare requires under all circumstances, and which the present situation renders more indispensable than ever, is, order in liberty and by liberty.

"*Vive la France!* Vive la République!

"*The representatives of the Seine:*

"Louis BLANC, V. SCHŒLCHER, Edmond ADAM, FLOQUET, Martin BERNARD, LANGLOIS, Edouard LOCKROY, FARCY, BRISSON, GREPPO, MILLIÈRE.

"*The maires and adjoints of Paris:*

"1st Arrondissement: Ad. ADAM, MELINE, adjoints.—2nd Arrondissement: TIRARD, maire, representative of the Seine; Ad. BRELAY, CHÉRON, LOISEAU-PINSON, adjoints.—3rd Arrondissement: BONVALET, maire; Ch. MURAT, adjoint.—4th Arrondissement: VAUTRAIN, maire; LOISEAU, CALLON, adjoints.—5th Arrondissement: JOURDAN, adjoint.—6th Arrondissement: HÉRISSON, maire; A. LEROY, adjoint.—7th Arrondissement: ARNAUD (de l'Ariége), maire, representative of the Seine.—8th Arrondissement: CARNOT, maire, representative of the Seine.—9th Arrondissement: DESMARET, maire.—10th Arrondissement: DUBAIL, maire; A. MURAT, DEGOUVES-DENUNQUES, adjoints.—11th Arrondissement: MOTU, maire, representative of the Seine; BLANCHON, POIRIER, TOLAIN, representative of the Seine.—12th Arrondissement: DENIZOT, DUMAS, TURILLON, adjoints.—13th Arrondissement: Léo MEILLET, COMBES, adjoints.—14th Arrondissement: HÉLIGON, adjoint.—15th Arrondissement: JOBBE-DUVAL, adjoint.—16th Arrondissement: Henri MARTIN, maire and representative of the Seine.—17th Arrondissement: FRANÇOIS FAVRE, maire; MALOU, VILLENEUVE, CACHEUX, adjoints.—18th Arrondissement: CLÉMENCEAU, maire and representative of the people; J. B. LAFONT, DEREURE, JACLARD, adjoints."

This proclamation has now been posted two hours, and I have not yet met a single person who does not approve of it entirely. The deputies of the Seine and the *maires* of Paris have, by the flight of the Government to Versailles, become the legitimate chiefs. We have elected them, it is for them to lead us. To them belongs the duty of reconciling the Assembly with the city; and it appears to us that they have taken the last means of bringing about that conciliation, by disengaging all that is legitimate and practical in its claims from the exaggeration of the *émeute*. Let them therefore have all praise for this truly patriotic attempt. Let them hasten to obtain from the Assembly a recognition of our rights. In acceding to the demands of the deputies and the *maires*, the Government will not be treating with insurrection; on the contrary, it will effect a radical triumph over it, for it will take away from it every pretext of existence, and will separate from it, in a definite way, all those men who have been blinded to the illegal and violent manner in which this programme is drawn up, by the justice of certain parts of it.

If the Assembly consent to this, all that will remain of the 18th of March will be the recollection—painful enough, without doubt—of one sanguinary day, while out of a great evil will come a great benefit.

Whatever may happen, we are resolute; we—that is to say, all those who, without having followed the Government of Versailles, and without having taken an active part in the insurrection, equally desire the re-establishment of legitimate power and the development of municipal liberties—we are resolved to follow where our deputies and the *maires* may lead us. They represent at this moment the only legal authority which seems to us to have fairly understood the difficulties of the situation, and if, in the case of all hope of conciliation being lost, they should tell us to take up arms, we will do so.

VIII.

PARIS has this evening, the 21st of March, an air of extraordinary contentment; it has belief in the deputies and the *maires*, it has trust even in the National Assembly. People talk of the manifestation of the Friends of Order and approve of it. A foreigner, a Russian, Monsieur A—— J——, who has inhabited Paris for ten years, and is consequently Parisian, has given me the following information, of which I took hasty note:—

"At half-past one o'clock to-day a group, of which I made one, was formed in the place of the New Opera-house. We numbered scarcely twenty persons, and we had a flag on which was inscribed, 'Meeting of the Friends of Order.' This flag was carried by a soldier of the line, an employé, it is said, of the house of Siraudin, the great confectioners. We marched along the boulevards as far as the Rue de Richelieu; windows were opened as we passed, and the people cried, '*Vive l'Ordre! Vive l'Assemblée Nationale! A bas la Commune!*' Few as we were at starting, our numbers soon grew to three hundred, to five hundred, to a thousand. Our troop followed the Rue de Richelieu, increasing as it went. At the Place de la Bourse a captain at the head of his National Guards tried to stop us. We continued our course, the company saluted our flag as we passed, and the drums beat to arms. After having traversed, still increasing in numbers, the streets which surround the Bourse, we returned to the boulevards, where the most lively enthusiasm burst out around us. We halted opposite the Rue Drouot. The *mairie* of the Ninth Arrondissement was occupied by a battalion attached to the Central Committee—the 229th, I believe. Although there was some danger of a collision, we made our way into the street, resolved to do our duty, which was to protest against the interference with order and the disregard for established laws; but no resistance was opposed to us. The National Guards came out in front of the door of the *mairie* and presented arms to us, and we were about to continue our way, when some one remarked that our flag, on which, as I have already said, were the words 'Meeting of the Friends of Order,' might expose us to the danger of being taken for '*réactionnaires*,' and that we ought to add the words '*Vive la République!*' Those who headed the manifestation came to a halt, and a few of them went into a café, and there wrote the words on the flag with chalk. We then resumed our march, following the widest and most frequented paths, and were received with acclamations everywhere. A quarter of an hour later we arrived at the Rue de la Paix and were marching towards the Place Vendôme, where the battalions of the Committee were collected in masses, and where, as is well known, the staff of the National Guard had its head-quarters. There, as in the Rue Drouot, the drums were beaten and arms presented to us; more than that, an officer came and informed the leaders of the manifestation that a delegate of the Central Committee begged them to proceed to the staff quarters. At this moment I was carrying the flag. We advanced in silence. When we arrived beneath the balcony, surrounded by National Guards, whose attitude was generally peaceful, there appeared on the balcony a rather young man, without uniform, but wearing a red scarf, and surrounded by several superior officers; he came forward and said—'Citizens, in the name of the Central Committee . . . .' when he was interrupted by a storm of hisses and by cries of '*Vive l'Ordre! Vive l'Assemblée Nationale! Vive la République!*' In spite of these daring interruptions we were not subjected to any violence, nor even to any threats, and without troubling ourselves any more about the delegate, we marched round the column, and having regained the boulevards proceeded towards the Place de la Concorde. There, some one proposed that we should visit Admiral Saisset, who lived in the Rue Pauquet, in the quarter of the Champs Elysées, when a grave looking man with grey hair said that Admiral Saisset was at Versailles. 'But,' he added, 'there are several admirals amongst you.' He gave his own name, it was Admiral de Chaillé. From that moment he headed the manifestation, which passed over the Pont de la Concorde to the Faubourg St. Germain. Constantly received with acclamations, and increasing in numbers, we paraded successively all the streets of the quarter, and each time that we passed before a guard-house the men presented arms. On the Place St. Sulpice a battalion drew up to allow us to pass. We afterwards went along the Boulevard St. Michel and the Boulevard de Strasbourg. During this part of our course we were joined by a large group, preceded by a tricolor flag with the inscription, '*Vive l'Assemblée Nationale!*' From this time the two flags floated side by side at the head of the augmented procession. As we were about to turn into the Boulevard Bonne-Nouvelle, a man dressed in a paletot and wearing a grey felt hat, threw himself upon me as I was carrying the standard of the Friends of Order, but a negro, dressed in the uniform of the National Guard, who marched beside me, kept the man off, who thereupon turned against the person that carried the other flag, wrested it from him, and with extraordinary strength broke the staff, which was a strong one, over his knee. This incident caused some confusion; the man was seized and carried off, and I fear he was rather maltreated. We then made our way back to the boulevards. At our appearance the enthusiasm of the passers-by was immense;

and certainly, without exaggeration, we numbered between three and four thousand persons by the time we got back to the front of the New Opera-house, where we were to separate. A Zouave climbed up a tree in front of the Grand Hotel, and fixed our flag on the highest branch. It was arranged that we should meet on the following day, in uniform but without arms, at the same place."

This account differs a little from those given in the newspapers, but I have the best reason to believe it absolutely true.

What will be the effect of this manifestation? Will those who desire "Order through Liberty and in Liberty" succeed in meeting in sufficiently large numbers to bring to reason, without having recourse to force, the numerous partizans of the Commune? Whatever may happen, this manifestation proves that Paris has no intention of being disposed of without her own consent. In connection with the action of the deputies in the National Assembly, it cannot have been ineffective in aiding the coming pacification.

Many hopeful promises of concord and quiet circulate this evening amongst the less violent groups.

IX.

WHAT is this fusillade? Against whom is it directed? Against the Prussians? No! Against Frenchmen, against passers-by, against those who cry "*Vive la République et vive l'Ordre.*" Men are falling dead or wounded, women flying, shops closing, amid the whistling of the bullets,—all Paris terrified. This is what I have just seen or heard. We are done for then at last. We shall see the barricades thrown up in our streets; we shall meet the horrid litters, from which hang hands black with powder; every woman will weep in the evening when her husband is late in returning home, and all mothers will be seized with terror. France, alas! France, herself a weeping mother, will fall by the hands of her own children.

I had started, in company with a friend, from the Passage Choiseul on my way to the Tuileries, which has been occupied since yesterday by a battalion devoted to the Central Committee. On arriving at the corner of the Rue St. Roch and the Rue Neuve des Petits Champs we perceived a considerable crowd in the direction of the Rue de la Paix. "What is going on now?" said I to my friend. "I think," said he, "that it is an unarmed manifestation going to the Place Vendôme; it passed along the boulevards a short time since, crying "*Vive l'Ordre.*"

As we talked we were approaching the Rue de la Paix. All at once a horrible noise was heard. It was the report of musketry. A white smoke rose along the walls, cries issued from all parts, the crowd fled terrified, and a hundred yards before us I saw a woman fall. Is she wounded or dead? What is this massacre? What fearful deeds are passing in open day, in this glorious sunshine? We had scarcely time to escape into one of the cross-streets, followed by the frightened crowd, when the shops were closed, hurriedly, and the horrible news spread to all parts of terrified Paris.

Reports, varying extremely in form, spread with extraordinary rapidity; some were grossly exaggerated, others the reverse. "Two hundred victims have fallen," said one. "There were no balls in the guns," said another. The opinions regarding the cause of the conflict were strangely various. Perhaps we shall never know, with absolute certainty, what passed in the Place Vendôme and the Rue de la Paix. For myself, I was at once too far and too near the scene of action; too near, for I had narrowly missed being killed; too far, for I saw nothing but the smoke and the flight of the terrified crowd.

One thing certain is that the Friends of Order who, yesterday, succeeded in assembling a large number of citizens, had to-day tried to renew its attempt at pacification by unarmed numbers. Three or four thousand persons entered the Rue de la Paix towards two o'clock in the afternoon, crying, "*L'Ordre! L'Ordre! Vive l'Ordre!*" The Central Committee had doubtless issued severe orders, for the foremost sentinels of the Place, far from presenting arms to the "Friends of Order," as they had done the day before, formally refused to let them continue their way. And then what happened? Two crowds were face to face, one unarmed, the other armed, both under strong excitement, one trying to press forward, the other determined to oppose its passage. A pistol-shot was heard. This was a signal. Down went the muskets, the armed crowd fired, and the unarmed dispersed in mad flight, leaving dead and wounded on their path.

But who fired that first pistol-shot? "One of the citizens of the demonstration; and moreover, the sentinels had their muskets torn from them," affirm the partisans of the Central Committee, and they bring forward, among other proofs, the evidence of an eye-witness, a foreign general, who saw it all from a window of the Rue de la Paix. But these assertions are but little to be relied upon. Can it be seriously believed that a crowd, to all appearance peaceful, would commit such an act of aggression? Who would have been insane enough to expose a mass of unarmed people to such dire revenge, by a challenge as criminal as it was useless? The account according to which the pistol was fired by an officer of the Federal guard from the foot of the Place Vendôme, thus giving the signal to those under his orders to fire upon the citizens, improbable as appears such an excess of cold-blooded barbarity, is much the more credible. And now how many women mourn their husbands and sons wounded, and perhaps dead? How many victims have fallen? The number is not yet known. Monsieur Barle, a lieutenant of the National Guard, was shot in the stomach. Monsieur Gaston Jollivet, who some time ago committed the offence, grave in our eyes, of publishing a comic ode in which he allows himself to ridicule our illustrious and beloved master, Victor Hugo, but was certainly guilty of none in desiring a return to order, had his arm fractured, it is said. Monsieur Otto Hottinger, one of the directors of the French Bank, fell, struck by two balls, while raising a wounded man from the ground.

One of my friends assures me that half-an-hour after the fusillade he was fired at, as he was coming out from a *porte-cochère*,* by National Guards in ambuscade.

At four o'clock, at the corner of the Rue de la Paix and the Rue Neuve des Petits Champs, an old man, dressed in a blouse, still lay where he had fallen across the body of a *cantinière*, and beside him a soldier of the line, the staff of a tricolour flag grasped in his dead hand. Is this soldier the same of whom my friend Monsieur A—— J—— speaks in his account of the first demonstration, and who was said to be an employé at Siraudin's?

There were many other victims—Monsieur de Péne, the editor of *Paris-Journal*, dangerously wounded by a ball that penetrated the thigh; Monsieur Portel, lieutenant in the Eclaireurs Franchetti, wounded in the neck and right foot; Monsieur Bernard, a merchant, killed; Monsieur Giraud, a stockbroker, also killed. Fresh names are added to the funereal list every moment.

Where will this revolution lead us, which was begun by the murder of two Generals and is being carried on by the assassination of passers-by?

X.

In the midst of all this horror and terror I saw one little incident which made me smile, though it was sad too; an idyl which might be an elegy. Three hired carriages descended the Rue Notre-Dame-de-Lorette. It was a wedding. In the first carriage was the bride, young and pretty, in tears; in the second, the bridegroom, looking anything but pleased. As the horses were

---

* Porte-cochère (carriage gateway).

proceeding slowly on account of the hill, I approached and inquired the cause of the discontent. A disagreeable circumstance had happened, the *garçon d'honneur* told me. They had been to the *mairie* to be married, but the *mairie* had been turned into a guard-house, and instead of the *maire* and his clerks, they found soldiers of the Commune. The sergeant had offered to replace the municipal functionary, but the grands-parents had not consented to such an arrangement, and they were forced to return with the connubial knot still to be tied. An unhappy state of things. "Pooh!" said an old woman who was passing by, "they can marry to-morrow.—There is always time enough to commit suicide."

It is true, they can marry to-morrow; but these young people wished to be married to-day. What are revolutions to them? What would it have mattered to the Commune had these lovers been united to-day? Is one ever sure of recovering happiness that has once escaped? Ah! this insurrection, I hate it for the men it has killed, and the widows it has made; and also for the sake of those pretty eyes that glistened with tears under the bridal wreath.

XI.

The *mairie* of the Second Arrondissement seems destined to be the centre of resistance to the Central Committee. The Federals have not been able, or have not dared, to occupy it. In the quarter of the Place de la Bourse and the Place des Victoires, National Guards have assembled and declared themselves Friends of Order. But they are few in number. Yesterday morning, the 23rd of March, they were reinforced by battalions that joined them, one by one, from all parts of Paris. They obey the orders, they say, of Admiral Saisset, raised to the superior command of the National Guard. It is believed that there are mitrailleuses within the Bourse and in the court of the Messageries. The massacre of the Rue de la Paix decided the most timorous. There is a determination to have done, by some means or other, with tyrants who represent in fact but a small part of the population of Paris, and who wish to dominate over the whole city. The preparations for resistance are being made between the Hôtel de Ville on the one hand, where the members of the Committee are sitting, formidably defended, and the Place Vendôme, crammed with insurgents, on the other. Is it civil war—civil war, with all its horrors, that is about to commence? A company of Gardes Mobiles has joined the battalions of Order. Pupils of the Ecole Polytechnique come and go between the *mairie* of the Second Arrondissement and the Grand Hôtel, where Admiral Saisset and his staff are said to be installed.* A triple line of National Guards closes the entrance of the Rue Vivienne against carriages and everybody who does not belong to the quarter. Nevertheless, a large number of people, eager for information, manage to pass the sentries in spite of the rule. On the Place de la Bourse a great crowd discusses, and gesticulates around the piled bayonets which glitter in the sun. I notice that the pockets of the National Guards are crammed full; a large number of cartridges has been distributed.

The orders are strict: no one is to quit his post. There are men, however, who have been standing there, without sleep, for twenty-four hours. No one must leave the camp of the Friends of Order even to go and dine. Those who have no money either have rations given them or are provided at the expense of the *mairie*, from a restaurant of the Rue des Filles Saint-Thomas, with a dinner consisting of soup and bouilli, a plate of meat, vegetables, and a bottle of wine. I hear one of them exclaim,

* Lieutenant-Colonel de Beaugrand had improvised staff-quarters at the Grand Hôtel, and the nomination of Admiral Saisset, together with M. Schœlcher and Langlois, had strengthened the enmity of the two parties. The Central Committee, seeing the danger which threatened, announced that the Communal elections were adjourned to Sunday the 26th March.

"If the Federals knew that we not only get our pay, but are also fed like princes, they would come over to us, every man of them. As for us, we are determined to obey the *maires* and deputies of Paris." Much astonishment is manifested at the absence of Vice-Admiral Saisset; as he has accepted the command he ought to show himself. Certain croakers even insinuate that the vice-admiral hesitates to organise the resistance, but we will not listen to them, and are on the whole full of confidence and resolution. "We are numerous, determined; we have right on our side, and will triumph."

At about four o'clock an alarm is sounded. We hear cries of "To arms! To arms!" The drums beat, the trumpets sound, the ranks are formed. The ominous click, click, as the men cock their rifles, is heard on all sides. The moment of action has arrived. There are more than ten thousand men, well armed and determined. A company of Mobiles and the National Guards defend the entrance of the Rue Vivienne. All this tumult is caused by one of the battalions from Belleville, passing along the boulevards with three pieces of cannon.

What is about to happen? When the insurgents reach the top of the Rue Vivienne they seem to hesitate. In a few seconds the boulevards, which were just now crowded, are suddenly deserted; and even the cafés are closed.

At such a moment as this, a single accidental shot (several such have happened this morning; a woman standing at a window at the corner of the Rue Saint Marc was nearly killed by the carelessness of one of the Guards),—a single shot, a cry even, or a menacing gesture would suffice to kindle the blaze. Nobody moves or speaks. I feel myself tremble before the possibility of an irreparable disaster; it is a solemn and terrible moment.

The battalion from Belleville presents arms; we reply, and they pass on. The danger is over; we breathe again. In a few seconds the crowd has returned to the boulevards.

XII.

It is two in the morning. Tired of doing nothing I take out my note-book, seat myself on a doorstep opposite the Restaurant Oatelain, and jot down my memoranda by the light of a street lamp.

As soon as night came on, every measure of precaution was taken. We have no idea by whom we are commanded, but it would appear that a serious defence is contemplated, and is being executed with prudence. Is it Admiral Saisset who is at our head? We hope so. Although we have been so often disappointed in our chiefs, we have not yet lost the desire to place confidence in some one. To-night we believe in the admiral. Ever and anon our superior officers retire to the *mairies*, and receive strict orders concerning their duty. We are quite an army in ourselves; our centre is in the Place de la Bourse, our wings extend into the adjoining streets. Lines of Nationals guard all the openings; sentinels are posted sixty feet in front to give the alarm. Within the enclosed space there is no one to be seen, but the houses are inhabited as usual. The doors have been left open by order, and also all the windows on the first floors. Each company, divided under the command of sergeants, has taken possession of three or four houses. At the first signal of alarm the street-doors are to be closed, the men to rush to the windows, and from there to fire on the assailants. "Hold yourselves in readiness; it is very possible you may be attacked. On the approach of the enemy the guards in the streets are to fall back under fire towards the houses, and take shelter there. Those posted at the windows are to keep up an unceasing fire on the insurgents. In the meantime the bulk of our forces will come to our aid, and clear the streets with their mitrailleuses."

So we waited, resolved on obedience, calm, with a silent but fervent prayer that we might not be obliged to turn our arms against our fellow-townsmen.

The night is beautiful. Some of our men are talking in groups on the thresholds of the doors, others, rolled in their blankets, are lying on the ground asleep. In the upper storeys of some of the houses lights are still twinkling through the muslin curtains; lower down all is darkness. Scarcely a sound is to be heard, only now and then the rumble of a heavy cart, or perhaps a cannon in the distance; and nearer to us the sudden noise of a musket that slips from its resting-place on to the pavement. Every hour the dull sound of many feet is heard; it is the patrol of Mobiles making its round. We question them as they pass.—"Anything fresh?"—"Nothing," is the invariable reply.—"How far have you been?"—"As far as the Rue de la Paix," they answer, and pass on. Interrupted conversations are resumed, and the sleepers, who had been awakened by the noise, close their eyes again. We are watching and waiting,—may we watch and wait in vain!

XIII.

NEVER have I seen the dawn break with greater pleasure. Almost everyone has some time in his life passed such sleepless nights, when it seems to him that the darkness will never disappear, and the desire for light and day becomes a fearful longing. Never was dawn more grateful than after that wretched night. And yet the fear of a disastrous collision did not disappear with the night. It was even likely that the Federals might have waited for the morning to begin their attack, just when fatigue is greatest, sleep most difficult to fight against, and therefore discipline necessarily slackened. Anyhow, the light seemed to reassure us; we could scarcely believe that the crime of civil war could be perpetrated in the day-time. The night had been full of fears, the morning found us bright and happy. Not all of us, however. I smile as I remember an incident which occurred a little before daylight. One of our comrades, who had been lying near me, got up, went out into the street, and paced up and down some time, as if to shake off cramp or cold. My eyes followed him mechanically; he was walking in front of the houses, the backs of which look out upon the Passage des Panoramas, and as he did so he cast furtive glances through the open doorways. He went into one, and came out with a disappointed expression on his face. Having repeated this strange manœuvre several times, he reached a *porte cochère* that was down by the side of the Restaurant Catelain. He remained a few minutes, then reappeared with a beaming countenance, and made straight for where I was standing, rubbing his hands gleefully.

"Monsieur," said he, in a low voice, so as not to be overheard, "do you approve of this plan of action, which consists, in case of attack, of shooting from the windows on the assailants?"—"A necessity of street fighting," said I. "Let us hope we shall not have to try it."—"Oh! of course; but I should have preferred it if they had taken other measures."—"Why?" I asked.—"Why, you see, when we are in the houses the insurgents will try to force their way in."—I could not see what he was driving at, so I said, "Most probably."—"But if they do get in?" he insisted.—"I will trust to our being reinforced from the Place de la Bourse before they can effect an entrance."—"Doubtless! doubtless!" he answered; but I saw he was anything but convinced.—"But you know reinforcements often arrive too late, and if the Federals should get in, we shall be shot down like dogs in those rooms overhead."—I acknowledged that this would be, to say the least, disagreeable, but argued that in time of war one must take one's chance.—"Do you think, then, monsieur," he continued, "that if in the event of the insurgents entering we were to look out for a back door to escape by, we should be acting the part of cowards?"—"Of cowards? no; but of excessively prudent individuals? yes."—"Well, monsieur, I am prudent, and there is an end of it!" exclaimed my comrade, with an air of triumph, "and I think I have found——"

—"The back door in question?"—"Just so; look down that passage in front of us; at the end there is a door which leads—where do you think?"—"Into the Passage des Panoramas, does it not?"—"Yes, monsieur, and now you see what I mean."—I told him I did not think I did.—"Why, you see," he explained, "when the enemy comes we must rush into that passage, shut the lower door, and make for our post at the windows, where we will do our duty bravely to our last cartridge. But suppose, in the meantime, that those devils succeed in breaking open the lower door with the butt end of their muskets—and it is not very strong—what shall we do then?"—"Why, of course," I said, "we must plant ourselves at the top of the staircase and receive them at the point of our bayonets."—"By no means," he expostulated.—"But we must; it is our duty."—"Oh! I fancied we might have gained the door that leads into the passage," he went on, looking rather shame-faced.—"What, run away!"—"No, not exactly; only find some place of safety!"—"Well, if it comes to that," I replied, "you may do just as you like; only I warn you that the passage is occupied by a hundred of our men, and that all the outlets are barricaded."—"No, not all," he said with conviction, "and that is why I appeal to you. You are a journalist, are you not?"—"Sometimes."—"Yes, but you are; and you know actors and all those sort of people, and you go behind the scenes, I dare say, and know where the actors dress themselves, and all that."—I looked at my brave comrade in some surprise, but he continued without noticing me, "And you know all the ins and outs of the theatre, the corridors, the trap-doors."—"Suppose I do, what good can that do you?"—"All the good in the world, monsieur; it will be the saving of me. Why we shall only have to find the actors' entrance of the *Variétés*, which is in the passage, then ring at the bell; the porter knows you, and will admit us. You can guide us both up the staircase and behind the scenes, and we can easily hunt out some hole or corner in which to hide until the fight is over."—"Then," said I, feeling rather disgusted with my companion, "we can bravely walk out of the front door on the boulevards, and go and eat a comfortable breakfast, while the others are busy carrying away our dead comrades from the staircase we ought to have helped to defend!"

The poor man looked at me aghast, and then went off. I saw that I had hurt his feelings, and I thought perhaps I had been wrong in making him feel the cowardice of his proposition. I had known him for some months; he lived in the same street as I did, and I remembered that he had a wife and children. Perhaps he was right in wishing to protect his life at any price. I thought it over for a minute or two, and then it went out of my mind altogether.

At four in the morning we had another alarm; in an instant every one was on foot and rushing to the windows. The house to which I was ordered was the very one that had inspired my ingenious friend with his novel plan of evasion. I found him already installed in the room from whence we were to fire into the street.—"You do not know what I have done," said he, coming up to me.—"No."—"Well, you know the door which opens on to the passage; you remember it?"—"Of course I do."—"I found there was a key; so what do you think I did? I double-locked the door, and went and slipped the key down the nearest drain! Ha! ha! The fellow who tries to escape that way will be finely caught!"

I seized him cordially by the hand and shook it many times. He was beaming, and I was pleased also. I could not help feeling that however low France may have fallen, one must never despair of a country in which cowards even can be brave.

XIV.

On Friday, the 24th of March, at nine in the morning, we are still in the quarter of the Bourse. Some of the men have not slept for forty-eight hours. We are tired but still resolved. Our numbers are increasing every hour. I have just seen three battalions, with trumpeters and all complete, come up and join us. They will now be able to let the men who have been so long on duty get a little rest. As to what is going on, we are but very incompletely informed. The Federals are fortifying themselves more strongly than ever at the Place de l'Hôtel de Ville and the Place Vendôme. They are very numerous, and have lots of artillery. Why do they not act on the offensive? Or do they want, as we do, to avoid a conflict? Certainly our hand shall not be the first to spill French blood. These hours of hesitation on both sides calm men's minds. The deputies and mayors of Paris are trying to obtain from the National Assembly the recognition of the municipal franchise. If the Government has the good sense to make these concessions, which are both legitimate and urgent, rather than remain doggedly on the defensive, with the conviction that it has right on its side; if, in a word, it remembers the well-known maxim, "*Summum jus, summa injuria,*" the horrors of civil war may be averted. We are told, and I fancy correctly, that the Federal Guards are not without fear concerning the issue of the events into which they have hurried. The chiefs must also be uneasy. Even those who have declared themselves irreconcileable in the hour of triumph would not perhaps be sorry now if a little condescension on the part of the Assembly furnished them with a pretext of not continuing the rebellion. Just now, several Guards of the 117th Battalion, a part of which has declared for the Central Committee, who happened to be passing, stopped to chat with our outposts. Civil war to the knife did not at all appear to be their most ardent desire. One of them said: "We were called to arms, what could we do but obey? They give us our pay, and so here we are." Were they sincere in this? Did they come with the hope of joining us, or to spy into what we were doing? Others, however, either more frank or less clever at deception, declared that they wanted the Commune, and would have it at any price.

F

This, however, was by far the smaller number; the majority of the insurgents are of the opinion of these men who joined in conversation with us. It is quite possible to believe that some understanding might be brought about. A fact has just been related to me which confirms me in my opinion.

The Comptoir d'Escompte was occupied by a post of Federals. A company of Government Guards from the 9th Arrondissement marched up to take possession. "You have been here for two whole days; go home and rest," said the officer in command of the latter. But the Federals obstinately refused to be sent away. The officer insisted.—" We are in our own quarter, you are from Belleville; it is our place to guard the Comptoir d'Escompte."— It was all of no avail until the officer said : "Go away directly, and we will give you a hundred francs."—They did not wait for the offer to be repeated, but accepted the money and marched off. Now men who are willing to sell their consciences at two francs a head—for there were fifty of them—cannot have any very formidable political opinions. I forgot to say that this post of Federals was commanded by the Italian Tibaldi, the same who had been arrested in one of the passages of the Hôtel de Ville during the riots of the 31st October.

XV.

THE news is excellent, in a few hours perhaps it will be better. We rejoice beforehand at the almost certain prospect of pacification. The sun shines, the boulevards are crowded with people, the faces of the women especially are beaming. What is the cause of all this joy? A placard has just been posted up on all the walls in the city. I copy it with pleasure.

"DEAR FELLOW CITIZENS,—I hasten to announce to you that together with the Deputies of the Seine and the Mayors of

Paris, we have obtained from the Government of the National Assembly: 1st. The complete recognition of your municipal franchises; 2nd. The right of electing all the officers of the National Guard, as well as the general-in-chief; 3rd. Modifications of the law on bills; 4th. A project for a law on rents, favourable to tenants paying 1,200 francs a year, or less than that sum. Until you have confirmed my nomination, or until you name some one else in my stead, I shall continue to remain at my post to watch over the execution of these conciliatory measures that we have succeeded in obtaining, and to contribute to the well-being of the Republic!

" The Vice-Admiral and
" Provisional Commander,
" Paris, 23rd March. " SAISSET."

Well! this is opportune and to the purpose. The National Assembly has understood that, in a town like Paris, a revolution in which a third of the population is engaged, cannot be alone actuated by motives of robbery and murder;* and that if some of the demands of the people are illegitimate or premature, there are at least others, which it is but right should obtain justice. Paris is never entirely in the wrong. Certainly among the authors and leaders of the 18th March, there are many who are very guilty. The murderers of General Lecomte and General Clément Thomas should be sought out and punished. All honest men must demand and expect that a minute inquiry be instituted concerning the massacres in the Place Vendôme. It must be acknowledged that all the Federals, officers and soldiers,

* At the same time that the proclamation of Admiral Saisset encouraged the partizans of the Assembly, proofs were not wanting of the poverty of the Commune in money as well as men: a new loan obtained from the Bank of France, which had already advanced half a million of francs, and the military nominations which raised Brunel, Eudes, and Duval from absolute obscurity to the rank of general. These were indications decidedly favourable to the party of order.

are not devils or drunkards. A few hundred men getting drunk in the cabarets—(I have perhaps been wrong to lay so much stress here upon the prevalence of this vice among the insurrectionists)—a few tipsy brutes, ought not to be sufficient to authorise us to condemn a hundred thousand men, among whom are certainly to be found some right-minded persons who are convinced of the justice of their cause. These unknown and suddenly elevated chiefs, whom the revolution has singled out, are they all unworthy of our esteem, and devoid of capacity? They possess, perhaps, a new and vital force that it would be right and perhaps necessary to utilise somehow. The ideas which they represent ought to be studied, and if they prove useful, put into practice. This is what the Assembly has understood and what it has done. By concessions which enlarge rather than diminish its influence, it puts all right-minded men, soldiers and officers, under the obligation of returning to their allegiance. Those who, having read the proclamation of Admiral Saisset, still refuse to recognise the Government, are no longer men acting for the sake of Paris and the Republic, but rioters guilty of pursuing the most criminal paths, for the gratification of their own bad passions. Thus the tares will be separated from the wheat, and torn up without mercy. Yesterday and the day before, at the Place de la Bourse, at the Place des Victoires and the Bank, we were resolved on resistance —resistance, nothing more, for none of us, I am sure, would have fired a shot without sufficient provocation—and even this resolution cost us much pain and some hesitation. We felt that in the event of our being attacked, our shots might strike many an innocent breast—and perhaps at the last moment our hearts would have failed us. Now, no thoughts of that kind can hinder us. In recognising our demand, the Assembly has got right entirely on its side, we shall now consider all rebellion against the authority of which it makes so able a use, as an act entailing immediate punishment. Until now, fearing to be abandoned or misunderstood by the Government, we had determined to obey the mayors and deputies elected by the people, but the Assembly, by its judicious conduct, has shown itself worthy confidence. Let them command, we are ready to obey.

Truly this change in the attitude of the Government is at once strange and delightful. No later than yesterday their language was quite different. The manner in which the majority received the mayors did not lead us to expect a termination so favourable to the wishes of all concerned. But this is all past, let us not recriminate. Let us rather rejoice in our present good fortune, and try and forget the dangers which seemed but now so imminent. I hear from all sides that the Deputies of the Seine and the mayors, fully empowered, are busy concluding the last arrangements. Municipal elections are talked of, for the 2nd April; thus every cause for discontent is about to disappear. Capital! Paris is satisfied. Shops re-open. The promenades are crowded with people; the Place Vendôme alone does not brighten with the rest, but it soon will. The weather is lovely, people accost each other in the streets with a smile; one almost wonders they do not embrace. Is to-day Friday? No, it is Sunday. Bravo! Assembly.

XVI.

On the ground-floor of the house of my neighbour there is an upholsterer's workshop. The day before yesterday the master went out to fetch some work, and this morning he had not yet returned. In an agony of apprehension his wife went everywhere in search of him. His body has just been found at the Morgue with a bullet through its head. Some say he was walking across the Rue de la Paix on his way home, and was shot by accident; but the *Journal Officiel* announces that this poor man, Wahlin, was a national guard, assassinated by the revolvers of the manifestation. Whom are we to believe? Anyhow, the man is to be buried tomorrow, and his poor wife is a widow.

XVII.

WHAT is the meaning of all this! Are we deceiving ourselves, or being deceived? We await in vain the consummation of Admiral Saisset's promises. In officially announcing that the Assembly had acceded to the just demands of the mayors and deputies, did he take upon himself to pass delusive hopes as accomplished facts? It seems pretty certain now that the Government will make no concessions, that the proclamation is only waste paper, and that the Provisional Commander of the National Guard has been leading us into error—with a laudable intention doubtless—or else has himself been deceived likewise. The united efforts of the Deputies of the Seine and the Mayors of Paris have been unequal to rouse the apathy of the Assembly.* In vain did Louis Blanc entreat the representatives of France to approve the conciliatory conduct of the representatives of Paris. "May the responsibility of what may happen be on your own heads!" cried M. Clémenceau. He was right; a little condescension might have saved all; such obstinacy is fatal. Deprived of the countenance of the Assembly, and left to themselves, the Deputies and Mayors of Paris, desirous above all of avoiding civil war, have been obliged to accede to the wishes of the Central Committee, and insist upon the municipal elections being proceeded with immediately. They could not have acted otherwise, and yet it is humiliating for them to have to bow before superior force, and

* The news of the check which the Maires of Paris had suffered in the Assembly suddenly loosened the bond which for two days had united the friends of order, and profound discouragement seized upon the public mind. It was at this moment that the deputies from the Committee presented themselves at the Mairie of the first arrondissement, preceded by three pieces of artillery, a very warlike accompaniment to a deputation. It was arranged that the Communal election should be managed by the existing Maires, and that the battalions of each quarter of the city, whether federal or not, should occupy the voting places of their sections; but this did not prevent the Committee on the following morning occupying the Mairie of Saint-Germain-l'Auxerrois, in spite of the arrangement, by their most devoted battalions.

their authority is compromised by so doing. What the Assembly, representing the whole of France, could have done with no loss of dignity, and even with honour to itself, the former accomplish only at the risk of losing their influence; what to the Assembly would have been an honourable concession is to them dangerous although necessary submission. The Committee would have been annulled if the Government had consented to the municipal elections, but thanks to a tardy consent, rung from the Deputies and Mayors of Paris, it triumphs. The result of the humiliation to which the representatives of Paris have been forced to submit to prevent the effusion of blood, will be the entire abdication of their authority, which will remain vested in the Central Committee until the members of the Commune are elected. Abandoned by the Government since the departure of the chief of the executive power and the ministers, we rallied round the representatives, who, unsustained by the Government, are obliged to submit to the revolutionists. We must now choose between the Commune and anarchy.

Therefore, to-day, Sunday, the 26th March, the male population of Paris is hurrying to the poll. It is in vain that the journals have begged the people not to vote; the elections were only announced yesterday, and the electors have had no time to reconsider the choice they have to make, and yet they insist on voting. Those who decline to obey the suggestions of the Central Committee, will re-elect the late mayors or choose among the deputies, but vote they will. The present attitude of the regular Government has done much towards furthering the revolution. The mistakes of the Assembly have diminished in the eyes of the public the crime of revolt. Everywhere the murder of Generals Clément Thomas and Lecomte is openly regretted; but those who repeat that the Central Committee declares having had nothing to do with it, are listened to with patience. The rumour that they were shot by soldiers gains ground, and seems less incredulously received. As to the massacres of the Rue de la Paix, we are told that this event is enveloped in mystery, that the evidence is most contradictory, &c., &c.* There is evidently a decided reactionary movement in favour of the partizans of the Commune. Without approving their acts their activity is incontestable. They have done much in a short time. People exclaim, "There are men for you!" This state of things is very alarming to all those who have remained faithful to the Assembly, which in spite of its errors has not ceased to be the legal representative of the country. It is a cruel position for the Parisians who are obliged to choose between a regular Government which they would desire to obey, but which by its faults renders such obedience impossible, and an illegitimate power, that, although guilty in its acts, and stained with crime, still represents the opinions of the republican majority. By to-night, therefore, the Commune will have been called into existence; an illegal existence it may be argued, doubtless, by the partizans of constitutional legality, who would consider as null and void elections carried on without the consent of the nation, as represented by the Assembly. Legal or not, however, the elections have taken place, and the fact alone is of some importance. In a few hours the Executive Power of the Republic will have to treat,

---

* The following are the terms in which the Commune spoke of the events of the 18th March, and excused the murder of the two generals:

"CITIZENS,—The day of the 18th of March, which for interested reasons has been travestied in the most odious manner, will be called in history, The Day of the People's Justice!

"The Government, now subverted—always maladroit—rushed into a conflict without considering either its own unpopularity, or the fraternal feeling that animates the armies; the entire army, when ordered to commit fratricide, replied with cries of 'Vive la Republique!' 'Vive la Garde Nationale!'"

"Two men alone, who had rendered themselves unpopular by acts which we now pronounce as iniquitous, were struck down in a moment of popular indignation.

"The Committee of the Federation of the National Guard, in order to render homage to truth, declare it was a stranger to these two executions.

"At the present moment the ministries are constituted, the prefect of police has assumed his duties, the public offices are again active, and we invite all citizens to maintain the utmost calmness and order."

whether it will or no, with a force which has constituted itself with as much legality as it had in its power to assume under the circumstances.

XVIII.

CROWDS in the streets and promenades. This evening all the theatres will be re-opened. In the meantime the voting is going on. The weather is delightful, so I take a stroll along the promenades. Under the colonnade of the Châtelet there is a long line of electors awaiting their turn. I fancy that in this quarter the candidates of the Central Committee will be surely elected. Women, in bright-coloured dresses and fresh spring bonnets, are walking to and fro. I hear some one say that there are a great many cannon at the Hôtel de Ville. Two friends meet together in the square of the Arts et Métiers.—"Are you alone, madame? says one lady to another.—" Yes, madame; I am waiting for my husband, who is gone to vote."

A child, who is skipping, cries out, "Mama, mama, what is the Commune?"

The fiacre drivers make the revolution an excuse for asking extravagant fares; this does not prevent their having very decided political opinions. One who drove me would scarcely have been approved of by the Central Committee.—"*Cocher*, what is the fare?" I ask.—"Five francs, monsieur."—"All right; take me to the mairie Place Saint-Sulpice."—"Beg pardon, monsieur, but if you are going to vote, it will be ten francs!"

On the Boulevard de Strasbourg there are streams of people dressed in holiday attire; itinerant dealers in tops, pamphlets, souvenirs of the siege—bits of black bread, made on purpose, and framed and glazed, also bits of shells—and scented soap, and coloured pictures; crowds of beggars everywhere. In this part of the town the revolution looks very much like a fair.

At the mairie of the 6th Arrondissement there are very few people. I enter into conversation with one of the officials there. He tells me he has never seen voting carried on with greater spirit.

I meet a friend who has just returned from Belleville, and ask him the news, of course.—"The voting is progressing in capital order," he tells me; "the men go up to the poll as they would mount the breach. They have no choice but to obey blindly."—" The Central Committee?" I inquire.—" Yes, but the Committee itself only obeys orders."—" Whose?"—" Why those of the International, of course."

At a corner near the boulevards, a compact little knot of people is stationed in front of a poster. I fancy they are studying the proclamation of one of the candidates, but it turns out only to be a play-bill. The crowd continues to thicken; the cafés are crammed; gold chignons are plentiful enough at every table; here and there a red Garibaldi shirt is visible, like poppies amongst the corn. Every now and then a horseman gallops wildly past with dispatches from one section to another. The results of some of the elections are creeping out. At Montrouge, Bercy, Batignolles, and the Marais, they tell us the members of the Central Committee are elected by a very large majority. Here the hoarse voice of a boy strikes in,—" Buy the account of the grand conspiracy of Citoyen Thiers against the Republic!" Then another chimes in with wares of a less political and more vulgar nature. The movement to and fro and the excitement is extraordinary. While the populace basks in the sun the destiny of the city is being decided.—" M. Desmarest is elected for the 9th Arrondissement," says some one close to me.—" Lesueur is capital in the 'Partie de Piquet,'" says another. Oh! people of Paris!

XIX.

It is over. We have a "Municipal Council," according to some; a "Commune," according to others. Not quite legally elected, but sufficiently so. Eighty councillors, sixty of whom are quite unknown men. Who can have recommended them, or, rather, imposed them on the electors? Can there really be some occult power at work under cover of the ex-Central Committee? Is the Commune only a pretext, and are we at the début of a social and political revolution? I overheard a partizan of the new doctrines say,—"The Proletariat is vindicating its rights, which have been unjustly trampled on by the aristocratic bourgeoisie. This is the workman's 1789!"

Another person expresses the same thing in rather a different form. "This is the revolt of the *canaille* against all kind of supremacy, the supremacy of fortune, and the supremacy of intellect. The equality of man before the law has been acknowledged, now they want to proclaim the equality of intellect. Soon universal suffrage will give place to the drawing of lots. There was a time in Athens when the names of the archontes were taken haphazard out of a bag, like the numbers at loto."

However, the revolution has not yet clearly defined its tendencies, and in the meantime what are we to think of the unknown beings who represent it? A man in whom I have the greatest confidence, and who has passed his life in studying questions of social science, and who therefore has mixed in nearly all the revolutionary circles, and is personally acquainted with the chiefs, said to me just now, in speaking of the new Municipal Council,*—

---

* The *Figaro* gives the following list of those who held service under the Commune:—

Anys-el-Bittar, Librarian MSS. Department, Bibliothèque Nationale. (Egyptian.)
Biondetti, Surgeon 233rd Battalion. (Italian.)
Babick, a Member of the Commune. (Pole.)

"It will be an assemblage of a very motley character. There will be much good and much bad in it. We may safely divide it into

Becka, Adjutant to the 207th Battalion. (Pole.)
Cluseret, General, Delegate of War. (American.)
Cernatesco, Surgeon of Francs Tireurs. (Pole.)
Crapulinski, Colonel of Staff. (Pole.)
Carneiro de Cunha, Surgeon 38th Battalion. (Portuguese.)
Charalambo, Surgeon of the Federal Scouts. (Pole.)
Dombrowski, General. (Russian.)
Dombrowski (his brother), Colonel of Staff. (Russian.)
Durnoff, Commandant of Legion. (Pole.)
Echenlaub, Colonel. (German.)
Ferrera Gola, General Manager of Field Hospitals. (Portuguese.)
Frankel, a Member of the Commune. (Prussian.)
Giorok, Commandant of the Fort d'Issy. (Valachian.)
Grejorok, Commandant of the Artillery at Montmartre. (Valachian.)
Kertzfeld, Chief Manager of Field Hospitals. (German.)
Iziquerdo, Surgeon of the 88th Battalion. (Pole.)
Jalowski, Surgeon of the Zouaves de la République. (Pole.)
Kobosko, Despatch Bearer.
La Cecilia, General. (Italian.)
Landowski, Aide-de-Camp of General Dombrowski. (Pole.)
Mizara, Commandant of the 104th Battalion. (Italian.)
Maratuch, Surgeon's mate of the 72nd Battalion. (Hungarian.)
Moro, Commandant of the 22nd Battalion. (Italian.)
Okolowicz and his brothers, General and Staff Officers. (Poles.)
Ostyn, a Member of the Commune. (Belgian.)
Olinski, Chief of the 17th Legion. (Pole.)
Pisani, Aide-de-Camp of Flourens. (Italian.)
Potampenki, Aide-de-Camp of General Dombrowski. (Pole.)
Ploubinski, Staff Officer. (Pole.)
Pazdzierswski, Commandant of the Fort de Vanves. (Pole.)
Piazza, Chief of Legion. (Italian.)
Pugno, Music-manager at the Opera-house. (Italian.)
Romanelli, Manager of the War Offices. (Italian.)
Rozyski, Surgeon of the 144th Battalion. (Pole.)
Rubinowicz, Surgeon of the Marines. (Pole.)
Syneok, Surgeon of the 151st Battalion. (German.)
Skalski, Surgeon of the 240th Battalion. (Pole.)
Soteriade, Surgeon. (Spaniard.)
Thaller, Under Governor of the Fort de Bicêtre. (German.)
Van Ostal, Commandant of the 115th Battalion. (Dutch.)
Vetzel, Commandant of the Southern Forts. (German.)
Wroblewski, General Commandant of the Southern Army. (Pole.)
Witton, Surgeon of the 72nd Battalion. (American.)
Zengerler, Surgeon of the 74th Battalion. (German.)

three distinct parts: firstly, ten or twelve men belonging to the International, who have both thought and studied and may be able to act, mixed with these several foreigners; secondly, a number of young men, ardent but inexperienced, some of whom are imbued with Jacobin principles; thirdly, and by far the largest portion, unsuccessful plotters in former revolutions, journalists, orators, and conspirators,—noisy, active, and effervescent, having no particular tie amongst themselves except the absence of any common bond of unity with the two former divisions, and being confounded now with one, now with the other. The members of the International alone have any real political value; they are Socialists. The Jacobin element is decidedly dangerous."—If in reality the Communal Assembly is thus composed, how will it act? Let us wait and see; in the meantime the city is calm. Never did so critical a moment wear so calm an exterior. By the bye, where are the Prussians?*

XX.

Who can help being carried away by the enthusiasm of a crowd? I am not a political man, I am only an observer who sees, hears, and feels.

I was on the Place de l'Hôtel de Ville at the moment when the names of the successful candidates were proclaimed, and the emotion is still fresh upon me.† There were perhaps a hundred thousand men there, assembled from all quarters of the city. The

---

* The Prussians and the Commune, see Appendix 3.

† The result of the voting was made known at four o'clock on the 28th March. The papers devoted to the Commune asserted, on the following day, that *two hundred and fifteen* battalions were assembled on that day, and that the average strength of each corps was one thousand men. Who could have believed that the Place de l'Hôtel de Ville was capable of accommodating so many! This farcical assertion of the two hundred and fifteen battalions has passed into a proverb.

neighbouring streets were also full, and the bayonets glittering in the sun filled the Place with brilliant flashes like miniature lightning. In the centre of the façade of the building a platform was erected, over which presided a statue of the Republic, wearing a Phrygian cap. The bronze basso-relievo of Henry IV. had been carefully hidden with clusters of flags. Each window was alive with faces. I saw several women on the roof, and the *gamins* were everywhere, hanging on to the sculptured ornaments, or riding fearlessly on the shoulders of the marble busts. One by one the battalions had taken up their position on the Place with their bands. When they were all assembled they struck up the Marseillaise, which was re-echoed by a thousand voices. It was grand in the extreme, and the magnificent hymn, which late defeats had shorn of its glory, swelled forth again with all its old splendour revived. Suddenly the cannon is heard, the voices rise louder and louder; a sea of standards, bayonets, and human heads waves backwards and forwards in front of the platform. The cannon roars, but we only hear it between the intervals of the hymn. Then all the sounds are confounded in one universal shout, that shout of the vast multitude which seems to have but one heart and one voice. The members of the Committee, each with a tricolor scarf across his breast, have taken their places on the platform. One of them reads out the names of the elected councillors. Then the cannon roars once more, but is almost drowned by the deafening huzzas of the crowd. Oh! people of Paris, who on the day of the "*Crosse en l'air*"* got tipsy in the wine-shops of Montmartre, whose ranks furnished the murderers of Thomas and Lecomte, who in the Rue de la Paix shot down unconscious passengers, who are capable of the wildest extravagance and most execrable deeds, you are also in your days of glory, grand and magnificent, when a volcano of generous passions rages within, and the hearts even of those who condemn you most, are scorched in the flames.

* When they turned the butt-ends (*crosses*) of their guns in the air, as a sign they would not fight.

XXI.

"Citizens," says the *Official Journal* this morning, "your Commune is constituted." Then follows decree upon decree. White posters are being stuck up everywhere. Why are they at the Hôtel de Ville, if not to publish decrees? The conscription is abolished. We shall see no more poor young fellows marching through the town with their numbers in their caps, and fired with that noble patriotism which is imbibed in the cabarets at so much a glass. We shall have no more soldiers, but to make up for that we shall all be National Guards. There's a glorious decree, as Edgar Poë says. As to the landlords, their vexation is extreme; even the tenants do not seem so satisfied as they ought to be. Not to have to pay any rent is very delightful, certainly, but they scarcely dare believe in such good fortune. Thus when Orpheus, trying to rescue Eurydice from "the infernal regions," interrupts with "his harmonious strains" the tortures of eternal punishment, Prometheus did not doubtless show as much delight as he ought to have done, on discovering that the beak of the vulture was no longer gnawing at his vitals, "scarcely daring to believe in such good fortune." Orpheus is the Commune; Eurydice, Liberty; "the infernal regions," the Government of the 4th September; "the harmonious strains," the decrees of the Commune; Prometheus, the tenant; and the vulture, the landlord!

In plain terms, however—forgive me for joking on such a subject—the decree which annuls the payment of the rents for the quarters ending October 1870, January 1871, and April 1871, does not appear to me at all extravagant, and really I do not see what there is to object to in the following lines which accompany it:—

"In consideration of the expenses of the war having been chiefly sustained by the industrial, commercial, and working portion of the population, it is but just that the proprietors of houses and land should also bear their part of the burthen...."

Let us talk it over together, Mr. Landlord. You have a house and I live in it. It is true that the chimneys smoke, and that you most energetically refuse to have them repaired. However, the house is yours, and you possess most decidedly the right of making a profit by it. Understand, once for all, that I never contest your right. As for me, I depend upon my wit, I do not possess much, but I have a tool—it may be either a pen, or a pencil, or a hammer—which enables me, in the ordinary course of things, to live and to pay with more or less regularity my quarter's rent. If I had not possessed this tool, you would have taken good care not to let me inhabit your house or any part or portion thereof, because you would have considered me in no position to pay you your rent. Now, during the war my tool has unquestionably rendered me but poor service. It has remained ignobly idle in the inkstand, in the folio, or on the bench. Not only have I been unable to use it, but I have also in some sort lost the knack of handling it; I must have some time to get myself into working order again. While I was working but little, and eating less, what were you doing? Oh! I do not mean to say that you were as flourishing as in the triumphant days of the Empire, but still I have not heard of any considerable number of landlords being found begging at the corners of the streets, and I do not fancy you made yourselves conspicuous by your assiduous attendance at the Municipal Cantines. I have even heard that you or many of your brother-landlords took pretty good care not to be in Paris during the Prussian siege, and that you contented yourselves with forming the most ardent wishes, for the final triumph of French arms, from beneath the wide-spreading oaks of your châteaux in Touraine and Beauce, or from the safe haven of a Normandy fishing village; while we, accompanied it is true by your most fervent prayers, took our turn at mounting guard, on the fortifications during the bitter cold nights, or knee-deep in the mud of the trenches. However, I do not blame those who sought safety in flight; each person is free to do as he pleases; what I object to is your coming back and saying, "During seven or eight months you have done no work, you have been obliged to pawn your furniture to buy bread for your wife and children; I pity you from the bottom of my heart—be so kind as to hand me over my three quarters' rent." No, a thousand times no; such a demand is absurd, wicked, ridiculous; and I declare that if there is no possible compromise between the strict execution of the law and this decree of the Commune, I prefer, without the least hesitation, to abide by the latter; I prefer to see a little poverty replace for a time the long course of prosperity that has been enjoyed by this very small class of individuals, than to see the last articles of furniture of five hundred thousand suffering wretches, put up to auction and knocked down for one-twentieth part of their value. There must, however, be some way of conciliating the interests of both landlords and tenants. Would it be sufficient to accord delays to the latter, and force the former to wait a certain time for their money? I think not; if I were allowed three years to pay off my three quarters' rent, I should still be embarrassed. The tool of the artisan is not like the peasant's plot of ground, which is more productive after having lain fallow. During the last few sad months, when I had no work to do, I was obliged to draw upon the future, a future heavily mortgaged; when I shall perhaps scarcely be able to meet the expenses of each day, will there be any possibility of acquitting the debts of the past? You may sell my furniture if the law gives you the right to do so, but I shall not pay!!

The only possible solution, believe me, is that in favour of the tenants, only it ought not to be applied in so wholesale a fashion. Inquiries should be instituted, and to those tenants from whom the war has taken away all possibility of payment, an unconditional receipt should be delivered: to those who have suffered less, a proportionate reduction should be allowed; but those whom the invasion has not ruined or seriously impoverished—and the number is large, among provision merchants, café keepers, and private residents—let those pay directly. In this way the landlords will lose less than one may imagine, because it will be the lowest rents that will be forfeited. The decree of the Commune is based on a right principle, but too generally applied.

The new Government—for it is a Government—does not confine itself to decrees. It has to install itself in its new quarters and make arrangements.* In a few hours it has organized more than ten committees—the executive, the financial, the public-service, the educational, the military, the legal, and the committee of public safety. No end of committees and committee-men: it is to be hoped that the business will be promptly despatched!

* Organisation of the Commissions on the 31st of March:

Executive Commission.—Citizens Eudes, Tridou, Vaillant, Lefrançais, Duval, Félix Pyat, Bergeret.

Commission of Finance.—Victor Clément, Varlin, Jourde, Beslay, Régère.

Military Commission.—General E. Duval, General Bergeret, General Eudes, Colonel Chardon, Colonel Flourens, Colonel Pindy, Commandant Ranvier.

Commission of Public Justice.—Ranc, Protot, Léo Meillet, Vermorel, Ledroit, Babick.

Commission of Public Safety.—Raoul Rigault, Ferré, Assy, Cournet, Oudet, Chalain, Gérardin.

Victualling Commission.—Dereure, Champy, Ostyn, Clément, Parizel, Emile Clément, Fortuné Henry.

Commission of Industry and Trade.—Malon, Frankel, Theiz, Dupont, Avrial, Loiseau-Pinson, Eugène Gérardin, Puget.

Commission of Foreign Affairs.—Delescluze, Ranc, Paschal Grousset, Ulysse Parent, Arthur Arnould, Antoine Arnauld, Charles Gérardin.

Commission of Public Service.—Ostyn, Billioray, Clément (J. B.) Martelet, Mortier, Rastoul.

Commission of Education.—Jules Vallès, Doctor Goupil, Lefèvre, Urbain,* Albert Leroy, Verdure, Demay, Doctor Robinet.

* Memoir, see Appendix XIII.

XXII.

Come, let us understand each other. Who are you, members of the Commune? Those among you who are in some sort known to the public do not possess, however, enough of its confidence to make up for the want of knowledge it has of the others. Have a care how you excite our mistrust. You have published decrees that certainly are open to criticism, but that are not entirely obnoxious, for their object is to uphold the interests of that portion of the population, which you most particularly represent, and from whom you hold your commission. We will forgive the decrees if you do nothing worse. Yesterday, the 30th March, during the night (why in the night?) some men wearing a red scarf and followed by several others with arms, presented themselves at the Union Insurance Company. On the porter refusing to deliver up the keys of the offices he was arrested. They then proceeded to break open the doors with the butt-end of their muskets, and put seals on the strong box. What can this portend? Have you been elected to break open private offices and put seals on cash-boxes? That same night, a friend of mine who happened to be passing across one of the bridges on his way home, noticed that the windows of the Hôtel de Ville were brilliantly lighted. Could they be having a ball already? he wondered. He made inquiries and discovered that it was not a ball, but a banquet: three or four hundred National Guards from Belleville had invaded the apartments and had ordered a dinner to be served to them. They were accompanied by a corresponding number of female companions, and were drinking, talking, and singing to their hearts' content. What do you mean by that, members of the Commune? Have you been elected to keep open-house, and do you propose to inscribe over the entrance of the municipal palace: "Ample accommodation for feasts and banquets," as a companion to your motto of "Liberty, Equality, and Fraternity?"

XXIII.

"I TELL you, you shall not go!"—"But I will."—"Well, *you* may, but not your furniture."—"And who shall prevent my carrying off my furniture if I choose?"—"I will."—"I defy you!"—"Thief!"—"Robber!"

THIS animated discussion was being carried on at the door of a house, in front of which a cart filled with furniture was standing; a crowd of street boys was fast assembling, and the heads of curious neighbours appeared grinning in all the windows.

A partizan of the Commune had determined to profit by the decree. Matters at first had seemed to go on quietly. The concierge, taken aback by the sudden apparition of the van, had not summoned up courage to prevent the furniture from being stowed away in it. The landlord, however, had got scent of the affair, and had hastened to this spot. Now, the tenant was a determined character, and as the van-men refused to mix themselves up in the fray, he himself shouldered his last article of furniture and carried it to the van. He was about to place it within cover of the awning, when the landlord, like a miser deprived of his treasure, seized it and deposited it on the pavement. The tenant re-grasped his spoil and thrust it again into the cart, from whence it was instantly drawn forth again by the enraged landlord. This game was carried on for some time, each as determined as the other, grasping, snatching, and pulling this unfortunate piece of furniture until one wrench, stronger than the former, entirely dislocated its component parts, and laid it in a ruined heap upon the ground. This was the moment for the tenant to show himself a man of spirit. Taking advantage of the surprise of the landlord, he swept the broken remains of his property deftly into the van, bounded on to the driver's seat, shook the reins, cracked his whip, and started off at a thundering gallop, pursued by the huzzas of the crowd, the cries of the van-men, and the oaths of the disappointed landlord. The van and its team of lean cattle were soon lost to view, and the landlord was left alone on his doorstep, shaking his fist, and muttering "Brigand!"

XXIV.

WHAT a quantity of luggage! Even those who had the good fortune of witnessing the emigration before the siege would never have supposed that there could be so much luggage in Paris. Well-to-do looking trunks with brass ornaments, black wooden boxes, hairy trunks, leathern hat-boxes, and cardboard bonnet-boxes, portmanteaux and carpet bags are piled up on vehicles of every description, of which more than ten thousand block up the roads leading to the railway stations. Everybody is wild to get away; it is whispered about that the Commune, the horrid Commune, is about to issue a decree forbidding the Parisians to quit Paris. So all prudent individuals are making off, with their bank-notes and shares in their pocket-books. I see a man I know, walking very fast, wearing a troubled expression on his face. I ask him where he is going.—"You do not know what has happened to me?" he cries. I confess I do not.—"The most extraordinary thing: I am condemned to death!"—"You!" I exclaim.—"Yes! by the Commune!"—"And wherefore?" I ask. —"Because I write on the *Figaro*."—"Why, I never knew that!"—"Oh! not very often; but last year I addressed a letter to the Editor, to explain to him that my new farce called 'My Aunt's Garters' had nothing at all to do with 'My Uncle's Braces,' which is by somebody else. You understand that I did not want to change the title, which is rather good of its kind, so I wrote to the *Figaro*, and as my letter was inserted, and as the Commune condemns all the contributors . . . You see . . . !"—

"Perfectly! Why, my dear fellow, you ought to have been off before. Of course you go to Versailles?"—"Why, yes."—"By the railway?" I cannot help having a joke at his expense.—"Yes, of course."—"Well, if I were you, I would not really; the engine might blow up, or you might run into a luggage train. Such things do happen in the best of times, and I think the Commune capable of anything to get rid of so dangerous an adversary."—"You don't mean to say," says the poor little man in a tremor, "that they would go to such lengths! Well, at any rate I will travel by the road."*

A little farther up the Boulevard des Italiens I see another acquaintance. "What, still in Paris?" I say, shaking hands with him.—"I am off this evening," he answers.—"Are you condemned to death?"—"No, but I shall be tried to-night."—"The devil! Do you write on the *Figaro?*"—"No, no, it is quite a long story. Three years ago, I made the acquaintance of a charming blonde, who reciprocated my advances, and made herself highly agreeable. In a word, I was smitten. Unfortunately there was a husband in the case!"—"The devil there was!"—"He made inquiries, and found out who I was, and . . . ."—"And invited you to mortal combat?"—"Oh! no, he is a hosier. But from that day forth he became my most bitter enemy."—"Very disagreeable of him, I am sure, but I do not see how the enmity of this retail dealer obliges you to quit Paris?"—"Why, you see he has a cousin who is elected a member

---

* The following is a document which completely justifies these apprehensions:—

"30th March—The Commune of Paris—Orders from the Central Committee to the officer in command of the battalion on guard at the station of Ouest-Ceinture.

"To stop all trains proceeding in the direction of Paris at the Ouest-Ceinture station.

"To place an energetic man night and day at this post. This man is to mount guard with a beam, which he is to throw across the rails at the arrival of each train, so as to cause it to run off the rails, if the engine-driver refuses to stop.

"HENRI, Chief of a Legion."

of the Commune."—"I understand your uneasiness; you fear the latent revenge of this unreasonable hosier."—"I am to be tried to-night, but it is not the fear of death which makes me fly. It is worse than that. Those Hôtel de Ville people are capable of anything, and I hear they are going to make a law on divorce. I know the malignity of the lady's husband—and I believe he is capable of getting a divorce, and forcing me to marry her!"

So, under one pretext and another, almost everyone is going away. As for me, I am like a hardened Parisian—my boots have a rooted dislike to any other pavement than that of the boulevards. Who is right, I, or those who are rushing off? Is there really danger here for those who are not ardently attached to the principles of the Commune? I try to believe not. True there have been arrests—domiciliary visits and other illegal and tyrannical acts—but I do not think it can last.* May we not hope that the dangerous element in the Commune will soon be neutralised by the more intelligent portion of the Municipal Council, if, indeed, that portion exists? I cannot believe that a revolution, accomplished by one-third of the population of Paris, and tolerated by another (the remaining fraction having taken flight), can be entirely devoid of the spirit of generosity and usefulness, capable only of appropriating the funds of others, and unjustly imprisoning innocent citizens. Besides, even if the Commune, instead of trying to make us forget the bloody deeds with which it preceded its establishment, or seeking to repair the faults of which it has been guilty, on the contrary continues to commit such excesses, thus hurrying to its ruin a city which has

---

* Vexatious measures accumulated:

The pacific M. Glais-Bizoin was arrested in a tobacconist's shop, where he was, doubtless, lighting a reactionary cigar. He fancied at first that there had been a mistake, but he was taken before the Committee, which caused him, however, to be liberated.

M. Maris Proth, a writer in *Charivari*, which is certainly not a royalist journal, was arrested on the following day, and detained for a longer time.

On the same day a search was made at the house of the publisher Lacroix.

already suffered so much, even then I will not leave it. I will cling to it to the last, as a sailor who has grown to love the ship that has borne him gallantly in so many voyages, clings to the wreck of his favourite, and refuses to be saved without it.

GAMBON.

XXV.

GARIBALDI is expected. Gambon has gone to Corsica to meet him. He is to be placed at the head of the National Guard. It is devoutly to be hoped that he will not come.*

* The Citizen Gambon, representative of the Department of the Seine, left Paris charged with a mission to seek Garibaldi, but was arrested at Bonifacio, in the island of Corsica, just as he was embarking for Caprera.
For Memoir, see Appendix 4.

Firstly, because his presence at this moment would create new dangers; and secondly, because this admirable and honoured man would compromise his glory uselessly in our sorry discords. If I, an obscure citizen, had the honour of being one of those to whom the liberator of Naples lends an ear, I would go to him without hesitation, and, after having bent before him as I would before some ancient hero arisen from his glorious sepulchre, say to him,—"General, you have delivered your country. At the head of a few hundred men you have won battles and taken towns. Your name recalls the name of William Tell. Wherever there were chains to rend and yokes to break, you were seen to hasten. Like the warriors Hugo exalts in his *Légende des Siècles*, you have been the champion of justice, the knight-errant of liberty. You appear to us victorious in a distant vision, as in the realm of legend. For the glory of our age in which heroes are wanting, it befits you to remain that which you are. Continue afar off, so that you may continue great. It is not that your glory is such that it can only be seen at a distance, and loses when regarded too nearly. Not so! But you would be hampered amongst us. There is not space enough here for you to draw your sword freely. We are adroit, strange, and complicated. You are simple, and in that lies your greatness. We belong to our time, you have the honour to be an anachronism. You would be useless to your friends, destructive to yourself. What would you, a giant fighting with the sword, do against dwarfs who have cannon? You are courageous, but they are cunning, and would conquer you. For the sake of the nineteenth century you must not be vanquished. Do not come; in your simplicity you would be caught in the spider's web of clever mediocrity, and your grand efforts to tear yourself free would only be laughed at. Great man, you would be treated like a pigmy."

It is probable, however, that if I held such a discourse to General Garibaldi, General Garibaldi would politely show me the door. Other and more powerful counsellors have inspired him with different ideas. Friendship dangerous indeed! How deeply painful is it that no man, however intelligent or great, can clearly distinguish the line, where the mission for which Heaven has endowed him ceases, and, disdaining all celebrity foreign to his true glory, consent to remain such as future ages will admire.*

---

* Garibaldi was chosen by the Central Committee for Commander-in-Chief of the National Guard, but he refused in the following terms, pretending not to be aware of the condition of Paris:—

"Caprera, 28th March, 1871.

"CITIZENS,—

"Thanks for the honour you have conferred upon me by my nomination as Commander-in-Chief of the National Guard of Paris, which I love, and whose dangers and glory I should be proud to share.

"I owe you, however, the following explanations:—

"A commandant of the National Guard of Paris, a commander of the army of Paris, and a directing committee, whatever they may be, are three powers which are not reconcilable with the present situation of France.

"Despotism has the advantage over us, the advantage of the concentration of power, and it is this same centralisation which you should oppose to your enemies.

"Choose an honest citizen, and such are not wanting: Victor Hugo, Louis Blanc, Félix Pyat, Edgar Quinet, or another of the elders of radical democracy, would serve the purpose. The generals Cremer and Billot, who, I see, have your confidence, may be counted in the number.

"Be assured that one honest man should be charged with the supreme command and full powers; such a man would choose other honest men to assist him in the difficult task of saving the country.

"If you should have the good fortune to find a Washington, France will recover from shipwreck, and in a short time will be grander than ever.

"These conditions are not an excuse for escaping the duty of serving republican France. No! I do not despair of fighting by the side of these *braves*, and I am,

"Yours devotedly,
(Signed), "G. GARIBALDI."

XXVI.

Monday, the 3rd of April.* A fearful day! I have been hurrying this way and that, looking, questioning, reading. It is now ten o'clock in the evening. And what do I know? Nothing certain; nothing except this, which is awful,—they are fighting.

Yes, at the gates of Paris, Frenchmen against Frenchmen, beneath the eyes of the Prussians, who are watching the battle-field like ravens: they are fighting. I have seen ambulance waggons pass full of National Guards. By whom have they been wounded? By Zouaves. Is this thing credible, is it possible? Ah! those guns, cannon, and mitrailleuses, why were they not all claimed by the enemy—all, every one, from soldiers and Parisians alike? But little hindrance would that have proved. It had been resolved—by what monstrous will?—that we should be

* On the 1st of April several shots were fired under the walls of Fort Issy, but it was not until the next day, the 2nd of April, at nine o'clock in the morning, that the action commenced in earnest at Courbevoie, by an attack of the Versailles army. The Federals, who thought themselves masters of the place, were stopped by the steady firing of a regiment of gendarmerie and heavy cannonading from Mont Valérien. At first the National Guards retreated, then disputed every foot of ground with much courage. In the neighbourhood the desolation and misery was extreme.

The revolution had now entered a new phase; the military proceedings had begun, and it was about to be proved that the Communist generals had even less genius than those of the Défense Nationale, although it must be admitted that the latter did not know the extent of the resources they had at their disposal. When we remember the small advantage those generals managed to derive from the heroism of the Parisian population, who, during the second siege showed that they knew how to fight and how to die, it is marvellous that many people have gone so far as to regret that the émeute of the 31st of October was not successful, believing that if the Commune had triumphed at that time, Paris would have been saved. All this seems very doubtful now, and opinions have veered round considerably, for it is not such men as Duval, Cluseret, La Cécilia, Eudes, or Bergeret, who could have protected Paris against the science of the Prussian generals.

THE BARRICADE: EVENING MEAL—SOUP AND CIGARS, AND A "PETIT VERRE."

hurled to the very bottom of the precipice. These Frenchmen, who would kill Frenchmen, would not be checked by lack of arms. If they could not shoot each other, they would strangle each other.

This, indeed, was unlooked for. An insurrection was feared; men thought of the June days; that evening when the battalions devoted to the National Assembly camped in the neighbourhood of the Bank, we imagined, as a horrible possibility, muskets pointed from between the stones of barricades, blood flowing in the streets, men killed, women in tears. But who could have foretold that a new species of civil war was preparing? That Paris, separated from France, would be blockaded by Frenchmen? That it would once more be deprived of communication with the provinces; once more starved perhaps? That there would be, not a few men struggling to the death in one of the quarters of the town, but two armies in presence, each with chiefs, fortifications and cannon? That Paris, in a word, would be besieged anew? How abominable a surprise of fate!

The cannonading has been heard since morning. Ah! that sound, which, during the siege, made our hearts beat with hope, —yes, with hope, for it made us believe in a possible deliverance —how horrible it was this morning. I went towards the Champs Elysées. Paris was deserted. Had it understood at last that its honour, its existence even, were at stake in this revolution, or was it only not up yet? Battalions were marching along the boulevards, with music playing. They were going towards the Place Vendôme, and were singing. The *cantinières* were carrying guns. Some one told me that men had been at work all night in the neighbourhood of the Hôtel de Ville, and that the streets adjoining it were blocked with barricades. But in fact no one knows anything, except that there is fighting in Neuilly, that the "Royalists" have attacked, and that "our brothers are being slaughtered." A few groups are assembled in the Place de la Concorde. I approach, and find them discussing the question of the rents,—yes, of the rents! Ah! it is certain those who are

THE BARRICADE: EVENING MEAL—SOUP AND CIGARS, AND A "PETIT VERRE."

hurled to the very bottom of the precipice. These Frenchmen, who would kill Frenchmen, would not be checked by lack of arms. If they could not shoot each other, they would strangle each other.

This, indeed, was unlooked for. An insurrection was feared; men thought of the June days; that evening when the battalions devoted to the National Assembly camped in the neighbourhood of the Bank, we imagined, as a horrible possibility, muskets pointed from between the stones of barricades, blood flowing in the streets, men killed, women in tears. But who could have foretold that a new species of civil war was preparing? That Paris, separated from France, would be blockaded by Frenchmen? That it would once more be deprived of communication with the provinces; once more starved perhaps? That there would be, not a few men struggling to the death in one of the quarters of the town, but two armies in presence, each with chiefs, fortifications and cannon? That Paris, in a word, would be besieged anew? How abominable a surprise of fate!

The cannonading has been heard since morning. Ah! that sound, which, during the siege, made our hearts beat with hope, —yes, with hope, for it made us believe in a possible deliverance —how horrible it was this morning. I went towards the Champs Elysées. Paris was deserted. Had it understood at last that its honour, its existence even, were at stake in this revolution, or was it only not up yet? Battalions were marching along the boulevards, with music playing. They were going towards the Place Vendôme, and were singing. The *cantinières* were carrying guns. Some one told me that men had been at work all night in the neighbourhood of the Hôtel de Ville, and that the streets adjoining it were blocked with barricades. But in fact no one knows anything, except that there is fighting in Neuilly, that the "Royalists" have attacked, and that "our brothers are being slaughtered." A few groups are assembled in the Place de la Concorde. I approach, and find them discussing the question of the rents,—yes, of the rents! Ah! it is certain those who are being killed at this moment will not have to pay their landlord. On reaching the Rond Point I can distinctly perceive a compact crowd round the Triumphal Arch, and I meet some tired National Guards who are returning from the battle. They are ragged, dusty, and dreary. "What has happened?"—"We are betrayed!" says one.—"Death to the traitors!" cries another.

No certain news from the field of battle. A runaway, seated outside a café amidst a group of eager questioners, recounts that the barricade at the Neuilly bridge has been attacked by *sergents de ville* dressed as soldiers, and Pontifical Zouaves carrying a white flag.—"A parliamentary flag?" asks some one.—"No! a royalist flag," answered the runaway.—"And the barricade has been taken?"—"We had no cartridges; we had not eaten for twenty-four hours; of course we had to decamp."

Farther on a soldier of the line affirms that the barricade has been taken again. The cannon roars still. Mont Valérien is firing, it is said, on the Courbevoie barracks, where a battalion of Federal guards was stationed yesterday.—"But they were off before daybreak," adds the soldier.

As I continue my road the groups become more numerous. I lift my head and see a shell burst over the Avenue of the Grande Armée, leaving a puff of white smoke hanging for a few seconds like a cloud-flake detached by the wind.

On I go still. The height on which the Arc de Triomphe stands is covered with people; a great many women and children among them. They are mounted on posts, clinging to the projections of the Arch, hanging to the sculpture of the bas-reliefs. One man has put a plank upon the tops of three chairs, and by paying a few *sous* the gapers can hoist themselves upon it. From this position one can perceive a motionless, attentive crowd reaching down the whole length of the Avenue of the Grande Armée, as far as the Porte Maillot, from which a great cloud of white smoke springs up every moment followed by a violent explosion,—it is the cannon of the ramparts firing on the Rond Point

PLACE DE LA CONCORDE AND CHAMPS ELYSÉES, FROM THE GARDENS OF THE TUILERIES—FEDERALISTS GOING OUT TO FIGHT THE VERSAILLAIS.

This panorama gives an idea of the theatre of operations of the Second Siege of Paris. The Prussians closed the eastern *enceinte*, whilst the Federals held the southern forts to the last, with the exception of Issy and Vanves that were abandoned. Point-du-Jour and Porte Maillot were the parts particularly attacked; the former being defended by the Federal gunboats on the Seine. Mont Valérien, it will be seen, commands the whole of the distant plateau. About one mile and a half beyond the Triumphal Arch the river Seine intersects the space from south to north, enclosing the Bois de Boulogne and the villages of Neuilly, Villiers, and Courcelles, being a sort of outer fortification. The walls of Paris follow the same line, falling about half a mile on the other side of the Arch, and parallel runs a line of railway within the fortified wall.

This view exhibits the portion the Prussians were permitted to occupy for two days: all the outlets, except the west, being barricaded and defended.

of Courbevoie; and beyond this the Avenue de Neuilly stretching far out in the sunshine, deserted and dusty, a human form crossing it rapidly from time to time; and farthest of all, beyond the Seine, beyond the Avenue de l'Empereur, deserted too, the hill of Courbevoie, where a battery of the Versailles troops is established. But stretch my eyes as I may I cannot distinguish the guns; but a few men, sentinels doubtless, can be made out. They are *sergents de ville*, says my right-hand neighbour; but he on my left says they are Pontifical Zouaves. They must have good eyes to recognise the uniforms at this distance. The most contradictory rumours circulate as to the barricade on the bridge; it is impossible for one to ascertain whether it has remained in the possession of the soldiers or the Federals. There has been but little fighting, moreover, since I came. A little later, at twelve o'clock, the fusillade ceases entirely. But the battery on the ramparts continues to fire upon Courbevoie, and Mont Valérien still shells Neuilly at intervals. Suddenly a flood of dust, coming from Porte Maillot, thrusts back the thick of the crowd, and as it flies, widening, and whirling more madly as it comes, everyone is seized with terror, and rushes away screaming and gesticulating. A shell has just fallen, it is said, in the Avenue of the Grande Armée. Not a soul remains about the Triumphal Arch. The adjoining streets are filled with people who have run to take shelter there. By little and little, however, the people begin to recover themselves, the flight is stopped in the middle, and, laughing at their momentary panic, they turn back again. A quarter of an hour afterwards the crowd is everywhere as compact as before.

This spectacle, however, of combatants and gapers distresses me, and in despair of learning anything I return into the city.

At some distance from the scene of events one gets better information, or, at any rate, a great deal more of it. Imagination has better play when it is farther from the fact. A hundred absurd stories reach me. What appears tolerably certain is, that the

Federals have received a check, not very important in itself, the Versailles troops having made but little advance, but at any rate a check which might have some influence on the resolution of the National Guards. They have been told that the army would not fight, that the soldiers of the line would turn the butt-ends of their guns into the air at Neuilly as they had done at Montmartre. But now they begin to believe that the army will fight, and those who cry the loudest that it was the *sergents de ville* and Charette's Zouaves who led the attack alone, seem as if they said it to give themselves courage and keep up their illusions.

But from which side did the first shot come? On this point everyone has something to say, and no one knows what to believe. Official reports are looked for with the utmost impatience. The walls, generally so communicative, are mute up to this hour. The least improbable of the versions circulated is the following: At break of day some shots are said to have been exchanged between the Federal advanced guard and the patrols of the Versailles troops. None dead or wounded; only powder wasted, happily. A little later, and a few minutes after the arrival of General Vinoy at Mont Valérien, a messenger with a flag of truce, preceded by a trumpeter and accompanied by two *sergents de ville* (inevitably), is said to have presented himself at the bridge of Courbevoie. The name of the messenger has been given,—Monsieur Pasquier, surgeon-in-chief to the regiment of mounted *gendarmes*. Two of the National Guards go to meet him; after some words exchanged, one of the Federals blows out Monsieur Pasquier's brains with his revolver, and ten minutes later Mont Valérien opens a formidable fire, which continues as fiercely four hours afterwards.

Meanwhile the drums beat to arms on all sides. A considerable number of battalions defile along the Boulevard Montmartre; more than twenty thousand men, some say, who pretend to know. On they march, singing and shouting "*Vive la Commune! Vive la République!*" They are answered by a few shouts. These are not the Montmartre and Belleville guards alone; peaceful faces of citizens and merchants may be seen under the military *képis*, and many hands are white as no workman's are. They march in good order; they are calm and resolved; one feels that these men are ready to die for a cause that they believe to be just. I raise my hat as they pass; one must do honour to those who, even if they be guilty, push their devotion so far as to expose themselves to death for their convictions.

But what are these convictions? What is the Commune? The men who sit at the Hôtel de Ville have published no programme, yet they kill and are killed for the sake of the Commune. Oh, words! words! What power they have over you, heroic and most simple people!

In the evening out came a proclamation. There was so great a crowd wherever it was posted up that I had not the chance of copying it; but it ran somewhat in these terms:—

"CITIZENS,—This morning the Royalists have ATTACKED.

"Impatient, before our moderation they have ATTACKED.

"Unable to bring French bayonets against us, they have opposed us with the Imperial Guard and Pontifical Zouaves.

"They have bombarded the inoffensive village of Neuilly.

"Charette's *chouans*, Cathelineau's *Vendéens*, Trochu's *Bretons*, Valentin's *gendarmes*, have rushed upon us.

"There are dead and wounded.

"Against this attack, renewed from the Prussians, Paris should rise to a man.

"Thanks to the support of the National Guard, the victory will be ours!"

Victory! What victory? Oh, the bitter pain! Paris shedding the blood of France, France shedding the blood of Paris! From whatever side the triumph comes, will it not be accursed?

GENERAL BERGERET.

XXVII.

To whom shall we listen? Whom believe? It would take a hundred pages, and more, to relate all the different rumours which have circulated to-day, the 4th of April, the second day of the horrible struggle. Let us hastily note down the most persistent of these assertions; later I will put some order into this pell-mell of news.

All through the night the drums beat to arms in every

quarter of the town. Companies assembled rapidly, and directed their way towards the Place Vendôme or the Porte Maillot, shouting, "*A Versailles!*"

Since five this morning, General Bergeret has occupied the Rond-Point of Courbevoie. This position has been evacuated by the troops of the Assembly. How was this? Were the Federals not beaten yesterday?

(One thing goes against General Bergeret in the opinion of his troops: he drives to battle in a carriage.)

He has formed his troops into columns. No less than sixty thousand men are under his orders; two batteries of seven guns support the infantry; omnibuses follow, filled with provisions. They march towards the Mont Valérien; after having taken the fort, they will march on Versailles by Rueil and Nanterre.* After they have taken the Mont Valérien! there is not a moment's doubt about the success of the enterprise. "We were assured," said a Federal general to me, "that the fort would open its doors at the first sight of us." But they counted without General Cholleton, who commands the fortress. The advance-guard of the Federals is received by a formidable discharge of shot and shells. Panic! Cries of rage! A regular rout to the words, "We are betrayed!"† The army of the Commune is divided into two fragments: one — scarcely three battalions strong — flies in the direction of Versailles, the other regains Paris

---

* The combined plan of the three generals of the Commune consisted, like the famous plan of General Boum, in proceeding by three different roads: the first column, under the orders of Bergeret, seconded by Flourens, went by Rueil; the second, commanded by Duval, marched upon Versailles by lower Meudon, Chaville, and Viroflay; covered by the fire of Fort Issy, and the redoubt of Moulineaux; and lastly, the third, with General Eudes at its head, took the Clamart road, protected by the fort of Vanves.

† Though no fort covered Bergeret's eight battalions with its fire, yet Bergeret was so sure that the artillerymen of Mont Valérien would do as the line did on the 18th of March, *i.e.*, refuse to fire, that he advanced boldly as far as the bridge of Neuilly, and had made a halt at the Rond-Point des Bergères, when a heavy cannonading from Mont Valerien separated a part of the column from its main body.

with praiseworthy precipitation. Must the Parisian combatants be accused of cowardice for this flight? No! They were surprised; had never expected such a reception from Mont Valérien; had they been warned, they would have held out better. After all, there was more fright than harm done in the affair; the huge fortress could have annihilated the Communists, and it was satisfied with dispersing them. But what has become of the three battalions that passed Mont Valérien? Bravely they went forward.

In the meantime another movement was being made upon Versailles by Meudon and Clamart. A small number of battalions had marched out during the night, and are massed under cover of the forts of Issy and Vanves. They have managed to establish a battery of a few guns on a wooded eminence, at the foot of the glacis of Fort Issy, and their pieces are firing upon the batteries of the Versailles troops at Meudon, which are answering them furiously. It is a duel of artillery, as in the time —the good time, alas!—of the Prussians.

Up to this moment the information is tolerably clear; probable even, and one is able to come to some idea of the respective positions of the belligerents. But towards two o'clock in the afternoon, all the reports get confused and contradictory.

An estafette, who has come from the Porte Maillot, cried to a group formed on the place of the New Opera-house, "We are victorious! Flourens has entered Versailles at the head of forty thousand men. A hundred deputies have been taken. Thiers is a prisoner."

Elsewhere it is said that in the rout of that morning, at the foot of Mont Valérien, Flourens had disappeared. And where could he have found the forty thousand men to lead them to Versailles?

At the same time a rumour spreads that General Bergeret has been grievously wounded by a shell. "Pure exaggeration!" some one answers. "The General has only had two horses killed under him."

Before him, rather, since he drives to battle.

What appears most certain of all is that there is furious fighting going on between Sèvres and Meudon. I hear it said that the 113th of the line have turned the butts of their guns into the air, and that the Parisians have taken twelve mitrailleuses from the Versailles troops.

There is fighting, too, at Châtillon. The Federals have won great advantages. Nevertheless an individual who went out that side to investigate, announces that he saw three battalions return with very little air of triumph, and that other battalions, forming the reserve, had refused to march.

A shower of contradictions, in which the news for the most part has no other source than the opinion and desire of the person who brings it. It is by the result alone that we can appreciate what is passed. At one moment I give up trying to get information as a bad job, but I begin questioning again in spite of myself; the desire to know is even stronger than the very strong certainty that I shall be able to learn nothing.

I turn to the Champs Elysées. The cannon is roaring; ambulance waggons descend the Avenue, and stop before the Palais de l'Industrie; over the way Punch is making his audience roar with laughter as usual. Oh! the miserable times! The horrible fratricidal struggle! May those who were its cause be accursed for ever!

While some are killing and others dying, the members of the Commune are rendering decrees, and the walls are white with official proclamations.

> "Messieurs Thiers, Favre, Picard, Dufaure, Simon and Pothuan are impeached; their property will be seized and sequestrated until they deliver themselves up to public justice."

This impeachment and sequestration, will it bring back husbands to the widows and fathers to the orphans?

> "The Commune of Paris adopts the families of citizens who

have fallen or may fall in opposing the criminal aggression of the Royalists, directed against Paris and against the French republic."

Infinitely better than adopting the orphans would be to save the fathers from death. Oh! these absurd decrees! You separate the Church from the State; you suppress the budget of public worship; you confiscate the property of the clergy. A pretty time to think about such acts! What is necessary, what is indispensable, is to restore quiet, to avoid massacres, and to stifle hatred. That you will not decree. No! no! That which is now happening you have desired, and you still desire it; you have profited by the provocations you have received to bring about the most frightful conflict which the history of unfortunate France records; and you will persevere, and, in order to revive the fainting courage of those whom you have devoted to inevitable defeat and death, you bring into action all the hypocrisy with which you have charged your enemies!

"Bergeret and Flourens have joined their forces; they are marching on Versailles. Success is certain!"

You cause this announcement to be placarded in the street—false news, is it not? But men can only be led to their ruin by being deceived. You add:

"The fire of the army of Versailles has not occasioned us any appreciable loss."

Ah! As to this let us ask the women who await at the gates of the city the return of your soldiers, and crowd sobbing round the bloody litters!

XXVIII.

Every hour that flies by, becomes more sinister than the last. They fight at Clamart as they fight at Neuilly, at Meudon and at Courbevoie. Everywhere rage the mitrailleuses, the cannon, and the rifle; the victories of the Communalists are lyingly proclaimed. The truth of their pretended triumphs will soon be known; and unhappily victory will be as detestable as defeat.

General Duval has been made prisoner and put to death. "If you had taken me," asked General Vinoy, "would you not have shot me?"—"Without hesitation," replied Duval. And Vinoy gave the word of command, "Fire!"

But this anecdote, though widely spread, is probably false. It is scarcely likely that a Commander-in-Chief of the Versailles troops would have consented to hold such a dialogue with an "insurgent."

Flourens also is killed. Where and how is not yet known with any certainty. Several versions are given. Some speak of a ball in the head, or the neck, or the chest; others spread the report that his skull was cut open by a sword.

Flourens is thought about and talked of by men of the most opposite opinions. This singular man inspires no antipathy even amongst those who might hold him in the greatest detestation. I shall one day try to account for the partiality of opinion in favour of this young and romantic insurgent.

Duval shot, Flourens killed, Bergeret lying in the pangs of death; the enthusiasm of the Federals might well be cooled down. Not in the least! The battalions that march along the boulevards have the same resolute air, as they sing and shout "*Vive la Commune!*" Are they the dupes of their chiefs to that extent as to believe the pompous proclamations with their hourly announcements of attacks repelled, of redoubts taken, of soldiers of the line made prisoners? It is not probable. And besides, the guards of the respective quarters must see the return of those who have been to the fight, and whose anxious wives are waiting on the steps of the doors; must learn from them that the forward marches have in reality been routs, and that many dead and wounded have been left on the field, when the Commune reports only declare "losses of little importance." Whence comes this ardour that the first rush and defeat cannot check? Is it nourished by the reports, true or false, of the cruelties of the Versaillais which are spread by the hundred? The "murder" of Duval, the "assassination" of Flourens, prisoners shot, *vivandières* violated, all these culpable inventions—can they be inventions, or does civil war make such barbarians of us?—are indeed of a nature to excite the enthusiasm of hate, and the men march to a probable defeat with the same air as they would march to certain victory. Ah! whether led astray or not, whether guilty, even, or whatever the motive that impels them, they are brave! And when they pass thus they are grand. Yes! in spite of the rags that serve the greater number of them for uniforms, in spite of the drunken gait of some, as a whole they are superb! And the reason of the coldest partisan of order at any price, struggles in vain against the admiration which these men inspire as they march to their death.

It must be admitted, too, that there is much less disorder in the command than might be expected. The battalions all know whom they are to obey. Some go to the Hôtel de Ville, others to the Place Vendôme, many to the forts, a few to the advanced posts; marches and counter-marches are managed without confusion; and the combatants are in general well provided with ammunition, and supplied with provisions. Far as one is from esteeming the chiefs of the Federals, one is obliged to admit that there is something remarkable in this rapid organisation of a whole army in the midst of one of the most complete political convulsions. Who, then, directs? Who commands? The members of the Commune, divided as they are in opinion, do not appear capable, on account of their number and lamentable inexperience, of taking the sole lead in military affairs. Is there not some one either amongst them or in the background, who knows how to think, direct, and act? Is it Bergeret? Is it Cluseret? The future perhaps will unravel the mystery. In the meantime, and in spite of the reverses to which the Federals have had to submit during these last days, the whole of Paris unites in unanimous surprise at the extreme regularity with which the administrative system of the war seems to work, the surprise being the greater that, during the siege, the "legitimate" chiefs with much more powerful means, and having disciplined troops at their command, did not succeed in obtaining the same striking results.

But would it not have been better far that that order had never existed? Better a thousand times that the command had been less precise than that those commanded should have been led to a death without glory? For the last few days Neuilly, so joyous in times gone by with its busy shops, its frequented *restaurants* and princely parks; Neuilly, with the Versailles batteries on one side and the Paris guns on the other, under an incessant rain of shells and *mitraille* from Mont Valérien; Neuilly, with her bridge taken and re-taken, her barricades abandoned and re-conquered, has been for the last few days like a vast abyss, into which the Federal battalions, seized with mortal giddiness, are precipitated one after another. Each house is a fortress. Yesterday, the *gendarmes* had advanced as far as the market of Sablonville; this morning they were driven back beyond the church. Upon this church, a child, the son of Monsieur Leullier, planted a red flag amidst a shower of projectiles. "That child will make a true man," said Cluseret, the war delegate. Ah, yes! provided he is not a corpse ere then. Shots are fired from window to window. A house is assaulted; there are encounters on the stairs; it is a horrible struggle in which no quarter is given, night and day, through all hours. The rage and fury on both sides are terrific. Men that were friends a week ago have but one desire—to assassinate each other. An inhabitant of Neuilly, who succeeded in escaping, related this to me: Two enemies, a soldier of the line and a Federal, had an encounter in the bathing establishment of the Avenue de Neuilly, a little above the Rue des Huissiers. Now pursuing, now flying from each other in their bayonet-fight, they reached the roof of the house, and there, flinging down their arms, they closed in a mad struggle. On the sloping roof, the tiles of which crush beneath them, at a hundred feet from the ground, they struggled without mercy, without respite, until at last the soldier felt his strength give way, and endeavoured to escape from the gripe of his adversary. Then, the Federal—the person from whom I learnt this was at an opposite window and lost not a single one of their movements—the Federal drew a knife from his pocket and prepared himself to strike his half-prostrate antagonist, who, feeling that all hope was lost, threw himself flat on the roof, seized his enemy by the leg, and dragging him with him by a sudden movement, they rolled over and fell on to the pavement below. Neither was killed, but the soldier had his face crimsoned with blood and dust, and the Federal, who had fallen across his adversary, despatched him by plunging his knife in his chest.

Such is this infamous struggle! Such is this savage strife! Will it not cease until there is no more blood to shed?

In the meantime, Paris of the boulevards, the elegant and fast-living Paris, lounges, strolls, and smiles. In spite of the numerous departures there are still enough *blasé* dandies and beauties of light locks and lighter reputation to bring the blush to an honest man's cheek. The theatres are open; "*La Pièce du Pape*" is being played. Do you know "The Pope's Money?" It is a suitable piece for diverting the thoughts from the horrors of civil war. A year ago the Pope was supported by French bayonets, but his light coinage would not pass in Paris. Now Papal zouaves are killing the citizens of Paris, and we take light silver and lighter paper. The piece is flimsy enough. It is not its political significance that makes it diverting, but the *double-entendre* therein. One must laugh a little, you understand. Men are dying out yonder, we might as well laugh a little here. Low whispers in the *baignoires*, munching of sugared violets in the stage boxes—everything's for the best. Mademoiselle Nénuphar (named so by antithesis) is said to have the most beautiful eyes in the world. I will wager that that handsome man behind her has already compared them to mitraille shot, seeing the ravages they commit. It would be impossible to be more complimentary,—more witty and to the point. Ah! look you, those who are fighting at this moment, who to-day by their cannon and chassepots are exposing Paris to a terrible revenge, guilty as these men are, I hold them higher than those who roar with laughter when the whole city is in despair, who have not even the modesty to hide their joys from our distresses, and who amuse themselves openly with shameless women, while mothers are weeping for their children!

On the boulevards it is worse still; there, vice exhibits itself and triumphs. Is it then true what a young fellow, a poor student and bitter philosopher, said to me just now: "When all Paris is destroyed, when its houses, its palaces, and its monuments thrown down and crushed, strew its accursed soil and form but one vast ruin beneath the sky, then, from out of this shapeless mass will rise as from a huge sepulchre, the phantom of a woman, a skeleton dressed in a brilliant dress, with shoulders bared, and a toquet on its head; and this phantom, running from ruin to ruin, turning its head every now and then to see if some libertine is following her through the waste—this phantom is the leprous soul of Paris!"

When midnight approaches, the *cafés* are shut. The delegates of the Central Committee at the ex-prefecture have the habit of sending patrols of National Guards to hasten and overlook the closing of all public places. But this precaution, like so many others, is useless. There are secret doors which escape the closest investigations. When the shutters are put up, light filters through the interstices of the boards. Go close up to them, apply your eye to one of those lighted crevices, listen to the cannon roaring, the mitrailleuses horribly spitting, the musketry cracking, and then look into the interior of the closed rooms. People are talking, eating, and smoking; waiters go to and fro. There are women too. The men are gay and silly. Champagne bottles are being uncorked. "Ah! ah! it's the fusillade!" Lovers and mistresses are in common here. This orgie has the most telling effect, I tell you, in the midst of the city loaded with maledictions, a few steps from the battle-field where the bayonets are dealing their death thrusts, and the shells are scattering blood. And later, after the laughter and the songs and the drink, they take an open carriage, if the night is fine, and go to the Champs Elysées, and there mount upon the box by the coachman to try and see the fight—if "those people" knew how to die as well as they know how to laugh it would be better for them.

Other *bons viveurs*, more discreet, hide themselves on the first floors of some houses and in some of the clubs. But they are betrayed by the sparkle of the chandeliers which pierces the heavy curtains. If you walk along by the walls you will hear the conversation of the gamesters and the joyous clink of the gold pieces.

Ah! the cowardice of the merry ones! Oh, thrice pardonable anger of those who starve!

XXIX.

At one o'clock this morning, the 5th of April, on my return from one of these nightly excursions through Paris, I was following the Rue du Mont Thabor so as to gain the boulevards, when on crossing the Rue Saint-Honoré I perceived a small number of National

ABBÉ DEGUERRY,
Curé of the Madeleine.

Guards ranged along the pavement. The incident was a common one, and I took no notice of it. In the Rue du Mont Thabor not a person was to be seen; all was in silence and solitude. Suddenly a door opened a few steps in front of me; a man came out and hurried away in the direction opposite to that of the church. This departure looked like a flight. I stopped and lent my attention. Soon two National Guards rushed out by the same door, ran, shouting as they went, after the fugitive, who had had but a short start of them, and overtaking him, without difficulty brought him back between them, while the National Guards that I had seen in the Rue Saint-Honoré ran up at the noise. The exclamations and insults of all kinds that were vociferated led me to ascertain that the man they had arrested was the Abbé Deguerry, *curé* of the Madeleine. He was dragged into the house, the door was shut, and all sank into silence again.

That morning I learned that Monseigneur Darboy, the Archbishop of Paris, was taken at the same hour and in almost similar circumstances.

The arrests of several other ecclesiastics are cited. The *curé* of St. Séverin and the *curé* of St. Eustache have been made prisoners, it is said; the first in his own house, the second at the moment when he was leaving his church. The *curé* of Notre-Dame-des-Victoires was to have been arrested also, but warned in time, he was able to place himself in safety.

Monseigneur Darboy, being conducted to the ex-prefecture (why the *ex*-prefecture? It seems to me it works just as well as when it was purely and simply a prefecture), was cross-examined there by the citizen delegate Rigault. It must be said that Monsieur Rigault had begun to make himself talked about during these last few days. He is evidently a man who has a natural vocation for the employment he has chosen, for he arrests, and arrests, and still arrests. He is young, cold, and cynical. But his cynicism does not exclude him from a certain gaiety, as we shall see. It was the Citizen Rigault, then, who examined the Archbishop of Paris. I am not inordinately curious, but I should very much like to know what the cynical member of the Commune could ask of Monseigneur Darboy. Having committed apparently

RAOUL RIGAULT.*

* Rigault became connected with Rochefort in the year 1869, and with him was engaged on the journal called the *Marseillaise*, and produced articles which subjected him more than once to fine and imprisonment. In the month of September, 1870, he was appointed by the Government of the National Defence, Commissaire of Police, but having taken part in the insurrection of the 31st of October, he was, on the following day, dismissed from office. Shortly after this he made his appearance as a writer in Blanqui's paper, the *Patrie en Danger*; but, presently, he took a military turn, and got himself elected to the command of a battalion of the National Guard. He seems to have been born an informer or police spy, for we are told that when at school, he used to amuse himself by filling up lists of proscriptions, with the names of his fellow-pupils. With such charming natural instincts, it is not at all surprising that he was on the 18th of March, appointed by the Commune Government, Prefect of Police.

MONSEIGNEUR DARBOY,

but one crime, that of being a priest, and having no inclination to disguise it, it is difficult to know what the interrogatory could turn upon. Monsieur Rigault's imagination furnished him no doubt with ample materials for the interview, and he has probably as much vocation for the part of a magistrate as for that of a police officer. But however it may be, the journals of the Commune record this fragment with ill-disguised admiration.

"My children"—the white-haired Archbishop of Paris is reported to have said at one moment.

"Citizen," interrupted the Citizen Rigault, who is not yet thirty, "you are not before children, but before magistrates."

That was smart! And I can conceive the enthusiasm with which Monsieur Rigault inspires the members of the Commune. But this excellent citizen did not confine himself to this haughty repartee. I am informed (and I have reason to believe with truth) that he added: "Moreover, that's too old a tale. You have been trying it on these eighteen hundred years."

Now everyone must admit that this is as remarkable for its wit as for its elegance, and it is just what might be expected of the amiable delegate, who, the other day, in a moment of exaggerated clemency, permitted an abbé to visit a prisoner in the Conciergerie, and furnished him with a *laisser-passer* that ran thus: "Admit the bearer, who styles himself the servant of one of the name of God." Oh! what graceful, charming wit!

XXX.

I AM beginning to feel decidedly uncomfortable. This new decree of the Commune seriously endangers the liberty of all those who are so unfortunate as to have incurred the ill-will of their concierge, or whose dealings with his next-door neighbour have not been of a strictly amicable nature. Let us copy the 1st article of this ferocious decree.

"All persons accused of complicity with the Government of Versailles shall be immediately taken and incarcerated."*

Pest! they do not mince matters! Why, the first good-for-nothing rascal—to whom, perhaps, I refused to lend five francs seven years ago—may go round to Citizen Rigault and tell him that I am in regular communication with Versailles, whereupon I am immediately incarcerated. For, I beg it may be observed, it is not necessary that the complicity with "the traitors" should be proved. The denunciation is quite sufficient for one to be

---

* DECREE CONCERNING THE SUSPECTED.
"Commune of Paris:

"Considering that the Government of Versailles has wantonly trampled on the rights of humanity, and set at defiance the rights of war; that it has perpetrated horrors such as even the invaders of our soil have shrunk from committing;

"Considering that the representatives of the Commune of Paris have an imperative duty devolving upon them,—that of defending the lives and honour of two millions of inhabitants, who have committed their destinies to their charge; and that it behoves them at once to take measures equal to the gravity of the situation;

"Considering that the politicians and magistrates of the city ought to reconcile the general weal with respect for public liberty,

"Decrees:

"Art. 1. All persons charged with complicity with the Government of Versailles will be immediately brought to justice and incarcerated.

"Art. 2. A 'jury of accusation' will be summoned within the twenty-four hours to examine the charges brought before it.

"Art. 3. The jury must pass sentence within the forty-eight hours.

"Art. 4. All the accused, convicted by the jury, will be retained as hostages by the People of Paris.

"Art. 5. Every execution of a prisoner of war, or of a member of the regular Government of the Commune of Paris, will be at once followed by the execution of a triple number of hostages, retained by virtue of article 4, who will be chosen by lot.

"Art. 6. All prisoners of war will be summoned before the 'jury of accusation,' who will decide whether they be immediately set at liberty or retained as hostages."

sent to contemplate the blue sky through the bars of the Conciergerie.* Besides, what do the words "complicity with the Government of Versailles" mean? All depends upon the way one looks at those things. I am not sure that I am innocent. I remember distinctly having several times bowed to a pleasant fellow—I say pleasant fellow, hoping that these lines will not fall under the observation of any one at the Prefecture of Police—who at this very moment is quite capable, the rogue, of eating a comfortable dinner at the Hôtel des Réservoirs at Versailles in company with one or more of the members of the National Assembly. You can understand now why I am beginning to feel rather uncomfortable. To know a man who knows a deputy, constitutes, I am fully persuaded—otherwise I am unworthy to live under the paternal government of the Commune—a most decided complicity with the men of Versailles. I really think it would be only commonly prudent to steal out of Paris in a coal sack, as a friend of mine did the other day, or in some other agreeable fashion.† See what may come of a bow!

XXXI.

FLOURENS is dead: we heard that last night for certain. A National Guard had previously brought back the colonel's horse from Bougival, but it was only a few hours ago that we heard any details. An attempt was made to take him prisoner at Rueil. A gendarme called out to him to surrender, he replied by a pistol shot; another gendarme advanced, and wounded him in the side,

---

* Prison of Detention.
† The following is still more naïve:—A man takes a return-ticket for the environs, and sometimes finds a guard silly enough to allow him to pass on the supposition that such a ticket was sufficient proof of his intention of returning to Paris.
Others get into the waiting-room without tickets, under the pretext of speaking to some one there.
M. Bergerat, a poet, passed the barrier in a cart-load of charcoal.

COLONEL FLOURENS.*

a third cleft his skull with a sabre cut. Some people do not believe in the pistol shot, and talk of assassination. How many such

* Flourens was born in 1838, and was the son of the well-known *savant* and physiologist of this name. He completed his studies with brilliancy, and succeeded his father as professor of the Collége de France. His opening lecture on the History of Man made a profound impression on the scientific world. However, he retired from this post in 1864, and turned his undivided attention to the political questions of the day. Deeply compromised by certain pamphlets written by him, he left France for Candia, where he espoused the popular cause against the Turks. On his return to France he was imprisoned for three months for political offences. Rochefort's candidature was hotly supported by him. In 1870 he rose against the Government, with a large force of the Belleville *faubouriens*. He was prosecuted, and took refuge in London. After the fourth of September he was placed at the head of five battalions of National Guards. He was again imprisoned for having instigated the rising of October, and it was not till the twenty-second of March that he was set at liberty. On the second of April he set out for Versailles at the head of an insurgent troop. He was met midway by a mounted patrol, and in the *mêlée* that ensued he was killed.

events are there, the truth of which will never be clearly proved! One thing certain is, that Flourens is dead. His body was recognised at Versailles by some one in the service of Garnier frères. His mother started this morning to fetch the corpse of her son. It is strange that one is so painfully affected by the violent death of this man. He has been mixed up in all the revolutionary attempts of the last few years, and ought to be particularly obnoxious to all peaceful and order-loving citizens; but the truth is, his was a sincerely ardent and enthusiastic spirit. He was a thorough believer in the principles he maintained. Whatever may be the religion he professes, the apostle inspires esteem, and the martyr compassion. This apostle, this martyr, was born to affluence; son of an illustrious savant, he may be almost said to have been born to hereditary distinction. He was still quite young when he threw himself heart and soul into politics. There was fighting in Crete, and so off he went. There he revolted against the revolt itself, got imprisoned, escaped, outwitted the gendarmes, got retaken: his adventures sound like a legend or romance. It is because he was so romantic, that he is so interesting. He returned to France full of generous impulses. He was as prodigal of his money as he had been of his blood. In the bitter cold winters he fed and clothed the poor of Belleville, going from attic to attic with money and consolation. You remember what Victor Hugo says of the sublime Pauline Roland. The spirit of Flourens much resembled hers. The patriot could act the part of a sister of charity. At other times, an enthusiast in search of a social Eldorado, he would put himself at the service of the most forlorn cause; never was anyone so imprudent. He was of a most active and critical disposition: it was impossible for him to remain quiet. When he was not seemingly employed, he was agitating something in the shade. His friendship for Rochefort was great. These two turbulent spirits, one with his pen, the other with his physical activity, remind us each of the other. Both ran to extremes, Rochefort in his literary invectives, Flourens in his hairbreadth adventures. Although they were often allied, these two, they were sometimes opposed. Have you never seen two young artists in a studio performing the old trick, one making a speech, while the other, with his head and body hidden in the folds of a cloak, stretches forth his arms and executes the most extravagant gestures? Rochefort and Flourens performed this farce in politics, the former talking, the latter gesticulating; but on the day of the burial of Victor Noir they went different ways. On that day Rochefort, to do him justice, saved a large multitude of men from terrible danger. Flourens, always the same, wished the body to be carried to Père Lachaise; on the road there must have been a collision; that was what he desired, but he was defeated. The tongue prevailed, a hundred thousand cries of vengeance filled the air, but they were only cries, and no mischief was done, except to a few graves in the Neuilly cemetery. Flourens awaited a better occasion, but by no means passively. He was a man of barricades; he did not seem to think that paving-stones were made to walk on, he only cared to see them heaped up across a street for the protection of armed patriots. Although he always wore the dress of a gentleman, he was not one of those black-coated individuals who incite the men to rebellion and keep out of the way while the fight is going on; he helped to defend the barricades he had ordered to be thrown up. Wherever there was a chance of being killed, he was sure to be; and in the midst of all this he never lost his placid expression, nor the politeness of a gentleman, nor the look of extreme youth which beamed from his eyes, and must have been on his face even when he fell under the cruel blows of the gendarmes. Now he is dead. He is judged harshly, he is condemned, but he cannot be hated. He was a madman, but he was a hero. The conduct of Flourens at the Hôtel de Ville in the night of the 31st October is hardly in keeping with so favourable a view. The French forgive and forget with facility—let that pass.

XXXII.

In the midst of so many horrible events, which interest the whole mass of the people, ought I to mention an incident which broke but one heart? Yes, I think the sad episode is not without importance, even in so vast a picture. It was a child's funeral. The little wooden coffin, scantily covered with a black pall, was not larger, as Théophile Gautier says, "than a violin case." There were few mourners. A woman, the mother doubtless, in a black stuff dress and white crimped cap, holding by the hand a boy, who had not yet reached the age of sorrowing tears, and behind them a little knot of neighbours and friends. The small procession crept along the wide street in the bright sunlight.

When it reached the church they found the door closed, and yet the money for the mass had been paid the night before, and the hour for the ceremony fixed. One of the women went forward towards the door of the vestry, where she was met by a National Guard, who told her with a superfluity of oaths that she must not go in, that the —— curé, the sacristan, and all the d—— fellows of the church were locked up, and that they would no longer have anything to do with patriots. Then the mother approached and said, "But who will bury my poor child if the curé is in prison?" and then she began to weep bitterly at the thought that there would be no prayers put up for the good of the little spirit, and that no holy water would be sprinkled on its coffin. Yes, members of the Commune, she wept, and she wept longer and more bitterly later at the cemetery, when she saw them lower the body of her child into the grave, without a prayer or a recommendation to God's mercy. You must not scoff at her, you see she was a poor weak woman, with ideas of the narrowest sort; but there are other mothers like her, quite unworthy of course to bear the children of patriots, who do not want their dear ones to be buried like dogs; who cannot understand that to pray is a crime, and to kneel down before God an offence to humanity, and who still are weak enough to wish to see a cross planted on the tombs of those they have loved and lost!

Not the cross of the nineteenth century—a red flag! *

COLONEL ASSY.

XXXIII.

COMMUNAL fraternity is decidedly in the ascendant; it is putting into practice this admirable precept, "Arrest each other." They say M. Delescluze has been sent to the Conciergerie. Yesterday Lullier was arrested, to-day Assy. It was not sufficient to change Executive Committees—if I may be allowed to say so—with no more ceremony than one would change one's boots; the

---

* Early in April the Commune forbade divine service in the Pantheon. They cut off the arms of the cross, and replaced it by the red flag during a salute of artillery.

PLACING THE RED FLAG ON THE PANTHEON.

Commune conducts itself in respect to those members that become obnoxious to it, absolutely as if they were no more than ordinary archbishops.

What! Assy—Assy* of Creuzot—who signed before all his comrades the proclamations of the Central Committee, in virtue, not only of his ability, but in obedience to the alphabetical order of the thing—Assy no longer reigns at the Hôtel de Ville!

* Assy, who first became publicly known as the leader of the strike at Messrs. Schneider's works at Creuzot, was an engineer. He was born in 1840. He became a member of the International Society, and was selected in 1870 to organise the Creuzot strike. Being threatened with arrest, he went to Paris, but did not remain there long, and on the 21st of March in that year, a few days after his return to Creuzot, the strike of the miners commenced. Assy was, finally, arrested and tried before the Correctional Tribune of Paris as chief and founder of a secret society, but he was acquitted of that charge.

At the siege of Paris, Assy was appointed as an officer in a free guerilla corps of the Isle of France. Subsequently he was a lieutenant in the 192nd battalion of the National Guard. Getting on the Central Committee, he took an active share in the events that occurred. Appointed commander of the 67th battalion on the 17th March, we find him on the morning of the 18th as Governor of the Hôtel de Ville, and colonel of the National Guard, organising with the members of the committee the means of a serious resistance—giving orders for the construction of barricades—stopping the transport of munitions and provisions from Paris. Becoming a member of the Commune, he took an active part in carrying into effect the decrees which led, among other things, to the demolition of the Vendôme Column and of the house of M. Thiers. He was arrested in April, and was succeeded as Governor of the Hôtel de Ville by one Pindy, who retained the office till the army entered Paris. Assy was held prisoner, *sur parole*, at the Hôtel de Ville, till the 19th April, when he was liberated. After this Assy was engaged in superintending the manufacture of munitions of war. He was the sole superintendent of the supply, especially as regards quality. Among the warlike stores manufactured were incendiary shells filled with petroleum, intended to be thrown into Paris during the insurrection. It is certain that these engines of destruction could only have been made at the factory superintended by Assi. He was arrested on the 21st May. Assy was one of the chiefs of the insurrection; he denied signing the decrees for the execution of the hostages, or order for the enrolment of the military in the National Guard. Assy was condemned by the tribunal of Versailles, Sept. 2, to confinement for life in a French fortress—a light penalty for the deeds of this important insurgent.

—publishes no more decrees, discusses no longer with F. Cournet, nor with G. Tridon. Wherefore this fall after so much glory? It is whispered about that Assy has thought it prudent to put aside a few rolls of bank notes found in the drawers of the late Government. What, is that all? How long have politicians been so scrupulous? Members of the Commune, how very punctilious you have grown. Now if the Citizen Assy were accused of having in 1843 been intimately acquainted with a lady whose son is now valet to M. Thiers' first cousin, or if he had been seen in a church, and it were clearly proved that he was there with any other intention than that of delicately picking the pockets of the faithful, then I could understand your indignation. But the idea of arresting a man because he has appropriated the booty of the traitors, is too absurd; if you go on acting in that way people will think you are growing conscientious!

As to Citizen Lullier,* who was one of the first victims of "fraternity," he is imprisoned because he did not succed in capturing Mont Valérien. I think with horror that if I had been in the place of Citizen Lullier I should most certainly have had to undergo the same punishment, for how in the devil's name I could have managed to transport that impregnable fortress on to the council-table at the Hôtel de Ville I have not the least conception. It is as bad as if you were in Switzerland, and asked the first child you met to go and fetch Mont Blanc; of course the child would go and have a game of marbles with his companions, and come back without the smallest trace of Mont Blanc in his arms, thereupon you would whip the youngster within an ace of his life. However, it appears that M. Lullier objected to being whipped, or rather imprisoned, and being as full of cunning as of valour he managed to slip out of his place of confinement, without drum or trumpet. "Dear Rochefort," he writes to the editor of *Le Mot d'Ordre*, "you know of what infamous machinations I have been the victim." I suppose M. Rochefort does, but I am obliged to confess that I have not the least idea, unless

* Memoir, see Appendix 5.

indeed M. Lullier means by "machinations" the order that was given him to bring Mont Valérien in his waistcoat pocket. "Imprisoned without motive," he continues, "by order of the Central Committee, I was thrown. . . ." (Oh! you should not have *thrown* M. Lullier) "into the Prefecture of Police," (the ex-Prefecture, if you please), "and put in solitary confinement at the very moment when Paris was in want of men of action and military experience." Oh, fie! men of the Commune, you had at your disposal a man of action—who does not know the noble actions of Citizen Lullier? A man of military experience—who does not know what profound experience M. Lullier has acquired in his numerous campaigns—and yet you put him, or rather throw him, into the Prefecture! This is bad, very bad. "The Prefecture is transformed into a state prison, and the most rigorous discipline is maintained." It appears then that the Communal prison is anything but a fool's paradise. "However, in spite of everything, I and my secretary managed to make our escape calmly . . ."—the calm of the high-minded—"from a cell where I was strictly guarded, to pass two court-yards and a dozen or two of soldiers, to have three doors opened for me while the sentinels presented arms as I passed . . ." What a wonderful escape : the adventures of Baron Munchausen are nothing to it. What a fine chapter poor old Dumas might have made of it. The door of the cell is passed under the very nose of the jailer, who has doubtless been drugged with some narcotic, of which M. Lullier has learnt the secret during his travels in the East Indies ; the twelve guards in the court-yards are seized one after another by the throat, thrown on the ground, bound with cords, and prevented from giving the alarm by twelve gags thrust into their twelve mouths ; the three doors are opened by three enormous false keys, the work of a member of the Commune, locksmith by trade, who has remained faithful to the cause of M. Lullier ; and last, but not least, the sentinels, plunged in ecstasy at the sight of the glorious fugitive, present arms. What a scene for a melodrama! The most interesting figure, however, in my opinion, is the secretary. I have the greatest respect for that secretary, who never dreamt one instant of abandoning his master, and I can see him, while Lullier is accomplishing his miracles, calmly writing in the midst of the danger, with a firm hand, the faithful account of these immortal adventures. "I have now," continues the ex-prisoner of the ex-Prefecture, "two hundred determined men, who serve me as a guard, and three excellent revolvers, loaded, in my pocket. I had foolishly remained too long without arms and without friends; now I am resolved to blow the brains out of the first man who tries to arrest me!" I heard a bourgeois who had read this exclaim, that he wished to Heaven each member of the Commune would come to arrest him in turn. Oh! blood-thirsty bourgeois! Then Lullier finishes up by declaring that he scorns to hide, but continues to show himself freely and openly on the boulevards. What a proud, what a noble nature! Oh, ye marionettes, ye fantoccini! Yet let me not be unjust; I will try and believe in you once more, in spite of armed requisitions, in spite of arrests, of robberies—for there have been robberies in spite of your decrees—I will try and believe that you have not only taken possession of the Hôtel de Ville for the purpose of setting up a Punch and Judy show and playing your sinister farces; I want to believe that you had and still have honourable and avowable intentions; that it is only your natural inexperience joined to the difficulties of the moment which is the cause of your faults and your follies; I want to believe that there are among you, even after the successive dismissal of so many of your members, some honourable men who deplore the evil that has been done, who wish to repair it, and who will try to make us forget the crimes and forfeits of the civil war by the benefits which revolution sometimes brings in its train. Yes, I am naturally full of hope, and will try and believe this; but, honestly, what hope can you have of inspiring confidence in those who are not prejudiced as I am in favour of innovators, when they see you arrest each other in this fashion, and know that you have among you such generals as Bergeret, such honest citizens as Assy, and such escaped lunatics as Lullier?

GENERAL CLUSERET.

XXXIV.

The fighting still continues, the cannonading is almost incessant. However, the damage done is but small. To-day, the 7th April, things seem to be in pretty much the same position as they were after Bergeret had been beaten back and Flourens killed. The forts of Vanves and Issy bombard the Versailles batteries, which in their turn vomit shot and shell on Vanves and Issy. Idle spectators, watching from the Trocadéro, see long lines of white smoke arise in the distance. Every morning, Citizen Cluseret,* the war delegate, announces that an assault of gendarmes has been victoriously repulsed by the garrisons in the

* The biography of this general of the Commune is very imperfect, down to the time when he was elected for the 1st Arrondissement of Paris, and was thereupon appointed Minister of War, or in Communal

forts. It is quite certain that if the Versaillais do attack they are repulsed, as they make no progress whatever; but do they attack, that is the question? I am rather inclined to think that these attacks and repulses are mere inventions. It seems evident to me that the generals of the National Assembly, who are now busy establishing batteries and concentrating their forces, will not make a serious attempt until they are certain of victory. In the meantime they are satisfied to complete the ruin of the forts which were already so much damaged by the Prussians.

Between Courbevoie and the Porte Maillot the fighting is continual. Ground is lost and gained, such and such a house that was just now occupied by the Versaillais is now in the hands of the Federals, and *vice versâ*. Neither side is wholly victorious, but the fighting goes on. What! is there no one to cry out "Enough! Enough blood, enough tears! Enough Frenchmen

phraseology, Delegate at the War Department. He seems to have been one of those beings, without country or family, but who are blessed, by way of compensation, with a plurality of names; we do not know whether Cluseret was really his own, or how many aliases he had made use of.

It is said that he was formerly captain in a battalion of Chasseurs d'Afrique, but was dismissed the army upon being convicted of defalcations, in connection with the purchase of horses, and, that soon after his dismissal from the French army, he went to the United States, where he served in the revolutionary war, and attained to the rank of General. Then we have another story, to the effect that having been entrusted with the care of a flock of lambs, the number of the animals decreased so rapidly, that nothing but the existence of a large pack of wolves near at hand, could possibly have accounted for it in an honest way; this affair is said to have occurred at Churchill. Such vague charges as these however deserve but little credit.

After closing his career as a shepherd, he became a defender of the Pope's flock, enlisting in the brigade against which Garibaldi took the field. The next we hear of him is that he joined the Fenians, and made an attempt to get possession of Chester Castle, but that he fell under suspicion of being a traitor, and was glad to escape to France, where, report says, he found refuge with a religious community.

> "When the devil was sick,
> The devil a monk would be;
> But when the devil was well,
> The devil a monk was he!"

killed by Frenchmen, Republicans killed by Republicans." Men fall on each side with the same war cry on their lips. Oh! when will all this dreadful misunderstanding cease?

XXXV.

THIRTY men carrying muffled drums, thirty more with trumpets draped in crape, head a long procession; every now and then the drums roll dismally, and the trumpets give a long sad wail.

Numerous detachments of all the battalions come next, marching slowly, their arms reversed. A small bunch of red immortelles is on every breast. Has the choice of the colour a political signification, or is it a symbol of a bloody death?

Next appears an immense funeral car draped with black, and drawn by four black horses; the gigantic pall is of velvet, with silver stars. At the corners float four great trophies of red flags.

Then another car of the same sort appears, another, and again another; in each of them there are thirty-two corpses. Behind the cars march the members of the Commune bare-headed, and wearing red scarfs. Alas! always that sanguinary colour! Last of all, between a double row of National Guards, follows a vast multitude of men, women, and children, all sorrowful and dejected, many in tears.

The procession proceeds along the boulevards; it started from the Beaujon hospital, and is going to the Père Lachaise; as it passes all heads are bared. One man alone up at a window remains covered; the crowd hiss him. Shame on him who will not bow before those who died for a cause, whether it may be a worthy one or not! On looking on those corpses, do not remember the evil they caused when they were alive. They are dead now, and have become sacred. But remember, oh! remember, that it is to the crimes of a few that are due the deaths of so many, and let us help to hasten the hour when the criminals, whoever they be, and to whatever party they belong; will feel the weight of the inexorable Nemesis of human destiny.

XXXVI.

WE are to have no more letters! As in the time of the siege, if you desire to obtain news of your mother or your wife, you have no other alternative than to consult a somnambulist or a fortune-teller. This is not at all a complicated operation; of course you possess a ribbon or a lock of hair, something appertaining to the absent person. This suffices to keep you informed, hour by hour, of what she says, does, and thinks. Perhaps you would prefer the ordinary course of things, and that you would rather receive a letter than consult a charlatan. But if so, I would advise you not to say so. They would accuse you of being, what you are doubtless, a reactionist, and you might get into trouble.

Yesterday a young man was walking in the Champs Elysées, a Guard National stalked up to him and asked him for a light for his cigar.—" I am really very sorry," said he, " but my cigar has gone out."—" Oh! your cigar is out, is it? Oh! so you blush to render a service to a patriot! Reactionist that you are!" Thereupon a torrent of invectives was poured on the poor young man, who was quickly surrounded by a crowd of eager faces. One charming young person exclaimed, " Why, he is a disguised sergent-de-ville!"—" Yes, yes; he is a gendarme!" is echoed on all sides.—" I think he looks like Ernest Picard," says one.— " Throw him into the Seine," says another.—" To the Seine, to the Seine, the spy!" and the unfortunate victim is pushed, jostled, and hurried off. A dense crowd of National Guards, women, and children had by this time collected, all crying out at the top of their voices, and without any idea of what was the matter, " Shoot him! throw him in the water! hang him!" Superstitious individuals leaned towards hanging for the sake of the cords.

As to the original cause of the commotion, no one seemed to remember anything about it. I overheard one man say,—" It appears that they arrested him just as he was setting fire to the ambulance at the Palais de l'Industrie!" As to what became of the young man I do not know; I trust he was neither hanged, shot, nor drowned. At any rate, let it be a lesson to others not to get embroiled in dangerous adventures of that kind; and whatever your anxiety may be concerning your family or affairs, you would do well to hide it carefully under a smiling exterior. Suppose you meet one of your friends, who says to you, " My dear fellow, how anxious you must be?" You must answer, "Anxious! oh, not at all. On the contrary, I never felt more free of care in my life."—" Oh! I thought your aunt was ill, and as you do not receive any letters . . . "—" Not receive any letters!" you continue in the same strain, " who told you that? Not receive any letters! why, I have more than I want! what an idea!"—" Then you must be strangely favoured," says your mystified companion; "for since Citizen Theiz* has taken possession of the Post-office, the communications are stopped."—" Don't believe it. It is a rumour set on float by the reactionists. Why, those terrible reactionists go so far as to pretend that the Commune has imprisoned the priests, arrested journalists, and stopped the newspapers!"—" Well, you may say what you please, but a proclamation of Citizen Theiz announces that communication with the departments will not be re-established for some days."—" Nothing but modesty on his

* A working chaser, and one of the most active and influential members of the International Society. He was among the accused who were tried in July, 1870, and was condemned to two years' imprisonment. On the formation of the Central Committee, he was appointed Vice-President. It was Theiz who saved the General Post Office, Rue J. J. Rousseau, from the total destruction decreed by other members of the Commune. His fate is not well known. Director of the General Post-office in the Rue J. J. Rousseau, he is said to have saved that important establishment, doomed to destruction by the Commune. Theiz escaped from Paris to London on the 29th of July; he took an active part in the struggle to the last, and was close to Vermorel when wounded at the barricade of the Château d'Eau.

part; he has only to show himself at the Post-office, and the service, which has been put out of order by those wretched reactionists, will be immediately reorganised."—"So I am to understand that you have news every day of your aunt."—"Of course."—"Well, I am delighted to hear it; for one of my friends, who arrived from Marseilles this morning, told me that your aunt was dead."—"Dead, good heavens! what do you mean? Now I think of it, I did not get a letter this morning."—"There you see!"

You must not, however, allow your sorrow to carry you away, at the risk of your personal safety, but answer readily. "I see it all, for a wonder I did not get a letter this morning; Citizen Theiz is a kind-hearted man, and did not want to make me unhappy."

XXXVII.

THE queen of the age is the Press. Lately dethroned and somewhat shorn of her majesty, but still a queen. It is in vain that the press has sometimes degraded itself in the eyes of honest men by stooping to applaud and approve of crimes and excesses, that journalists have done what they can to lower it; still the august offspring of the human mind, the press, has really lost neither its power nor its fascination. Misunderstood, misapplied, it may have done some harm, but no one can question the signal service which it has been able to render, or the nobility of its mission. If it has sometimes been the organ of false prophets, its voice has also been often raised to instruct and encourage.

When last night you went secretly, in a manner worthy of the act, to seize on the printing presses of the *Journal des Débats*, the *Paris Journal*, and the *Constitutionnel*, were you aware of what you were doing? You imagined, perhaps, this act would have no other result than that of suppressing violently a private concern —which is one kind of robbery—and of reducing to a state of beggary—which is a crime—the numerous individuals, journalists, printers, compositors, and others who are employed on the journal, and who live by its means. You have done worse than this. You have stopped, as far as it was in your power, the current of human progress. You have suppressed man's noblest right—the right of expressing his opinions to the world; you are no better than the pickpocket who appropriates your handkerchief. You have taken our freedom of thought by the throat, and said, "It is in my way, I will strangle it." Wherefore have you acted thus? To shut the mouths of those who contradict you, is to admit that you are not so very sure of being in the right. To suppress the journals is to confess your fear of them; to avoid the light is to excite our suspicion concerning the deeds you are perpetrating in the darkness. We shut our windows when we do not desire to be seen. Little confidence is inspired by closed doors. Your councils at the Hôtel de Ville are secret as the proceedings of certain legal cases, the details of which might be hurtful to public morality. Again I say, wherefore this mystery? What strange projects have you on foot? Do you discuss among you, propositions of a nature which your modesty declines to make known to the world? This fear of publicity, of opposition, you have proved afresh, by the nocturnal visits of your National Guards to the printing offices, wherein they forced an entrance like housebreakers. Shall we be reduced to judge of your acts, and of the bloody incidents of the civil war, only by your own asseverations and those of your accomplices? You must be very determined to act guiltily and to be obliged to tell lies, as you take so much trouble to get rid of those, who might pass sentence on you, and who might convict you of falsehood. Therefore you have not only committed a crime in so doing, but made a great mistake as well. No one can meddle with the liberty of the press with impunity. The persecution of the press always brings with it its own punishment. Look back to the many years of the Imperial Government, to the few months of the Government of the 4th of September; of all the crimes perpetrated by the former, of all the errors committed by the latter, those crimes and errors which most particularly hastened the end were those that were levelled against the freedom of the press. The most valable excuse in favour of the revolt of the 18th of March was certainly the suppression of several journals by General Vinoy, with the consent of M. Thiers. How can you be so rash as to make the very same mistakes which have been the destruction of former governments, and also so unmindful of your own honour as to commit the very crime which reduces you to the same level as your enemies?

Ah! truly those who were ready to judge you with patience and impartiality, those who at first were perhaps, on the whole, favourable to you, because it seemed to them that you represented some of the legitimate aspirations of Paris; even those, seeing you act like thoughtless tyrants, will feel it quite impossible to blind themselves any longer to your faults; those who having wished to esteem you for the sake of liberty, will for the sake of liberty, be obliged to despise you!

XXXVIII.

It cannot be true. I will not believe it. It cannot be possible that Paris is to be again bombarded: and by whom? By Frenchmen! In spite of the danger I was told there was to be apprehended near Neuilly, I wished to see with my own eyes what was going on. So this morning, the 8th April, I went to the Champs Elysées.

Until I reached the Rond Point there was nothing unusual, only perhaps fewer people to be seen about. The omnibus does not go any farther than the corner of the Avenue Marigny. An Englishwoman, whom the conductor had just helped down, came up to me and asked me the way; she wanted to go to the Rue Galilée, but did not like to walk up the wide avenue. I pointed out to her a side-street, and continued my way. A little higher up a line of National Guards, standing about ten feet distant from each other, had orders to stop passengers from going any farther. "You can't pass."—"But . . .," and I stopped to think of some plausible motive to justify my curiosity. However, I was saved the trouble. Although I had only uttered a hesitating "but," the sentinel seemed to consider that sufficient, and replied, " Oh, very well, you can pass."

The avenue seemed more and more deserted as I advanced. The shutters of all the houses were closed. Here and there a passenger slipped along close to the walls of the houses, ready to take refuge within the street-doors, which had been left open by order, directly they heard the whizzing of a shell. In front of the shop of a carriage-builder, securely closed, were piled heaps of rifles; most of the National Guards were stretched on the pavement fast asleep, while some few were walking up and down smoking their pipes, and others playing at the plebeian game of "bouchon." *
I was told that a shell had burst a quarter of an hour before at the corner of the Rue de Morny. A captain was seated there on the ground beside his wife, who had just brought him his breakfast; the poor fellow was literally cut in two, and the woman had been carried away to a neighbouring chemist's shop dangerously wounded. I was told she was still there, so I turned my steps in that direction. A small group of people were assembled before the door. I managed to get near, but saw nothing, as the poor thing had been carried into the surgery. They told me that she had been wounded in the neck by a bit of the shell, and that she was now under the care of one of the surgeons of the Press Ambulance. I then continued my walk up the avenue. The cannonading, which had seemed to cease for some little time, now began again with greater intensity than ever. Clouds of white smoke arose in the direction of the Porte Maillot, while bombs from Mont Valérien burst over the Arc de Triomphe. On

* The game of pitch-halfpenny, in which, in France, a cork (*bouchon*), with halfpence on the top of it, is placed on the ground.

the right and left of me were companies of Federals. A little further on a battalion, fully equipped, with blankets and saucepans strapped to their knapsacks, and loaves of bread stuck aloft on their bayonets, moved in the direction of Porte Maillot. By the side of the captain in command of the first company marched a woman in a strange costume, the skirt of a vivandière and the jacket of a National Guard, a Phrygian cap on her head, a chassepot in her hand, and a revolver stuck in her belt. From the distance at which I was standing she looked both young and pretty. I asked some Federals who she was; one told me she was the wife of Citizen Eudes,* a member of the Commune, and another that she was a newspaper seller in the Avenue des Ternes, whose child had been killed in the Rue des Acacias the night before by a fragment of a shell; and that she had sworn to revenge him. It appeared the battalion was on its way to support the combatants at Neuilly, who were in want of help. From what I

* General Eudes was the Alcibiades, or rather the Saint Just, of the Commune. He had the face and manners of a fashionable *tenorino*, the luxurious taste of the Athenian, the cruel inflexibility of Robespierre's protégé. He was born at Bonay, in the arrondissement of Coutances. His father was a tradesman of the Boulevard des Italiens. In his examination before the Council of War in August, 1870, Eudes called himself a shorthand writer and law student, though his real position was said to be that of a linendraper's clerk. His first notable exploit was the assassination of a fireman at La Villette. For this crime he was brought before the First Council of War at Paris. Here he informed the President, in somewhat unparliamentary terms, that "the betrayers of the country were not the Republicans, and that to destroy the Imperial Government was to annihilate the Prussians." In spite of the eloquent appeal of his counsel, he was condemned to death. The events of the fourth of September prevented the execution of this sentence, and he lived to take an active part in the agitation of the thirty-first of October. He was again tried for this conduct and acquitted, together with Vermorel, Ribaldi, Lefrançais and others. Eudes' name figures in the first decrees of the Commune, and on the last of those of the Committee of Public Safety. On the second of April he was appointed Delegate for War, and, conjointly with Cluseret, organised ten corps of the Enfants Perdus of Belleville. He promised to each of his volunteers an annuity of 300 francs and a decoration. Eudes was an atheist of the most violent type, and sayings are attributed to him which make one shudder.

hear the gendarmes and sergents de ville had fought their way as far as the Rue des Huissiers. Now I had no doubt the Versailles generals had made use of the gendarmes and sergents de ville, who were most of them old and tried soldiers, but if in very truth they were wherever the imagination of the Federals persisted in placing them, they must either have been as numerous as the grains of sand on the sea-shore, or else their leaders must have found out a way of making them serve in several places at once. Having followed the battalion, I found myself a few yards in front of the Arc de Triomphe. Suddenly a hissing, whizzing sound is heard in the distance, and rapidly approaches us; it sounds very much like the noise of a sky-rocket. "A shell!" cried the sergeant, and the whole battalion to a man, threw itself on the ground with a loud jingling of saucepans and bayonets. Indeed there was some danger. The terrible projectile lowered as it approached, and then fell with a terrific noise a little way from us, in front of the last house on the left-hand side of the avenue. I had never seen a shell burst so near me before; a good idea of what it is like may be had from those sinister looking paintings, that one sees sometimes suspended round the necks of certain blind beggars, supposed to represent an explosion in a mine. I think no one was hurt, and the mischief done seemed to consist in a wide hole in the asphalte and a door reduced to splinters. The National Guards got up from the ground, and several of them proceeded to pick up fragments of the shell. They had, however, not gone many yards when another cry of alarm was given, and again we heard the ominous whizzing sound; in an instant we were all on our faces. The second shell burst, but we did not see it; we only saw at the top of the house that had already been struck, a window open suddenly and broken panes fall to the ground. The shell had most likely gone through the roof and burst in the attic. Was there anyone in those upper stories? However, we were on our legs again and had doubled the Arc de Triomphe. I had succeeded in ingratiating myself with the men of the rear-guard, and I hoped to be able to go as far with them as I pleased. Strange enough, and I confess it with *naif* delight, I did not feel at all afraid. Although half an inch difference in

THE ARC DE TRIOMPHE, EAST SIDE (THE FINEST), UNINJURED.

Damaged on the other side. During the Prussian siege it was defended from injury, though no shells reached it. Uncovered before the civil war.

the inclination of the cannon might have cost me my life, still I felt inclined to proceed on my way. I begin to think that it is not difficult to be brave when one is not naturally a coward ! Beneath the great arch were assembled a hundred or so of persons who seemed to consider themselves in safety, and who from time to time ventured a few steps forward, for the purpose of examining the damage done to Etex's sculptured group by three successive shells. But in the Avenue de la Grande Armée only three Federals were to be seen, and I think I was the only man in plain clothes they had allowed to go so far. I could distinctly perceive a small barricade erected in front of the Porte Maillot on this side of the ramparts. The bastion to the right was hard at work cannonading the heights of Courbevoie; great columns of smoke, succeeded by terrific explosions, testified to the zeal of the Communist artillerymen. Beyond the ramparts the Avenue de Neuilly extended, dusty and deserted. Unfortunately the sun blinded me, and I could not distinguish well what was going on in the distance. By this time the sound of musketry was heard distinctly. I was told they were fighting principally at Saint James and in the park of Neuilly. I tried to pass out of the gates with the battalion, but an officer caught sight of me, and in no measured tones ordered me back. I ought not to complain, however, he rendered me good service; for although the fire of the Versaillais had somewhat diminished, I do not think the place could have been much longer tenable, to judge from the quantities of bits of shell that strewed the road; from the numerous litters that were being borne away with their bloody burthens; from the railway-station in ruins, and the condition of the neighbouring houses, which had nearly all of them great black holes in their fronts. The Federals did not seem at all impressed by their critical position; sounds of laughter reached me from the interior of a casemate, from the chimney of which smoke was arising, and guards running hither and thither were whistling merrily the *Chant du Départ*, with a look of complete satisfaction.

I managed to reach the Rue du Débarcadère, which is situated close to the ramparts. An acquaintance of mine lives there. I knew he was away, but I thought the porter would recognise and allow me to take up a position at one of the windows. Next door, the corner house, I found a shell had gone into a wine-merchant's shop there, who could very well have dispensed with such a visitor, and had behaved in the most unruly fashion, breaking the glass, smashing the tables and counter, but neither killing nor wounding anybody. The porter knew me quite well, and invited me to walk upstairs to the apartments of my friend, situated on the third floor. From the windows I could not see the bastion, which was hidden by the station; but to the left, in the distance, beyond the Bois de Boulogne, wherein I fancied I perceived troops moving between the branches, but whether Versaillais or Parisians I could not tell, arose the tremendous Mont Valérien bathed in sunlight. The flashes from the cannon, which in daylight have a pale silver tint, succeeded each other rapidly; the explosions were formidable, and the fort was crowned with a wreath of smoke. They appeared to be firing in the direction of Levallois, rather than on the Porte Maillot. The Federals did not seem to attempt to reply. Turning myself towards the right I could scan nearly the whole length of the Avenue de Neuilly. The bare piece of ground which constitutes the military zone was completely deserted; several shells fell there that had been aimed doubtless at the Porte Maillot or the bastion. The position I had taken up at the window was rather a perilous one. I was just behind the bastion. Beyond the military zone most of the houses seemed uninhabited, but I saw distinctly the National Guards in front of the Restaurant Gilet, making their soup on the side-walk. I was too far away to judge of the extent of the mischief done by the cannonading, but I was told that several roofs had fallen in and many walls had been thrown down in that quarter. All that I could see of the market-place was empty; but the sound of musketry, and the smoke which issued from the houses on one side of it, told me

HORSE CHASSEUR ACTING AS A COMMUNIST ARTILLERY MAN, ATTENDED BY A GAMIN SPONGER.

that the Federals were there in sufficient numbers. A little further on I saw the barrels of the rifles sticking out of the windows, with little wreaths of smoke curling out of them; small knots of armed men every now and then marched hurriedly across the avenue, and disappeared into the opposite houses. Partly on account of the distance, and partly on account of the blinding sun, and partly, perhaps, on account of the emotion I experienced, which made me desire and yet fear to see, I could distinguish the bridge but indistinctly, with the dark line of a barricade in front of it. What surprised me most in the battle which I was busily observing, was the extraordinarily small number of combatants that were visible, when suddenly—it was about two o'clock in the afternoon—the Versailles batteries at Courbevoie, which had been silent for some time, began firing furiously. The horrid screech of the mitrailleuse drowned the hissing of the shells; the whole breadth of the long avenue was covered by a kind of white mist. The bastion in front of me replied energetically. It seemed to me as if the interior part of my ear was being rent asunder, when suddenly I heard a dull heavy sound, such as I had not heard before, and I felt the house tremble beneath me. Loud cries arose from the National Guards on the ramparts. I fancied that a rain of shot and shell had destroyed the drawbridge of the Porte Maillot; but it was not so; in the distance I saw that the clouds of smoke were rolling nearer and nearer, and that the roar of the musketry, which had greatly increased, sounded close by. I felt sure that a rush was being made from Courbevoie—that the Versaillais were advancing. The shells were flying over our heads in the direction of the Champs Elysées. I began to distinguish that a tumultuous mass of human beings were marching on in the smoke, in the dust, in the sun. The guns on the bastion now thundered forth incessantly. There was no mistaking by this time, there were the Versaillais; I could see the red trowsers of the men of the line. The Federals were shooting them down from the windows. Then I saw the advanced guard stop, hesitate beneath the balls which seemed to rain on them from the Place du Marché, and presently retire. Whereupon a large number of Federals poured forth from the houses, and, walking close to the walls, to be as much as possible out of the way of the projectiles, hurried after the retreating enemy. But suddenly, when they had arrived a little too far for me to distinguish anything very clearly, they in their turn came to a standstill, and then retraced their steps, and returned to their positions within the houses. The fire from the Versaillais then sensibly diminished, but that of the bastions continued its furious attack. It was thus that I witnessed one of those *chassé-croisés* under fire, which have become so frequent since this dreadful civil war was concentrated at Neuilly.

As it would have been most imprudent to follow the railway cutting, or to have gone back by the Avenue de la Grande Armée, where the Versailles shells were still falling, I walked up the Rue du Débarcadère, and then turned into the Rue Saint-Ferdinand, and soon found myself in the Place des Ternes, in front of the church. There was a most dismal aspect about the whole of this quarter. Situated close to the ramparts, it is very much exposed, and had suffered greatly. Nearly all the shops were shut; some of the doors, however, of those where wine or provisions are sold, were standing open, while on the shutters of others were inscribed in chalk, "The entrance is beneath the gateway." I was astonished to see that the church was open, a rare sight in these days. Why, is it possible that the Commune has committed the unqualifiable imprudence of not arresting the curé of Saint-Ferdinand, and that she is weak enough—may she not have to regret it!—to permit the inhabitants of Ternes to be baptised, married, and buried according to the deplorable rites and ceremonies of Catholicism, which has happily fallen into disuse in the other quarters of Paris? I can now understand why the shells fall so persistently in this poor arrondissement: the anger of the goddess of Reason (shall we not soon have a goddess of Reason?) lies heavily on this quarter, the shame of the capital, where the inhabitants still try to look as if they believed in heaven! In spite of everything, however, I entered the church; there were a great many women on their knees, and several men too. The prayers of the dead were being said over the coffin of a woman who, I was told, was killed yesterday by a ball in the chest, whilst crossing the Avenue des Ternes, just a little above the railway bridge. A ball, how strange! yet I was assured such was the case. It is pretty evident, then, that the Versaillais were considerably nearer to Paris, on this side at least, than the official despatches lead us to suppose.

On returning to the street I directed my steps in the direction of the Place d'Eylau. Two National Guards passed me, bearing a litter between them.—"Oh, you can look if you like," said one. So I drew back the checked curtain. On the mattress was stretched a woman, decently dressed, with a child of two or three years lying on her breast. They both looked very pale; one of the woman's arms was hanging down; her sleeve was stained with blood; the hand had been carried away.—"Where were they wounded?" I asked.—"Wounded! they are dead. It is the wife and child of the velocipede-maker in the Avenue de Wagram; if you will go and break the news to him you will do us a good service."

It was therefore quite true, certain, incontestable. The balls and shells of the Versaillais were not content with killing the combatants and knocking down the forts and ramparts. They were also killing women and children, ordinary passers-by; not only those who were attracted by an imprudent curiosity to go where they had no business, but unfortunates who were necessarily obliged to venture into the neighbouring streets, for the purpose of buying bread. Not only do the shells of the National Assembly reach the buildings situated close to the city walls, but they often fall considerably farther in, crushing inoffensive houses, and breaking the sculpture on the public monuments. No one can deny this. I have seen it with my own eyes. Anyhow, the projectiles fall nearer and nearer the centre. Yesterday they fell in the Avenue de la Grande Armée; to-day they fly over the Arc de Triomphe, and fall in the Place d'Eylau and the Avenue d'Uhrich. Who knows but what to-morrow they will have reached the Place de la Concorde, and the next day perhaps I may be killed by one on the Boulevard Montmartre ? Paris bombarded ! Take care, gentlemen of the National Assembly ! What the Prussians did, and what gave rise to such a clamour of indignation on the part of the Government of the 4th September, it will be both infamous and imprudent for you to attempt. You kill Frenchmen who are in arms against their countrymen,—alas ! that is a horrible necessity in civil war,—but spare the lives and the dwellings of those who are not arrayed against you, and who are perhaps your allies. It is all very well to argue that guns are not endowed with the gifts of intelligence and mercy, and that one cannot make them do exactly what one likes; but what have you done with those marvellous marksmen who, during the siege, continually threw down the enemy's batteries and interrupted his works with such extraordinary precision, and who pretended that at a distance of seven thousand metres they could hit the gilded spike of a Prussian helmet? Wherefore have they become so clumsy since they changed places with their adversaries ? Joking apart, in a word, you are doing yourself the greatest injury in being so uselessly cruel; every shell overleaping the fortifications is not only a crime, but a great mistake. Remember, that in this horrible duel which is going on, victory will not really remain with that party which shall have triumphed over the other, by the force of arms (yours undoubtedly), but to the one who, by his conduct, shall have succeeded in proving to the neutral population, which observes and judges, that right was on his side. I do not say but what your cause is the best ; for although we may have to reproach you with an imprudent resistance, unnecessary attacks, and a wilful obstinacy not to see what was legitimate and honourable in the wishes of the Parisians, still we must consider that you represent, legally, the whole of France. I do not say, therefore, but what your cause is the best ; frankly though, can you hope to bring over to your side that large body of citizens, whose confidence you

MARINE GUNNER AND STREET-BOY.

During the Prussian siege the sailors of the French navy played an important part, their bravery, activity, and ingenuity being much esteemed by the Parisians. Some of them took the red side, and manned the gun-boats on the Seine. Knowing the prestige attached to the brave marines, the Communist generals made use of the naval clothes found in the marine stores, and dressed therein some of the valliant heroes of Belleville and Montmartre.

had shaken, by massacring innocent people in the streets, and destroying their dwellings? If this bombardment continues, if it increases in violence as it seems likely to do, you will become odious, and then, were you a hundred times in the right, you will still be in the wrong. Therefore, it is most urgent that you give orders to the artillerymen of Courbevoie and Mont Valérien, to moderate their zeal, if you do not desire that Paris—neutral Paris—should make dangerous comparisons between the Assembly which flings us its shells, and the Commune which launches its decrees, and come to the conclusion that decrees are less dangerous missiles than cannon-balls. As to the legality of the thing, we do not much care about that; we have seen so many governments, more or less legal, that we are somewhat *blasés* on that point; and a few millions of votes have scarcely power enough to put us in good humour with shot and shell. Certainly the Commune, such as the men at the Hôtel de Ville have constituted it, is not a brilliant prospect. It arrests priests, stops newspapers, wishes to incorporate us, in spite of ourselves, in the National Guard; robs us—so we are told; lies inveterately—that is incontestable, and altogether makes itself a great bore; but what does that matter?—human nature is full of weaknesses, and prefers to be bored than bombarded.

XXXIX.

WHERE is Bergeret? What have they done with Bergeret? We miss Bergeret. They have no right to suppress Bergeret, who, according to the official document, was "himself" at Neuilly; Bergeret, who drove to battle in an open carriage; who enlivened our ennui with a little fun. They were perfectly at liberty to take away his command and give it to whomsoever they chose; I am quite agreeable to that, but they had no right to take him away and prevent him amusing us. Alas! we do not have the chance so often!*

Rumours are afloat that he has been taken to the Concier-

* General Bergeret, Member of the Central Committee, Delegate of War, &c., was a bookseller's assistant. He emerged in 1869 from a printing-office to support the irreconcileable candidates in the election meetings.

Events progressed, and on the 18th of March Victor Bergeret reappeared, resplendent in gold lace and embroidery, happy to have found at last a government, to which Jules Favre did not belong.

When Bergeret, who never had any higher grade than that of sergeant in the National Guard, was made general, he believed himself to be a soldier. A friend of this pasteboard officer said one day, "If Bergeret were to live a hundred years, he would always swear he had been a general."

On the 8th April, Victor Bergeret was arrested by order of the Executive Commission for having refused obedience to Cluseret, a general too, and his superior, and he was incarcerated in the prison of Mazas, where he remained for a short time, until the day when Cluseret was shut up there himself. In fact, Cluseret went into the very cell which Bergeret had just quitted, and found an autograph note written on the wall by his predecessor, and addressed to himself. The words ran thus:—

"CITIZEN CLUSERET,—

"You have had me shut up here, and you will be here yourself before eight days are over.

"GÉNÉRAL BERGERET."

On leaving the prison of Mazas, Bergeret was still kept a prisoner for a time in a magnificent apartment of the Hôtel de Ville, decorated with gilded panneling and cerise-coloured satin. His wife was allowed to join him here, and he also obtained permission to keep with him a little terrier, of which he was extremely fond. Shortly afterwards he was reinstated, took his place again in the Communal Assembly, and was attached to the commission of war. The beautiful palace of the president of the Corps Législatif was now his residence, and there he delighted in receiving the friends who had known him when he was poor. His invariable home-dress in palace as in prison was red from head to foot: red jacket, red trousers, and red Phrygian cap.

One day, a short time after his release from prison, he said to an intimate friend:—"Affairs are going well, but the Commune is in need of money, I know it, and they are wrong not to confide in me. I would lend them ten thousand francs willingly." The generalship had singularly enriched the bookseller's assistant, Victor Bergeret.

CORPS LEGISLATIF.—THE HEAD-QUARTERS OF GENERAL BERGERET.

gerie. Poor Bergeret! and why is he so treated? Because he got the Federals beaten in trying to lead them to Versailles?

Citizens, if you will allow me to express my humble opinion on the subject, I shall take the opportunity of insinuating that the plan of Citizen Bergeret—which has, I acknowledge, been completely unsuccessful—was the only possible one capable of transforming into a triumphant revolution, the émeute of Montmartre, now the Commune of Paris.

Let us look at it from a logical point of view, if you please. Does it seem possible to you, that Paris can hold its own against the whole of the rest of France? No, most certainly not. To-day, especially, after the disasters that have occurred to the communal insurrectionists of Marseilles, Lyons, and Toulouse—disasters which your lying official reports have in vain tried to transform into successes; to-day, I say, you cannot possibly nourish any delusive hopes of help from the provinces. In a few days, you will have the whole country in array in front of your ramparts and your ruined fortresses, and then you are lost; yes, lost, in spite of all the blinded heroism of those whom you have beguiled to the slaughter. The only hope you could reasonably have conceived was that of profiting by the first moment of surprise and disorder, which the victorious revolt had occasioned among the small number of hesitating soldiery which then constituted the whole of the French army; to surprise Versailles, inadequately defended, and seize, if it were possible, on the Assembly and the Government. Your sudden revolution wanted to be followed up by a brusque attack, there would then have been some hope—a faint one, I confess, but still a hope, and this plan of Bergeret, by the very reason of its audacity, should not have been condemned by you, who have only succeeded through violence and audacity, and can only go on prospering by the same means. Now, what do you mean to do? To resist the whole of France? To resist your enemies inside the walls, besides those enemies outside, who increase in numbers and confidence every day? Your defeat is certain, and from this day forth is only a question of time. You were decidedly wrong to put Bergeret " in the shade," as they say at the Hôtel de Ville,—firstly, because he amused us; and secondly, because he tried the only thing that could possibly have succeeded—an enterprise worthy of a brilliant madman.

GENERAL DOMBROWSKI.

XL.

WHO takes Bergeret's place? Dombrowski.* Who had the idea of doing this? Cluseret. First of all we had the Central

* There are two versions of Dombrowski's earlier history. By his admirers he was said to have headed the last Polish insurrection: the party of order stigmatise him as a Russian adventurer, who had fought in Poland, but against the Poles, and in the Caucasus, in Italy, and in France—wherever; in fine, blows were to be given and money earned. He entered France, like many other adventurous knights, in Garibaldi's suite, came to Paris after the siege, and immediately after the outbreak of the eighteenth of March was created general by the Commune, and gathered round him in guise of staff the most illustrious, or least ignoble, of those foreign parasites and vagabonds, who have made of Paris a grand occidental Bohemian

Committee, then we had the Commune, and now we have Cluseret. It looks as if Cluseret had swallowed the Commune, which had previously swallowed and only half digested the Central Committee. We are told that Cluseret is a great man, that Cluseret is strong, that Cluseret will save Paris. Cluseret issues decrees, and sees that they are executed. The Commune says, "*we wish;*" but Cluseret says, "*I wish.*" It is he who has conceived and promulgated the following edict:

> "In consideration of the patriotic demands of a large number of National Guards, who, although they are married men, wish to have the honour of defending their municipal rights, even at the expense of their lives . . ."

I should like to know some of those National Guards who attach so little importance to their lives! Show me two, and I will myself consent to be the third. But I am interrupting Dictator Cluseret.

> "The decree of the fifth of April is therefore modified:"

The decree of the fifth of April was made by the Commune, but Cluseret does not care a straw for that.

> "From seventeen to nineteen, service in the marching companies is voluntary, but from nineteen to forty it is obligatory for the National Guards, married or unmarried.
>
> "I recommend all good patriots to be their own police, and to

Babel. These soldiers of fortune, most of whom had been "unfortunate" at home, formed the marrow of the Commune's military strength.

Dombrowski had gained a name for intrepidity even among these men of reckless courage and adventurous lives. He maintained strict discipline, albeit to a not very moral purpose. Whoever dared connect his name with the word defeat was shot. Like many other Communist generals he took the most stringent measures for concealing the truth from his soldiers, and thus staved off total demoralisation until the Versailles troops were in the heart of Paris. His relations with the Federal authorities were not of an uniformly amiable character.

see that this edict is carried out in their respective quarters, and to force the refractory to serve."

Ingenious decree! See how logically he draws his conclusions. Another than Cluseret would have accepted the patriotic offers of this large body of married National Guards, who were determined to leave their wives and families, even at the risk of their lives,—would have accepted their services with thanks; but Cluseret does better than this. Several men want to get killed, he says to himself; then they must all go and get killed. Most logical! Suppose my neighbour has an attack of brain fever and throws himself out of window, and suppose my doctor orders me, on the instant, to precipitate myself head foremost from my fourth floor on to the pavement. In vain I plead that I have not got brain fever; it does not matter at all, my neighbour is attacked with it, that is more than sufficient, and if I say another word, I am threatened with the police.

As to the last paragraph of Cluseret's decree it is impossible to joke about it, it is by far too odious. This exhortation in favour of a press-gang,—this wish that each man should become a spy upon his neighbour (he says it in so many words), fills me with anger and disgust. What! I may be passing in the streets, going about my own business, and the first Federal who pleases, anybody with dirty hands, a wretch you may be sure, for none but a wretch would follow the *recommendations* of Cluseret,—an escaped convict, may take me by the collar and say, "Come along and be killed for the sake of my municipal independence." Or else I may be in bed at night, quietly asleep, as it is clearly my right to be, and four or five fellows, fired with patriotic ardour, may break in my door, if I do not hasten to open it on the first summons like a willing slave, and, whether I like it or not, drag me in night-cap and slippers, in my shirt perhaps, if it so pleases the brave *sans-culottes*, to the nearest outpost. Now I swear to you, Cluseret, I would not bear this, if I had not, during the last few hungry days of the siege, sold to a curiosity-dealer—your colleague now in the Commune—my revolver, which I had hoped naïvely might defend me against the Prussians! Think, a revolver with six balls, if you please, and which, alas! I forgot to discharge!

We can only hope that even at this moment, when the revolution has brought out of the darkness into the light, so many rascals and cowards, just as the sediment rises to the top when the wine is shaken, we must hope, that there will be found in Paris, nobody to undertake the mean office of spy and detective; and that the decree of M. Cluseret will remain a dead-letter, like so many other decrees of the Commune. I will not believe all I am told; I will not believe that last night several men, without any precise orders, without any legal character whatever, merely National Guards, introduced themselves into peaceful families; waking the wife and children, and carrying off the husband as one carries off a housebreaker or an escaped convict. I am told that this is a fact, that it has happened more than fifty times at Montmartre, Batignolles, and Belleville; yet I will not believe it.* I prefer to believe that these tales are "inventions of Versailles" than to admit the possibility of such infamy.

Come now, Cluseret, War Delegate, whatever he likes to call himself. Where does he come from, what has he done, and what services has he rendered, to give him a right thus to impose his sovereign wishes upon us?

He is not a Frenchman; nor is he an American; for the honour of France I prefer his being an American. His history is as short as it is inglorious. He once served in the French army, and left, one does not know why; then went to fight in America during the war. His enemies affirm that he fought for the Slave States, his friends the contrary. It does not seem very clear which side he was on—both, perhaps. Oh, America!

---

* A poor Italian smith told me he had three men seized. They had taken a stove near the fortifications of Ternes, when they were arrested. "But we are Italians!" they cried. It was no excuse, for the Federals replied, "Italians! so much the better; you shall serve as Garibaldians!"

you had taken him from us, why did you not keep him? Cluseret came back to us with the glory of having forsworn his country. Immediately the revolutionists received him with open arms. Only think, an American! Do you like America? People want to make an America everywhere. Modern Republics have had formidable enemies to contend with—America and the revolution of '93. We are sad parodists. We cannot be free in our own fashion, but are always obliged to imitate what has been or what is. But that which is adapted to one climate or country, is it always that which is the fittest thing for another? I will return, however, to this subject another time. America, who is so vaunted, and whom I should admire as much as could reasonably be wished, if men did not try to remodel France after her image, one must be blind not to see what she has of weakness and of narrowness, amid much that is truly grand. It was said to me once by some one, "The American mind may be compared to a compound liqueur, composed of the yeast of Anglo-Saxon beer, the foam of Spanish wines, and the dregs of the *petit-bleu* of Suresnes, heated to boiling point by the applause and admiration given by the genuine pale ale, the true sherry, and authentic Château-Margaux to these their deposits. From time to time the caldron seethes with a little too much violence, and the bubbling drink pours over upon the old world, bringing back to the pure source, to the true vintage, their deteriorated products. Oh! The poor wines of France! How many adulterations have they been submitted to!" Calumny and exaggeration no doubt; but I am angry with America for sending Cluseret back, as I am angry with the Commune for having imposed him on Paris. The Commune, however, has an admirable excuse: it has not, perhaps, found among true Frenchmen one with an ambition criminal enough to direct, according to her wishes, the destruction of Paris by Paris, and France by France.

XLI.

It was not enough that men should be riddled with balls and torn to pieces by shells. The women are also seized with a strange enthusiasm in their turn, and they too fall on the battle-field, victims of a terrible heroism. What extraordinary beings are these who exchange the needle for the needle-gun, the broom for the bayonet, who quit their children that they may die by the sides of their husbands or lovers? Amazons of the rabble, magnificent and abject, something between Penthesilea and Théroigne de Méricourt. There they are seen to pass as cantinières, among those who go forth to fight. The men are furious, the women are ferocious,—nothing can appal, nothing discourage them. At Neuilly, a vivandière is wounded in the head; she turns back a moment to staunch the blood, then returns to her post of danger. Another, in the 61st Battalion, boasts of having killed three *gardiens de la paix* * and several *gendarmes*. On the plain of Châtillon a woman joins a group of National Guards, takes her stand amongst them, loads her gun, fires, re-loads and fires again, without the slightest interruption. She is the last to retire, and even then turns back again and again to fire. A *cantinière* of the 68th Battalion was killed by a fragment of shell which broke the little spirit-barrel she carried, and sent the splinters into her stomach. After the engagement of the 3rd of April, nine bodies were brought to the *mairie* of Vaugirard. The poor women of the quarter crowd there, chattering and groaning, to look for husbands, brothers and sons. They tear a dingy lantern from each other, and put it close to the pale faces of the dead, amongst whom they find the body of a young woman literally riddled with shot. What means the wild rage that seizes upon these furies? Are they conscious of the crimes they commit; do they understand the

---

* The Gardiens de la Paix replaced the Sergents de Ville. They carried no sword, and wore a cap with a tricoloured band and cockade; in fact were the policemen of Paris. The Gendarmerie are the country police.

cause for which they die? Yesterday, in a shop of the Rue de Montreuil, a woman entered with her gun on her shoulder and her bayonet covered with blood. "Wouldn't you do better to stay at home and wash your brats?" said an indignant neighbour. Whereupon arose a furious altercation, the virago working herself into such a fury that she sprang upon her adversary, and bit her violently in the throat, then withdrew a few steps, seized her gun, and was going to fire, when she suddenly turned pale, her weapon fell from her hands, and she sank back dead. In her wild passion she had broken a blood vessel. Such are the women of the people in this terrible year of 1871. It has its *cantinières* as '93 had its *tricoteuses*,* but the cantinières are preferable, for the horrible in them partakes of a savage grandeur. Fighting as they are against brothers and kinsfolk, they are revolting, but against a foreign enemy, they would have been sublime.

Children, even, do not remain passive in this fearful conflict. The children! you cry,—but do not smile; one of my friends has just seen a poor boy whose eye has been knocked in with the point of a nail. It happened thus. It was on Friday evening in the principal street of Neuilly. Two hundred boys—the eldest scarcely twelve years old—had assembled there; they carried sticks on their shoulders, with knives and nails stuck at the end of them. They had their army roll, and their numbers were called over in form, and their chiefs—for they had chiefs—gave the order to form into half sections, then to march in the direction of Charenton; a mite of a child trudged before, blowing in a penny trumpet bought at a toy-shop, and they had a cantinière, a little girl of six. Soon, they met another troop of children of about the same numbers. Had the encounter been previously arranged? Had it been decided that they should give battle? I cannot tell you this, but at all events the battle took place, one party being for the Versailles troops, the other for

---

* Tricoteuses (knitters), women who attended political clubs—working whilst they listened—1871 refined upon the idea of 1793. The first revolution had its Tricoteuses, that of 1871 its Petroleuses!!!

the Federals. Such a battle, that the inhabitants of the quarter had the greatest difficulty in separating the combatants, and there were killed and wounded, as the official despatches of the Commune would give it; Alexis Mercier, a lad of twelve, whom his comrades had raised to the dignity of captain, was killed by the blow of a knife in the stomach.

Ah! believe it, these women drunk with hate, these children playing at murder, are symptoms of the terrible malady of the times. A few days hence, and this fury for slaughter will have seized all Paris.

XLII.

May conciliation be hoped for yet? Alas! I can scarcely think so. The bloody fight will have a bloody end. It is not alone between the Commune of Paris and the Assembly of Versailles that there lies an abyss which only corpses can fill. Paris itself, at this moment—I mean the Paris sincerely desirous of peace—is no longer understood by France; a few days of separation have caused strange divisions in men's minds; the capital seems to speak the country's language no longer. Timbuctoo is not as far from Pekin, as Versailles is distant from Paris. How can one hope under such circumstances, that the misunderstanding, the sole cause of our misfortunes, can be cleared away? How can one believe that the Government of Monsieur Thiers will lend an ear to the propositions carried there by the members of the Republican Union of the rights of Paris,* by the delegates of

---

* The citizens, united under the denomination of the League of Republican Union of the Rights of Paris, had adopted the following programme, which seemed to them to express the wishes of the population:—

"Recognition of the Republic.

"Recognition of the rights of Paris to govern itself, to regulate its police, its finances, its public charities, its public instruction, and the

Parisian trade and by the emissaries of the Freemasons;* when the principal object of all these propositions is the definitive establishment of the Republic, and the full and entire recognition of our municipal liberties. The National Assembly is at the same point as it was on the eve of the 18th of March; it disregards now, as it did then, the legitimate wishes of the population, and, moreover, it will not perceive the fact that the triumphant insurrection—in spite of the excesses that everyone condemns—has naturally added to the validity of our just revendications. The "Communists" are wrong, but the Commune, the true Commune,

exercise of its religious liberty by a council freely elected and all-powerful within the scope of its action.

"The protection of Paris exclusively confided to the National Guard, formed of all citizens fit to serve.

"It is to the defence of this programme that the members of the League wish to devote their efforts, and they appeal to all citizens to aid them in the work, by making known their adhesion, so that the members of the League, thereby strengthened and supported, may exercise a powerful mediatory influence, tending to bring about the return of peace, and to secure the maintenance of the Republic.

"Paris, 6th April, 1871."

Here follow the signatures of former representatives, *maires*, doctors, lawyers, literary men, merchants, and others.

---

* MANIFESTO OF THE FREEMASONS.

"In the presence of the fearful events which make all France shudder and mourn, in the sight of the precious blood that flows in streams, the Freemasons, who represent the sentiments of humanity and have spread them through the world, come once more to declare before you, government and members of the Assembly, and before you, members of the Commune, these great principles which are their law and which ought to be the law of every one who has the heart of a man.

"The flag of the Freemasons bears inscribed upon it, the noble device — Liberty, Equality, Fraternity, Union. The Freemasons uphold peace among men, and, in the name of humanity, proclaim the inviolability of human life. The Freemasons detest all wars, and cannot sufficiently express grief and horror at civil warfare. Their duty and their right are to come between you and to say:

"'In the name of humanity, in the name of fraternity, in the name of the distracted country, put a stop to this effusion of blood; we ask of you, we implore of you, to listen to our appeal.'"

is right; this is what Paris believes, and, unhappily, this is what Versailles will not understand; it wants to remain, as to the form of its government, weakly stationary; it makes a municipal law that will be judged insufficient; and, as it obstinately persists in errors which were worn out a month ago and are rotten now, they will soon consider the "conciliators" whose ideas have progressed from day to day, as the veritable agents of the insurrection, and send them, purely and simply, about their business.

Nevertheless, the desire of seeing this fratricidal war at an end, is so great, so ardent, so general, that convinced as we are of the uselessness of their efforts, we admire and encourage those who undertake the almost hopeless task of pacification with persistent courage. True Paris has now but one flag, which is neither the crimson rag nor the tricolour standard, but the white flag of truce.

XLIII.

Do you know what the Abbaye de Cinq-Pierres is, or rather what it was? Mind, not Saint-Pierre, but Cinq-Pierres (Five Stones). Gavroche,* who loves puns and is very fond of slang, gave this nickname to a set of huge stones which stood before the prison of La Roquette, and on which the guillotine used to be erected on the mornings when a capital punishment was to take place. The executioner was the Abbé de Cinq-Pierres, for Gavroche is as logical as he is ingenious. Well! the abbey exists no longer, swept clean away from the front of the Roquette prison. This is splendid! and as for the guillotine itself, you know what has been done with that. Oh! we had a narrow escape! Would you believe that that infamous, that abominable

---

* Gavroche is a street boy of Paris, a *gamin* immortalized by Victor Hugo in "Les Misérables," a master of Parisian *argot* (slang).

Government of Versailles, conceived the idea, at the time it sat in Paris, of having a new and exquisitely improved guillotine, constructed by anonymous carpenters? It is exactly as I have the honour of telling you. You can easily verify the fact by reading the proclamation of the "*sous-comité en exercice.*" What is the "active under-committee?". I admit that I am in total ignorance on the subject; but, what does it matter! In these times when committees spring up like mushrooms, it would be absurd to allow oneself to be astonished at a committee—and especially a sub-committee—more or less. Here is the proclamation:—

"CITIZENS,—Being informed that a guillotine is at this moment in course of construction, . . ." Dear me, yes, while you were fast asleep and dreaming, with no other apprehension than that of being sent to prison by the members of the Commune, a guillotine was being made. Happily, the sub-committee was not asleep. No, not they! ". . . a guillotine ordered and paid for . . .". Are you quite sure it was paid for, good sub-committee? For that Government, you know, had such a habit of cheating poor people out of their rights. ". . . . by the late odious government; a portable and rapid guillotine." Ha! What do you say to that? Does not that make your blood run cold? Rapid, you understand; that is to say, that the guillotining of twelve or fifteen hundred patriots in a morning would have been play to the Abbé of Cinq-Pierres. And portable, too! A sort of pocket guillotine. When the members of the Government had a circuit to make in the provinces, they would have carried their guillotine with their seals of office, and if, at Lyons, Marseilles, or any other great town, they had met a certain number of scoundrels—Snip, snap! In the twinkling of an eye, no more scoundrels left. Oh! how cunning! But let us go on reading. "The sub-committee of the eleventh arrondissement . . ." Oh! so there is a sub-committee for each arrondissement, is there? ". . . has had these infamous instruments of monarchical domination . . ." One for you, Monsieur Thiers! ". . . seized, and has voted their destruction for ever." Very good intentions, sub-committee, but you can't write grammar. "In consequence, they will be burnt in front of the *mairie*, for the purification of the arrondissement and the preservation of the new liberties." And accordingly, a guillotine was burnt on the 7th of April, at ten o'clock in the morning, before the statue of Voltaire.

The ceremony was not without a certain weirdness. In the midst of a compact crowd of men, women, and children, who shook their fists at the odious instrument, some National Guards of the 137th Battalion fed the huge flames with broken pieces of the guillotine, which crackled, blistered, and blazed, while the statue of the old philosopher, wrapped in the smoke, must have sniffed the incense with delight. When nothing remained but a heap of glowing ashes, the crowd shouted with joy; and for my own part, I fully approved of what had just been done as well as of the approbation of the spectators. But, between you and me, do you not think that many of the persons there had often stationed themselves around the guillotine with rather different intentions than that of seeing it burnt? And then, if in reducing this instrument of death to ashes, they wished to prove that the time is past when men put men to death, it seems to me that they ought not to stop at this. While we are at it, let us burn the muskets too,—what say you?

XLIV.

I HAVE just witnessed a horrible scene. Alas! what harrowing spectacles meet our eyes on every side, and will still before all this comes to an end. I accompanied a poor old woman to a cemetery in the east of Paris. Her son, who had engaged himself in a battalion of Federal guards, had not been home for five days. He was most likely dead, the neighbours said, and one bade her "go

and look at the Cimetière de l'Est, they have brought in a load of bodies there." Imagine a deep trench and about thirty coffins placed side by side. Numbers of people came there to claim their own among the dead. To avoid crowding, the National Guards made the people walk in order, two or three abreast, and thus they were marshalled among the tombs and crosses. The poor woman and I followed the others. From time to time I heard a burst of sobs; some one amongst the dead had been recognised. On we go slowly, step by step, as if we were at the doors of a theatre. At last we arrive before the first coffin. The poor mother I have come with is very weak and very sad; it is I who lift up the thin lid of the coffin. A grey-haired corpse is lying within it, from the shoulders downwards nothing but a heap of torn flesh, and clothes, and congealed blood. We continue on. The second coffin also contains the body of an old man; no wounds are to be seen; he was probably killed by a ball. Still we advance. I observe that the old men are in far greater number than the young. The wounds are often fearful. Sometimes the face is entirely mutilated. When I had closed the lid of the last coffin the poor mother uttered a cry of relief; her son was not there! For myself, I was stupefied with horror, and only recovered my senses on being pushed on by the men behind me, who wanted to see in their turn. "Well! when will he have done?" said one. "I suppose he thinks that it is all for him."

XLV.

WHAT is absolutely stupefying in the midst of all this, is the smiling aspect of the streets and the promenades. The constantly increasing emigration is only felt by the diminution in the number of depraved women and dissipated men; enough, however, remain to fill the cafés and give life to the boulevards. It might almost be said that Paris is in its normal state.

Every morning, from the Champs Elysées, Les Ternes, and Vaugirard, families are seen removing into the town, out of the way of the bombardment, as at the time when Jules Favre anathematised the barbarity of the Prussians. Some pass in cabs, others on foot, walking sadly, with their bedding and household furniture piled on a cart. If you question these poor people, they will all tell you of the shells from the Versailles batteries, destroying houses and killing women and children. What matters it? Paris goes her usual round of business and pleasure. The Commune suppresses journals and imprisons journalists. Monsieur Richardet, of the *National*, was marched off to prison yesterday, for the sole crime of having requested a passport of the savage Monsieur Rigault; the Commune thrusts the priests into cells, and turns out the young girls from the convents, imprisons Monsieur O'yan, one of the directors of the Seminary of St. Sulpice; hurls a warrant of arrest at Monsieur Tresca, who escapes; tries to capture Monsieur Henri Vrignault, who however, succeeds in reaching a place of safety; the Commune causes perquisitions to be made by armed men in the banking houses, seizes upon title deeds and money; has strong-boxes burst open by willing locksmiths; when the locksmiths are tired, the soldiers of the Commune help them with the butt-ends of their muskets. They do worse still, these Communists—they do all that the consciousness of supreme power can suggest to despots without experience; each day they send honest fathers of families to their death, who think they are suffering for the good cause, when they are only dying for the good pleasure of Monsieur Avrial and Monsieur Billioray. Well! and what is Paris doing all this time? Paris reads the papers, lounges, runs after the last news and ejaculates: "Ah! ah! they have put Amouroux into prison! The Archbishop of Paris has been transferred from the Conciergerie to Mazas! Several thousand francs have been stolen from Monsieur Denouille!

Diable! Diable!" And then Paris begins the same round of newspaper reading, lounging, and gossiping again. Nothing seems changed. Nothing seems interrupted. Even the proclamation of the famous Cluseret, who threatens us all with active service in the marching regiments, has not succeeded in troubling the tranquillity and indifference of the greater number of Parisians. They look on at what is taking place, as at a performance, and only bestow just enough interest upon it to afford them amusement. This evening the cannonading has increased; on listening attentively, we can distinguish the sounds of platoon-firing; but Paris takes its glass of beer tranquilly at the Café de Madrid and its Mazagran at the Café Riche. Sometimes, towards midnight, when the sky is clear, Paris goes to the Champs Elysées, to see things a little nearer, strolls under the trees, and smoking a cigar exclaims: "Ah! there go the shells." Then leisurely compares the roar of the battle of to-day to that of yesterday. In strolling about thus in the neighbourhood of the shells, Paris exposes itself voluntarily to danger; Paris is indifferent, and use is second nature. Then bed-time comes, Paris looks over the evening papers, and asks, with a yawn, where the devil all this will end? By a conciliation? Or the Prussians perhaps? And then Paris falls asleep, and gets up the next morning, just as fresh and lusty as if Napoleon the Third were still Emperor by the grace of God and the will of the French nation.

XLVI.

An insertion in the *Journal Officiel* of Versailles has justly irritated the greater part of the French press. This is the paragraph. "False news of the most infamous kind has been spread in Paris where no independent journal is allowed to appear."

From these few lines it may be concluded, that in the eyes of the Government of Versailles the whole of the Paris newspapers, whose editors have not deserted their posts, have entirely submitted to the Commune, and only think and say what the Commune permits them to think and say. This is an egregious calumny. No, thank heaven! The Parisian press has not renounced its independence, and if no account is taken (as is perfectly justifiable) of a heap of miserable little sheets which no sooner appear than they die, and of some few others edited by members of the Commune, one would be obliged to acknowledge, on the contrary, that since the 18th of March the great majority of journals have exhibited proofs of a proud and courageous independence. Each day, without allowing themselves to be intimidated, either by menaces of forcible suppression or threats of arrest, they have fearlessly told the members of the Commune their opinion without concealment or circumlocution. The French press has undoubtedly committed many offences during the last few years, and is not altogether irresponsible for the troubles which have overwhelmed the unhappy country; but reparation is being made for these offences in this present hour of danger, and the fearless attitude which it has maintained before these men of the Hôtel de Ville, atones nobly for the past. It has constituted itself judge; condemns what is condemnable, resists violence, endeavours to enlighten the masses. Sometimes too—and this is perhaps its greatest crime in the eyes of the Versailles Government—it permits itself to disapprove entirely of the acts of the National Assembly; some journals going as far as to insinuate that the Government is not altogether innocent of the present calamities. But what does this prove? That the press is no more the servant of the Assembly than it is the slave of the Commune; in a word, that it is free.

And what false news is this of which the *Journal Officiel* of Versailles complains, and against which it seems to warn us? Does it think it likely that we should be silly enough to give credence to the shouts of victory that are recorded each morning, on the handbills of the Commune? Does it suppose that we look upon the deputies as nothing but a race of anthropophagi who dine every day off Communists and Federals at the *tables d'hôte* of the Hôtel des Réservoirs? Not at all. We easily unravel the truth, from the entanglement of exaggerations forged by the men of the Hôtel de Ville; and it is precisely this just appreciation of things that we owe to those papers which the *Journal Officiel* condemns so inconsiderately.

But it is not of false news alone, probably, that the Versailles Assembly is afraid. It would not perhaps be sorry that we should ignore the real state of things, and I wager that if it had the power it would willingly suppress ill-informed journals—although they are not Communist the least in the world—who allow themselves to state that for six days the shells of Versailles have fallen upon Les Ternes, the Champs Elysées and the Avenue Wagram, and have already cost as many tears and as much bloodshed, as the Prussian shells of fearful memory.

XLVII.

WEDNESDAY, 12th April.—Another day passed as yesterday was, as to-morrow will be. The Versaillais attack the forts of Vanves and Issy and are repulsed. There is fighting at Neuilly, at Bagneux, at Asnières. In the town requisitions and arrests are being made. A detachment of National Guards arrives before the Northern railway-station. They inquire for the director, but director there is none. Embarrassing situation this. The National Guards cannot come all this way for nothing. Determined on arresting some one, they carry off M. Félix Mathias, head of the works, and M. Coutin, chief inspector. An hour later other National Guards imprison M. Lucien Dubois, general inspector of markets, in the depôt of the ex-Prefecture of Police. Here and there a few journalists are arrested without cause, to serve as examples; some priests are despatched to Mazas, among others M. Lartigues, *curé* of *Saint Leu*. Yesterday the following was placarded on the shut doors of the church at Montmartre:

> "Since priests are bandits and churches retreats where they have morally assassinated the masses, causing *France to cower beneath the clutches of the infamous Bonapartes, Favres, and Trochus*, the delegates of the stone masons at the ex-Prefecture of Police give orders that the church of Saint-Pierre (not Cinq-Pierres this time) shall be closed, and decrees the imprisonment of its priests and its *Frères Ignorantins*. Signed by Le Moussu."

To-day it is the turn of the church of Notre Dame de Lorette. A considerable number of worshippers had assembled in the holy place. The National Guards arrive, headed by men in plain clothes. Under the Empire such men were called spies. The women found praying are turned out, those who do not obey promptly enough, with blows. This done, the guards retire. What they had come there for is not known. But what we are certain of is, that they will begin again to-morrow in this same church, or in another. The days resemble each other as the children of an accursed family. What frightful catastrophe will break this shameful monotony?

XLVIII.

EH! What? It is impossible! Are your brains scattered? I speak figuratively, awaiting the time when they will be scattered in earnest. It must be some miserable jester who has worded, printed, and placarded this unconscionable decree. But no, it is in the usual form, the usual type. This is rather too much, Gentlemen of the Commune; it outsteps the bounds of the ridiculous; you count a little too much this time on the complicity of some of the population, and on the patience of others. Here is the decree:

THE COLUMN IN THE PLACE VENDÔME.

Erected by the first Napoleon to commemorate his German campaign of 1805.
An imitation of the Column of Trajan, at Rome, slightly taller.
It cost 1,500,000 francs!

"THE COMMUNE OF PARIS,

"Considering that the Imperial column of the Place Vendôme is a monument of barbarism, a symbol of brute force, of false glory, an encouragement of military spirit, a denial of international rights, a permanent insult offered by the conquerors to the conquered, a perpetual conspiracy against one of the great principles of the French Republic, namely: Fraternity,

"Decrees:

"*Sole article.*—The Colonne Vendôme is to be demolished."

Now I must tell you plainly, you are absurd, contemptible, and odious! This sorry farce outstrips all one could have imagined, and all that the Versailles papers said of you must have been true; for what you are doing now is worse than anything they could ever have dared to imagine. It was not enough to violate the churches, to suppress the liberties,—the liberty of writing, the liberty of speaking, the liberty of free circulation, the liberty of risking one's life or not. It was not enough that blood should be recklessly spilled, that women should be made widows and children orphans, trade stopped and commerce ruined; it was not enough that the dignity of defeat—the only glory remaining—should be swallowed up in the shameful disaster of civil war; in a word, it was not sufficient to have destroyed the present, compromised the future; you wish now to obliterate the past! Funereal mischief! Why, the Colonne Vendôme is France, and a trophy of its past greatness,—alas, at present in the shade—is not the monument, but the record of a victorious race who strode through the world conquering as they went, planting the tricolour everywhere. In destroying the Colonne Vendôme, do not imagine that you are simply overthrowing a bronze column surmounted by the statue of an emperor; you disinter the remains of your forefathers to shake their fleshless bones, and say to them, "You were wrong in being brave and proud and great; you were wrong to conquer towns, to win battles; you were wrong to astound the universe by raising the vision of France glorified. It is scattering to the wind the ashes of heroes! It is telling those aged soldiers, seen formerly in the streets (where are they now? Why do we meet them no longer? Have you killed them, or does their glory refuse to come in contact with your infamy?) It is telling the maimed soldiers of the Invalides, "You are but blockheads and brigands. So you have lost a leg, and you an arm! So much the worse for you idle scamps. Look on these rascals crippled for their country's honour!" It is like snatching from them the crosses they have won, and delivering them into the hands of the shameless street urchins, who will cry, "A hero! a hero!" as they cry "Thief! thief!" There is certainly purer and less costly grandeur than that which results from war and conquests. You are free to dream for your country a glory different to the ancient glory; but the heroic past, do not overthrow it, do not suppress it, now especially, when you have nothing with which to replace it, but the disgraces of the present. Yet, no! Complete your work, continue in the same path. The destruction of the Colonne Vendôme is but a beginning, be logical and continue; I propose a few decrees:

> "The Commune of Paris, considering that the Church of Notre Dame de Paris is a monument of superstition, a symbol of divine tyranny, an affirmation of fanaticism, a denial of human rights, a permanent insult offered by believers to atheists, a perpetual conspiracy against one of the great principles of the Commune, namely, the convenience of its members,
>
> "Decrees:

"The Church of Notre Dame shall be demolished."

What say you to my proposition? Does it not agree with your dearest desire? But you can do better and better: believe me you ought to have the courage of your opinions.

> "The Commune of Paris, considering that the Museum of the Louvre contains a great number of pictures, of statues, and other objects of art, which, by the subjects they represent, bring eternally to the mind of the people the actions of gods, and kings, and priests; that these actions indicated by flattering brush or chisel are often delineated in such a way as to diminish the hatred that priests, kings, and gods should

inspire to all good citizens; moreover, the admiration excited by the works of human genius is a perpetual assault on one of the great principles of the Commune, namely, its imbecility,

"Decrees:

"*Sole article.*—The Museum of the Louvre shall be burned to the ground."

Do not attempt to reply that in spite of the recollections of religion and despotism attached to these monuments you would leave Notre Dame and the Museum of the Louvre untouched for the sake of their artistic importance. Beware of insinuating that you would have respected the Colonne Vendôme had it possessed some merit as a work of art. You! respect the masterpieces of human art! Wherefore? Since when, and by what right? No, little as you may have been known before you were masters, you were yet known enough for us to assert that one of you—whom I will name: M. Lefrançais—wished in 1848 to set fire to the *Salon Carré*; there is another of you—whom I will also name: M. Jules Vallès—asserts that Homer was an old fool. It is true that M. Jules Vallès is Minister of Public Instruction. If you have spared Notre Dame and the Museum of the Louvre up to this moment, it is that you dared not touch them, which is a proof, not of respect but of cowardice.

Ah! our eyes are open at last! We are no longer dazzled by the chimerical hopes we nourished for a moment, of obtaining through you communal liberties. You did but adopt those opinions for the sake of misleading us, as a thief assumes the livery of a house to enter his master's room and lay hands on his money. We see you now as you are. We had hoped that you were revolutionists, too ardent, too venturous perhaps, but on the whole impelled by a noble intention; you are nothing but insurgents, insurgents whose aim is to sack and pillage, favoured by disturbances and darkness. If a few well-intentioned men were among you, they have fled in horror. Count your numbers, you are but a handful. If there still remain any among you, who have not lost all power of discriminating between justice and injustice, they look towards the door, and would fly if they dared. Yet this handful of furious fools governs Paris still. Some among us have been ordered to their death, and they have gone! How long will this last? Did we not surrender our arms? Can we not assemble, as we did a month ago near the Bank, and deal justice ourselves without awaiting an army from Versailles? Ah! we must acknowledge that the deputies of the Seine and the Maires of Paris, misled like ourselves, erred in siding with the insurrectionists. They wished to avert street fighting. Is the strife we are witnessing not far more horrible than that we have escaped? One day's struggle, and it would have ended. Yes, we were wrong to lay down our arms; but who could have believed—the excesses of the first few days seemed more like the sad consequences of popular effervescence than like premeditated crimes—who could have believed that the chiefs of the insurrection lied with such impudence as is now only too evident, and that before long the Commune would be the first to deprive us of the liberties it was its duty to protect and develope? The "Rurals" were right then,—they who had been so completely in the wrong in refusing to lend an attentive ear to the just prayers of a people eager for liberty, they were right when they warned us against the ignorance and wickedness of these men. Ah! were the National Assembly but to will it, there would yet be time to save Paris. If it really wished to establish a definite Republic, and concede to the capital of France the right, free and entire, of electing an independent municipality, with what ardour should we not rally round the legitimate Government! How soon would the Hôtel de Ville be delivered from the contemptible men who have planted themselves there. If the National Assembly could only comprehend us! If it would only consent to give Paris its liberty, and France its tranquillity, by means of honourable concessions!

XLIX.

The delegates of the League of the Republican Union of the Rights of Paris returned from Versailles to-day, the 14th April, and published the following reports:—

"Citizens,—The undersigned, chosen by you to present your programme to the Government of Versailles, and to proffer the good offices of the League to aid in the conclusion of an armistice, have the honour of submitting you an account of their mission.

"The delegates, having made known to Monsieur Thiers the programme of the League, he replied that as chief of the sole legal government existing in France he had not to discuss the basis of a treaty, but notwithstanding he was quite ready to treat with such persons whom he considered as representing Republican principles, and to acquaint them with the intentions of the chief of the executive power.

"It is in accordance with these observations, which denote, in fact, the true character of our mission, that Monsieur Thiers has made the following declarations on different points of our programme.

"Respecting the recognition of the Republic, Monsieur Thiers answers for its existence as long as he remains in power. A Republican state was put into his hands, and he stakes his honour on its conservation."

Ay! it is precisely that which will not satisfy Paris—Paris sighing for peace and liberty. We have all the most implicit faith in Thiers' honour. We are assured that the words, "French Republic" will head the white Government placards as long as he remains in power. But when Thiers is withdrawn from power—National Assemblies can be capricious sometimes—what assures us that we shall not fall victims to a monarchical or even an imperial restoration? Ghosts can appear in French history as well as in Anne Radcliffe's novels. To attempt to consider the elected members who sit at Versailles as sincere Republicans is an effort beyond the powers of our credulity. You see that Thiers himself dares not speak his thoughts on what might happen were he to withdraw from power. Thus we find ourselves, as before, in a state of transition, and this state of transition is just what appals us. We address ourselves to the Assembly, and ask of it, "We are Republican; are you Republican?" And the Assembly pretends to be deaf, and the deputies content themselves with humming under their breaths, some the royal tune of "The White Cockade," and others the imperial air of "Partant pour la Syrie." This does not quite satisfy us. It is true that Thiers says he will maintain the form of government established in Paris as long as he possibly can; but he only promises for himself, and it results clearly from all this that we shall not keep the Republic long, since its definite establishment depends in fact on the majority in the Assembly, while the Assembly is royalist, with a slight sprinkle of imperialism here and there. But let us continue the reading of the reports.

> "Respecting the municipal franchise of Paris, Monsieur Thiers declares that Paris will enjoy its franchise on the same conditions as those of the other towns, according to a common law, such as will be set forth by the Assembly of the representatives of all France. Paris will have the common right, nothing less and nothing more."

This again is little satisfactory. What will this common right be? What will the law set forth by the representatives of all France be worth? Once more we have the most entire confidence in Thiers. But have we the right to expect a law conformable to our wishes from an assembly of men who hold opinions radically opposed to ours on the point which is in fact the most important in the question—on the form of government?

> "Concerning the protection of Paris, now exclusively confided to

> the National Guards, Monsieur Thiers declares that he will proceed at once to the organization of the National Guard, but that cannot be to the absolute exclusion of the army."

In my personal opinion, the President is perfectly right here; but from the point of view which it was the mission of the delegates of the Republican Union to take, is not this third declaration as evasive as the preceding?

> "Respecting the actual situation and the means of putting an end to the effusion of blood, Monsieur Thiers declares that not recognising as belligerents the persons engaged in the struggle against the National Assembly, he neither can nor will treat the question of an armistice; but he declares that if the National Guards of Paris make no hostile attack, the troops of Versailles will make none either, until the moment, yet undetermined, when the executive power shall resolve upon action and commence the war."

Oh, words! words! We are perfectly aware that Thiers has the right to speak thus, and that all combatants are not belligerents. But what! Is it as just as it is legal to argue the point so closely, when the lives of so many men are at stake; and is a small grammatical concession so serious a thing, that sooner than make it one should expose oneself to all the horrible feelings of remorse that the most rightful conqueror experiences at the sight of the battle-field?

> "Monsieur Thiers adds: 'Those who abandon the contest, that is to say, who return to their homes and renounce their hostile attitude, will be safe from all pursuit.'"

Is Thiers quite certain that he will not find himself abandoned by the Assembly at the moment when he enters upon this path of mercy and forgiveness?

> "Monsieur Thiers alone excepts the assassins of General Lecomte and General Clément Thomas, who if taken will be tried for the crime."

And here he is undoubtedly right. We must have been blind indeed the day that this double crime failed to open our eyes to the true characters of the men who, if they did not commit it or cause it to be committed, made at least no attempt to discover the criminals!

> "Monsieur Thiers, recognising the impossibility for a great part of the population, now deprived of work, to live without the allotted pay, will continue to distribute that pay for several weeks longer.
> "Such, citizens, is, etc., etc."

This report is signed by A. Dessonnaz, A. Adam, and Bonvallet. Alas! we had foreseen what the result of the honourable attempt made by the delegates of the Republican Union would be. And this result proves that not only is the National Guard at war with the regular troops, but that a persistent opposition is also made by the National Assembly of Versailles to the most reasonable portion of the people of Paris. And yet the Assembly represents France, and speaks and acts only as she is commissioned to speak and act. The truth then is this,—Paris is republican and France is not republican; there is division between the capital and the country. The present convulsion, brought about by a group of madmen, has its source in this divergence of feeling. And what will happen? Will Paris, once more vanquished by universal suffrage, bend her neck and accept the yoke of the provincials and rustics? The right of these is incontestable; but will it, by reason of superiority of numbers, take precedence of our right, as incontestable as theirs? These are dark questions, which hold the minds of men in suspense, and which, in spite of our desire to bring the National Assembly over to our side, the greater part of whose members could not join us without betraying their trust, cause us to bear the intolerable tyranny of the men of the Hôtel de Ville, even while their sinister lucubrations inspire us with disgust.

L.

During this time the walls resound with fun. Paris of the street and gutter—Paris, Gavroche and blackguard, rolls with laughter before the caricatures which ingenious salesmen stick with pins on shutters and house doors. Who designed these wild pictures, glaringly coloured and common, seldom amusing and often outrageously coarse? They are signed with unknown names—pseudonyms doubtless; their authors, amongst whom it is sad to think that artists of talent must be counted, are like women, high born and depraved, mixing with their faces masked in hideous orgies.

These vile pictures with their infamous calumnies keep up and even kindle contempt and hatred in ignorant minds. Laughter is often far from innocent. But the passers-by think little of this, and are amused enough when they see Jules Favre's head represented by a radish, or the *embonpoint* of Monsieur Picard by a pumpkin. Where will all this unwholesome stuff be scattered in a few days? Flown away and dispersed. Eccentric amateurs will tear their hair at the impossibility of obtaining for their collections these frivolous witnesses of troubled times. I will make a few notes so as to diminish their despair as far as I am able.

A green soil and a red sky—In a black coffin is a half-naked woman, with a Phrygian cap on her head, endeavouring to push up the lid with all her might. Jules Favre, lean, small, head enormous, under lip thick and protruding, hair wildly flying like a willow in a storm, wearing a dress coat, and holding a nail in one hand and a hammer in the other, with his knee pressed upon the coffin-lid, is trying to nail it down, in spite of the very natural protestations of the half-naked woman. In the distance, and running towards them, is Monsieur Thiers, with a great broad face and spectacles, also armed with a hammer. Below is written: "If one were to listen to these accursed Republics, they would never die." Signed, Faustin.

Same author—Same woman. But this time she lies in a bed hung with red flags for curtains. Her shoulders a little too bare, perhaps, for a Republic, but she must be made attractive to her good friends the Federals. At the head of the bed a portrait of Rochefort; Rochefort is the favoured one of this lady, it seems. Were I he, I should persuade her to dress a little more decently. Three black men, in brigands' hats, their limbs dragging, and their faces distorted, approach the bed, singing like the robbers in Fra Diavolo: "Ad .... vance ... ad ... vance ... with ... pru ... dence ... !" The first, Monsieur Thiers, carries a heavy club and a dark lantern; Jules Favre, the second, brandishes a knife, and the third, carries nothing, but wears a peacock's feather in his hat, and ...... I have never seen Monsieur Picard, but they tell me that it is he.

The young Republic again, with shoulders bare and the style of face of a *petite dame* of the Rue Bossuet. She comes to beg Monsieur Thiers, cobbler and cookshop-keeper, who "finds places for pretenders out of employ, and changes their old boots for new at the most reasonable prices," to have her shoes mended. "Wait a bit! wait a bit!" says the cobbler to himself, "I'll manage 'em so as to put an end to her walking."

Here is a green monkey perched on the extreme height of a microscopic tribune. At the end of his tail he wears a crown; on his head is a Phrygian cap. It is Monsieur Thiers of course. "Gentlemen," says he, "I assure you that I am republican, and that I adore the vile multitude." But underneath is written: "We'll pluck the Gallic cock!" The author of this is also Monsieur Faustin. I have here a special reproach to add to what I have already said of these objectionable stupidities. I do not like the manner in which the author takes off Monsieur Thiers; he quite forgets the old and well-known resemblance of the chief of the executive power to Monsieur Prud'homme, or what is the same thing, to Prud'homme's inventor, Henri Monnier. One day Gil Perez the actor, met Henri Monnier on the Boulevard Montmartre. "Well, old fellow!" cried he, "are you back? When are you and I going to get at our practical jokes again?" Henri Monnier looked profoundly astonished; it was Monsieur Thiers!

The next one is signed Pilotel. Pilotel, the savage commissioner! He who arrested Monsieur Chaudey, and who pocketed eight hundred and fifteen francs found in Monsieur Chaudey's drawers. Ah! Pilotel, if by some unlucky adventure you were to succumb behind a barricade, you would cry like Nero: "Qualis artifex pereo!" But let us leave the author to criticise the work. A Gavroche, not the Gavroche of the *Misérables*, but the boy of Belleville, chewing tobacco like a Jack-tar, drunk as a Federal, in a purple blouse, green trousers, his hands in his pockets, his cap on the nape of his neck; squat, violent, and brutish. With an impudent jerk of the head he grumbles out: "I don't want any of your kings!" This coarse sketch is graphic and not without merit.

Horror of horrors! "Council of Revision of the Amazons of Paris," this next is called. Oh! if the brave Amazons are like these formidable monstrosities, it would be quite sufficient to place them in the first rank, and I am sure that not a soldier of the line, not a guardian of the peace, not a *gendarme* would hesitate a moment at the sight, but all would fly without exception, in hot haste and in agonised terror, forgetting in their panic even to turn the butt ends of their muskets in the air. One of these Amazons—but how has my sympathy for the amateurs of collections led me into the description of these creatures of ugliness and immodesty?—one of them . . . . but no, I prefer leaving to your imagination those Himalayan masses of flesh, and pyramids of bone—these Penthesileas of the Commune of Paris that are before me.

Ah! Here is choleric old "Father Duchesne" in a towering passion, with short legs, bare arms, and rubicund face, topped with an immense red cap. In one hand he holds a diminutive

Monsieur Thiers and stifles him as if he were a sparrow. Here, the drawing is not only vile, but stupid too.

This time we have the nude, and it is not the Republic, but France that is represented. If the Republic can afford to bare her shoulders, France may dispense with drapery entirely. She has a dove which she presses to her bosom. On one side is a portrait of Monsieur Rochefort. Again! Why this unlovely-looking journalist is a regular Lovelace. Finally, two cats (M. Jules Favre and M. Thiers) are to be seen outside the garret window with their claws ready for pouncing. "Poor dove!" is the tame inscription below the sketch.*

---

* As a power for the encouragement of virtue and the suppression of vice, caricature cannot be too highly estimated, though often abused. It is doubtful which exercises the greater influence, poem or picture. In England, perhaps, picture wields the greater power; in France, song. Yet, "let me write the ballads and you may govern the people," is an English axiom which was well known before pictures became so plentiful or so popular, or the refined cartoons of Mr. Punch were ever dreamt of. In Paris, where art-education is highly developed, fugitive designs seems to have, with but few exceptions, descended into vile abuse and indecent metaphor, the wildest invective being exhausted upon trivial matters—hence the failure.

The art advocates of the Commune, with but few exceptions, seem to have been of the most humble sort, inspired with the melodramatic taste of our Seven Dials or the New Cut, venting itself in ill-drawn heroic females, symbols of the Republic, clad in white, wearing either mural crowns or Phrygian caps, and waving red flags. They are the work of aspiring juvenile artists or uneducated men. I allude to art favourable to the Commune, and not that coëval with it, or the vast mass of pictorial unpleasantry born of gallic rage during the Franco-Prussian war, including such designs as the horrible allegory of Bayard, "Sedan, 1870," a large work depicting Napoleon III. drawn in a calèche and four, over legions of his dying soldiers, in the presence of a victorious enemy and the shades of his forefathers; and the well-known subject, so popular in photography, of "The Pillory," Napoleon between King William and Bismarck, also set in the midst of a mass of dead and dying humanity. Paper pillories are always very popular in Paris, and under the Commune the heads of Tropmann and Thiers were exhibited in a wooden vice, inscribed Pantin and Neuilly underneath. And, again, in another print, entitled "The Infamous," we have Thiers, Favre, and MacMahon, seen in a heavenly upper storey, fixed to stakes, contemplating a dead mother and her child, slain in their happy home, the wounds very sanguine and visible, the only

Next we find a Holy Family, by Murillo. Jules Favre, as Joseph, leads the ass by the reins, and a wet-nurse, who holds the Comte de Paris in her arms instead of the infant Jesus, is seated between the two panniers, trying to look at once like Monsieur Thiers and the Holy Virgin. The sketch is called "The Flight

remaining relict being a child of very tender years in an overturned cradle; beneath is the inscription "Their Works." Communal art seems also to have been very severe upon landlords, who are depicted with long faces and threadbare garments, seeking alms in the street, or flying with empty bags and lean stomachs from a very yellow sun, bearing the words "The Commune, 1871." Whilst as a contrast, a fat labourer, with a patch on his blouse, luxuriates in the same golden sunshine. As a sample of the better kind of French art, we give two fac-similes, by Bertal, from *The Grelot*, a courageous journal started during the Commune; it existed unmolested, and still continues. We here insert a fac-simile of a sketch called "Paris and his Playthings."

"What destruction the unhappy, spoiled, and ill-bred child whose name is Paris has done, especially of late!

"France, his strapping nurse, put herself in a passion in vain, the child would not listen to reason. He broke Trochu's arms, ripped up Gambetta, to see what there was inside. He blew out the lantern of Rochefort; as to Bergeret himself, he trampled him under foot.

"He has dislocated all his puppets, strewed the ground with the *débris* of his fancies, and he is not yet content.—'What do you want, you wretched baby?'—'I want the moon!' The old woman called the Assembly was right in refusing this demand.—'The moon, you little wretch, and what would you do with it if you had it?'—'I would pull it to bits, as I did the rest.'"

Further on will be found "Paris eating a General a day" (Chapter LXXVIII). Early in June, 1871 there appeared in the same journal "The International Centipede," "John Bull and the Blanche Albion." The Queen of England, clad in white, holding in her hands a model of the Palace of Westminster, and sundry docks, resists the approach of an interminable centipede, on which she stamps, vainly endeavouring to impede the progress of the coil of fire and blood approaching to soil and fire her fair robe; beside her stands John Bull, in a queer mixed costume, half sailor, with the smalls and gaiters of a coalheaver. He bears the Habeas Corpus Act under his arm, but stands aghast and paralysed, it never seeming to have occurred to the artist that this "Monsieur John Boule, Esquire," was well adapted by his beetle-crushers to stamp out the vermin. Perhaps, it is needless to add, that the snake-like form issues from a hole in distant Prussia, meandering through many nations, causing great consternation, and that M. Thiers is finishing off the French section in admirable style.

. . . . to Versailles." Oh! fie! fie! Messieurs the Caricaturists, can you not be funny without trenching on sacred ground?

We might refer to dozens more. Some date from the day when Paris shook off the Empire, and are so infamous that, by a natural reaction of feeling, they inspire a sort of esteem for those they try to make you despise; others, those which were seen by everyone during the siege, are less vile, because of the patriotic rage which originated them, and excused them; but they are as odious as they can be nevertheless. But the amateurs of collections who neglected to buy fly-sheets one by one as they appeared, must be satisfied with the above.

LI.

WHAT has Monsieur Courbet to do among these people? He is a painter, not a politician. A few beery speeches uttered at the Hautefeuille Café cannot turn his past into a revolutionary one, and an order refused for the simple reason that it is more piquant for a man to have his button-hole without ornament than with a slip of red ribbon in it, when it is well known that he disdains whatever every one else admires, is but a poor title to fame. To your last, Napoleon Gaillard!* To your paint-brushes, Gustave Courbet! And if we say this, it is not only from fear that the meagre lights of Monsieur Courbet are insufficient, and may draw the Commune into new acts of folly,—(though we scarcely know, alas! if there be any folly the Commune has left undone,)—but it is, above all, because we fear the odium and ridicule that the false politician may throw upon the painter. Yes! whatever may be our horror for the nude women and un-

---

* Gaillard Senior (a sort of Odger), cobbler of Belleville and democratic stump orator. Appointed, April 8, to the Presidency of the Commission of Barricades.

sightly productions with which Monsieur Courbet* has honoured the exhibitions of paintings, we remember with delight several, admirably true to nature, with sunshine and summer breezes playing among the leaves, and streams murmuring refreshingly over the pebbles, and rocks whereon climbing plants cling closely; and, besides these landscapes, a good picture here and there, executed, if not by the hand of an artist—for the word artist possesses a higher meaning in our eyes—at least by the hand of a man of some power, and we hate that this painter should be at the Hôtel de Ville at the moment when the spring is awakening in forest and field, and when he would do so much better to go into the woods of Meudon or Fontainebleau to study the waving of the branches and the eccentric twists and turns of the oak-tree's huge trunk, than in making answers to Monsieur Lefrançais — iconoclast in theory

---

* As a painter Courbet has been very diversely judged. He was the chief of the ultra-realistic school, and therefore a natural subject for the contempt and abuse of the admirers of "legitimate art." But his later use of the political power entrusted to him has drawn down upon him the wrath of an immense majority of the French public, which his artistic misdemeanours had scarcely touched. On the sixteenth of April he was elected a member of the Commune by the 6th arrondissement of Paris, and forthwith appointed Director of the Beaux Arts. Until this time his life had been purely professional, and consequently of mediocre interest for the general public. He was born at Ornans, department of the Doubs, in 1819, and received his primary instructions from the Abbé Gousset, afterwards Archbishop of Rheims. He first applied himself to the study of mathematics, painting the while, and apparently aiming at a fusion of both pursuits. He subsequently read for the bar for a short time, and, finally, adopting art as his sole profession, threw himself heart and soul into a Rénaissance movement as the apostle of a new style. The peculiarities of his manner soon brought him into notoriety, and a school of imitators grouped itself around him. His pride became a proverb. In 1870 he was offered the cross of the Legion of Honour, and refused it, arrogantly declaring that he would have none of a distinction given to tradesmen and ministers. The part he took in the destruction of the Colonne Vendôme is familiar to all readers of the English press. Three weeks after the fall of the Commune he was denounced by a Federal officer, and discovered at the house of a friend hiding in a wardrobe, and in September was condemned by the tribunal at Versailles to six months' imprisonment and a fine of 500 francs—a slight penalty that astonished everyone.

THE MODERN "EROSTRATE" GOURBET.

IN PROGRESS OF REMOVAL, JUNE 7. 1871.

only as yet—and to Monsieur Jules Vallès, who has read Homer in Madame Dacier's translation, or has never read it at all. That one should try a little of everything, even of politics, when one is capable of nothing else, is, if not excusable, at any rate comprehensible; but when a man can make excellent boots like Napoleon Gaillard, or good paintings like Gustave Courbet, that he should deliberately lay himself open to ridicule, and perhaps to everlasting execration, is what we cannot admit. To this Monsieur Courbet would reply: "It is the artists that I represent; it is the rights and claims of modern art that I uphold. There must be a great revolution in painting as in politics; we must federate too, I tell you; we'll decapitate those aristocrats, the Titians and Paul Veroneses; we'll establish, instead of a jury, a revolutionary tribunal, which shall condemn to instant death any man who troubles himself about the ideal—that king whom we have knocked off his throne; and at this tribunal I will be at once complainant, lawyer, and judge. Yes! my brother painters, rally around me, and we will die for the Commune of Art. As to those who are not of my opinion, I don't care the snap of a finger about them." By this last expression the friends of Monsieur Gustave Courbet will perceive that we are not without some experience of his style of conversation. Courbet, my master, you don't know what you are talking about, and all true artists will send you to old Harry, you and your federation. Do you know what an artistic association, such as you understand it, would result in? In serving the puerile ambition of one man—its chief, for there will be a chief, will there not, Monsieur Courbet?—and the puerile rancours of a parcel of daubers, without name and without talent. Artist in our way we assert, that no matter what painter, even had he composed works superior in their way to Courbet's "*Combat de Cerfs*" and "*Femme au Perroquet*," who came and said, "Let us federate," we would answer him plainly: "Leave us in peace, messieurs of the federation, we are dreamers and workers; when we exhibit or publish and are happy enough to meet with a man who will buy or print a few thousand copies of our work without reducing himself to beggary, we are happy. When that is done, we do not trouble ourselves much about our work; the indulgence of a few friends, and the indignation of a few fools, is all we ask or hope for. We federate? Why? With whom? If our work is bad, will the association with any society in the world make it good? Will the works of others gain anything by their association with ours? Let us go home, *messieurs les artistes*, let us shut our doors, let us say to our servants—if we have any—that we are at home to no one, and, after having cut our best pencil, or seized our best pen, let us labour in solitude, without relaxation, with no other thought than that of doing the best we can, with no higher judge than that of our own artistic conscience; and when the work is completed, let us cordially shake hands with those of our comrades who love us; let us help them, and let them bring help to us, but freely, without obligation, without subscriptions, without societies, and without statutes. We have nothing to do with these free-masonries, absurd when brought into the domain of intelligence, and in which two or three hundred people get together to do that, which some new-comer, however unknown his budding fame, would accomplish at a blow, in the face of all the associations in the world." This is what I should naïvely reply to Monsieur Courbet if he took it into his head to offer me any advice or compact whatsoever to sign.

The artists have done still better than we should; they have not answered at all, for one cannot call the " General Assembly of all the Artists in Design," presided over by Monsieur Gustave Courbet, and held on the 13th of April, 1871, in the great amphitheatre of the Ecole de Médecine, a real meeting of French artists. We know several celebrated painters, and we saw none of them there. The citizens Potier and Boulaix had been named secretaries. We congratulate them; for this high distinction may, perhaps, aid in founding their reputation, which was in great want of a basis of some kind. But there were some sculptors there, perhaps? We saw some long beards, beards that were quite unknown to us, and their owners may have been sculptors, perhaps. For Paris is a city of sculptors. But if artists were wanting, there were talkers enough. Have you ever remarked that there are no orators so indefatigable as those who have nothing to say? And the interruptions, the clamour, the apostrophising, more highly coloured than courteous! Such an overwhelming tumult was never heard:—

"No more jury!"
"Yes! yes! a jury! a jury!"
"Out with the reactionist!"
"Down with Cabanel!"
"And the women? Are the women to be on the jury?"
"Neither the women, nor the infirm."

And all the time there is Monsieur Gustave Courbet, the chairman, desperately ringing his bell for order, and launching some expressive exclamation from time to time. And the result of all this? Absolutely nothing at all! No! stop! There were a few statutes proposed—and every one amused himself immensely. "Well! so much the better," said one. "Every one laughed, and no harm was done to anybody."

We beg your pardon! There was a great deal of harm done—to Monsieur Courbet.

LII.

It is forbidden to cross the Place Vendôme, and naturally, walking there is prohibited too. I had been prowling about every afternoon for the last few days, trying to pass the sentinels of the Rue de la Paix, hoping that some lucky chance might enable me to evade the military order; all I got for my pains was a sharply articulated "*Passez au large!*" and I remained shut out.

To-day, as I was watching for a favourable opportunity, a *petite dame* who held up her skirts to show her stockings, which were as red as the flag of the Hôtel de Ville—out upon you for a female Communist!—approached the sentinel and addressed him with her most gracious smile. And oh, these Federals! The man in office forgot his duty, and at once began with the lady a conversation of such an intimate description, that for discretion's sake I felt myself obliged to take a slight turn to the left, and a minute later I had slipped into the forbidden Place.

A Place?—no, a camp it might more properly be called. Here and there are seen a crowd of little tents, which would be white if they were washed, and littered about with straw. Under the tents lie National Guards; they are not seen, but plainly heard, for they are snoring. You remember the absurd old bit of choplogic often repeated in the classes of philosophy? One might apply it thus: he sleeps well who has a good conscience; the Federals sleep well; ergo, the Federals have a good conscience. Guards walk to and fro with their pipes in their mouths. If I were to say that these honourable Communists show by their easy manner, gentlemanly bearing, and superior conversation, that they belong to the cream of Parisian society, you would perhaps be impertinent enough not to believe one word of what I said. I think it, therefore, preferable in every way to assert the direct contrary. There is a group of them flinging away their pay at the usual game of *bouchon*. "The Soldier's Pay and the Game of Cork" is the title that might be given by those who would write the history of the National Guard from the beginning of the siege to the present time. And if to the cork they added the bottle, they might pride themselves upon having found a perfect one. This is how it comes to pass. The wife is hungry, and the children are hungry, but the father is thirsty, and he receives the pay. What does he do? He is thirsty, and he must drink; one must think of oneself in this world. When he has satisfied his thirst, what remains? A few sous, the empty bottle, and the cork. Very good. He plays his last sou on the famous game, and in the evening, when he returns home, he carries to his family—what?—the empty bottle!

On the Place two barricades have been made, one across the Rue de la Paix, and the other before the Rue Castiglione. "Two formidable barricades," say the newspapers, which may be read thus: "A heap of paving stones to the right, and a heap of paving stones to the left." I whisper to myself that two small field-pieces, one on the place of the New Opera-house, and the other at the Rue de Rivoli, would not be long before they got the better of these two barricades, in spite of the guns that here and there display their long, bright cylinders.

The Federals have decidedly a taste for gallantry. About twenty women—I say young women, but not pretty women—are selling coffee to the National Guards, and add to their change a few ogling smiles meant to be engaging.

As to the Column, it has not the least appearance of being frightened by the decree of the Commune which threatens it with a speedy fall. There it stands like a huge bronze I, and the emperor is the dot upon it. The four eagles are still there, at the four corners of the pedestal, with their wreaths of immortelles, and the two red flags which wave from the top seem but little out of place. The column is like the ancient honour of France, that neither decrees nor bayonets can intimidate, and which in the midst of threats and tumult, holds itself aloft in serene and noble dignity.

LIII.

WHO would think it? They are voting. When I say "they are voting," I mean to say "they might vote;" for as for going to the poll, Paris seems to trouble itself but little about it. The

Commune, too, seems somewhat embarrassed. You remember Victor Hugo's song of the Adventurers of the Sea:

> "En partant du golfe d'Otrente
> Nous étions trente,
> Mais en arrivant à Cadix
> Nous n'étions que dix." *

The gentlemen of the Hôtel de Ville might sing this song with a few slight variations. The Gulf of Otranto was not their starting point, but the Buttes Montmartre; though to make up for it they were eighty in number. On arriving at C——, no, I mean, the decree of the Colonne Vendôme, they were a few more than ten, but not many. What charming stanzas in imitation of Victor Hugo might Théodore de Banville and Albert Glatigny write on the successive desertions of the members of the Commune. The first to withdraw were the *maires* of Paris, frightened to death at having been sent by the votes of their fellow-citizens into an assembly which was not at all, it appears, their ideal of a municipal council. And upon this subject Monsieur Desmarest, Monsieur Tirard, and their *adjoints* will perhaps permit me an unimportant question. What right had they to persuade their electors and the Friends of Order, to vote for the Commune of Paris if they were resolved to decline all responsibility when the votes had been given them? Their presence at the Hôtel de Ville, would it not have infused—as we hoped—a powerful spirit of moderation even in the midst of excesses that could even then be foretold? When they have done all they can to persuade people to vote, have they the right to consider themselves ineligible? In a word, why did they propose to us to elect the Commune of Paris if the Commune were a bad thing? and if it were a good thing, why did they refuse to take their part in it? Whatever the cause, no sooner were they

---

* On leaving the gulf of Otranto
There were thirty of us there,
But on arriving at Cadiz
There were no more than ten.

elected than they sent in their resignations. Then the hesitating and the timid disappeared one after another, not having the courage to continue the absurdity to the end. Add to all this the arrests made in its very bosom by the Assembly of the Hôtel de Ville itself, and you will then have an idea of the extent of the dilemma. A few days more and the Commune will come to an end for want of Communists, and then we shall cry, "Haste to the poll, citizens of Paris!" And the white official handbills will announce supplementary elections for Sunday, 16th of April.

But here comes the difficulty; there may be elections, but not the shadow of an elector. Of candidates there are enough, more than enough, even to spare; voting lists where the electors' names are inscribed; ballot-urns—no, ballot-boxes this time—to receive the lists; these are all to be found, but voters to put the lists into the ballot-boxes, to elect the candidates, we seek them in vain. The voting localities may be compared to the desert of Sahara viewed at the moment when not a caravan is to be seen on the whole extent of the horizon, so complete is the solitude wherever the eager crowd of voters was expected to hasten to the poll. Are we then so far from the day when the Commune of Paris, in spite of the numerous absentees, was formed—thanks to the strenuous efforts of the few electors left to us? Alas! At that time we had still some illusions left to us, whilst now.... Have you ever been at the second representation of a piece when the first was a failure? The first day there was a cram, the second day only the *claque* remained. People had found out the worth of the piece, you see. Nevertheless, though the place is peopled only with silence and solitude, the *claque* continues to do its duty, for it receives its pay. For the same reason one sees a few battalions marching to the poll, all together, in step, just as they would march to the fighting at the Porte Maillot; and as they return they cry, "Oh! citizens, how the people are voting! Never was such enthusiasm seen!" But behind the scenes,—I mean in the Hôtel de Ville,—authors and actors whisper to each other: "There is no doubt about it, it is a failure!"

LIV.

AND what has become of the Bourse? What are the brokers and jobbers saying and doing now? I ask myself this question for the first time, as in ordinary circumstances, the Bourse is of all sublunary things that which occupies me the least. I am one of those excessively stupid people, who have never yet been able to understand how all those black-coated individuals can occupy three mortal hours of every day, in coming and going beneath the colonnade of the "temple of Plutus." I know perfectly well that stockbrokers and jobbers exist; but if I were asked what these stockbrokers and jobbers do, I should be incapable of answering a single word. We have all our special ignorances. I have heard, it is true, of the *Corbeille*,* but I ingeniously imagined, in my simple ignorance, that this famous basket was made in wicker work, and crammed with sweet-scented leaves and flowers, which the gentlemen of the Bourse, with the true gallantry of their nation, made up into emblematical bouquets to offer to their lady friends. I was shown, however, how much I was deceived by a friend who enlightened me, more or less, as to what is really done in the Bourse in usual times, and what they are doing there now.

I must begin by acknowledging that in using the worn metaphor of the "temple of Plutus" just now, I knew little of what I was talking about.

The Bourse is not a temple; if it were it would necessarily be a church or something like one, and consequently would have been closed long ago by our most gracious sovereign, the Commune of Paris.

The Bourse, then, is open; but what is the good of that? you will say, for all those who haunt it now, could get in just as well

---

* A circular space in the great hall of the Bourse, enclosed with a railing, and in which the stockbrokers stand to take bids. It is nicknamed the basket (*corbeille*).

through closed doors and opposing railings; spectres and other supernatural beings never find any difficulty in insinuating themselves through keyholes and slipping between bars. Poor phantoms! Thanks to the weakness of our Government, which has neglected to put seals on the portals of the Bourse, they are under the obligation of going in and coming out like the most ordinary individuals; and a Parisian, who has not learned, by a long intimacy with Hoffmann and Edgar Poë, to distinguish the living from the dead, might take these ghosts of the money-market for simple *boursiers*. Thank heaven! I am not a man to allow myself to be deceived by specious appearances on such a subject, and I saw at once with whom I had to do.

On the grand staircase there were four or five of them, spectres lean as vampires who have not sucked blood for three months; they were walking in silence, with the creeping, furtive step peculiar to apparitions who glide among the yew-trees in churchyards. From time to time one of them pulled a ghost of a notebook from his ghost of a waistcoat-pocket, and wrote appearances of notes with the shadow of a pencil. Others gathered together in groups, and one could distinctly hear the rattling of bones beneath their shadowy overcoats. They spoke in that peculiar voice which is only understood by the *confrères* of the magi Eliphas Levy, and they recall to each other's mind the quotations of former days, Austrian funds triumphant, Government stock at 70 (*quantum mutata ab illâ!*), bonds of the city of Paris 1860-1869, and the fugitive apotheosis of the Suez shares. They said with sighs: "You remember the premiums? In former times there were reports made, in former times there were settling days at the end of the month, and huge pocket-books were so well filled, that they nearly burst; but now, we wander amidst the ruins of our defunct splendour, as the shade of Diomedes wandered amid the ruins of his house at Pompeii. We are of those who were; the imaginary quotations of shares that have disappeared, are like vain epitaphs on tombs, and we, despairing ghosts, we should die a second time of grief, if we were not allowed to appear to each other in this deserted palace, here to brood over our past financial glories!" Thus spoke the phantoms of the money market, and then added: "Oh! Commune, Commune, give us back our settling days?" From time to time a phantom, which still retains its haughty air, and in which we recognise a defunct of distinction, passes near them. In the days of Napoleon the Third and the Prussians this was a stockbroker; it passed along with a mass of documents under its arm,—as the father of Hamlet, rising from the grave, still wore his helmet and his sword. It enters the building, goes towards the *Corbeille*, shouts out once or twice, is answered only by an echo in the solitude, and then returns, saluted on his passage by his fellow-ghost. And to think that a little bombardment, followed by a successful attack, seven or eight houses set on fire by the Versailles shells, seven or eight hundred Federals shot, a few women blown to pieces, and a few children killed, would suffice to restore these desolate spectres to life and joy. But, alas! hope for them is deferred; the last circular of Monsieur Thiers announces that the great military operations will not commence for several days. They must wait still longer yet. The people who cross the Place de la Bourse draw aside with a sort of religious terror from the necropolis where sleep the three per cents. and the shares of the *Crédit Foncier;* and if the churches were not closed, more than one charitable soul would perhaps burn a candle to lay the unquiet spirits of these despairing jobbers.

LV.

THE game is played, the Commune is *au complet.* In the first arrondissement 21,260 electors are inscribed, and there were 9 voters! Monsieur Vésinier had 2 votes, and Monsieur Vésinier was elected. Monsieur Lacord—more clever still—has no votes at all, and, triumphing by the unanimity of his electors, Monsieur

Lacord will preside over the Commune of Paris in future. A very logical arrangement. It must be evident to all serious minds that the legislators of the Hôtel de Ville have promulgated *in petto* a law which they did not think it necessary to make known, but which exists nevertheless, and must be couched somewhat in the following terms:—" Clause 1st. The elections will not be considered valid, if the number of voters exceed a thousandth part of the electors entered.—Clause 2nd. Every candidate who has less than fifteen votes will be elected; if he has sixteen his election will be a matter of discussion." The poll is just like the game called, "He who loses gains, and he who gains loses;" and the probable advantages of such an arrangement are seen at once. Now let us do a bit of Communal reasoning. By whom was France led within an inch of destruction? By Napoleon the Third. How many votes did Napoleon the Third obtain? Seven millions and more. By whom was Paris delivered into the hands of the Prussians? By the dictators of the 4th September. How many votes did the dictators of the 4th September get for themselves in the city of Paris? More than three hundred thousand. *Ergo*, the candidates who obtain the greatest number of votes are swindlers and fools. The Commune of Paris cannot allow such abuses to exist; the Commune maintains universal suffrage—the grand basis of republican institutions—but turns it topsy-turvy. Michon has only had half a vote,—then Michon is our master!

Ah! you do not only make us tremble and weep, you make us laugh too. What is this miserable parody of universal suffrage? What is this farce of the will of the people being represented by a half a dozen electors? The unknown individual, who owes his triumph to the kindness of his concierge and his water-carrier, becomes a member of the Commune. I shall be governed by Vésinier, with Briosne and Viard as supporters. Do you not see that the few men, with any sense left, who still support you, have refused to present themselves as candidates, and that even amongst those who were mad enough to declare themselves eligible, there are some who dispute the validity of the elections? No; you see nothing of all this, or rather it suits you to be blind. What are right and justice to you? Let us reign, let us govern, let us decree, let us triumph. All is contained in that. Rogeard pleases us, so we'll have Rogeard. If the people won't have Rogeard, so much the worse for the people. Beautiful! admirable! But why don't you speak out your opinion frankly? There were some honest brigands (*par pari refertur*) in the Roman States who were perhaps no better than you are, but at least they made no pretension of being otherwise than lawless, and followed their calling of brigands without hypocrisy. When, by the course of various adventures, the band got diminished in numbers, they stuck no handbills on the walls to invite people to elect new brigands to fill up the vacant places; they simply chose among the vagabonds and such like individuals those, who seemed to them, the most capable of dealing a blow with a stiletto or stripping a traveller of his valuables, and the band, thus properly reinforced, went about its usual occupations. The devil! *Messieurs*, one must say what is what, and call things by their names. Let us call a cat a cat, and Pilotel a thief. The time of illusions is past; you need not be so careful to keep your masks on; we have seen your faces. We have had the carnival of the Commune, and now Ash-Wednesday is come. You disguised yourselves cunningly, *Messieurs*; you routed out from the old cupboards and corners of history the cast-off revolutionary rags of the men of '93; and, sticking some ornaments of the present fashion upon them,—waistcoats à la Commune and hats à la Fédération,—you dressed yourselves up in them and then struck attitudes. People perceived, it is true, that the clothes that were made for giants, were too wide for you pigmies; they hung round your figures like collapsed balloons; but you, cunning that you were, you said, "We have been wasted by persecution." And when, at the very beginning, some stains of blood were seen upon your old disguises; "Pay no attention," said you, "it is only the red flag we have in our pockets that is sticking out." And it happened that some few believed you. We ourselves, in the very face of all our suspicions, let ourselves be caught by the waving of your big Scaramouche sleeves, that were a great deal too long for your arms. Then you talked of such beautiful things: liberty, emancipation of workmen, association of the working-classes, that we listened and thought we would see you at your task before we condemned you utterly. And now we have seen you at your task, and knowing how you work, we won't give you any more work to do. Down with your mask, I tell you! Come, false Danton, be Rigault again, and let Sérailler's * face come out from behind that Saint Just mask he has on. You, Napoléon Gaillard, though you are a shoemaker, you are not even a Simon. Drop the Robespierre, Rogeard! Off with the trappings borrowed from the dark, grand days! Be mean, small, and ridiculous,—be yourselves; we shall all be a great deal more at our ease when you are despicable and we are despising you again.

Paris said to you yesterday just what I am telling you now. This almost general abstention of electors, compared with the eagerness of former times, is but the avowal of the error to which your masquerade has given rise. And what does it prove but the resolution to mix in your carnival no more? We see clearly through it now, I tell you, that the saturnalia is wearing to its end. In vain does the orchestra of cannon and mitrailleuses, under the direction of the conductor, Cluseret, play madly on and invite us to the fête. We will dance no more, and there is an end of it!

But it will be fatal to Paris if, after saying this, she sit satisfied. Contempt is not enough, there must be abhorrence too, and actual measures taken against those we abhor. It is not sufficient to neglect the poll, one abstains when one is in doubt, but now that we doubt no longer it is time to act. While wrongful work is being done, those that stand aside with folded arms become

---

* Sérailler, a member of the International, intrusted with a commission to London on behalf of the Central Committee to borrow cash for the daily pay of thirty sous to the National Guard.

accomplices. Think that for more than a fortnight the firing has not ceased; that Neuilly and Asnières have been turned into cemeteries; that husbands are falling, wives weeping, children suffering. Think that yesterday, the 18th of April, the chapel of Longchamps became a dependance—an extra dead-house—of the ambulances of the Press, so numerous were that day's dead. Think of the savage decrees passed upon the hostages and the refractory, those who shunned the Federates; of the requisitions and robberies; of the crowded prisons and the empty workshops; of the possible massacres and the certain pillage. Think of our own compromised honour, and let us be up and doing, so that those who have remained in Paris during these mournful hours, shall not have stood by her only to see her fall and die.

LVI.

PARIS! for once I defy you to remain indifferent. You have had much to bear during these latter days; it has been said to you, that you should kneel in your churches no more, and you have not knelt there; that the newspapers that pleased you, should be read no more, and you have not read them. You have continued to smile—with but the tips of your lips, it is true—and to promenade on the boulevards. But now comes stalking on that which will make you shudder indeed! Do you know what I have just read in the *Indépendance Belge?* Ah! poor Paris, the days of your glory are past, your ancient fame is destroyed, the old nursery rhyme will mock you, "*Vous n'irez plus au Bois, vos lauriers sont coupés.*" * This is what has happened; you are supplanted on the throne of fashion. The world, uneasy about the form of bonnet to be worn this sorrowful year, and seeing you occupied with your internal discords, anxiously turned to London for help, and London henceforth

---

* The refrain of a nursery song,—

"Go no more to the wood, for all the laurels are cut."

dictates to all the modistes of the universe. City of desolation, I pity you! No more will you impose your sovereign laws, concerning *Suivez-moi-jeune-homme* * and dog-skin gloves. No more will your boots and shirt-collars reach, by the force of their reputation, the sparely-dressed inhabitants of the Sandwich Islands. And, deepest of humiliations, it is your old rival, it is your tall and angular sister, it is the black city of London, who takes your glittering sword and transforms it into a policeman's baton of wood! You are destined to see within your walls—if any walls remain to you—your own wives and daughters clog their dainty tread with encumbrances of English leather, flatten their heads beneath mushroom-shaped hats, surround themselves with crinoline and flounces, and wear magenta, that abominable mixture of red and blue which always filled your soul with horror. Then, to increase the resemblance of your Parisian women with the Londoners or Cockneys (for it is time you learnt the fashionable language of England), your dentists will sell them new sets of teeth, called insular sets, which can be fitted over their natural front teeth, and will protrude about a third of an inch beyond the upper lip. And they will have corsets offered them whose aim is to prolong the waist to the farthest possible limits and compress the fairest forms—a fact, for report says they lace in London, whilst here we have nearly abandoned the corset. Well, my Paris, do you tremble and shiver? Oh! when those days of horror come to pass; when you see that not only have you forfeited your pride, but your vanity too; when you are convinced that the Commune has not only rendered you odious, but ridiculous as well; ah! then, when you wear bonnets that you have not invented, how deeply will you regret that you did not rebel on that day, when some of the best of your citizens were put *au secret* in the cells of Mazas prison!†

---

* The long floating ends of the neck ribbons.
† The Parisian play-writer's English exhibits all the typical peculiarities noted above. We have our ideal, if not typical, Frenchman, little less truthful perhaps—taken from refugees and excursionists,

LVII.

I HAVE just heard or read a touching story; and here it is as I remember it. In the Faubourg Saint Antoine lives a community of women with whom the aged of the poor find shelter; those who have become infirm, or have dropped into helpless childishness, whether men or women, are received there without question or payment. There they are lodged, fed and clothed, and humbly prayed for.

Last evening, sleep was just beginning to reign in the little community. The old people had been put to rest, each Little Sister had done her duty and was asleep, when the report of a gun resounded at the house-door. You can imagine the startings and the terror. The Little Sisters of the poor are not accustomed to have such noises in their ears, and there was a tumult and hubbub such as the house had never known, while they hurriedly rose, and the old people stared at each other from their white beds in the long dormitories. When the house-door was got open, a party of men, with a menacing look about them, strode in with their guns and swords, making a horrible racket. One of them was the chief, and he had a great beard and a terrible voice. All the Little Sisters gathered in a trembling crowd about the superior.

"Shut the doors," cried the captain, "and if one of these women attempt to escape—one, two, three, fire!" Then the Good Mother—that is the Little Sisters' name for their superior—made a step forward and said, "What do you wish, messieurs?"

"Citizens, *sacrebleu!*"

The Good Mother crossed herself and repeated, "What do you wish, my brothers?"

from the close-cropped, dingy denizen of Leicester Square; our tourist suits, heavy pedestrian boots, "wide-awakes," and faded fashions, used up in travel—all these things are put down to insular peculiarities.

FEDERAL VISIT to THE LITTLE SISTERS OF THE POOR.

Now, if Citizen Rigault, who put Monseigneur Darboy down so wittily, had been there, how briskly he would have told the stupid woman that these were National Guards, and not brothers, before her. But even Rigault cannot be everywhere at once. "We want to inspect your funds," replied the officer. The Good Mother signed to him to follow, opened a cupboard, pulled out a drawer, and said, "This is what we have." The box had twenty-two francs in it. "Is that all?" asked the captain in a suspicious tone.—"Nothing more, monsieur," she said; "besides, you can look everywhere for yourselves." So the National Guards spread through the house, opened the rooms, searched the cupboards and chests, and came at last, without having found anything, to the dormitories, where the Little Sisters' old nurselings were lying. Every head was upraised in astonishment and fear, and all, stammering and trembling, began jabbering out at once, "What are you doing here? You are not going to hurt the good Sisters? It's a shame! It's infamous! Go away! It's cowardly! My good monsieur, what will become of us if you take them away?" The old women were furious, and the old men in lamentations. Officer and men scarcely expected such a scene, and began to hesitate in their search. "Well, well, my good people," said the officer, who had been the most violent, and had now softened down, "we won't take the Little Sisters away, and we won't hurt them either. There, there—are you satisfied?" —and the men began to go downstairs again. — "My sister, you have not shut your drawer," said the captain, as he passed the cupboard.—"That is true, monsieur; I am not in the habit of doing it. In our house, you see, it is quite useless."—"Never mind, shut it to-day at any rate. How can I know all the men I have about me?" And as he spoke, the captain turned back, shut the drawer himself, without touching the contents, and gave the key to the superior. He seemed quite ill at ease, and got out at last, "We didn't know . . . . if we had known it was like this . . . . you see we had been told . . . . yes, yes, it is very good of you to take care of those poor old folks upstairs." Now that the man seemed embarrassed and showed some kindliness in his manner, a Little Sister who had quite got over her fear, went up to him and told him how frightened they had been for a whole month past; that they had been told that the Reds wanted to take their house. Ah! it was horrible! But monsieur would protect them, would he not?

"That I will," bravely answered the captain, "give me your hand. And now, if any one wants to harm you, he will have me to deal with first."

A few minutes later, the National Guards were gone, the Little Sisters and the old nurslings were at rest again, and the house was just as silent and peaceful as if it were no abominable resort of plotters and conspirators.

But if I had been the Commune of Paris, would I not have shot that captain!

LVIII.

THE people of the Hôtel de Ville said to themselves, "All our fine doings and talking come to nothing, the delegate Cluseret and the commandant Dombrowski send us the most encouraging despatches in vain, we shall never succeed in persuading the Parisian population, that our struggle against the army of Versailles is a long string of decisive victories; whatever we may do, they will finish by finding out that the federate battalions gave way strangely in face of the iron-plated mitrailleuses the day before yesterday at Asnières, and it would be difficult to make them believe that this village, so celebrated for fried fish and Paris Cockneys, is still in our possession, unless we can manage to persuade them that although we have evacuated Asnières, we still energetically maintain our position there. The fact is, affairs are taking a tolerably bad turn for us. How are we to get over the inconvenience of being vanquished? What are we to do to destroy the bad impression produced by our doubtful triumphs?" And thereupon the members of the Commune fell to musing. "Parbleu!" cried they, after a few moments' reflection—the elect of Paris are capable of more in a single second than all the deputies of the National Assembly in three years—" Let decrees, proclamations, and placards be prepared. By what means did we succeed in imposing on the donkeys of Paris? Why, by decrees, by proclamations, by placards. Courage, then, let us persevere. Ha! the traitors have taken the château of Bécon, and have seized upon Asnières. What matters! quick, eighty pens and eighty inkstands. To work, men of letters.; painters and shoemakers, to work! Franckel, who is Hungarian; Napoléon Gaillard, who is a cobbler; Dombrowski, who is a Pole; and Billioray, who writes *omelette* with an h, will make perhaps rather a mess of it. But, thank heaven! We have amongst us Félix Pyat, the great dramatist; Pierre Denis, who has made such bad verses that he must write good prose; and lastly, Vermorel, the author of '*Ces Dames*,' a little book illustrated with photographs for the use of schools, and '*Desperanza*,' a novel which caused Gustave Flaubert many a nightmare. To work, comrades, to work! We have been asked for a long time what we understand by the words—*La Commune*. Tell them, if you know. Write it, proclaim it, and we will placard it. Even if you don't know, tell them all the same; the great art of a good cook consists in making jugged hare without hare of any kind." And this is why there appeared this morning on the walls an immense placard, with the following words in enormous letters: "Declaration to the French people."

Twenty days ago a long proclamation, which pretended to express and define the tendencies of the revolution of the eighteenth of March, would perhaps have had some effect. To-day we have awaked from many illusions, and the finest phrases in the world will not overcome our obstinate indifference. Let us, however, read and note.

"In the painful and terrible conflict which once more imposes upon Paris the horrors of the siege and the bombardment,

VERMOREL,* DELEGATE OF PUBLIC SAFETY.

* He was born in 1841, in the department of the Rhône. His education was completed very early. At the age of twenty he was engaged on two journals of the opposition, *La Jeune France*, and *La Jeunesse*. These papers were soon suppressed, and their young contributor was imprisoned for three months. In 1864 he became one of the staff of the *Presse*, whence he passed to the *Liberté* in 1866. Two years later he founded the *Courrier Français*; but from the multiplicity of fines imposed upon it, and from the imprisonment of its founder, the new journal expired very shortly. After a year's incarceration at Sainte-Pélagie, Vermorel was engaged on the *Réforme*, which continued to appear until the fall of the Empire. During the siege he served as a private in the National Guard. He became a member of the Committee of Justice under the Commune, and was one of those who, at its fall, neither deserted nor disgraced it. He is reported to have mounted a barricade armed only with a cane, crying "I come here to die and not to fight." His mother obtained permission to transport his remains to Venice.

"which makes French blood flow, which causes our brothers, our wives, our children, to perish, crushed by shot and shell, it is urgent that public opinion should not be divided, that the national conscience should not be troubled."

That's right! I entirely agree with you; it is undoubtedly very urgent that public opinion should not be divided. But let us see what means you are going to take to obtain so desirable a result.

"Paris and the whole nation must know what is the nature, the reason, the object of the revolution which is now being accomplished."

Doubtless; but if that be indispensable to-day, would it have been less useful on the very first day of the revolution; we do not see why you have made us wait quite so long for it.

"The responsibility of the mourning, the suffering, and the misfortunes of which we are the victims should fall upon those who, after having betrayed France and delivered Paris to the foreigner, pursue with blind obstinacy the destruction of the capital, in order to bury under the ruins of the Republic and of Liberty the double evidence of their treason and their crime."

Heigho! what a phrase! These clear and precise expressions, that throw so much light on the gloom of the situation, are these yours, Félix Pyat? Did the Commune say "*Pyat Lux!*" Or were they yours, Pierre Denis? Or yours, Vermorel? I particularly admire the double evidence buried under the ruins of the Republic. Happy metaphor!

"The duty of the Commune is to affirm and determine the aspirations and the views of the population of Paris; to fix precisely the character of the movement of the 18th of March, misunderstood, misinterpreted, and vilified by the men who sit at Versailles."

Ah, yes, that is the duty of the Commune, but for heaven's sake don't keep us waiting, you see we are dying with impatience.

> "Once more, Paris labours and suffers for the whole of France, and by her combats and her sacrifices prepares the way for intellectual, moral, administrative and economic regeneration, glory and prosperity."

That is so true that since the Commune existed in Paris, the workshops are closed, the factories are idle, and France, for whom the capital sacrifices herself, loses something like fifty millions a day. These are facts, it seems to me; and I don't see what the traitors of Versailles can say in reply.

"What does Paris demand?"

Ah! yes, what does she ask?. Truly we should not be sorry to know. Or rather, what do you ask; for in the same way as Louis le Grand had the right to say, "The State, I am the State," you may say "Paris, we are Paris."

> "Paris demands the recognition and the consolidation of the Republic, the only form of government compatible with the rights of the people, and the regular and free development of society."

This once you are right. Paris demands the Republic, and must yearn for it eagerly indeed, since neither your excesses nor your follies have succeeded in changing its mind.

> "It demands the absolute entirety of the Commune extended to all the localities of France, ensuring to everyone the integrity of its rights, and to every Frenchman the free exercise of his faculties and abilities as man, citizen, and workman. The rights of the Commune should have no other limit but the equal rights of all other Communes adhering to the contract, an association which would assure the unity of France."

This is a little obscure. What I understand is something like this. You would make France a federation of Communes, but what is the meaning of words "adherence to the contract?" You admit then that certain Communes might refuse their adhesion. In that case what would be the situation of these rebels? Would you leave them free? Or would you force them to obey the conventions of the majority? Do you think it would be sufficient, in the case of such a town as Pezenas, for example, refusing to adhere, that the association would be incomplete? That is to say, that French unity would not exist? Are you very sure about Pezenas? Who tells you that Pezenas may not have its own idea of independence, and that we may not hear presently that it has elected a duke who raises an army and coins money. Duke of Pezenas! that sounds well. Remember, also, that many other localities might follow the example of Pezenas, and perhaps in order to insure the entirety of the Commune, it might have been wise to have asked them if they wanted it. Now, what do you understand by "localities?" Marseilles is a locality; an isolated farm in the middle of a field is also a locality. So France would be divided into an infinite number of Communes. Would they agree amongst themselves, these innumerable little states? Supposing they are agreed to the contract, it is not impossible that petty rivalries should lead to quarrels, or even to blows; an action about a party-wall might lead to a civil war. How would you reduce the recalcitrant localities to reason? for even supposing that the Communes have the right to subjugate a Commune, the disaffected one could always escape you by declaring that it no longer adheres to the social compact. So that if this secession were produced not only by the vanity of one or more little hamlets, but by the pride of one or more great towns, France would find herself all at once deprived of her most important cities. Ah! messieurs, this part of your programme certainly leaves something to be desired, and I recommend you to improve it, unless indeed you prefer to suppress it altogether.

"The inherent rights of the Commune are 'the vote of the

Communal budget, the levying and the division of taxes, the direction of the local services, the organisation of the magistrature, of the police, and of education, and of the administration of the property belonging to the Commune.'"

This paragraph is cunning. It does not seem so at first sight, but look at it closely, and you will see that the most Machiavellic spirit has presided over its production. The ability consists in placing side by side with the rights which incontestably belong to the Commune, other rights which do not belong to it the least in the world, and in not appearing to attach more importance to one than to the other, so that the reader, carried away by the evident legitimacy of many of your claims, may say to himself, " Really *all* that is very just." Let us unravel if you please this skein of red worsted so ingeniously tangled. The vote of the Communal budget, receipts and expenses, the levying and division of taxes, the administration of the Communal property, are rights which certainly belong to the Commune; if it had not got them it would not exist. And why do they belong to it? Because it alone could know what is good for it in these matters, and could come to such decision upon them, as it thought fit, without injuring the whole country. But it is not the same as regards measures concerning the magistracy, the police, and education. Well, suppose one fine day a Commune should say, "Magistrates? I don't want any magistrates; these black-robed gentry are no use to me; let others nourish these idlers, who send brave thieves and honest assassins to the galleys; I love assassins and I honour thieves, and more, I choose that the culprits should judge the magistrates of the Republic." Now, if a Commune were to say that, or something like that, what could you answer in reply? Absolutely nothing; for, according to your system, each locality in France has the right to organise its magistracy as it pleases. As regards the police and education, it would be easy to make out similar hypotheses, and thus to exhibit the absurdity of your Communal pretensions. Should a Commune say, " No person shall be arrested in future, and it is prohibited under pain of death to learn by heart the fable of the wolf and the fox." What could you say to that? Nothing, unless you admitted that you were mistaken just now in supposing, that the integrity of the Commune ought to have no other limit but the right of equal independence of all the other Communes. There exists another limit, and that is the general interests of the country, which cannot permit one part of it to injure the rest, by bad example or in any other way; the central power alone can judge those questions where a single absurd measure—of which more than one "locality" may probably be guilty—might compromise the honour or the interests of France; the magistracy, the police, and education, are evidently questions of that nature.

The other rights of the Commune are, always be it understood, according to the declaration made to the French people:

- "The choice by election or competition; with the responsibility and the permanent right of control over magistrates and communal functionaries of every class;
- "The absolute guarantee of individual liberty, of liberty of conscience, and of liberty of labour;
- "The permanent participation of the citizens in Communal affairs by the free manifestations of their opinions, and the free defence of their interests: guarantees to this effect to be given by the Commune, the only power charged with the surveillance and the protection of the full and just exercise of the rights of meeting and publicity;
- "The organisation of the city defences and of the National Guard, which elects its own officers, and alone ensures the maintenance of order in the city."

With regard to the affirmation of these rights we may repeat that which we have said above, that some of them really belong to the Commune, but that the greater part of them do not.

" Paris desires nothing more in the way of local guarantees, on

> condition, let it be understood, of finding in the great central administration . . ."

Notice that they do not say "government," but it would be nearly the same under another name, would it not?

> ". . . In the great central administration appointed by the federated Commune the realisation and the practice of the same principles."

That is to say, in other words, that Paris will consent willingly to be of the same opinion as others, if all the world is of the same opinion as itself.

> "But, thanks to its independence, and profiting by its liberty of action, Paris reserves to itself the right of effecting, as it pleases, the administrative and economic reforms demanded by the population; to create proper institutions for the development and propagation of instruction, production, commerce, and credit; to universalize power and property, . . ."

Whew! Universalize property! Pray what does that mean, may I ask? Communalism here presents a singular likeness to Communism!

> ". . . According to the necessities of the moment, the desire of those interested, and the lessons furnished by experience:
> "Our enemies deceive themselves or the country when they accuse Paris of wishing to impose its will or its supremacy on the rest of the nation, and to pretend to a dictatorship which would be a positive offence against the independence and the sovereignty of the other Communes:
> "They deceive themselves, or they deceive the country, when they accuse Paris of desiring the destruction of French unity, constituted by the Revolution amid the acclamations of our fathers hurrying to the Festival of the Federation from all points of ancient France:

> "Political unity as imposed upon us up to the present time by the empire, the monarchy, and parliamentarism, is nothing more than despotic centralization, whether intelligent, arbitrary, or onerous.
>
> "Political unity, such as Paris demands, is the voluntary association of all local initiatives, the spontaneous and free co-operation of individual energies with one single common object—the well-being and the security of all.
>
> "The Communal revolution, inaugurated by the popular action of the 18th of March, ushers in a new era of experimental, positive, and scientific politics."

Do you not think that during the last paragraphs the tone of the declaration is somewhat modified? It would seem as though Felix Pyat had become tired, and handed the pen to Pierre Denis or to Delescluze,—after Communalism comes socialism.

> "Communal revolution is the end of the old governmental and clerical world, of militarism, of officialism (this new editor seems fond of words ending in ism), of exploitation, of commission, of monopolies, and of privileges to which the proletariat owes his thraldom, and the country her misfortunes and disasters."

Of course there is nothing in the world that would please me better; but if I were very certain that Citizen Rigault did not possess an improved glass enabling him to observe me from a distance of several miles, without leaving his study or his armchair, if I were very certain that Citizen Rigault could not read over my shoulder what I am writing at this moment, I might perhaps venture to insinuate, that the revolution of the 18th of March appears to me to be, at the present moment, the apotheosis of most of the crimes which it pretends to have suppressed.

> "Let then our grand and beloved country, deceived by falsehood and calumnies, be reassured!"

Well, in order that she may be reassured there is only one thing to be done,—be off with you!

> "The struggle going on between Paris and Versailles is one of those which can never be terminated by deceitful compromises. There can be no doubt as to the issue. (Oh, no! there is no doubt about it.) Victory, pursued with indomitable energy by the National Guard, will remain with principle and justice.
> "We ask it of France."

Where is the necessity, since you have the indomitable energy of the National Guard?"

> "Convinced that Paris under arms possesses as much calmness as bravery . . ."

You will find that a very difficult thing to persuade France to believe.

> ". . . That it maintains order with equal energy and enthusiasm . . ."

Order? No doubt, that which reigned at Warsaw; the order that reigned on the day after the 2nd of December.

> ". . . That it sacrifices itself with as much judgment as heroism . . ."

Yes; the judgment of a man who throws himself out of a fourth-floor window to prove that his head is harder than the paving-stones.

> ". . . That it is only armed through devotion for the glory and liberty of all—let France cause this bloody conflict to cease!"

She'll cause it to cease, never fear, but not in the way you understand it.

"It is for France to disarm Versailles . . ."

Up to the present time she has certainly done precisely the contrary.

"... by the manifestations of her irresistible will. As she will be partaker in our conquests, let her take part in our efforts, let her be our ally in this conflict, which can only finish by the triumph of the Communal idea, or the ruin of Paris."

The ruin of Paris! That is only, I suppose, a figurative expression.

"For ourselves, citizens of Paris, it is our mission to accomplish the modern revolution, the grandest and most fruitful of all those that have illuminated history.

"Our duty is to struggle and to conquer!

"THE COMMUNE OF PARIS."

Such is this long, emphatic, but often obscure declaration. It is not wanting, however, in a certain eloquence; and, although frequently disfigured by glaring exaggerations, it contains here and there some just ideas, or at least, such as conform to the views of the great majority. Will it destroy the bad effect produced by the successive defeats of the Federals at Neuilly and at Asnières? Will it produce any good feeling towards the Commune in the minds of those who are daily drawing farther and farther from the men of the Commune? No; it is too late. Had this proclamation been placarded fifteen or twenty days sooner, some parts of it might have been approved and the rest discussed. To-day we pass it by with a smile. Ah! many things have happened during the last three days. The acts of the Commune of Paris no longer allow us to take its declarations seriously, and we look upon its members as too mad—if not worse—to believe that by any accident they can be reasonable. These men have finished by rendering detestable whatever good there originally was in their idea.

LIX.

We have a court-martial; it is presided over by the citizen Rossel, chief of the grand staff of the army. It has just condemned to death the Commandant Girod, who refused to march against the "enemy." The Executive Committee, however, has pardoned Commandant Girod. Let us look at this matter a little. If the Executive Committee occupies its time in undoing what the court-martial has done, I can't quite understand why the executive has instituted a court-martial at all. If I were a member of the latter I should get angry. "What! I should say, they instal me in the hall where the courts-martial are held, they appoint guards to attend upon me, and my president has the right to say, 'Guards, remove the prisoner.' In a word, they convert me into something which resembles a judge as much as a parody can resemble the work burlesqued, and when I, a member of the court-martial, desire to take advantage of the rights that have been conferred upon me, and order the Commandant Girod to be shot, they stand in the way of justice, and save the life of him I have condemned. This is absurd! I had a liking for this commandant, and I wished him to die by my hands."

Never mind, court-martial, take it coolly; you will have your revenge before long. At this moment there are at least sixty-three ecclesiastics in the prisons of Mazas, the Conciergerie, and La Santé. Although they are not precisely soldiers, they will be sent before you to be judged, and you may do just what you like with them, without any fear of the executive commission interposing its veto. The refractory also will give you work to do, and against them you can exercise your pleasure. As to the Commandant Girod, his is a different case, you understand. He is the friend of citizen Delescluze. The members of the Commune have not so many friends that they can afford to have any of them suppressed. But don't be downcast; a dozen priests are well worth a major of the National Guard.

LX.

It is precisely because the men that the Commune sends to the front, fight and die so gloriously, that we feel exasperated against its members. A curse upon them, for thus wasting the moral riches of Paris! Confusion to them, for enlisting into so bad a service, the first-rate forces which a successful revolt leaves at their disposal. I will tell you what happened yesterday, the 22nd of April, on the Boulevard Bineau; and then I think you will agree with me that France, who has lost so much, still retains some of the bright, dauntless courage which was her pride of old.

A trumpeter, a mere lad of seventeen, was marching at the head of his detachment, which had been ordered to take possession of a barricade that the Versailles troops were supposed to have abandoned. When I say, "he marched," I am making a most incorrect statement, for he turned somersets and executed flying leaps on the road, far in advance of his comrades, until his progress was arrested by the barricade; this he greeted with a mocking gesture, and then, with a bound or two, was on the other side. There had been some mistake, the barricade had not been abandoned. Our young trumpeter was immediately surrounded by a pretty large number of troops of the line, who had lain hidden among the sacks of earth and piles of stones, in the hope of surprising the company which was advancing towards them. Several rifles were pointed at the poor boy, and a sergeant said: "If you move a foot, if you utter a sound, you die!"—The lad's reply was to leap to the highest part of the barricade and cry out, with all the strength of his young voice, "Don't come on! They are here!" Then he fell backwards, pierced by four balls, but his comrades were saved!

LXI.

ANOTHER, and a sadder scene happened in the Avenue des Ternes. A funeral procession was passing along. The coffin, borne by two men, was very small, the coffin of a young child. The father, a workman in a blouse, walked behind with a little knot of other mourners. A sad sight, but the catastrophe was horrible. Suddenly a shell from Mont Valérien fell on the tiny coffin, and, bursting, scattered the remains of the dead child upon the living father. The corpse was entirely destroyed, with the trappings that had surrounded it. Massacring the dead! Truly those cannons are a wonderful, a refined invention!

LXII.

AT last the unhappy inhabitants of Neuilly are able to leave their cellars. For three weeks, they have been hourly expecting the roofs of their houses to fall in and crush them; and with much difficulty have managed during the quieter moments of the day to procure enough to keep them from dying of starvation. For three weeks they have endured all the terrors, all the dangers of battle and bombardment. Many are dead—they all thought themselves sure to die. Horrible details are told. A little past Gilet's restaurant, where the omnibus office used to be, lived an old couple, man and wife. At the beginning of the civil war, two shells burst, one after another, in their poor lodging, destroying every article of furniture. Utterly destitute, they took refuge in the cellar, where after a few hours of horrible suspense, the old man died. He was seventy, and the fright killed him; his wife was younger and stronger, and survived. In

FEMALE CURIOSITY AT PORTE MAILLOT.
"Prenez garde, Mam'zelle."

the rare intervals between the firing she went out and spoke to her neighbours through the cellar gratings.—" My husband is dead. He must be buried; what am I to do?"—Carrying him to the cemetery was of course out of the question; no one could have been found to render this mournful duty. Besides, the bearers would probably have met a shell or a bullet on the way, and then others must have been found to carry them. One day, the old woman ventured as far as the Porte Maillot, and cried out as loud as she could, " My husband is dead in a cellar; come and fetch him, and let us both through the gates!"—The sentinel facetiously (let us hope it was nothing worse) took aim at her with his rifle, and she fled back to her cellar. At night, she slept by the side of the corpse, and when the light of morning filtered into her dreary place of refuge, and lighted up the body lying there, she sobbed with grief and terror. Her husband had been dead four days, when putrefaction set in, and she, able to bear it no longer, rushed out screaming to her neighbours: " You must bury him, or I will go into the middle of the avenue and await death there!"—They took pity on her, and came down into her cellar, dug a hole there and put the corpse in it. During three weeks she continued there, resting herself on the newly-turned earth. To-day, when they went to fetch her she fainted with horror; the grave had been dug too shallow, and one of the legs of the corpse was exposed to gaze.

This morning, the 25th of April, at nine o'clock, a dense crowd moved up the Champs Elysées: pedestrians of all ages and classes, and vehicles of every description. The truce obtained by the members of the *Republican Union of the rights of Paris* was about to begin, and relief was to be carried to the sufferers at Neuilly. However, some precautions were necessary, for neither the shooting nor the cannonade had ceased yet, and every moment one expected to see some projectile or other fall among the advancing multitude. In the Avenue de la Grande Armée a shell had struck a house, and set fire to it. Gradually the sound of the artillery diminished, and then died away entirely; the crowd hastened to the ramparts.

PORTE MAILLOT AND CHAPEL OF ST. FERDINAND.
The chapel was erected by Louis Philippe in memory of the Duke of Orleans, killed on the spot, July 13th, 1842.

The Porte Maillot has been entirely destroyed for some time, in

THE INHABITANTS OF NEUILLY ENTERING PARIS DURING THE ARMISTICE OF THE 25TH OF APRIL.

The firing ceased from nine in the morning until five in the afternoon, when Paris cabs, furniture-vans, ambulance-waggons, hand-barrows, and all sorts of vehicles were requisitioned to bring in the sad remains and dilapidated household goods of the surburban *bombardés*. They entered by the gate of Ternes—for that of Porte Maillot was in ruins and impassable. Many went to the Palais de l'Industrie, in the Champs Elysées, where a commission sat to allot vacant apartments in Paris. On this occasion some robberies were committed, and refractories escaped: it is even said that hard-hearted landlords wished to prevent their lodgers from departing—an object in which the proprietors were not very successful. The poor woman perched on the top of her relics, saved from the cellar in which she had lived in terror for fourteen days, deplores the loss of her husband and the shapeless mass of ruin and rubbish she once called her happy home ; whilst her boys bring in green stuff from the surburban gardens, and a middle-aged neighbour stalks along with his pet parrot, the bird all the while amusing himself with elaborate imitations of the growl of the mitrailleuse and the hissing of shells ending with terrific and oft-repeated explosions.

spite of what the Commune has told us to the contrary; the drawbridge is torn from its place, the ruined walls and bastions have fallen into the moat. The railway-station is a shapeless mass of blackened bricks, broken stones, glass, and iron-work; the cutting where the trains used to pass is half filled up with the ruins. It is impossible to get along that way. Fancy the hopeless confusion here, arising among this myriad of anxious beings, these hundreds of carts and waggons, all crowding to the same spot. Each one presses onwards, pushing his neighbour, screaming and vociferating; the National Guards try in vain to keep order. To add to the difficulties there is some form to be gone through about passes. I manage to hang on to a cart which is just going over the bridge; after a thousand stoppages and a great deal of pushing and squeezing, I succeeded in getting out, my clothes in rags. A desolate scene meets my eyes. In front of us, is the open space called the military zone, a dusty desert, with but one building remaining, the chapel of Longchamps; it has been converted into an ambulance, and the white flag with the red cross is waving above it. Truly the wounded there must be in no little danger from the shells, as it lies directly in their path. To the left is the Bois de Boulogne, or rather what used to be the wood, for from where I stand but few trees are visible, the rest is a barren waste. I hasten on, besides I am hard pressed from behind. Here we are in Neuilly, at last. The desolation is fearful, the reality surpassing all I could have imagined. Nearly all the roofs of the houses are battered in, rafters stick out of the broken windows; some of the walls, too, have fallen, and those that remain standing are riddled with blackened holes. It is there that the dreadful shells have entered, breaking, grinding furniture, pictures, glasses, and even human beings. We crunch broken glass beneath our feet at every step; there is not a whole pane in all the windows. Here and there are houses which the bullets seemed to have delighted to pound to atoms, and from which dense clouds of red and white dust are wafted towards us. Well, Parisians, what do you say to that? Do you not think that Citizen Cluseret, although an American, is an excellent patriot, and is it not the moment to publish such a decree as the following :—

> "In consideration of Neuilly being in ruins, and of this happy result being chiefly due to the glorious resistance organized by the delegate Citizen Cluseret, decrees : That the destroyer of Neuilly, Citizen Cluseret, has merited the gratitude of France and the Republic."

Out of all the houses, or rather from what was once the houses, emerge the inhabitants carrying different articles of furniture, tables, mattresses, boxes. They come out as it were from their graves. Relations meet and embrace, after having suffered almost the bitterness of death. Thousands run backwards and forwards; the carts are heaped up to overflowing, everything that is not destroyed must be carried away. A large van filled with orphan children moves on towards the barrier; a sister of charity is seated beside the driver. The most impatient of the refugees are already through the Porte Maillot; who will give them hospitality there? No one seems to think of that. The excitement caused by all this movement is almost joyous under the brilliant rays of the sun. But time presses, in a few minutes the short truce will have expired. Stragglers hurry along with heavy loads. At the gates, the crowding and confusion are greater than in the morning. Carts heavily laden, move slowly and with difficulty; the contents of several are spilled on the highway. More shouting, crowding, and pushing, until the gates are passed at last, and the emigrant crowd disperses along the different streets and avenues into the heart of Paris. A happy release from bondage, but what a dismal promised land !

Then the cannonading and musketry on either side recommences. Destroy, kill, this horrible quarrel can only end with the annihilation of one of the two parties engaged. Go on killing each other if you will have it so, combatants, fellow-countrymen.

Some wretched women and children will at least sleep in safety to-night, in spite of you!

Yes, my good friends and idlers, the sad scene would not have

Federal Officer. Pardon, Monsieur, but we cannot allow civilians to remain here.
Monsieur. I wait for Valérien to open upon us.

been complete without your presence to relieve its sadness. If respect for your persons kept you away from danger, it at least gives zest to the place, a locality that in a few short minutes will

MDLLE. ET SES COUSINES.

5.30. Great guns of Valérien, why do you not begin? Know you that tubes charged with bright eyes are directed against you?

be dangerous again. At five the armistice was over, but for all that, the National Guard had great difficulty in clearing the ground, until real danger, the excitement sought for, arrived, and sent the spectators much further up the Avenue de la Grande Armée.

LXIII.

I HAD almost made up my mind not to continue these notes. Tired and weary, I remained two days at home, wishing to see nothing, hear nothing, trying to absorb myself in my books, and to take up the lost thread of my interrupted studies, but all to no purpose.

It is ten in the morning, and I am out again in search of news. How many things may have happened in two days! Not far from the Hôtel de Ville excited groups are assembled at the corners of the streets that lead out of the Rue de Rivoli. They seem waiting for something—what are they waiting for? Vague rumours, principally of a peaceful and conciliatory nature, circulate from group to group, where women decidedly predominate.

"If *they* help us we are saved!" says a workwoman, who is holding a little boy in the dress of a national guard by the hand. —"Who?" I ask.—"Ah! Monsieur, it is the Freemasons who are taking the side of the Commune; they are going to cross Paris before our eyes. The Commune must be in the right if the Freemasons think so."—"Here they come!" says the little boy, pulling his mother along with all his strength.

The vehicles draw up on one side to make room, the crowd presses to the edge of the pavement. The drums beat, a military band strikes up the "Marseillaise." First come five staff-officers, and then six members of the Commune, wearing their red scarfs, fringed with gold. I fancy I recognize Citizens Delescluze and Protot among them. "They are going to the Hôtel de Ville!"

cries an enthusiastic butcher-boy, holding a large basket of meat on his head, which he steadies with one hand, while with the other he makes wild signs to two companions on the other side of the way. "I saw them this morning in the Place du Carrousel," he continues in the same strain. "That was fine, I tell you! And then this battalion came to fetch them, with the music and

PROTOT,* DELEGATE OF JUSTICE.

all. Now they are going to salute the Republic; come along, I say. Double quick time!" So the butcher-boy, and the woman with the child, and myself, and all the rest of the bystanders, turn and follow the eight or ten thousand members of Parisian freemasonry who are crowding along the Rue de Rivoli. In the front

* Memoir, see Appendix 6.

and rear of the procession I notice a large number of unarmed men, dressed in loose Zouave trousers of dark-blue cloth, with white gaiters, white bands, and blue jackets. Their heads are mostly bare. I am told these are the Communist sharpshooters. Ever so far on in front of us a large white banner is floating, bearing an inscription which I cannot manage to read on account of the distance. However, the butcher-boy has made it out, and informs us that "Love one another" is written there. Happy, delusive Freemasons! "Tolerate one another" is scarcely practicable! In the meantime we continue to follow at the heels of the procession. There is much shouting and noise, here and there a feeble "*Vive la Commune!*" But the principal cries are, "Down with the murderers! Death to assassins! Down with Versailles!" A Freemason doffs his hat and shouts, "*Vive la Paix!* It is peace we are going to seek!"

I am still sadly confused, and cannot make up my mind what all this is about. Patience, however, I shall know all at the Hôtel de Ville. Here we are. The National Guard keeps the ground, and the whole procession files into the Cour d'Honneur. Carried on by the crowd, I find myself near the entrance and can see what is going on inside. The whole of the Commune is out on the balcony, at the top of the grand staircase, in front of the statue of the Republic, which like the Communists wears a red scarf. Great trophies of red flags are waving everywhere. Men bearing the banners of the society are stationed on every step; on each is inscribed, in golden letters, mottos of peace and fraternity. A patriarchal Freemason, wearing his collar and badges, has arrived in a carriage; they help him to alight with marks of the greatest respect. The court is by this time full to overflowing, an enthusiastic cry of "Vive la Franc Maçonnerie! Vive la République Universelle!" is re-echoed from mouth to mouth. Citizen Félix Pyat, member of the Commune, who is on the balcony, comes forward to speak. I congratulate myself on being at last about to hear what all this means. But I am

FÉLIX PYAT.*

* Félix Pyat was born in 1810 at Vierzon. He came to Paris for the purpose of studying law, but soon abandoned his intention for the more genial profession of journalist. He contributed to the *Figaro*, the *Charivari*, the *Revue de Paris*, and the *National*. In 1848 he was named Commissary-General, and subsequently deputy of the department of the Cher. Having signed Ledru-Rollin's call to arms, he was obliged after the events of June to take refuge in England. Profiting by the amnesty of the fifteenth of August, 1869, he returned to France, but made himself so obnoxious to the Government by his virulent abuse of the Empire, that he was again expelled. The revolution of the fourth of September allowed him to re-enter France. He commenced an immediate and violent attack on the new government, which he continued until his journal, *Le Combat*, was suppressed. Needless to say that he was one of the chief actors in the insurrections of the thirty-first of October and the twenty-second of January. He was elected deputy, but soon resigned, for the purpose of connecting himself with the cause of the Commune. He edited the *Vengeur* and the *Commune* newspapers, and obtained a decree suppressing nearly all rival or antagonistic publications. At the fall of the Commune he fled no one knows where.

disappointed. The pushing and squeezing is unbearable. I have vigorously to defend my hat, stick, purse, and cigar-case, and am half stifled besides. I almost despair of catching a single word, but at last succeed in hearing a few detached sentences:—
"Universal nationality .... liberty, equality, and fraternity .... manifestos of the heart ...." (what is that?) "the standard of humanity .... ramparts ...." If I could only get a little nearer—the words "homicidal balls .... fratricidal bullets .... universal peace ...." alone reach me. Is it to hear such stuff as this, that the Freemasons have come to the Hôtel de Ville? I suppose so, for after a little more of the same kind the whole is drowned in a stupendous roar of "Vive la Commune!" and "Vive la République!" I have given up all hope of ever understanding.

"They have come to draw lots to see who is to go and kill M. Thiers," cries a red-haired gamin.—"Idiot," retorts his comrade, "they have no arms!"—"Listen, and you will hear," says the first, which is capital advice, if I could but follow it. The pushing becomes intolerable, when suddenly the bald head of an unfortunate citizen executes a fatal plunge—I can breathe at last—and the following words reach me pretty clearly:—"The Commune has decided that we shall choose five members who are to have the honour of escorting you, and we are to draw lots ...."—"There! was I not right?" cries he of the carrotty hair; "I knew they were going to draw lots!" A cleverly administered blow, however, soon silences his elation, and we hear that the lots have been drawn, and that five members are chosen to aid "this glorious, this victorious act." There seems more rhyme than reason in this. "An act that will be read of in the future history of France and of humanity." Here the irrepressible breaks out again:—"Now I am sure they are going to kill M. Thiers!" Whereupon his irritated adversary seizes him by the collar, gives his head some well-applied blows against the curb-stone, and then, pushing through the crowd, carries him off bodily. As for me, my curiosity unsatisfied, I grow resigned—may the will of the Commune be done—and I give it up. More hopeless mystification from the Citizen Beslay, who regrets not having been chosen to aid in this "heroic act." He also alludes to the drawing of lots, and I begin after all to fancy poor M. Thiers must be at the bottom of it all, but he continues:—" Citizens, what can I say after the eloquent discourse of Félix Pyat? You are about to interest yourselves in an act of fraternity . . . ." (then something horrible is surely contemplated) " in hoisting your banner on the walls of our city, and mixing in our ranks against our enemies of Versailles." A sudden light breaks upon me. In the meantime Citizen Beslay is embracing the nearest Freemason, while another begs the honour of being the first to plant his banner, the Persévérance, which was unfurled in 1790, on the ramparts. Here a band plays the "Marseillaise," horribly out of tune; a red flag is given to the Freemasons, with an appropriate harangue; then the Citizen Térifocq takes back the flag, with another harangue, and ends by waving it aloft and roaring, "Now, citizens, no more words; to action!"

This is clear, the Freemasons are to hoist their banner on to the walls of Paris side by side with the standard of the Commune; and who is blind enough to imagine, that the shells and bullets, indiscriminately homicidal, fratricidal, and infanticidal as they prove, are imbued with tact sufficient to steer clear of the Freemasons' banners, and injure in their flight only those of the Commune? As the Versailles projectiles have only one end in view, that of piercing both the Parisians and their standards, as a national consequence if both Parisians and standards are pierced, it is likewise most probable that the Masonic banners will not remain unscathed in so dangerous a neighbourhood. And if so, what will be the result? According to Citizen Térifocq "the Freemasons of Paris will call to their aid the direst vengeance; the Masons of all the provinces of France will follow their example; everywhere the brothers will fraternise with the troops which are marching on to help Paris. On the other hand, if the Versailles gunners do not aim at the Masons, but only at the

National Guards (*sic!*), then the Masons will join the battalions in the field, and encourage by their example the gallant soldiers, defenders of the city."

This is all rather complicated—what can come of it? Escorted by an ever-increasing crowd, we reach the Place de la Bastille. Several discourses are spouted forth at the foot of the column, but the combined effects of noise, dust, and fatigue have blunted my senses, and I hear nothing; it seems, however to be about the same thing over again, for the same acclamations of the crowd greet the same gestures on the part of the orators.

We are off again down the Boulevards; the long procession, with its waving banners and glittering signs, is hailed by the populace with delight. Having reached the Place de la Concorde, I loiter behind. Groups are stationed here and there. I go from one to another, trying to gather what these open-air politicians think of all this Masonic parade. Shortly fugitives are seen hurrying back from the Champs Elysées, shouting and gesticulating. "Horror! Abomination! They respect nothing! Vengeance!" I hear a brother-mason has been killed by a shell opposite the Rue du Colysée; that the white flag is riddled with shot; that the Versailles rifles have singled out, killed and wounded several masons.

In a very short time the terrible news, increased and exaggerated as it spread, filled every quarter of Paris with consternation. I returned home in a most perplexed state of mind, from which I could not arouse myself until the arrival, towards evening, of a friend, a freemason, and consequently well informed. This, it appears, is what took place.

"At the moment when the procession arrived in the Champs Elysées it formed itself into several groups, each choosing a separate avenue or street. One followed the Faubourg St. Honoré and the Avenue Friedland as far as the Triumphal Arch, till it reached the Porte Maillot; a second proceeded to the Porte des Ternes by the Avenue des Ternes; a third to the Porte Dauphine by the Avenue Uhrich. Not a single freemason was wounded on

Q

THE FREEMASONS AT THE RAMPARTS.   GAMINS COLLECTING SHELLS.

the way, though shells fell on their passage from time to time. The VV∴ of each lodge marched at the head, displaying their masonic banners.

"As soon as the white flag was seen flying from the bastion on the right of the Porte Maillot, the Versailles batteries ceased firing. The freemasons were then able to pass the ramparts and proceed towards Neuilly. There they were received rather coldly by the colonel in command of the detachment. The officers, including those in high command, were violently indignant against Paris. But the soldiers themselves seemed utterly weary of war.

"After some parleying the members of the manifestation obtained leave to send a certain number of delegates to Versailles, in order to make a second attempt at conciliation with the Government."

Will this new effort be more successful than the preceding one? Will the company of freemasons obtain what the Republican Union failed in procuring? I would fain believe it, but cannot. The obstinacy of the Versailles Assembly has become absolute deafness, though we must admit that the freemasons' way of trying to bring about reconciliation was rather singular, somewhat like holding a knife at Monsieur Thiers' throat and crying out, "Peace or your life!"

LXIV.

No! no! Monsieur Félix Pyat, you must remain, if you please. You have been of it, you are of it, and you shall be of it. It is well that you should go through all the tenses of the verb. I am not astonished that a man as clever as you, finding that things were taking a bad turn, should have thought fit to give in your resignation. When the house is burning, one jumps out of window. But your cleverness has been so much pure loss, for your amiable confederates are waiting in the street to thrust you back into the midst of the flames again. It is in vain that you have written the following letter, a chef-d'œuvre in its way, to the president of the Commune:—

> "CITIZEN PRESIDENT,—If I had not been detained at the Ministry of War on the day when the election took place, I should have voted with the minority of the Commune. I think that the majority, for this once, is in the wrong."

"For this once" is polite.

> "I doubt if she will ever retrieve her error."

If the Commune were to retrace its steps at each error it made, it would advance slowly.

> "I think that the elected have not the right of replacing the electors. I think that the representatives have not the right of taking the place of the sovereign power. I think that the Commune cannot create a single one of its own members, neither make them nor unmake them; and, therefore, that it cannot of itself furnish that which is wanted to legalise their nominations."

Oh! Monsieur Félix Pyat, legality is strangely out of fashion, and it is well for Versailles that it is so.

> "I think also, seeing that the war has changed the population . . . ."

Yes; the war has changed the population, if not in the way you understand it, at least in this sense, that a great many reasonable people have gone mad, and that many—ah! how many?—are now dead.

> "I think that it was more just to change the law than to violate it. The ballot gave birth to the Commune, and in completing itself without it, the Commune commits suicide. I will not be an accomplice in the fault."

We understand that; it is quite enough to be an accomplice in the crime.

"I am so convinced of this truth, that if the Commune persist in what I call an usurpation of the elective power, I could not reconcile the respect due to the vote of the majority with the respect due to my own conscience; I shall therefore be obliged, much to my regret, to give in my resignation to the Commune before the victory.

"*Salut et Fraternité.*

"Félix Pyat."

"Before the victory" is exquisitely comic! But, carried away by the desire of exhibiting the wit of which he is master, Monsieur Félix Pyat fails to perceive that his irony is a little too transparent, that "before the victory" evidently meant "before the defeat," and that consequently, without taking into account the excellent reasons given in his letter to the president of the Commune, we shall only recollect that rats run away when the vessel is about to sink. But this time the rats must remain at the bottom of the hold. Your colleagues, Monsieur Pyat, will not permit you to be the only one to withdraw from the honours, since you have been with them in the strife. Not daring to fly themselves, they will make you stay. Vermorel will seize you by the collar at the moment you are about to open the door and make your escape; and Monsieur Pierre Denis,* who used to be a poet as well as a cobbler, will murmur in your ear these verses of Victor Hugo †, which, with a few slight modifications, will suit your case exactly:—

> "Maintenant il se dit: 'L'empire est chancelant;
>   La victoire est peu sûre.'
> Il cherche à s'en aller, furtif et reculant.
>   Reste dans la mesure!

---

* A writer in the *Vengeur*.
† For translation, see Appendix 7.

> "Tu dis : 'Le plafond croule ; ils vont, si l'on me voit,
>   Empêcher que je sorte.'
> N'osant rester ni fuir, tu regardes le toit,
>   Tu regardes la porte.
>
> "Tu mets timidement la main sur le verrou ;
>   Reste en leurs rangs funèbres !
> Reste ! La loi qu'ils ont enfouie en un trou
>   Est là dans les ténèbres.
>
> "Reste ! Elle est là, le flanc percé de leurs couteaux,
>   Gisante, et sur sa bière
> Ils ont mis une dalle. Un pan de ton manteau
>   Est pris sous cette pierre.
>
> "Tu ne t'en iras pas ! Quoi ! quitter leur maison !
>   Et fuir leur destinée !
> Quoi ! tu voudrais trahir jusqu'à la trahison
>   Elle-même indignée !
>
> "Quoi ! n'as-tu pas tenu l'échelle à ces fripons
>   En pleine connivence ?
> Le sac de ces voleurs ne fut-il pas, réponds,
>   Cousu par toi d'avance ?
>
> "Les mensonges, la haine au dard froid et visqueux,
>   Habitent ce repaire ;
> Tu t'en vas ! De quel droit, étant plus renard qu'eux
>   Et plus qu'elle vipère ?"

And Monsieur Félix Pyat will remain, in spite of the thousand and one good reasons he would find to make a short tour in Belgium. His colleagues will try persuasion, if necessary—"You are good, you are great, you are pure ; what would become of us without you?" and they will hold on to him to the end, like cowards who in the midst of danger cling to their companions, shrieking out, "We will die together!" and embrace them convulsively to prevent their escape.

LXV.

AN anonymous writer, who is no other, it is said, than the citizen Delescluze, has just published the following :—

"The Commune has assured to itself the receipt of a sum of 600,000 francs a day—eighteen millions a month."

There was once upon a time a French forger, named Collé, celebrated for the extent and importance of his swindling, and who possessed, it was said, a very large fortune. When questioned upon the subject, he used to answer : "I have assured to myself a receipt of a hundred francs a day—three thousand francs a month."

Between Collé and the Commune there exists a difference, however : in the first place, Collé affected a particular liking for the clergy, whose various garbs he used frequently to assume, and the Commune cannot endure *curés* ; and secondly, while Collé, in assuring himself a receipt of three thousand francs a month, had done all that was possible for him to do, the Commune puts up with a miserable eighteen millions, when it might have ensured to itself a great deal more. It is astounding, and, I may add, little in accordance with its dignity, that it should be satisfied with so moderate an allowance. You show too much modesty; it is not worth while being victorious for so little. Eighteen millions—a mere nothing ! Your delicacy might be better understood were you more scrupulous as to the choice of your means. Thank Heaven ! you do not err on that score. Come ! a little more energy, if you please. "But !" sighs the Commune, "I have done my best, it seems to me. Thanks to Jourde,[*] who throws Law into the shade,

---

[*] Jourde occupied the position of Financial Minister under the Commune Government. He is well-educated, and is said to be one of the most intellectually distinguished of the Federal functionaries. He is a medical student, and said to be twenty-seven years of age. See Appendix 8.

and to Dereure,* the shoemaker—Financier and Cobbler of La Fontaine's Fable—I pocket daily the gross value of the sale of tobacco, which is a pretty speculation enough, since I have had to pay neither the cost of the raw materials nor of the manufacture. I have besides this, thanks to what I call the 'regular income from the public departments,' a good number of little revenues which do not cost me much and bring me in a good deal. Now there's the Post, for instance. I take good care to despatch none of the letters that are confided to me, but I manage to secure the price of the postage by an arrangement with my employés. This shows cleverness and tact, I think. Finally, in addition to this, I get the railway companies to be kind enough to drop into my pockets the sum of two millions of francs: the Northern Railway Company will supply me with three hundred and ninety-three thousand francs; the Western, with two hundred and seventy-five thousand; the Eastern, three hundred and fifty-four thousand francs; the Lyons Railway Company, with six hundred and ninety-two thousand francs; the Orleans Railway, three hundred and seventy-six thousand francs. It is the financial delegate, Monsieur Jourde, who has the most brains of the whole band, who planned this ingenious arrangement. And, in truth, I consider that I have done all that is in my power, and you are wrong in trying to humiliate me by drawing comparisons between myself and Collé, who had some good in him, but who was in no way equal to me." My dear, good Commune, I do not deny that you have the most excellent intentions; I approve the tobacco speculation and the funds drawn from the public service money, in which you include, I suppose, the profits made in your nocturnal visits to the public and other coffers, and your fruitful rounds in the

* A working cobbler, and member of the International Society, which he represented at the Congress of Bâle. He occupied a post on the *Marseillaise* newspaper, became a Commissary of Police after the fourth of September, and took part on the popular side in the outbreak of the thirty-first of October. He was deprived of his office by General Trochu's government, and appointed one of the delegates for justice by the authorities of the Commune.

churches. As to the tax levied on railways, it inspires me with an admiration approaching enthusiasm. But, for mercy's sake, do not allow yourself to stop there. Nothing is achieved so long as anything remains to be done. You waste your time in counting up the present sources of your revenues, while so many opportunities remain of increasing them. Are there no bankers, no stockbrokers, no notaries, in Paris? Send a few of these honest patriots of yours to the houses of the reactionaries. A hundred thousand francs from one, two hundred thousand francs from another; it is always worth the taking. From small streams come great rivers. In your place I would not neglect the shopkeepers' tills either, or the money-chests of the rich. They are of the *bourgeoisie*, those people, and the *bourgeois* are your enemies. Tax them, *morbleu!* Tax them by all means. Have you not all your friends and your friends' friends to look after? Is it false keys that fail you? But they are easily made, and amongst your number you will certainly find one or two locksmiths quite ready to help you. Take Pilotel, for instance: a sane man, that! There were only eight hundred francs in the escritoire of Monsieur Chaudey, and he appropriated the eight hundred francs. Thus, you see, how great houses and good governments are founded. And when there is no longer any money, you must seize hold of the goods and furniture of your fellow-citizens. You will find receivers of stolen goods among you, no doubt. They told me yesterday that you had sent the Titiens and Paul Veroneses of the Louvre to London, in order to be able to make money out of them. A most excellent measure, that I can well explain to myself, because I can understand that Monsieur Courbet must have a great desire to get rid of these two painters, for whom he feels so legitimate and profound a hatred. But, alas! it was but a false report. You confined yourselves to putting up for sale the materials composing the Column of the Place Vendôme; dividing them into four lots, two lots of stone and cement, and two lots of metal. Two lots only? Why! you know nothing about making the best of your merchandise. There is something better than stone and metal in this column. There is that in it which a number of silly people used to call in other times the glory of France. What a pretty spectacle—when the sale by auction is over—to see the buyers carrying away under their arms—one, a bit of Wagram; another, a bit of Jena; and some, who had thought to be buying a pound or two of bronze, having made the acquisition of the First Consul at Arcole or the Emperor at Austerlitz. It is a sad pity that you did not puff up the value and importance of your sale to the bidders. Your speculation would then have turned out better. You have managed badly, my dear Commune; you have not known how to take advantage of your position. Repair your faults, impose your taxes, appropriate, confiscate! All may be yours, disdain nothing, and have no fear of resistance; everyone is afraid of you. Here! I have five francs in my own pocket, will you have them?

LXVI.

"The social revolution could end but in one great catastrophe, of which the immediate effects would be—

"To make the land a barren waste:

"To put a strait jacket upon society:

"And, if it were possible that such a state of things could be prolonged for several weeks—

"To cause three or four millions of human beings to perish by horrible famine.

"When the Government shall be without resources, when the country shall be without produce and without commerce:

"When starving Paris, blockaded by the departments, will no longer discharge its debts and make payments, no longer export nor import:

"When workmen, demoralised by the politics taught at the clubs and the closing of the workshops, will have found a means of living, no matter how:

"When the State appropriates to itself the silver and ornaments of the citizens for the purpose of sending them to the Mint:

"When perquisitions made in the private houses are the only means of collecting taxes:

"When hungry bands spread over the country, committing robbery and devastation:

"When the peasant, armed with loaded gun, has to neglect the cultivation of his crops in order to protect them:

"When the first sheaf shall have been stolen, the first house forced, the first church profaned, the first torch fired, the first woman violated:

"When the first blood shall have been spilt:

"When the first head shall have fallen:

"When abomination and desolation shall have spread over all France—

"Oh! then you will know what we mean by a social revolution:

"A multitude let loose, arms in hand, mad with revenge and fury:

"Soldiers, pikes, empty homes, knives and crowbars:

"The city, silent and oppressed; the police in our very homes, opinions suspected, words noted down, tears observed, sighs counted, silence watched; spying and denunciations:

"Inexorable requisitions, forced and progressive loans, paper money made worthless:

"Civil war, and the enemy on the frontiers:

"Pitiless proconsuls, a supreme committee, with hearts of stone—

"This would be the fruits of what they call democratic and social revolution."

Who wrote this admirable page?—Proudhon.

O all-merciful Providence! Take pity on France, for she has come to this.

LXVII.

A BALLOON! A balloon! Quick! A balloon! There is not a moment to be lost. The inhabitants of Brive-la-Gaillarde and the mountaineers of Savoy are thirsting for news; let us shower manna on them. Write away! Pierre Denis! Pump in your gas, emulators of Godard! And may the four winds of heaven carry our "Declarations" to the four quarters of France! Ah! ah! The Versaillais—band of traitors that they are!—did not calculate on this. They raise soldiers, the simpletons; they bombard our forts and our houses, the idiots! But *we* make decrees, and distribute our proclamations throughout the country by means of an unlimited number of revolutionary aëronauts. May they be guided by the wind which blows across the mountains! How the honest labourers, the good farmers, the eager workers of the departments will rejoice when they receive, dropping from the sky, the pages on which are inscribed the rights and duties of the man of the present day! They will not hesitate one single instant. They will leave their fields, their homes, their workshops, and cry, "A musket! a musket!" with no thought that they leave behind them women without husbands, and children without fathers! They will fly to us, happy to conquer or die for the glory of Citizen Delescluze and Citizen Vermorel! What ardour! What patriotism! Already they are on their way; they are coming, they are come! Those who had no fire-arms have seized their pickaxes or pieces of their broken ploughs! Hurrah! Forward! March! To arms, citizens, to arms! Hail to France, who comes to the rescue of Paris!

All to no purpose. I tell you the people of Brive-la-Gaillarde and the mountaineers of Savoy have not once thought of taking up arms. They have never been more tranquil or more resolute on remaining in peace and quiet than now. When they see one of your balloons—always supposing that it has any other end in view than of depositing repentant communists in safe, snug corners, pass the lines of the Versailles troops—when they see one of your balloons, they simply exclaim, "Hulloa! Here's a balloon! Where in the world can it come from?" If some printed papers fall from the sky, the peasant picks them up, saying, "I shall give them to my son to read, when he returns from school." The evening comes, the son spells them out, while the father listens. The son cannot understand; the father falls asleep. "Ah! those Parisians!" cries the mother. Can you wonder? These people are born to live and die without knowing all that is admirable in the men of the Hôtel de Ville. They are fools enough to cling to their own lives and the lives of those near them. They do not go to war amongst themselves; they are poor ignorant creatures, and you will never make them believe that when once they have paid their taxes, worked, fed their wives and children, there still remains to them one duty to fulfil, more holy, more imperative than all others,—that of coming to the Porte-Maillot to receive a ball or a fragment of shell in their skulls.

But these balloons might be made of some use, nevertheless. Pick out one, the best made, the largest in size, the best rigged; put in Citizen Félix Pyat—who, you may be sure, will not be the last to sit down—and Citizen Delescluze too, nor must we omit Citizen Cluseret, nor any of the citizens who at the present moment constitute the happiness of Paris and the tranquillity of France! Now inflate this admirable balloon, which is to bear off all your hopes, with the lightest gases. Then blow, ye winds, terrifically, furiously, and bear it from us! Balloons can be capricious at times. Have you read the story of Hans Pfaal? Good Heavens! if the wind could only carry them away, up to the moon, or even a great deal further still.

LXVIII.

I am surprised myself, as I re-read the preceding pages, at the strange contradictions I meet with. During the first few days I was almost favourable to the Commune; I waited, I hoped. To-day all is very different. When I write down in the evening what I have seen and thought in the day, I allow myself to blame with severity men that inspired me formerly with some kind of sympathy. What has taken place? Have my opinions changed? I do not think so. Besides, I have in reality but one opinion. I receive impressions, describing these impressions without reserve, without prejudice. If these stray leaves should ever be collected in a volume, they will at least possess the rare merit of being thoroughly sincere. Is it then, that my nature is modified? By no means. If I were indulgent a month ago, it was that I did not know those of whom I spoke, and that I am of a naturally hopeful and benevolent disposition: if I now show myself severe, it is that—like the rest of Paris—I have learned to know them better.

LXIX.

The Commune has naturally brought an infinite number of journals into existence. Try, if you will, to count the leaves of the forest, the grains of sand on the seashore, the stars in the heavens, but do not, in your wildest dreams, attempt to enumerate the newspapers that have seen the light since the famous day of the 18th of March. Félix Pyat has a journal, *Le Vengeur;* Vermorel has a journal, *Le Cri du Peuple;* Delescluze has a journal, *Le Reveil;* there is not a member of the Commune but indulges in the luxury of a sheet in which he tells his colleagues daily all the evil he thinks of them. It must be acknowledged that these gentlemen have an extremely bad opinion one of the other. I defy even the *Gaulois* of Versailles—yes, the *Gaulois* itself—to

VERMESCH (PÈRE DUCHESNE).*

* Vermesch, who was born at Lille, in 1845, though not an official member of the Commune, was one of its most powerful champions. He was founder and principal editor of the *Père Duchesne*, a poor imitation of the journal, published under the same title, by Hébert, in the time of the first Revolution. This paper, one of the most characteristic of the Commune, was filled with trivialities, in the vilest taste and slang, which cannot be rendered in English. The first number of Vermesch's journal was published on the 6th of March, but was suppressed by General Vinoy; it re-appeared, however, on the eighteenth of the same month, and met with such prodigious success, that even its editor himself was astonished. Intoxicated with the result, the writers became more and more virulent, and not content with penning the vilest personal abuse, Vermesch assumed the *rôle* of public informer. For instance, he denounced M. Gustave Chaudey, a writer in the *Siècle*, in the *Père Duchesne* of the

treat Félix Pyat as Vermorel treats him, and if it be remembered on the other hand what Félix Pyat says of Vermorel, the *Gaulois* will be found singularly good-natured. Napoleon cautioned us long ago " to wash our dirty linen at home," but good patriots cannot be expected to profit by the counsels of a tyrant. So the columns of the Commune papers are devoted to the daily and mutual pulling to pieces of the Commune's members. But where will these ephemeral sheets be in six months, in one month, or in a week's time perhaps? The wind which wafts away the leaves of the rose and the laurel, will be no less cruel for the political leaves. Let us then, for the sake of posterity, offer a specimen of what is—or as we shall soon say, what was—the Communalist press of to-day. Be they edited by Marotteau, or Duchesne, or Paschal Grousset, or by any other emulator of Paul-Louis Courier, these worthy journals are all much alike, and one example will suffice for the whole.

First of all, and generally in enormous type, stand the LATEST NEWS, the news from the Porte Maillot where the friends of the Commune are fighting, and the news from Versailles where the enemies of the country are sitting. They usually run somewhat in this style :—

> " It is more and more confirmed that the Assembly of Versailles is surrounded and made prisoner by the troops returned from Germany. The generals of the Empire have newly proclaimed

---

12th of April, and that journalist was arrested in consequence on the following day. The journal became, not only the medium of all kinds of personal abuse and vengeance, but did the duty of inquisitor for the Communal Government, for whom it produced a terrible crop of victims. The *Official Journal* contained a number of decrees, the drafts of which at first appeared in *Père Duchesne*.

Amongst other acts, Vermesch organised what he called the battalion of the Enfants of the *Père Duchesne*, and considering the origin of this corps, the character of the rabble which filled its ranks may easily be imagined. The children of such a father could only be found amidst the lowest dregs of the Parisian population; fit instruments for the infamous work which was afterwards to be done.

Napoleon the Third, Emperor. After a violent quarrel about two National Guards whom Marshal MacMahon had had shot, but had omitted to have cooked for his soldiers, Monsieur

PASCHAL GROUSSET, DELEGATE FOR FOREIGN AFFAIRS.*

* Paschal Grousset prepared himself for politics by the study of medicine; from the anatomy of heads he passed to the dissection of ideas. Having turned journalist, he wrote scientific articles in *Figaro*, contributed to the *Standard*, and was one of the editors of the *Marseillaise* when the challenge, which gave rise to the death of Victor Noir and the famous trial at Tours, was sent to Prince Pierre Bonaparte. Immediately after the revolution of the eighteenth of March he started the *Nouvelle Republique*, an ephemeral publication which only lived a week. On the second of April he commenced the *Affranchi*, or journal of free men, as he called it, Vesinier joining him in the management of it. The popularity of Grousset caused him to be elected a member of the Commune in April, and the Government soon appointed him Minister of Foreign Affairs. He communicated

Thiers sent a challenge to the Marshal, by his two seconds These seconds were no other than the Comte de Chambord and the Comte de Paris. Marshal MacMahon chose the ex-Emperor and Paul de Cassagnac. The duel took place in the Rue des Reservoirs, in the midst of an immense crowd. The Marshal was killed, and was therefore obliged to renounce the command of the troops. But the Assembly would not accept his resignation.

"We are in the position to assert that a company of the 132nd Battalion has this morning surrounded fifteen thousand gendarmes and sergents-de-ville, in the park of Neuilly. Seeing that all resistance was useless, the supporters of Monsieur Thiers surrendered without reserve. Among them were seventeen members of the National Assembly, who, not content with ordering the assassination of our brothers, had wished also to be present at the massacre.

"A person worthy of credit has related to us the following fact:—A *cantinière* of the 44th Battalion (from the Batignolles quarter), was in the act of pouring out a glass of brandy for an artilleryman of the Fort of Vanves, when suddenly the artilleryman was cut in two by a Versailles shell; the brave *cantinière* drank off the contents of the

circulars to the representatives of different nations at Paris, in order to obtain a recognition of the Commune; he also sent proclamations to the large towns of France, appealing to arms. But his means of communication with other governments, and indeed with his own envoys, was very restricted.

He was one of those who took refuge at the *Mairie* of the Eleventh Arrondissement, and who, knowing well that the struggle was really over, said to the silly heroes who protected them, "All is well. The Versailles mob is turned, and you will soon join your brethren in the Champs Elysées." Many of them that night entered the valley of the shadow of death! On the third of June the ex-Minister of Foreign Affairs was arrested in the Rue Condorcet, dressed as a woman, and marched off to Versailles.

glass just poured out for the dead man who lay in bits at her feet, and took his place at the guns. She performed her new part of artilleryman so bravely, that ten minutes later there was not a single gun uninjured in the Meudon battery. As to those who were serving the pieces there, they were all hurled to a distance of several miles, and amongst them were said to have been recognised—we give this news however with great reserve—Monsieur Ollivier, the ex-minister of the ex-Emperor, and Count von Bismarck, who wished to verify for himself the actual range of the guns that he had lent to his good friends of Versailles."

After the LATEST NEWS come the reports of the day, the *bulletin du jour* as it is called now, and it is in this that the editor, a member of the Commune, reveals his talent. We trust that the following example is not quite unworthy of the pen of Monsieur Félix Pyat, or the signature of Monsieur Vermorel:—

"Paris, 29th April, 1871.

"They are lying in wait for us, these tigers athirst for blood.

"They are there, these Vandals, who have sworn that in all Paris not a single man shall be spared, nor a single stone left standing.

"But we are not in their power yet. No, nor shall we ever be.

"The National Guard is on the watch; victorious and sublime, their soldierly breasts are not of flesh and blood, but of bronze, from which the balls rebound as they stand, dauntless, before the enemy.

"Ah! so these lachrymose Jules Favres, these fat Picards, these hungry Jules Ferrys, said amongst themselves, 'We will take Paris, we will tear it up, and its soil shall be divided after the victory between the wives of the *sergents de ville!'*

"They are beginning to understand all the insanity of their plan. Why, it is Paris that will take Versailles, that will take all those blear-eyed old men who, because they cannot look steadily at Monsieur Thiers' face, fancy that it is the sun.

"It is in vain that they gorge with blood and wine their deceived soldiers; the moment is approaching when these men will no longer consent to march against the city which is fighting for them. Already, yesterday, the mêlée of a battle could be distinguished from the fort of Vanves; the line had come to blows with the *gendarmes* of Valentin and Charette's Zouaves. Courage, Parisians! A few more days and you will have triumphed over all the infamy that dares to stop the march of the victorious Commune!

"But it is not enough to vanquish the enemies without, we must get rid also of the enemies that are within.

"No more pity! no more vacillation! The justice of the people is wearied of formalities, and cries out for vengeance. Death to spies! Death to the *réactionaires!* Death to the priests! Why does the Commune feed this collection of malefactors in your prisons, while the money they cost us daily would be so useful to the women and children of those who are fighting for the cause of Paris? We are assured that one of the prisoners ate half a chicken for his dinner yesterday; how many good patriots might have been saved from suffering with the sum which was taken from the chests of the Republic for this orgie! There is no longer time to hesitate; the Versaillais are shooting and mutilating the prisoners; we must revenge ourselves! We must show them such an example, that in perceiving from afar the heads of their infamous accomplices, the traitors of Versailles, stuck upon our ramparts, confounded by the magnanimity of the Commune, they will lay down their arms at last, and deliver themselves up as prisoners.

"As to the refractory of Paris, we cannot find words to express the astonishment we experience at the weakness that has been shown with regard to them.

"What! we permit that there should still be cowards in Paris? I thought they were all at Versailles. We allow still to remain amongst us men who are not of our opinion? This state of things has lasted too long. Let them take their muskets or die. Shoot them down, those who refuse to go forward. They have wives and children, they are fathers of families, they say; a fine reason indeed! The Commune before everything! And, besides, there must be no pity for the wives of *réactionaires* and the children of spies!"

The *bulletins du jour* are sometimes set forth in gentler terms; but we have chosen a fair average specimen between the lukewarm and the most violent.

Then comes the solid, serious article, generally written by a pen invested with all due authority, by the man who has the most head in the place. The subject varies according to circumstances; but the main point of the article is generally to show that Paris has never been so rich, so free, nor so happy, as under the government of the Commune; and this is a truth that is certainly not difficult to prove. Is not the fact of being able to live without working the best possible proof that people are well off? Well! look at the National Guards; they have not touched a tool for a whole month, and they have such a supply of money that they are obliged to make over some of it to the wineshop-keepers in exchange for an unlimited number of litres and sealed bottles. Then, who could say that we are not free? The journals that allowed themselves to assert the contrary have been prudently suppressed. Besides, is it not being free to have shaken off the shameful yoke of the men who sold France; to be no longer subjected to the oppression of snobs, *réactionaires*, and traitors?

And as to the most perfect happiness, it stands to reason, since we are both free and rich, that we must be in the incontestable enjoyment of it. Finally, after the official dispatches edited in the style you are acquainted with, and after the accounts of the last battles, come the miscellaneous news, the *faits divers;* and here it is that the ingenuity of the writers displays itself to the greatest advantage.

"Yesterday evening, towards ten o'clock, the attention of the passers-by in the Rue St. Denis was attracted by cries which seemed to proceed from a four-storied house situated at the corner of the Rue Sainte-Apolline. The cries were evidently cries of despair. Some people went to the nearest guard-house to make the fact known, and four National Guards, preceded by their corporal, entered the house. Guided by the sound of the cries they arrived at the fourth storey, and broke open the door. A horrible spectacle was then exposed to the view of the Guards and of the persons who had followed them in their quest. Three young children lay stretched on the floor of the room, the disorder of which denoted a recent struggle. The poor little things were without any covering whatever, and there were traces of blows upon their bodies; one of them had a cut across the forehead. The National Guards questioned the children with an almost maternal kindness. They had not eaten for four days, and, in consequence of this prolonged fast, they were in such a state of moral and physical abasement that no precise information could be obtained from them. The corporal then addressed himself to the neighbours, and soon became acquainted with a part of the terrible truth.

"In this room lived a poor work-girl, young and pretty. One day, as she was carrying back her work to the shop, she observed that she was followed by a well-dressed man, whose physiognomy indicated the lowest passions. He spoke to her, and was at first repulsed; but, like the tempter Faust offering jewels to Marguerite, he tempted her with bright promises, and the poor girl, to whom work did not always come, listened to the base seducer. Blame her not too harshly, pity her rather, and reserve all your indignation for the wretch who betrayed her.

"After three years, which were but anguish and remorse to the miserable woman, and during which she had no other consolation but the smiles of the children whose very existence was a crime, she was becoming reconciled at last to her life, when the father of her children deserted her.

"This desertion coincided with the glorious revolution of the 18th of March; and the poor work-girl, who had still room in her heart for patriotism, found some consolation in reflecting that the day, so miserable for her, had at least brought happiness to France.

"A fortnight passed, the poor abandoned mother had given up all hope of ever seeing the father of her three children again, when one evening—it was last Friday—a man, wrapped in a black cloak, introduced himself into the house, and made inquiries of the *concierge*—a great patriot, and commander of the 114th Battalion—whether Mademoiselle C . . . were at home? Upon an answer in the affirmative from the heroic defender of Right and Liberties of Paris, the man mounted the stairs to the poor workwoman's rooms. It was he—the seducer; the *concierge* had recognised him. What passed between the murderer and his victims? That will be known, perhaps—never! But certain it is, that an hour afterwards he went out, still enveloped in his black mantle.

"The next day, and the days following, the *concierge* was much astonished not to see his lodger of the fourth floor, who was accustomed to stop and talk with him on her way to fetch her *café au lait*. But his deep sense of duty as commander of the 114th Battalion occupied his mind so thoroughly, that he paid but little attention to the incident. Neither did he regard the sighs and sobs which were heard from the upper stories. He can scarcely be blamed for this negligence; he was studying his *vade-mecum*.

"On the fourth day, however, the cries were so violent that they began to inspire the passers-by with alarm, and we have related how four men, headed by their *caporal*, were sought for to inquire into the cause.

"We have already told what was seen and heard, but the explanations of the neighbours were not sufficient to clear up the darkest side of the mystery, and perhaps the truth would never have been known if the *caporal*—exhibiting, by a rare proof of intelligence, how far he was worthy of the grade with which his comrades had honoured him—had not been inspired with the idea of lifting up the curtain of the bed.

"Horror! Upon the bed lay stretched the corpse of the unhappy mother, a dagger plunged into her heart, and in her clutched hand was found a paper upon which the victim, before rendering her last breath, had traced the following lines:—

"'I die, murdered by him who has betrayed me; he would have murdered also my three children, if a noise in the next room had not caused him to take flight. He had come from Versailles for the express purpose of accomplishing this quadruple crime, and, by this means, obliterate every trace of his past villany. His name is Jules Ferry. You who read this, revenge me!'"

LXX.

"Issy is taken!
"Issy is not taken!
"Mégy* has delivered it up!
"Eudes holds it still."

* Mégy, the famous governor of the Fort of Issy, was implicated in the last, supposed, plot against the life of Napoleon III. Having shot one of the police agents charged with his arrest, he was tried and condemned to death. He was, however, delivered from prison on the

I have heard nothing but contradictory news since this morning. Is Fort Issy in the hands of the Versailles troops—yes or no? Hoping to get better information by approaching the scene of conflict, I went to the Porte d'Issy, but returned without having succeeded in learning anything.

There were but few people in that direction; some National Guards, sheltered by a casemate, and a few women, watching for the return of their sons and husbands, were all I saw. The cannonading was terrific; in less than a quarter of an hour I heard five shells whistle over my head.

Towards twelve o'clock the drawbridge was lowered, and I saw a party of about sixty soldiers, dusty, tired, and dejected, advancing towards me. These were some of the "revengers of the Republic."

"Where do you come from?" I asked them.

"From the trenches. There were four hundred of us, and we are all that remain."

But when I asked them whether the Fort of Issy were taken, they made no answer.

Following the soldiers came four men, bearing a litter, on which a dead body lay stretched; and it was with this sad procession that I re-entered Paris. From time to time the men deposited their load on the ground, and went into a wine-shop to drink. I took advantage of one of these moments when the corpse lay abandoned, to lift the cloak that had been spread over it. It was the body of a young man, almost a lad; his wound was hidden, but the collar of his shirt was dyed crimson with blood. When the men returned for the third time, their gait was so unsteady that it was with difficulty they raised the poor boy's bier, and then went off staggering. At the turning of a street

---

fourth of September, and appointed to the command of a battalion of National Guards, with which he marched against the Hôtel de Ville on the thirty-first of October and the twentieth of January. He was named a member of the Commune on the eighteenth of March, and set fire to the Cour des Comptes and the Palace of the Légion d'Honneur on the twenty-third of May, 1871.

the corpse fell, and I ran up as it was being picked from the ground; one of the drunken men was shedding tears, and maudling out, "My poor brother!"

LXXI.

WE shall see no more of Cluseret! Cluseret is done for, Cluseret is in prison!* What has he done? Is he in disgrace on account of Fort Issy? This would scarcely be just, considering that if the fort were evacuated yesterday it was reoccupied this morning; by the bye, I cannot explain satisfactorily to myself why the Versaillais should have abandoned this position, which they seem to have considered of some importance. If it is not on account of Fort Issy that Cluseret was politely asked to go and keep Monseigneur Darboy company, why was it? I remember hearing yesterday and the day before something about a letter of General Fabrice, in which that amiable Prussian, it is reported, begged General Cluseret to intercede with the Commune in behalf of the imprisoned priests. Is it possible that the Communal delegate, at the risk of passing for a Jesuit, could have made the required demand? Why, M. Cluseret, that was quite enough for you to be put in prison, and shot too into the bargain. However, you did not intercede for anybody, for the very excellent

* General Cluseret was a great personage for a time with the Communists, and his military talents were lauded to the skies, but suddenly he was committed to prison, and was succeeded in the command of the army by Rossel. The cause of his imprisonment is not clear. Some say that he was discovered to be in correspondence with the Thiers government, others that he was suspected of aiming at the Dictatorship. During the confusion that occurred on the first entry of the Versailles troops into Paris, when the Archbishop of Paris and the other so-called "hostages" had been barbarously assassinated, when the Louvre, the Palais Royal, and the Hôtel de Ville were in flames, Cluseret escaped from prison, and was not heard of again until it was reported that his body had been found buried beneath the rubbish of the last barricade. Was report correct?

reason that General Fabrice no more thought of writing to you, than of giving back Alsace and Lorraine. So we must search somewhere else for the motive of this sudden eclipse. Some say there was a quarrel with Dombrowski, that the latter thought fit to sign a truce without the authority of Cluseret—a truce, what an idea! Has Dombrowski any scruples about slaughter?— that Cluseret flew into a great rage, but that his rival got the best of it in the end. You see if one is an American and the other a Pole, the Commune must have a hard time of it between the two!

No, neither the evacuation of Fort Issy—in spite of what the *Journal Officiel* says—Monseigneur Darboy, nor the quarrel with Dombrowski are the real causes of the fall of Cluseret. Cluseret's destiny was to fall; Cluseret has fallen because he did not like gold lace and embroidery—"that is the question," all the rest are pretexts.

So the noble delegate imagined he could quietly issue a proclamation one morning commanding all the officers under his orders to rip off the gold and silver bands which luxuriantly ornament their sleeves and caps!* He thought his staff would forego epaulets and other military gewgaws. Why, the man must have

---

* "THE MINISTER OF WAR TO THE NATIONAL GUARD.

"CITOYENS,—I notice with pain that, forgetful of our modest origin, the ridiculous mania for trimmings, embroidery, and shoulder-knots has begun to take hold upon you.

"To work! You have for the first time accomplished a revolution by, and for, labour.

"Let us not forget our origin, and, above all, do not let us be ashamed of it. Workmen we were! workmen let us remain!

"In the name of virtue against vice, of duty against abuse, of austerity against corruption, we have triumphed; let us not forget the fact.

"Let us be, above all, men of honour and duty; we shall then found an austere Republic, the only one that has or can have reason for its existence.

"I appeal to the good sense of my fellow-citizens: let us have no more tags and lace, no more glitter, no more frippery which costs so little at the shops yet is so dear to our responsibility.

"In future, anyone who cannot deduce proof of his right to wear the insignia of his nominal rank, or, who shall add to the regular uni-

been mad! What would Cora or Armentine have said if they had seen their military heroes stalk into the Café de Suède or the Café de Madrid, shorn of all their brilliant appendages, which made them look so wonderfully like the monkey-general at the Neuilly fair, in the good old times, when there were such things as fairs, and before Neuilly was a ruin. Ask any soldier, Federal or otherwise, if he will give up his pay, or his jingling sword, or even his rank; he may perhaps consent, but ask him to rip off his embroidery, and he will answer, never! How can you imagine a man of sense consenting not to look like a mountebank?

Another of these absurd prescriptions has done much to lower Cluseret in public estimation. One day he took it into his head to prevent his officers from galloping in the streets and boulevards, under the miserable pretext that the rapid evolutions of these horsemen had occasioned several accidents. Well, and if they had, do you think a gallant captain of horse is going to deprive himself of the pleasure of curvetting within sight of his lady love, for the pitiful reason, that he may perchance upset an old woman or two or three children? Citizen Cluseret does not know what he is talking about! It is certain that if this valiant general has such a very great horror of accidents, he should begin by stopping the firing at Courbevoie, which is a great deal more dangerous than the galloping of a horse on the Boulevard Montmartre. As you may imagine, the officers went on galloping and wearing their finery under the very nose of the general, while he walked about stoically in plain clothes. However, although they did not obey him, they owed him a grudge for the orders he had given. Opposition was being hatched, and was ready to burst forth on the first opportunity, which happened

---

form of the National Guard, tags, lace, or other vain distinctions, will be liable to be punished.

"I profit by this occasion to remind each of you of the necessity of absolute obedience to the authorities, for in obeying those whom you have elected you are only obeying yourselves.

"The Delegate of War,
"Paris, April 7th, 1871.   (Signed)   "E. CLUSERET."

to be the evacuation of Fort Issy.* Cluseret has fallen a victim to his taste for simplicity, but he carries with him the regrets of all the illused cab-horses which, in the absence of thoroughbreds, have to suffice the gallant staff, and who, poor creatures, were only too delighted not to gallop.

LXXII.

SUPPOSE that a man in disguise goes into the opera ball intoxicated, rushes hither and thither, gesticulating, insulting the women, mocking the men, turns off the gas, then sets light to some curtains, until such a hue and cry is raised that he is turned out of the place. Whereupon our mask runs off to the nearest costumier's, changes his clown's dress for that of a pantaloon, and returns to the opera to recommence his old tricks, saying, "I have changed my dress, no one will recognise me." But he is wrong, there is no mistaking his way of doing business.

The crowd surrounds him and cries, "We recognise you, *beau masque!*" and if he has had the imprudence to secure the doors, they throw him out of window.

We recognise you, Executive Commission;† it is in vain that

---

* The affair of the 30th of April signally disappointed the chiefs of the insurrection, who decreed the formation of a Committee of Public Safety, and caused Cluseret to disappear. "The incapacity and negligence of the Delegate of War having," they said, "almost lost them the possession of Fort Issy, the Executive Commission considered it their duty to propose the arrest of Citizen Cluseret, which was forthwith decreed by the Commune."

† The character and composition of the Executive Commission are settled by the following decree drawn up by the Commune at its meeting on the 20th of April:—

"The Commune of Paris decrees:—

"1. The executive power is and remains provisionally confided to the delegates of the nine commissions, amongst whom the Commune

you disguise yourself in the bloody rags of the Committee of Public Safety, you are still yourself, you are still Félix Pyat, you are still Ranvier, you have never ceased to be Gérardin; you hope to make yourself obeyed more readily under this lugubrious cos-

has distributed the work of the various departments of the Government.

" 2. The delegates will be named by the Commune, and by a majority of voices.

" 3. The delegates will meet daily and decide, by a majority of votes, all questions relative to the bodies they represent.

" 4. They will report each day to the Commune, in secret committee, the measures taken and the acts done by them, and the Commune will decide thereon.

" The following are appointed members of the Executive Committee:—

" Cluseret, *War*; Jourde, *Finance*; Viard, *Commissariat*; Paschal Grousset, *Foreign Affairs*; Franckel, *Industry and Exchange*; Protot, *Justice*; Andrieu, *Public Services*; Vaillant, *Public Instruction*; Rigault, *Public Safety*."

The following is another example of the 1793 pattern:—The Citizen Miot, in consequence of the gravity of circumstances, proposed the formation of a Committee of Public Safety. This motion, when brought before the Committee, encountered sharp opposition; nevertheless, the measure was declared urgent, each member giving the reason for his vote. The following are the most salient of the declarations made:—

For the motion.

" Seeing that the expression 'public safety' absolutely belongs to the same epoch as the titles *République Française*, and *Commune of Paris*, I vote for the proposition.—PYAT."

" With the hope that the Committee of Public Safety may be in 1871 what it is generally but erroneously believed to have been in 1793, I vote for the motion.—LÉO FRANCKEL."

" I vote for a Committee of Public Safety, because if the Commune has made itself beloved by all honest men, it has not yet taken the necessary measures for making cowards and traitors tremble.— BLANCHET DUPONT."

Against the motion.

" I do not believe in the efficacy of a Committee of Public Safety; it is nothing but a phrase, and the people have been too long played with by means of words. I vote against the motion.—A. VERMOREL."

" No! Because I do not like useless and ridiculous legislation, which, far from adding to our strength, takes away that which we have.—G. TRIDON."

" Considering that we cannot name any one for an office which appears to us as useless as it is fatal, and which foreshadows to our

tume, but you mistake. Command us to go and fight, and we will not budge; pursue us, and we will hardly run away; put us in

DUPONT, DELEGATE OF TRADE AND COMMERCE.

prison, and we will only laugh. You are no more a Terror, than mind a capitulation committee, we abstain from voting.—TRIDON, VERMOREL, AVRIAL, V. CLÉMENT, THEISZ, PINDY, GÉRARDIN."

In the end the affirmative was carried by a slight majority, and the following decree was the result:—

"Paris, May 1st, 1871.

The Commune decrees:

"Art. 1. A Committee of Public Safety shall be immediately organized.

"Art. 2. It will be composed of five members, nominated by the Commune and by ballot.

"Art. 3. The fullest powers over all the delegations and commissions are given to this committee, which is only responsible to the Commune.

"The following citizens are named members of the Committee of Public Safety:—Antoine Arnaud, Léo Meillet, Ranvier, Félix Pyat, and Charles Gérardin."

Gil-Pérez the actor is Talma; the knocks you receive have pushed aside your false nose; it is in vain that you decree, that you rob, that you incarcerate; you are too grotesque to be terrible. Even if you carried the parody out to the end, and thought fit to erect a guillotine and sharpen the knife, we should even then decline to look seriously upon you; and were we to see one by one five hundred heads fall into the basket, we should still persist in thinking that your axe was of wood, and your guillotine of cardboard!

LXXIII.

THE Parisian *Official Journal* says: "The members of the Commune are not amenable to any other tribunal than their own" (that of the Commune). Ah! truly, men of the Hôtel de Ville, you imagine that, do you? Have you forgotten that there are such tribunals as court-martials and assizes?

LXXIV.

M. ROSSEL is really very unfortunate! What is M. Rossel?* Why, the provisional successor of Citizen Cluseret. It was not a

---

* Colonel Rossel was one of the most capable members of the Commune Government. He was born in 1844, and was the son of Commandant Louis Rossel, an officer who acquired a high reputation in the Chinese war. The young Louis Rossel received a sound military education at the Prytanée of La Flèche, and subsequently at the École Polytechnique, at which latter institution he gained high honours. He served as captain of engineers in the army of Metz, and was one of the officers who signed the protestation against the surrender of Bazaine. He succeeded in eluding the vigilance of the Prussians, and appeared at Tours to offer his services to the Government of National Defence. Gambetta, then Minister of War, appointed Rossel to the rank of colonel in the so-called auxiliary army. After the signature of the

bad idea to put in the word *provisional*. The Commune had confided to him the care of military matters, which he had accepted, but with an air of condescension. This "Communeux" looks to me like an aristocrat. At any rate he has not been fortunate. Scarcely had he taken upon himself the safety of Paris, when the redoubt of Moulin-Saquet was surprised by the Versaillais. This accident was not calculated to enhance the courage of the Federals. The whole affair has been kept as dark as possible, but the porter of the house where I live, who was there, has told me strange things.

"Will you believe, Monsieur, that I had just finished a game of cards with the captain, and was preparing to have a bit of sleep, for it was near upon eleven o'clock, when I thought I heard something like the noise of troops marching. I looked round to see if any one heard it besides myself, but the men were already asleep, and a circular line of boots was sticking out all round the tents. The captain said: 'I daresay it is the patrol from the Rue de Villejuif.'—'Oh, yes,' said I, 'from the barricade,' and I fell to sleep without a thought of danger. In fact, there seemed nothing to fear, as the Moulin-Saquet overlooks the whole of the plain which stretches from Vitry to Choisy-le-Roi, and from Villejuif to the Seine. It was impossible for a man to approach the redoubt without being seen by the sentinel. I had, therefore, been asleep a few minutes when I was awoke by the following dialogue:—'Stop! who goes there?'—'The patrol.'—'Corporal, forward!'—Oh! said I to myself, it is our comrades come to see us; there will be some healths drunk before morning, and I got up to go and give them a welcome. The captain was also

---

peace preliminaries, the new government refused to ratify the promotion granted by Gambetta, but offered Rossel the rank of major. This seriously offended the ex-Dictator's ex-colonel, who shortly after the tenth of March, put his sword at the disposition of the Commune. He was at first appointed chief of the staff of General Cluseret, whom he subsequently replaced as delegate for war. On April 16 he became president of the Communist court-martial; he acted with great vigour in all military affairs until the 10th of May, when the Commune ordered his arrest.

astir. 'The pass-word!' he cried. The chief of the patrol came forward and answered—'Vengeance!' I remember wondering at the moment why he spoke so loud in giving the pass-word, when suddenly I saw three men rush forward, seize our captain, and throw him down. At the same time two or three hundred men, dressed as National Guards, threw themselves into the camp, rushed upon the sleeping artillery-men with their bayonets, and then fired several volleys into the tents where our poor comrades were asleep. What I had taken at first for National Guards were only those devils of sergents-de-ville dressed up! So, you see, as it was each man for himself, and the high road for everybody, I just threw myself down on my face, and let myself drop into the trenches. There was no fear of the noise of my fall being heard in the riot. I managed to hide myself pretty well in a hole I found there, and which had doubtless been made by a shell. I could not see anything, but I heard all that was going on. Clic! clac! clic! went the rifles, almost like the cracking of a whip, answered by the most dismal cries from the wounded. I could hear also the grinding of wheels, and made sure they were taking away our guns, the robbers! When all was silent except the groans of the dying men, I crept out of my hiding place. Would you believe it, Monsieur, I was the only one able to stand up; the Versaillais had taken all those who had not run away or were not wounded; I saw them, the pilfering thieves, making off towards Vitry, as fast as their legs could carry them!"

"You have no idea, lieutenant," I said to the porter, "how the Versaillais got to know the pass-word?"—"No, only the captain, who is an honest fellow enough, but rather too fond of the bottle, went in the evening to the route d'Orléans where there are lots of wine-shops . . ."—"And you think he got tipsy, and let the pass-word out to some spy or other?"—"I would not swear he did not; but what I am more sure of, is that we are betrayed!"

Alas! yes, unfortunates, you are betrayed, but not in the way you think. You are being cheated by these madmen and criminals who are busy publishing decrees at the Hôtel de Ville, while you are dying by scores at Issy, Vanves, Montrouge, Neuilly, and the Moulin-Saquet; they betray you when they talk of Royalists and Imperialists; they deceive you when they tell you, that victory is certain, and that even defeat would be glorious. I tell you, that victory is impossible, and that your defeat will be without honour; for when you fall, crying, "Vive la Commune!" "Vive la République!" the Commune is Félix Pyat, and the Republic, Vermorel.

LXXV.

MALEDICTION on the man who imagined this decree; malediction on the assembly that approved it; and cursed be the hand which shall first touch a stone of that tomb! Oh! believe me, I am not among those who regret the times of royal prerogatives, and who believe that everything would have gone well, in the most peaceful country in the world, if Louis XVII. had only succeeded to the throne after his father, Louis XVI. The author of the revolution of 1793 knew what he was about in multiplying such terrible catastrophes. The name of that author was Infallible Necessity. Indeed I am quite ready to confess that the indolent husband of Marie Antoinette had none of those qualities which make a great king, and I will even add, if you wish it absolutely, that the solitary fact of being a king is a crime worthy a thousand deaths. As to Marie Antoinette herself—"the Austrian," *Père Duchesne* would call her—I allow that in history she is not quite so amiable as she appears in the novels of Alexandre Dumas, and that her near relationship to the queen Caroline-Marie, whose little suppers at Naples, in company with Lady Hamilton, one is well acquainted with, gives some excuse for the calumnies of which she has been the object. Have I said enough to prevent myself being the recipient, in the event of a Bourbon restoration, of the most modest pension that ever came out of a royal treasury? Well, in spite of what I have said, and in spite of what I think,

CHAPELLE EXPIATOIRE.

I repeat, "Do not touch that tomb!" Like the Column Vendôme, which is the symbol of an heroic and terrible epoch in history, the Chapelle Expiatoire* is a souvenir of the old monarchical reign, an age which was neither devoid of sorrow, nor of honour for France. Can you not be republican without suppressing history, which was royalist? The last remains of monarchy repose in peace beneath that gloomy monument; may it be respected, as we respect the ashes of those who respected it; and you, breakers of images, profaners of past glory, do you not fear, in executing your decree, to produce an effect diametrically opposed to that which you desire? By persecuting kings even in their last resting-place, are you not afraid to excite the pity, the regret perhaps, of those whose consciences still hesitate? In the interest of the Republic, I say, take care! The memory of the dead stalks forth from open sepulchres!

LXXVI.

Rejoice, poor housewives, who, on days of poverty, were obliged to carry to the Mont-de-Piété † the discoloured remains of your wedding dress, or your husband's Sunday coat; rejoice, artisans, who, after a day of toil, thought your bed so hard since your last mattress was taken to the Rue des Blancs-Manteaux, to rejoin your last pair of sheets. The Commune has decreed that " all objects in pawn at the Mont-de-Piété, for a sum not exceeding twenty francs, shall be given back gratuitously to all persons who shall prove their legitimate right to the said objects." Thanks to this benevolent decree, you may now hope that things you have pawned will be restored to you before three or four hundred days!

* This chapel was erected by Louis XVIII. upon the spot where, during the Revolution of 1793, the remains of Louis XVI. and his Queen had been obscurely interred.
† The governmental pawnbroking establishments. All the pawnbroking is carried on by the Government.

Count on your fingers; the number of articles to which the decree applies is at least 1,200,000. As there are only three offices for the claimants to apply to, and considering the forms which have to be observed, I do not think more than three thousand objects can be given back daily; the Commune says four thousand, but the Commune does not know what it is talking about. However, even if we calculate four thousand a-day, the whole would take up ten or twelve months.

During this time men and women, whom poverty had long ere this taught the road to the Mont-de-Piété, would have to get up early, neglect the daily work by which they live, and go and stand awaiting their turn at the office, frozen in winter, baked in summer, thankful to obtain a moment's rest upon one of the wooden benches in the great bare hall; and when they have been there a long, weary time, to see their number, drawn by lot, put off to the next day or the day after, or the week or the month following perhaps.

Still we must not blame the Commune for the sad disappointment of this long delay, it would be impossible to shorten it.

One thing, which is less impossible, is to indemnify the administration of the Mont-de-Piété for this gratuitous restitution. Citizen Jourde, delegate of the finances, says, "I will give 100,000 francs a-week." Without stopping to consider where this able political economist means to get his weekly 100,000 francs, I will be content with remarking that this sum would in no wise cover the loss to the Mont-de-Piété, and that the Commune will only be giving alms out of other people's purses.

If, however, thanks to this decree, some few poor creatures are enabled to get back those goods and chattels which they were obliged to dispose of in the hour of need, there will not be much cause to complain. The Mont-de-Piété usually does a very good business, and there will always be enough misery in Paris for it to grow rich upon. Besides, the Commune owes the poor wounded, mutilated, dying fellows who have been brought from Neuilly and Issy, at least a mattress to die in some little comfort upon.

LXXVII.

They have put them into the prison of Saint-Lazare. Whom? The nuns of the convent of Picpus. They have put them there because they have been arrested. But why were they arrested? That is what Monsieur Rigault himself could not clearly explain. Some of the nuns are old. They have been living long in seclusion, and have only changed cells; having been the captives of Heaven, they have become the prisoners of Citizen Mouton. In such an abject place too, poor harmless souls! Victor Hugo has said, speaking of that wretched prison, "Saint-Lazare! we must crush that edifice." Yes, later, when we have the time; we must now pull down the Column Vendôme and the Chapelle Expiatoire. In the meantime these poor ladies are very sad. One of my friends went to see them; they have neither their prayer-books nor their crucifix; they have had even the amulets they wore round their necks taken from them. This seems nothing to you, citizens of the Commune. You are men of advanced opinions. You care as much about a crucifix as a fish for an apple; and perhaps you are right. You have studied the question, and you say in the evening, looking up at the stars, "There is no God." But you must understand that with these poor nuns it is quite a different matter. They have not read philosophical treatises; they still believe that the Almighty created the world in six days, and that the Son died on the cross for the sake of the world. When they were free, or rather when they were in a prison of their own choosing, they prayed in the morning, they prayed at noon, they prayed at night, and only interrupted this most pernicious occupation for the purpose of teaching poor little girls that it is good to be virtuous, honest, and grateful, and that Heaven rewards those who do rightly. That was their occupation, poor simple souls, and you have sent them to Saint Lazare for that. You should have chosen another prison, for their presence must be disagreeable to the usual female denizen of the place. But there, or elsewhere, they do not complain they only ask for a prayer-book and a wooden crucifix. Come Citizen Delegate of the ex-Prefecture, one little concession, and unless the future of the Republic is likely to be compromised by so doing, give them a cross. A cross is only two pieces of wood placed one on the other. I promise you there will be wood enough in the forest the day honest men make up their minds to exercise their muscles on your backs, you bullying slave-drivers.

LXXVIII.

AFTER Bergeret came Cluseret; after Cluseret, Rossel. But Rossel has just sent in his resignation. My idea is, that we take back Cluseret, that we may have Bergeret, and so on, unless we prefer to throw ourselves into the open arms of General Lullier. The choice of another general for the defence of Paris is however no business of mine; and the Commune, a sultan without a favourite, may throw his handkerchief if he pleases, to the tender Delescluze, as some say he has the intention—I have not the least objection. Why should not Delescluze* be an excellent general? He is a journalist, and what journalist does not know more about military matters than Napoleon I., or Von Moltke himself? In the meantime we are in mourning for our third War Delegate, and we shall no longer see Rossel on his dark bay, galloping between the Place Vendôme and the Fort Montrouge. He has just written the following letter to the members of the Commune:—

"CITIZENS, MEMBERS OF THE COMMUNE,—Having been charged

---

* PARIS AT DINNER.—An ogress, gentleman! A famished creature, faring sumptuously; her face flushed with wine, her eyes bright, her hands trembling.

Madame Lutetia is a strapping woman still, with a queenly air

QUELLE GOURMANDE!

PARIS AT TABLE

(BELECLUSE)
—WAITER— TWO OR THREE MORE STEWED GENERALS!
—WE ARE OUT OF THEM.
—VERY WELL, THEN A DOZEN COLONELS IN CAPER SA[UCE]
A DOZEN?— YES! DIRECTLY!!

by you with the War Department, I feel myself no longer capable of bearing the responsibility of a command wherein every one deliberates, and no one obeys.

"When it was necessary to organise the artillery, the Central Committee of Artillery deliberated, but nothing was done. After a month's revolution, that service is only carried on, thanks to the energy of a very small number of volunteers.

"On my nomination to the Ministry, I wanted to further the search for arms, the requisition of horses, and the pursuit of refractory citizens; I asked help of the Commune.

"The Commune deliberated, but passed no resolutions.

"Later, the Central Committee came and offered its services to the War Department; I accepted them in the most decisive manner, and delivered up to its members all the documents I had concerning its organisation. Since then the Central Committee has been deliberating, and has done nothing. During this time the enemy multiplied its venturesome attacks on Fort Issy; had I had the smallest military force at my command, I would have punished them for it.

"The garrison, badly commanded, took flight; the officers deliberated, and sent away from the fort Captain Dumont, an energetic man, who had been ordered to command them. Still deliberating, they evacuated the fort, after having stupidly talked of blowing it up,—as difficult a thing for them to do as to defend it.

about her, in spite of the red patches on her tunic; somewhat shorn of her ornaments, it is true, as she has had to pawn the greater part of her jewelry, but the orgie once over she will be again what she was before.

For the time being she is wholly absorbed in her gastronomic exertions. She has already devoured a Bergeret with peas, a Lullier with anchovy sauce, an Assy and potatoes, a Cluseret with tomatos, a Rossel with capers, besides a large quantity of small fry, and she is not yet appeased. The *maître-d'hôtel* Delescluze waits upon her somewhat in trepidation, with a sickly smile on his face. What if, after such a meal of generals and colonels, the ogress were to devour the waiter!—*Fac-simile of design from the "Grelot,"* 17th *May*, 1871.

"Even that was not enough. Yesterday, when every on[e] ought to have been at work or fighting, the chiefs we[re]

DELESCLUZE, DELEGATE OF WAR.*

deliberating upon another system of organisation from that which I had adopted, so as to make up for their want of

---

* Delescluze's wild life began at Dreux, in 1809. Driven from home on account of his bad conduct, he came to Paris, and obtained employment in an attorney's office, from which he was very soon afterwards, it is said, discharged for robbery. In 1834, he underwent the first of his long list of imprisonments, for the part he took in the April revolution, and in the following year, being compromised in a conspiracy against the safety of the state, he took refuge in Belgium, where he obtained the editorship of the *Courrier de Charleroi*.

In 1840 he returned to Paris, where he founded a journal called the *Révolution Démocratique et Sociale*, which brought him fifteen months' imprisonment and twenty thousand francs fine. After a long period of liberty of nearly eight years, he was condemned to transportation by the High Court of Justice, but the condemnation was given in his ab-

forethought and authority. The results of their council were a project, when we want men, and a declaration of principles, when we wanted acts.

"My indignation brought them back to other thoughts, and they promised me for to-day the largest force they could possibly muster,—an organised one of not more than 12,000 men. With these I undertook to march on the enemy. These men were to muster at eleven o'clock: it is now one, and they are not ready, and the promised 12,000 has dwindled to about 7,000, which is not at all the same thing.

"Thus, the utter uselessness of the artillery committee prevented the organization of the artillery; the hesitation of the Central Committee stopped all arrangements; the petty discussions of the officers, paralyses the concentration of the troops.

"I am not a man to mind having recourse to violence. Yesterday, while the chiefs discussed, a company of men with loaded rifles awaited in the court. But I did not want to take upon myself the initiative of so energetic a measure, or draw upon myself the odium of such executions as would have been necessary to extricate obedience and victory from

sence, for he had slipped over to England, where he remained until 1853. On his returning in that year to France he was immediately imprisoned at Mazas, transferred afterwards to Belle-Isle, and then successively to the hulks of Corte, Ajaccio, Toulon, Brest, and finally to Cayenne. These sojourns lasted until 1868, when the amnesty permitted him to return to France, where he made haste to bring out another new journal, *Le Réveil*, which of course earned him fines and imprisonments with great rapidity, three of each within the twelvemonth.

In the month of February, 1871, he was elected deputy by a large number of votes; and later, when the Assembly went to Bordeaux, sat there for some time, and then gave in his resignation, in order to take part with the Commune.

By the Commune he was made delegate at the Ministry of War, after the pretended flight of Rossel, and in a sitting of the 20th of April, in which the project of burning Paris was discussed, Delescluze ended his speech with the words—" If we must die, we will give to Liberty a pile worthy of her."

such a chaos. Even if I had been protected by the publicity of my acts, I need not have given up my position.

"But the Commune has not had the courage to confront publicity. Twice I wished to give some necessary explanations, and twice, in spite of me, it insisted on a secret council.

"My predecessor was wrong to remain in so absurd a position.

"Enlightened by his example, and knowing that the strength of a revolutionary, only consists in the clearness of his position, I have only two alternatives, either to break the chains which impede my actions, or to retire.

"I will not break the chains, because those chains are you, and your weakness,—I will not touch the sovereignty of the people.

"I retire; and have the honour to beg for a cell at Mazas.

"ROSSEL."*

Most certainly I do not like the Paris Commune, such as the men of the Hôtel de Ville understand it. Deceived at first by my own delusive hopes, I now am sure that we have nothing to expect from it but follies upon follies, crimes upon crimes. I hate it on account of the suppressed newspapers, of the imprisoned journalists, of the priests shut up at Mazas like assassins, of the nuns shut up at Saint-Lazare like courtesans; I hate it because it incites to the crime of civil war those who would have been ready to fight against the Prussians, but who do not wish to fight against Frenchmen; I hate it on account of the fathers of families sent to battle and to death; on account of our ruined ramparts, our dismantled forts, each stone of which as it falls wounds or

---

* He was convinced of the hopelessness of any further struggle after the capture of Fort Issy; gave in his resignation, and hid himself to escape the vengeance of his former colleagues. He was supposed to be in England or Switzerland, whereas, in fact, he had fled no farther than the Boulevard Saint Germain. He was arrested by the police on the ninth of June, disguised as an employé of the Northern Railway. He was first interrogated at the Petit Luxembourg, and afterwards conducted handcuffed to Versailles, where three months after he was tried by court-martial and sentenced to military degradation and death.

destroys; on account of the widowed women and the orphaned children, all of whom they can never pension in spite of their decrees; I cannot pardon them the robbing of the banks, nor the money extorted from the railway companies, nor the loan-shares sold to a money-changer at Liège; I hate it on account of Clémence the spy, and Allix the madman. I am sorry to think that two or three intelligent men should be mixed up with it, and have to share in its fall. I hate it particularly on account of the just principles it at one time represented, and of the admirable and fruitful ideas of municipal independence, which it was not able to carry out honestly, and which, because of the excesses that have been committed in their name, will have lost for ever, perhaps, all chance of triumphing.

Still, great as is my horror of this parody of a government to which we have had to submit for nearly two months, I could not forbear a feeling of repulsion on reading the letter of Citizen Rossel. It is a capitally written letter, firm, concise, conclusive, differing entirely from the bombastic, unintelligible documents to which the Commune has accustomed us; and besides, it brings to light several details at which I rejoice, because it permits me to hope that the reign of our tyrants is nearly at an end. I am glad to hear that the Commune, if it possesses artillery, is short of artillerymen. It delights me to learn that they can only dispose of seven thousand combatants. I had feared that it would be enabled to kill a great many more; and as to what Citizen Rossel says of the committees and officers who deliberate but do not act, it is most pleasant news, for it convinces me, that the Commune has not the power to continue much longer a war, which can but result in the death of Paris; and yet I highly disapprove of the letter of Citizen Rossel, because it is on his part an act of treachery, and it is not for the friends and servants of the Commune to reveal its faults and to show up its weaknesses. Who obliged Rossel, commander of the staff, to take the place of his general, disgraced and imprisoned? Did he not accept willingly a position, the difficulties of which he had already recognised? He says himself that his predecessor was wrong to have stayed in so absurd a position, and why did he voluntarily put himself there, where he blamed another for remaining? If the new delegate hoped by his own cleverness to modify the position, he ought not, the position remaining the same, accuse anything but his own incapacity. In a word, the conclusion at which we arrive is, that he only accepted power to be able to throw it off with effect, like Cato, who only went to the public theatres for the purpose of fussily leaving the place, at the moment when the audience called the actors before the curtain. Not being able or perhaps willing to save the Commune, M. Rossel desired to save himself at its expense. There is something ungentlemanly in this. Do not, however, imagine for a moment that I believe in M. Rossel having been bought by M. Thiers. All those ridiculous stories of sums of money having been offered to the members of the Commune, are merely absurd inventions.* What do you think they say of Cluseret? That he was in the habit of taking his breakfast at the Café d'Orsay, and afterwards playing a game of dominoes. One day his adversary is reported to have said to him, "If you will deliver the fort of Montrouge to the Versaillais, I will give you two millions." What fools people must be to believe such

---

* "A plot had just been discovered between Bourget of the Internationale, Billioray, member of the Commune, and Cérisier, captain of the 101st Battalion of the insurgent National Guard. For a certain sum of money they were to deliver Fort Issy into the hands of General Valentin, of the Versailles army. The succession of Rossel to the Ministry of War frustrated the whole project.

"In the night of the 17th of May another attempt of the same kind met with failure. The Communists Bourget, Billioray, Mortier, Cérisier, and Pilotel, the artist, traitors to their own treacherous cause, were to open the gates to the soldiers of Versailles, an hour after midnight, at the Point du Jour; the soldiers to be disguised as National Guards. But, at the appointed hour, Cérisier took fright, and contented himself with the money he had received on account (twenty-five thousand francs) in payment for his treachery, and did no more. When the Versailles troops presented themselves at the gates, they had to beat a retreat under a heavy fire of mitrailleuses."
Guerre des Communeux.

absurdities! Rossel has not sold himself, for the very good reason that nobody ever thought of buying him. It was his own idea to do what he did. For the pleasure of being insolent and showing his boldness, he has pulled down from its pedestal what he adored, consequently the most criminal among the members of the Commune, once a swindler, now a pilferer, is free to say to M. Rossel, who is, I am told, a man of intelligence and honesty, "You are worse than I am, for you have betrayed us!"

LXXIX.

I was told the following by an eye-witness of the scene. In a small room at the Hôtel de Ville five personages were seated round a table at dinner. The repast was of the most modest kind, and consisted of soup, one dish of meat, one kind of vegetable, cheese, and a bottle of *vin ordinaire* each. One would have thought oneself in a restaurant at two francs a head, if it had not been that the condiments had got musty during the siege; besides, there was something solemn and official in the very smell of the viands which took away one's appetite. However, our five personages swallowed their food as fast as they could. At the head of the table sat Citizen Jourde. Jourde looks about eight and twenty; he has a delicate looking, mathematical head, with brown curly hair and sallow complexion, a kind of Henri Heine of the Finance. Tall and thin, with his red scarf tied round his waist, he reminds us of one of the old Convention of '89. They sat for some time in silence, as if they were observing each other. At the end of the first course, Jourde took up a spoon and examined it, saying, "Silver! true there is silver at the Hôtel de Ville, I will send for it to-morrow!" One of the other guests said, "Pardon me, I have to answer for it, and shall not give it up."—"Oh, yes you will," answered Jourde, "I will have an order sent to you from the Domaine,"* and then, as if he were thinking aloud, goes on to express his satisfaction at having found an unexpected

FONTAINE, DIRECTOR OF PUBLIC DOMAINS AND REGISTRATION.†

sum of three hundred thousand francs, as it were on the dinner-table. A whole day's pay! He will be able to put by four millions

---

* The Commune occupied the Mint, and directed Citizen Camelinat, bronze-fitter, to manufacture gold and silver coin to the amount of 1,500,000 francs. Of that sum, 75,000 francs only was saved by the Versailles troops on their entry. The different articles of gold and silver found at the Hôtel des Monnaies represented a total weight of 1,186 lbs., and consisted of objects taken from the churches, religious houses, and government offices, Imperial plate, and presents to the city of Paris. All these objects have been sent to the repository of the Domaine, where they may be claimed on identification by their owners.

† Fontaine was nominated on the 18th of March director of the public domains and of registration. His name figures in the history of the revolutions, émeutes, and insurrections of Paris from 1848. He was a professional insurgent.

at the end of the week; he tries to be economical, but the war runs away with everything. "You must at least give me three days' notice for the payment of sums amounting to more than a hundred thousand francs," says he, with a shrug of the shoulders, particularly addressed to Beslay. Then he speaks of his hopes of reducing the Prussian debt before the year is out, if the Commune lives so long; touches on subjects connected with the taxes, patents and duties, "or else bank-notes worth five hundred francs in the morning, will only be worth twenty sous in the evening; money is scarce, it is leaving the city. I do not see much copper about, but if you leave me alone, I promise to succeed." All this was said in a tone of the most sincere conviction. When the dinner was over, he hastily bowed and rushed off, without having taken any notice of what was said to him. Every now and then cries arose in the streets, and made the members of the Commune start as they sat there behind their sombre curtains. "Do you think they can come in?" asked some one of Johannard, to which he replies, "What a wild idea! Delescluze knows it is impossible, and Dombrowski, a cold unexcitable fellow, only laughs when people mention it; does he not, Rigault?" Thereupon the personage addressed, who has not yet spoken, bows his head in sign of acquiescence. He looks young in spite of his thick, black beard; his eyes are weak, his expression is sly and disagreeable, and looks as if he might sometimes have his hours of coarse joviality. Then a *portière* was lowered, or a door shut, and the person who had overheard the preceding heard and saw no more.

LXXX.

I AM beginning to regret Cluseret. He was impatient, especially in speech. He used to say "Every man a National Guard!" But with Cluseret, as with one's conscience, there were possible conciliations. You had only to answer the decrees of the war delegate by an enthusiastic " Why I am delighted, indeed I was just going to beg you to send me to the Porte-Maillot;" which having done, one was free to go about one's business without fear of molestation. As to leaving Paris, in spite of the law which condemned every man under forty to remain in the city, nothing was easier. You had but to go to the Northern Railway Station, and prefer your request to a citizen, seated at a table behind a partition in the passport office.* When he asked you your age you had only to answer " Seventy-eight," passing your hand through your sable locks as you spoke—" Only that ? I thought you looked older," the accommodating individual would answer,

* The decree which rendered obligatory the service in the marching companies of the National Guard, and the establishment of courts-martial, spread terror among the population, and thousands of people thronged daily to the Prefecture of Police. Sometimes, the *queue* extended from the Place Dauphine to beyond the Pont Neuf. But soon afterwards, stratagems of every kind were put into requisition to escape from the researches of the Commune, which became more eager and determined, from day to day, after the publication of the following decree, the *chef-d'œuvre* of the too famous Raoul Rigault:—

" Ex-Prefecture of Police.
" Delivery of Passports.

" Considering that the civil authority cannot favour the non-execution of the decrees of the Commune, without failing in its duty, and that it is highly necessary that all communications with those who carry on this savage war against us should be prevented,

" The member of the Committee of Public Safety, Delegate at the Prefecture of Police,

" Decrees :—

" Art. 1. Passports can only be delivered on the production of satisfactory documents.

" Art. 2. No passport will be delivered to individuals between the ages of seventeen and thirty-five years; as such fall within the military law.

" Art. 3. No passport will be issued to any member of the old police, or who are in relation with Versailles.

" Art. 4. Any persons who come within the conditions of Articles 2 or 3, and apply for passports, will be immediately sent to the dépôt of the ex-Prefecture of Police.

(Signed) " Raoul Rigault,
" Member of the Committee of Public Safety."

at the same time putting into your hand a paper on which was written some cabalistic sign. One day I had taken it into my head to go and spend two hours at Bougival, and my pass bore the strange word "Carnivolus" written on it. Provided with this mysterious document, I was enabled to procure a first-class ticket and jump into the next train that started. I was free, and nothing could have prevented my going, if such had been my wish, to proclaim the Commune at Mont Blanc or Monaco.

How the times are changed! The Committee of Public Safety and the Central Committee now join together in making the lives of the poor *réfractaires** a burthen to them. I do not speak of the disarmaments, which have nothing particularly disagreeable about them, for an unarmed man may clearly nourish the hope that he is not to be sent to battle. But there are other things, and I really should not object to be a little over eighty for a few days. Domiciliary visits have become very frequent. Four National Guards walk into the house of the first citizen they please, and politely or otherwise, explain to him that it is his strict duty to go into the trenches at Vanves and kill as many Frenchmen as he can. If the citizen resists he is carried off, and told that on account of his resistance he will have the honour of being put at the head of his battalion at the first engagement. These visits often end in violence. I am told that in the Rue Oudinot a young man received a savage bayonet thrust because he resisted the corporal's order; and as these occurrences are not uncommon, the *réfractaires* cannot be said to live in peace and comfort. They are subject to continual terror, the sour visage of their *concierge* fills them with misgivings, he may be one of the Commune. As to going to bed, it must not be thought of; it is during the hours of night that the Communal agents are particularly active. This necessity of changing domicile has lead to certain Amélias and Rosalines and other ladies of that description having the words "Hospitality to *Réfractaires*" written in pencil on their cards. Men who decline to take advantage of such opportunities have to go about from

* Those who decline to join the Commune.

hotel to hotel, giving imaginary names, suspicious of the waiters, and awaking at the least sound, thinking it is the noise of feet ascending the stairs, or the rattle of muskets on the landing.

The day before yesterday a number of *réfractaires*, having the courage of despair, walked to the Porte Saint-Ouen—"Will you let us out?" asked they of the commanding officer, who answered in a decided negative; whereupon the party, which was three hundred strong, fell upon the captain and his men, whom they disarmed, and five minutes afterwards they were running free across the fields.

Others employ softer means of corruption; resort to the wine-shops of Belleville, where they make themselves agreeable in every way, and soon succeed in entering into friendly conversation with some of the least ferocious among the Federals of the place.

"You are on duty, Tuesday, at the Porte de la Chapelle?" —"Why, yes."—"So that you might very easily let a comrade out who wants to go and pay a visit at Saint-Denis?"—"Quite out of the question; the others would prevent me, or denounce me to the captain."—"You think there is nothing to be done with the captain?"—"Oh! no; he is a staunch patriot, he is!"— "How very tiresome; and I wanted most particularly to go to Saint-Denis on Tuesday evening. I would gladly give twenty francs out of my own pocket for the sake of a little walk outside the fortifications."—"There is only one way."—"And how is that?"—"You don't care much about going out by the door, do you?"—"Well, no; what I want is to get outside."—"Oh! then listen to me; come to La-Chapelle early on Tuesday evening, and walk up and down the rampart. I will try and be on duty at eight o'clock, and look out for you. When I see you I will take care not to say *qui vive*."—"That's easy enough; and what then?"—"Why, then I will secure around you a thick rope which of course you will have with you!"—"The devil!"—"And I will throw you into the trench."—"By Jove! That will be a leap."— "Oh! I will do it very carefully, without hurting you. I will let

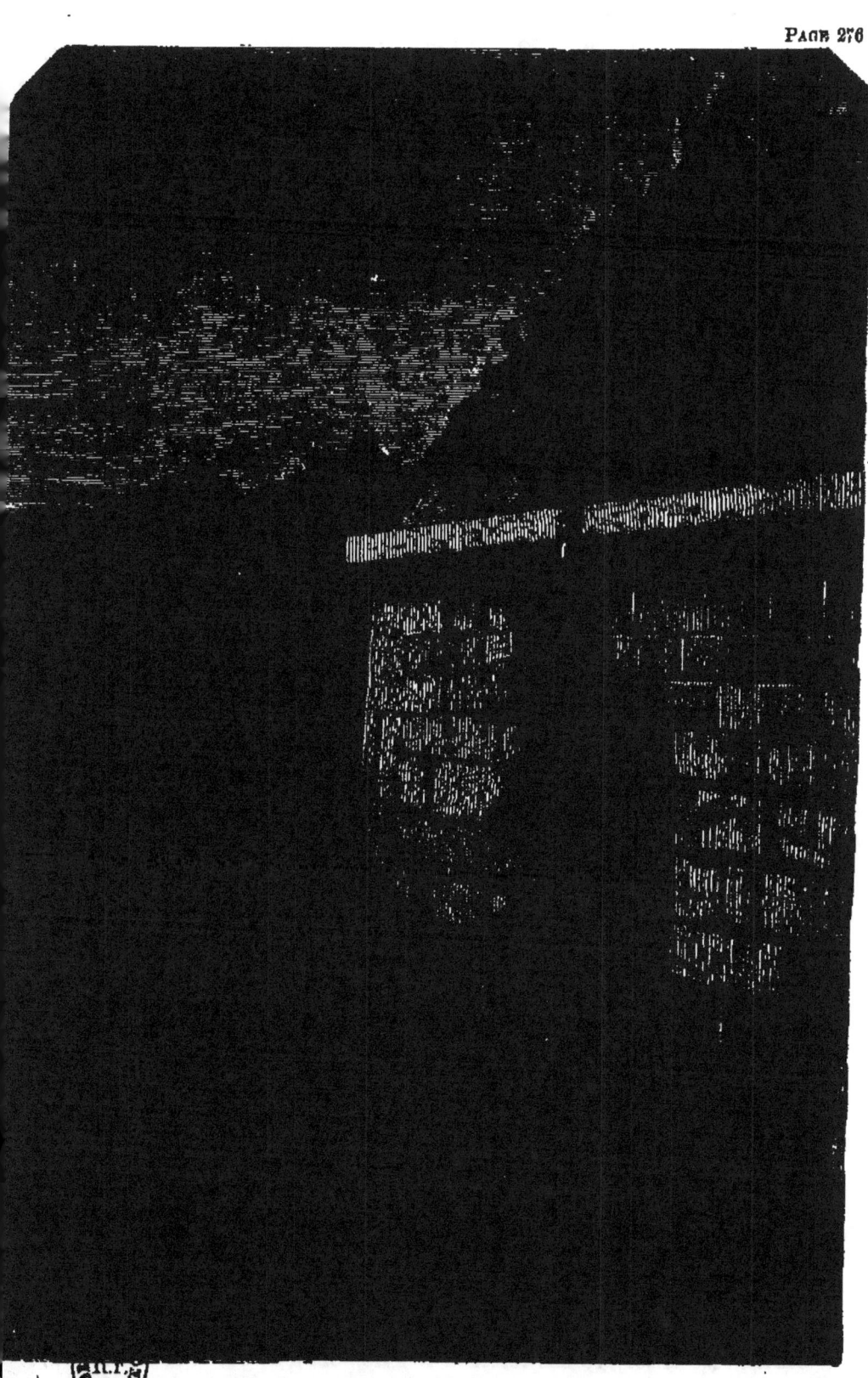

REFRACTORIES ESCAPING FROM PARIS.

you slip softly down the wall."—"Humph!"—"When you reach the ground below, in an instant you can be up and off into the darkness. Do you accept? Yes or no?"—"I should certainly prefer to drive out of the city in a coach and six, but nevertheless I accept."

Generally, this plan answers admirably. They say that the Federals of Belleville and Montmartre make a nice little income with this kind of business. Sometimes, however, the plan only half succeeds, and either the rope breaks, or the Federal considers, he may manage capitally to reconcile his interest with his duty, by sending a ball after the escaped *réfractaire*.

Disguises are also the order of the day. A poet, whose verses were received at the Comédie Française with enthusiasm during the siege, managed to get away, thanks to an official on the Northern Railway, who lent him his coat and cap. Another poet —they are an ingenious race—conceived a plan of greater boldness. One day on the Boulevard he called a fiacre, having first taken care to choose a coachman of respectable age. "*Cocher*, drive to the Rue Montorgueil, to the best restaurant you can find." On the way the poet reasoned thus to himself: "This coachman has in his pocket, as they all have, a Communal passport, which allows him to go out and come into Paris as he pleases; let me remember the fourth act of my last melodrama, and I am saved."

The cab stopped in front of a restaurant of decent exterior not far from Philippe's. The young man went in, asked for a private room, and told the waiter to send up the coachman, as he had something to say to him, and to procure a boy to hold the horse. The coachman walked into the room, where the breakfast was ready served.

"Now, coachman, I am going to keep you all day, so do not refuse to drink a glass with me to keep up your strength."

An hour after the poet and the coachman had breakfasted like old friends; six empty bottles testified that neither one nor the other were likely to die of thirst. The poet grumbled internally to himself as he thought of the three bottles of Clos-Vougeot, one of Léoville, two of Moulin-au-Vent, that had been consumed, and the fellow not drunk yet. Then he determined to try surer means, and called to the waiter to bring champagne. "It is no use, young fellow," laughed the coachman, who was familiar at least, if he was not drunk; "champagne won't make any difference; if you counted on that to get my passport, you reckoned without your host!"—"The devil I did," cried the poor young man, horrified to see his scheme fall through, and to think of the prodigious length of the bill he should have to pay for nothing.—"Others have tried it on, but I am too wide awake by half," said the coachman, adding as he emptied the last bottle into his glass, "give me two ten-franc pieces and I will get you through."—"How can I be grateful enough?" cried the poet, although in reality he felt rather humiliated to find that the grand scene in his fourth act had not succeeded.—"Call the waiter, and pay the bill." The waiter was called, and the bill paid with a sigh. "Now give me your jacket."—"My jacket?"—"Yes, this thing in velvet you have on your back." The poet did as he was bid. "Now your waistcoat and trousers."—"My trousers! Oh, insatiable coachman!"—"Make haste will you, or else I shall take you to the nearest guard-room for a confounded *réfractaire*, as you are." The clothes were immediately given up. "Very well; now take mine, dress yourself in them, and let's be off." While the young man was putting on with decided distaste the garments of the *cocher*, the latter managed to introduce his ponderous bulk into those of the poet. This done, out they went. "Get up on the box."—"On the box?"—"Yes, idiot," said the coachman, growing more and more familiar; "I am going to get into the cab, now drive me wherever you please." The plan was a complete success. At the Porte de Châtillon the disguised poet exhibited his passport, and the National Guard who looked in at the window of the carriage cried out, "Oh, he may pass; he might be my grandfather." The cab rolled over the draw-bridge, and it was in this way that M . . . .—ah! I was just going to let the cat out of the bag—it was in this way that our young poet broke the law of the Commune, and managed to dine that same evening at the Hôtel des Réservoirs at Versailles, with a deputy of the right on his left hand, and a deputy of the left on his right hand.

Shall I go away? Why not? Do I particularly wish to be shut up one morning in some barrack-room, or sent in spite of myself to the out-posts? My position of *réfractaire* is sensibly aggravated by the fact of my being in rather a dangerous neighbourhood. For the last few days, I have felt rather astonished at the searching glances that a neighbour always casts upon me, when we met in the street. I told my servant to try and find out who this man was. Great heavens! this scowling neighbour of mine is Gérardin—Gérardin of the Commune! Add to this the perilous fact that our *concierge* is lieutenant in a Federal battalion, and you will have good reason to consider me the most unfortunate of *réfractaires*. However, what does it matter? I decide on remaining; I will stay and see the end, even should the terrible Pyat and the sweet Vermorel both of them be living under the same roof with me, even if my *concierge* be M. Delescluze himself!

LXXXI.

Glorious news! I have seen Lullier again. We had lost Cluseret, lost Rossel; Delescluze does not suffice, and except for Dombrowski and La Cécilia with his prima-donna-like name, the company of the Commune would be sadly wanting in stars. Happily! Lullier has been restored to us. What had become of him? he only wrote seven or eight letters a day to Rochefort and Maroteau, that I can find out. How did he manage to employ that indomitable activity of his, and that of his two hundred friends, who with their red Garibaldis and blue sailor trousers made him the most picturesque escort you can imagine? Was he meditating some gigantic enterprise; the dictatorship that Cluseret had dreamed of and Rossel disdained, was he about

GENERAL LA CÉCILIA.*

to assume it for the good of the Republic? I have no idea; but whatever he has been doing, I have seen him again at the club held in the church of Saint Jacques.

Ha! ha! Worthless hypocrites and inquisitors, who for the last eighteen hundred years have crushed, degraded, and tortured the poor; you thought our turn was never to come, you monks, priests,

* A political refugee, who left his country in 1859 for Prussia, where he taught mathematics in the University of Ulm, and afterwards accepted service under Garibaldi.

and archbishops! Thanks to the Commune you now preach in

THE CHURCH OF SAINT EUSTACHE.
Used as a Red Club. Partly destroyed by fire.

the prisons of the Republic; you may confess, if you like, the spiders of your dungeons, and give the holy viaticum to the rats which play around your legs! You can no longer do any harm to patriots. No more churches, no more convents! Those who have not houses in the Champs Elysées shall lodge in your convents; in your churches shall be held honest assemblies, which will give the people their rights; as to their duties, that is an invention of reactionists. No more of your sermons or speeches: after Bossuet, Napoléon Gaillard!

On entering the church of Saint Eustache yesterday, I was agreeably surprised to find the font full of tobacco instead of holy-water, and to see the altar in the distance covered with bottles and glasses. Some one informed me that was the counter. In one of the lateral chapels, a statue of the Virgin had been dressed out in the uniform of a vivandière, with a pipe in her mouth. I was, however, particularly charmed with the amiable faces of the people I saw collected there. The sex to which we owe the *tricoteuses* was decidedly in the majority. It was quite delightful not to see any of those elegant dresses and frivolous manners, which have for so long disgraced the better half of the human race. Thank heaven! my eyes fell with rapture on the heroic rags of those ladies who do us the honour of sweeping our streets for us. Many of these female patriots were proud to bear in the centre of their faces a rubicund nose, that rivalled in colour the Communal flag on the Hôtel de Ville. Oh, glorious red nose, the distinguished sign of Republicanism! As to the men, they seemed to have been chosen among the first ranks of the new aristocracy. It was charming to note the military elegance with which their caps were slightly inclined over one ear; their faces, naturally hideous, were illuminated with the joy of freedom, and certainly the thick smoke which emanated from their pipes, must have been more agreeable as an offering, than the faint vapours of incense that used to arise from the gilded censers.

"Marriage, citoyennes, is the greatest error of ancient humanity. To be married is to be a slave. Will you be slaves?"—
"No, no!" cried all the female part of the audience, and the

INTERIOR OF THE CHURCH OF ST. EUSTACHE—COMMUNIST CLUB.

orator, a tall gaunt woman with a nose like the beak of a hawk, and a jaundice-coloured complexion, flattered by such universal applause, continued, "Marriage, therefore, cannot be tolerated any longer in a free city. It ought to be considered a crime, and suppressed by the most severe measures. Nobody has the right to sell his liberty, and thereby to set a bad example to his fellow citizens. The matrimonial state is a perpetual crime against morality. Don't tell me that marriage may be tolerated, if you institute divorce. Divorce is only an expedient, and if I may be allowed to use the word, an Orleanist expedient!" (Thunders of applause.) "Therefore, I propose to this assembly, that it should get the Commune of Paris to modify the decree, which assures pensions to the legitimate or illegitimate companions of the National Guards, killed in the defence of our municipal rights. No half measures. We, the illegitimate companions, will no longer suffer the legitimate wives to usurp rights they no longer possess, and which they ought never to have had at all. Let the decree be modified. All for the free women, none for the slaves!"

The orator descends from the pulpit amidst the most lively congratulations. I am told by some one standing near me, that the orator is a monthly nurse, who used to be a somnambulist in her youth. But the crowd opens now to give place to a male orator, who mounts the spiral staircase, passes his hand through his hair, and darts a piercing glance on the multitude beneath. It is Citizen Lullier.

This young man has really a very agreeable physiognomy; his forehead is intelligent, his eyes pleasant. Looking on M. Lullier's sympathetic face, one is sorry to remember his eccentricities. But what is all this noise about? What has he said? what has he done? I only heard the words "Dombrowski," and "La Cécilia." Every one starts to his feet, exasperated, shouting. Several chairs are about to be flung at the orator. He is surrounded, hooted. "Down with Lullier! Long live Dombrowski!" The tumult increases. Citizen Lullier seems perfectly calm in the midst of it all, but refuses to leave the pulpit; he tries in vain to speak and explain. Two women, two amiable hags, throw themselves upon him; several men rush up also; he is taken up bodily and carried away, resisting to the utmost and shouting to the last. The people jump up on the chairs, Lullier has disappeared, and I hear him no more; what have they done with him!

What do you think of all this, gentlemen and Catholics! Do you still regret the priests and choristers who used awhile ago to preach and chant in the Parisian churches? Where is the man, who at the very sight of this new congregation, so tolerant, so intelligent, listening with such gratitude to these noble lessons of politics and morality; where is the man, who could any longer blind himself to the admirable influence of the present revolution? Innumerable are the benefits that the Paris Commune showers upon us! As I leave the church, a little vagabond walks up to the font, and taking a pinch of tobacco,—" In the name of the * * *!" says he, then fills his pipe; " In the name of the * * *!" proceeding to strike a lucifer, adds, " In the name of the * * * * * *!"—" Confound the blasphemous rascal!" say I, giving him a good box on the ears. After having written these lines I felt inclined to erase them; on second thoughts I let them remain— they belong to history!

LXXXII.

This morning I took a walk in the most innocent manner, having committed no crime that I knew of. It was lovely weather, and the streets looked gay, as they generally do when it is very bright, even when the hearts of the people are most sad. I passed through the Rue Saint-Honoré, the Palais Royal, and finally the Rue Richelieu. I beg pardon for these details, but I am particularly careful in indicating the road I took, as I wish the inhabitants of the places in question, to bear witness that I did not steal in passing a single quartern loaf, or appropriate the smallest article of jewellery. As I was about to turn on to the boulevards, one of the four National Guards who were on duty, I do not know what for, at the corner of the street, cried out, "You can't pass!" All right, thought I to myself; there is nothing fresh I suppose, only the Commune does not want people to pass; of course, it has right on its side. Thereupon I began to retrace my steps. "You can't pass," calls out another sentinel, by the time I have reached the other side of the street.

This is strange, the Commune cannot mean to limit my walk to a melancholy pacing up and down between two opposite pavements. A sergeant came up to me; I recognised him as a Spaniard, who during the siege belonged to my company. "Why are you not in uniform?" he asked me, with a roughness that I fancied was somewhat mitigated by the remembrance of the many cigars I had given him, the nights we were on guard during the siege. I understood in an instant what they wanted with me, and replied unhesitatingly, "Because it is not my turn to be on guard."—"No, of course it's not, it never is. You have been taking your ease this long time, while others have been getting killed." It was evident this Spaniard had not taken the cigars I had given him, in good part, and was now revenging himself.— "What do you want with me?" I said; "let's have done with this." Instead of answering, he signed to two Federals standing near, who immediately placed themselves one on each side of me, and cried, "March!" I was perfectly agreeable, although this walk was not exactly in the direction I had intended. On the way I heard a woman say, "Poor young man! They have taken him in the act." I was conducted to the church of Notre-Dame-de-Lorette, and marched into the vestry, where about fifty *réfractaires* were already assembled.

Behind a deal table, on which were placed a small register, an inkstand stuck in a great bung, and two quill pens, sat three young men, almost boys, in uniform. You might have imagined them to be Minos, Æacus, and Rhadamanthus, at the age when they played at leap-frog. "Your name?" said Rhadamanthus, addressing me. I did not think twice about it, but gave them a name which has never been mine. Suddenly some one behind me burst out laughing; I turned round and recognised an old friend, whom I had not noticed among the other prisoners. "Your profession?" inquired Minos.—"Prizefighter," I answered, putting my arms akimbo and looking as ferocious as possible, by way of keeping up the character I had momentarily assumed. To the rest of the questions that were addressed to me, I replied in the same satisfactory manner. When it was over, Minos said to me, "That is enough; now go and sit down, and wait until you are called."—"Pardon me, my young friend, but I shall not go and sit down, nor shall I wait a moment more."—"Are you making fun of us? We are transacting most serious business, our lives are at stake. Go and sit down."—"I have already had the honour to remark, my dear Rhadamanthus, that I did not mean to sit down. Be kind enough to allow me to depart instantly."—"You ask *me* to do this?"—"Yes! you!" I shouted in a tremendous voice. The three judges looked at me in great perplexity, and began whispering amongst themselves. A prize fighter, by jingo! I thought the moment had come to strike a decisive blow, so I pulled out of my pocket a little green card, which I desired them to examine. Immediately Minos, Æacus, and Rhadamanthus got up, bowed to me most respectfully, and called out to two National Guards who were at the door, "Allow the citizen to pass."—"By-the-bye," said I, pointing to my friend, "this gentleman is with me."—"Allow both the citizens to pass," shouted the lads in chorus.—"This is capital," cried my friend as soon as we were well outside the door. —"How did you manage?"—"I have a pass from the Central Committee."—"In your own name?"—"No, I bought it of the widow of a Federal, who was on very good terms with Citizen Félix Pyat."—"Why, it is just like a romance."—"Yes, but a romance that allows me to live pretty safely in the midst of this strange reality. Anyhow, I think we had better look out for other lodgings."

LXXXIII.

At ten o'clock in the evening I was walking up the Rue Notre-Dame-de-Lorette. In these times the streets are quite deserted at that hour. Looking on in front I saw that the Place Saint-Georges was lighted up by long tongues of flame, that the wind blew hither and thither. I hastened on, and was soon standing in front of M. Thiers' house.* At the open gate stood a sentinel;

* It should be remarked that the destruction of M. Thiers' house coincided with the first success of the Versailles army; it was the spirit of hatred and mad destructiveness which dictated the following decree, issued by the Committee of Public Safety on the 10th of May:—

"Art. 1. The goods and property of Thiers (they even denied him the appellation of citizen) are seized by order of the administration of public domains.

"Art. 2. The house of Thiers, situated at the Place Saint-Georges, to be demolished."

On the following day the National Assembly, in presence of the activity exhibited by M. Thiers, declared that the proscribed, whose house was demolished, had exhibited proofs of an amount of patriotism and political ability which inspired every confidence in the future. On the 12th of the same month works were commenced at Versailles for the formation of a railway-station sufficient for all the wants of an important army, the initiation of which was due to M. Thiers; a conference was opened on the 19th April with the Western Railway Company, the plans were approved on the 22nd of the same month, and the preliminary works were commenced on the 12th of May. When these are terminated, they will consist of thirty-five parallel lines of rails, more than a mile in length. But the principal point in the plan is, that by means of branches to Pontoise and Chevreuse, this immense station may be placed in direct communication with all the lines of railway in France. It is easy enough to draw the following conclusion, namely, that if the necessity should ever again arise, Paris would cease to be the central depot for all commercial movements, and thus the paralysis of the affairs of the whole country would be avoided, in case the Parisian populace should again be bitten by the barricade mania.

At one time it was feared that the collections of M. Thiers were

a large fire had been lighted in the court by the National Guard

HOUSE OF M. THIERS, PLACE SAINT-GEORGES.

not that the night was cold, they seemed to have lighted it

destroyed in the conflagration at the Tuileries; but M. Courbet reports that on the 12th of May he asked what he ought to do about the different things taken at the house of M. Thiers, and if they were to

merely for the pleasure of burning furniture and pictures, that had been left behind by the Communal waggoners. They had already begun to pull down the right side of the house; a pickaxe was leaning against a loosened stone; the roof had fallen in, and a rafter was sticking out of one of the windows. The fire rose higher and higher; would it not be better that the flames should reach the house and consume it in an hour or two, than to see it being gradually pulled down, stone by stone, for many days to come? In the court I perceived several trucks full of books and linen. A National Guard picked up a small picture that was lying near the gate; I bent forward and saw that it was a painting of a satyr playing on a flute. How sad and cruel all this seemed! The men lounging about looked demoniacal in the red light of the fire. I turned away, thinking not of the political man, but of the house where he had worked, where he had thought, of the books that no longer stood on the shelves, of the favourite chair that had been burnt on the very hearth by which he had sat so long; I thought of all the dumb witnesses of a long life destroyed, dispersed, lost, of the relatives and friends whose traces had disappeared from the rooms empty to-day, in ruins to-morrow; I thought of all this, and of all the links that would be broken by a dispersion, and I trembled at the idea that some day—in these times anything seems possible—men may break open the doors of my modest habitation, knock about the furniture of which I have grown fond, destroy my books which have so long been the companions of my studies, tear the pictures from my walls, and burn the verses that I love for the sake of the

be sent to the Louvre or to be publicly sold, and he was then appointed a member of the commission to examine the case. Regarding his conduct at the time of the demolishing of the house of M. Thiers, he arrived too late, he says, to make an inventory; the furniture and effects had been already packed by the *employés* of the Garde Meuble: "I made some observations about it, and on going through the empty apartments, I noticed two small figures that I packed in paper, thinking they might be private *souvenirs*, and that I would return them some day to their owner. All the other things were already destroyed or gone."

U

trouble they have given me to make,—kill, in a word, all th[e]
renders life agreeable to me, more cruelly than if four Federa[ls]

HOUSE OF M. THIERS DURING DEMOLITION AND REMOVAL.

were to take me off and shoot me at the corner of a street. But
I am not a political man. I belong to no party—who would think

of doing me any injury? I am perfectly harmless, with my love-sick metaphor. Ah! how egotistical one is! It was of my own home that I thought while I stood in front of the ruin in the Place Saint-Georges. I confess that I was particularly touched by the misfortunes of that house, because it awakened in me the fear of my own misfortune, most improbable, and most diminutive, it is true, in comparison with that.

LXXXIV.

An anecdote: Parisian all over; but with such stuff are they amused!

Raoul Rigault, the man who arrests, was breakfasting with Gaston Dacosta, the man who destroys. These two friends are worthy of each other. Rigault has incarcerated the Archbishop of Paris, but Dacosta claims the merit of having loosened the first stone in M. Thiers' house. But however, Rigault would destroy if Dacosta were not there to do so; and if Rigault did not arrest, Dacosta would arrest for him.

They talked as they ate. Rigault enumerated the list of people he had sent to the Conciergerie and to Mazas, and thought with consternation that soon there would be no one left for him to arrest. Suddenly he stopped his fork on its way to his mouth, and his face assumed a most doleful expression.—" What's the matter?" cried Dacosta, alarmed.—" Ah!" said Rigault, tears choking his utterance, "Papa is not in Paris."—" Well, and what does it matter if your father is not here?"—" Alas!" exclaimed Rigault, bursting out crying, "I could have had him arrested!" *

* The illegality of his conduct, however, was too glaring even for the Commune, and he was removed from his post on a complaint made by Arthur Arnould, to the committee, concerning the arbitrary arrest of a number of persons. Cournet was appointed to the Préfecture in Rigault's stead, but the amateur policeman and informer did not

COURNET, MEMBER OF COMMITTEE OF GENERAL SAFETY.

LXXXV.

The horrible cracking sound that is heard at sea when a vessel splits upon a rock, is not a surer sign of peril to the terrified crew, than are the vain efforts, contradictions and agitation at the Hôtel de Ville, the forerunners of disaster to the men of the Commune. Listen! the vessel is about to heave asunder. Everybody gives orders, no one obeys them. One man looks defiantly at another; this man denounces that, and Rigault thinks seriously of arresting them both. There is a majority which is

renounce work; he found the greatest pleasure, as he himself expressed it, in acting the spy over the official spies. This man was a well-known frequenter of the low cafés of the Quartier Latin, and his face bore such evidences of his debauched life, that though only twenty-eight years of age, he looked nearer forty.

not united, and a minority that cannot agree amongst themselves. Twenty-one members retire, they do well.* I am glad to find on the list the names of the few that Paris still believes in, and whom, thanks to this tardy resignation, it will not learn to despise. For instance, Arthur Arnould. But why should they take the trouble to seek out a pretext? Why did they not say simply: "We have left them because we find them full of wickedness; we were blinded as you were at first, but now we in our turn see clearly; a good cause has been lost by madmen or worse, and we have abandoned it because, if we were to stay a moment longer, now that we are no longer blinded, we should be committing a criminal act." Such words as these would have opened

---

* An important document has just made the round of the Communal press—the manifesto of the minority of the Commune, in which twenty-one members declare their refusal to take any farther part in the deliberations of the body, which they accuse of having delivered its powers into the hands of the Committee of Public Safety, and thus rendering itself null. This declaration is signed by:—Arthur Arnould, Avrial, Andrieux, Arnold, Clémence, Victor Clément, Courbet, Franckel, Eugène Gérardin, Jourde, Lefrançais, Longuet, Malon, Ostyn, Pindy, Serailler, Tridon, Theisz, Varlin, Vermorel, Jules Vallès.

Adding to these twenty-one secessionists, twenty-one members who have resigned:—Adam, Barré, Brelay, Beslay, De Bouteiller, Chéron, Desmarest, Ferry, Fruneau, Goupil, Loiseau-Pinson, Leroy, Lefèvre, Méline, Murat, Marmottan, Nast, Ulysse Parent, Robineat, Rano, Tirard;

Three who have not sat: Briosne, Menotti Garibaldi, Rogeard;

Two dead: Duval, Flourens;

One captured: Blanqui;

One escaped: Charles Gérardin;

Five incarcerated: Allix, Panille dit Blanchet, Brunel, Emile Clément, Cluseret;—

Out of 101 members elected to the Commune on the 26th of March and the 16th of April, only forty-seven now remain:—Amouroux, Ant. Arnaud, Assy, Babick, Billioray, Clément, Champy, Chardon, Chalain, Demay, Dupont, Decamp, Dereure, Durant, Delescluze, Eudes, Henry Fortuné, Ferré, Gambon, Geresme, Paschal Grousset, Johannard, Ledroit, Langevin, Lonclas, Mortier, Léo Meiller, Martelet, J. Miot, Oudet, Protot, Paget, Pilotel, Félix Pyat, Philippe, Parisel, Pottier, Régère, Raoul Rigault, Sicard, Triquet, Urbain, Vaillant, Verdure, Vésinier, Viart.

the eyes of so many wretched beings, who are going to their

ARTHUR ARNOULD, COMMISSIONER OF FOREIGN AFFAIRS.*

deaths and think they do well to die! As to those who remain,

---

* Arnould is a man of about forty-seven years of age, small in stature, lively and intelligent. He has written in many of the Democratic journals of Paris and the provinces; and his literary talents are of a good kind. Being connected with Rochefort's journal, the *Marseillaise*, he was sent by the latter to challenge Pierre Bonaparte, and was a witness at the trial which followed the murder of Victor Noir.

Although naturally drawn by his connections into the movement of the eighteenth of March, he always protested loudly against the arbitrary acts of the Commune, and it is surprising that he did not fall under accusation by his colleagues. He opposed particularly the proposals for the suppression of newspapers. "It is prodigious to me," he said, in full meeting of the committee, "that people will still talk of arresting others for expressing their opinions."

He voted against the organisation of the Committee of Public Safety on the ground:—

"That such an institution would be directly opposed to the political

they must feel that their power is slipping from them. They did not arrest or detain Rossel; it would seem as if they dared not touch him because he was right in thinking what he said, although he was very wrong to say it as he did. While the Commune hesitates, the military plans of the Versaillais are being carried out. Vanves taken, Montrouge in ruins, breaches opened at the Point-du-Jour, at the Porte-Maillot, at Saint-Ouen; the Communists have only to choose now, between flight and the horrors of a terrible death struggle! May they fly, far, far away, beyond the reach of vengeance, despised, forgotten if that be possible! I am told that the Central Committee is trying now to substitute itself for the Commune, which was elected by its desire.* One born of the other, they will die together.

opinions of the electoral body, of which the Commune is the representative."

He protested most energetically against secret imprisonment—

"Secret incarceration has something immoral in it; it is moral torture substituted for physical.

"I cannot understand men who have passed their life in combating the errors of despotism, falling into the same faults when they arrive at power. Of two things one: either secret imprisonment is an indispensable and good thing; or, it is odious. If it was good it was wrong to oppose it, and if it be odious and immoral, we ought not to continue it."

What on earth had he then to do in the Commune?

"Que diable allait-il faire dans cette galère?"

* "REPUBLICAN FEDERATION OF THE NATIONAL GUARD.

"Central Committee.

"To the People of Paris! To the National Guard!

"Rumours of dissensions between the majority of the Commune and the Central Committee have been spread by our common enemies with a persistency which, once for all, must be crushed by public compact.

"The Central Committee, appointed to the administration of military affairs by the Committee of Public Safety, will enter upon office from this day.

"This Committee, which has upheld the standard of the Communal revolution, has undergone no change and no deterioration. It is to-day what it was yesterday, the legitimate defender of the Commune, the basis of its power, at the same time as it is the determined enemy

LXXXVI.

It was five o'clock in the afternoon. The day had been splendid and the sun shone brilliantly on Cæsar still standing on the glorious pedestal of his victories. Outside the barricades of the Rue de la Paix and the Rue Castiglione, the crowd was standing in a compact mass, as far as the Tuileries on one side and the New Opera House on the other. There must have been from twenty to twenty-five thousand people there. Strangers accosted each other by the title of Citizen. I heard some talking about an eccentric Englishman who had paid three thousand francs for the pleasure of being the last to climb to the summit of the column. Nearly every one blamed him for not having given the money to the people. Others said that Citizen Jourde would not manage to cover his expenses; Abadie* the engineer had asked thirty-two thousand francs to pull down the great trophy, and that the stone and plaster was after all, not covered with more than an inch or two of bronze, that it was not so many metres

of civil war; the sentinel placed by the people to protect the rights that they have conquered.

"In the name, then, of the Commune, and of the Central Committee, who sign this pact of good faith, let these gross suspicions and calumnies be swept away. Let hearts beat, let hands be ready to strike in the good cause, and may we triumph in the name of union and fraternity.

"Long live the Republic!
"Long live the Commune!
"Long live the Communal Federation!

"The Commission of the Commune, BERGERET, CHAMPY, GERESME, LEDROIT, LONCLAS, URBAIN.

"The Central Committee.

"Paris, 19th May, 1871."

* Abadie arranged to demolish the Colonne Vendôme for 32,000 or 35,000 francs, forfeiting 500 francs for every day's delay after the fourth of May. This reduced the sum to be paid to him by 6000 francs.

high, and would not make a great many two-sous pieces after all. These sous seemed to occupy the public mind exceedingly, but the

BARRICADE OF THE RUE CASTIGLIONE, FROM THE PLACE VENDOME.

principal subjects of conversation, were the fears concerning the probable effects of the fall.

The event was slow in accomplishment. The wide Place was thinly sprinkled with spectators, not more than three hundred in all, privileged beings with tickets, or wearing masonic badges; or officers of the staff. Bergeret at one of the windows was coolly smoking a cigarette; military bands were assembled at the four angles of the Place; the sound of female laughter reached us from the open windows of the Ministère de la Justice. The horses of the mounted sentinels curvetted with impatience; bayonets glittered in the sun; children gaped wearily, seated on the curbstone. The hour of the ceremony was past; a rope had broken. Around the piled faggots on which the column was to fall, great fascines of flags of the favourite colour were flying.

The crowd did not seem to enjoy being kept in suspense, and proclaimed their impatience by stamping with measured tread, and crying "Music!"

At half-past five there was a sudden movement and bustle around the barricade of the Rue Castiglione. The members of the Commune appeared with their inevitable red scarfs.* Then there was a great hush. At the same instant the windlass creaked; the ropes which hung from the summit of the column tightened; the gaping hole in the masonry below, gradually closed; the statue bent forward in the rays of the setting sun, and then suddenly describing in the air a gigantic sweep, fell among the flags with a dull, heavy thud, scattering a whirlwind of blinding dust in the air.

Then the bands struck up the "Marseillaise," and cries of "Vive la Commune" were re-echoed on all sides by the terror or the indifference of the multitude. In a marvellously short time,

* Regarding Courbet and the destruction of the Column, he rejects the accusation on the ground that this decree had been voted previously to his admission in the Commune, and on the request he had made under the Government of the 4th of May of removing the column to the esplanade of the Invalides. He affirms that the official paper has altered his own words at the Commune, and he pretends having proposed to the Government to rebuild the column at his own expense, if it can be proved that he has been the cause of its destruction.

however, all was quiet again, so quiet, indeed, that I distinctly heard a dog bark as it ran frightened across the Place.

I daresay the members of the Commune, who presided over the accomplishment of this disgraceful deed, exclaimed in the pride of their miserable hearts, "Cæsar, those whom you salute shall live!"

Everybody of course wished to get a bit of the ruin, as visitors to Paris eagerly bought bits of siege bread framed and glazed, and there was a general rush towards the place; but the National Guards crossed their bayonets in front of the barricade, and no one was allowed to pass. So that the crowd quickly dispersed to its respective dinners. "It is fallen!" said some to those who had not been fortunate enough to see the sight. "The head of the statue came off—no one was killed." The boys cried out, "Oh, it was a jolly sight all the same!" But the greater part of the people were silent as they trudged away.

Then night came on, and next day a land-mark and a finger-post seemed missing in our every-day journey. Until we lose a familiar object we hardly appreciate its existence.

LXXXVII.

On the sixteenth, I received a prospectus through my concierge. There was to be a concert, mixed with speeches—a sort of popular fête at the Tuileries. The places varied in price from ten sous to five francs. Five francs the Salle des Maréchaux; ten sous the garden, which was to be illuminated with Venetian lamps among the orange-trees; the whole to be enlivened by fireworks from the Courbevoie batteries.

I had tact enough not to put on white gloves, and set out for the palace.

It was not a fairy-like sight; indeed, it was a most depressing spectacle. A crowd of thieves and vagabonds, of dustmen and

THE PALACE OF THE TUILERIES, FROM THE GARDEN.

The last concert held in the Tuileries by the Commune took place on Sunday, the 21st March, when Auteuil and Passy had been in the power of the army for several hours. Two days later the old palace was in flames. Citizen Félix Pyat had advocated the preservation of the Tuileries in the *Vengeur*, proposing to convert it into an "asylum for the victims of work and the martyrs of the Republic. This residence," he wrote, "ought to be devoted to the people, who had already taken possession of it."

rag-pickers, with four or five gold bands on their sleeves and caps, (the insignia of officers of the National Guard), were hurrying along down the grand staircase, chewing "imperiales," spitting, and repeating the old jokes of '93. As to the women—they were sadly out of place. They simpered, and gave themselves airs, and some of them even beat time with their fans, as Mademoiselle Caillot was singing, to look as if they knew something about music.

The concert took place in the Salle des Maréchaux: a platform had been erected for the performers. The velvet curtains with their golden bees still draped the windows. From the gallery above I could see all that was going on. The Imperial balcony opens out of it; I went there, and leaned on the balustrade with a certain feeling of emotion. Below were the illuminated gardens, and far away at the end of the Champs Elysées, almost lost in the purple of the sky, rose the Arc de Triomphe de l'Etoile.

The roaring of the cannon at Vanves and Montrouge reached me where I stood. When the duet of the "*Maître de Chapelle*" was over, I returned into the hall; the distant crashing of the mitrailleuse at Neuilly, borne towards us on the fresh spring breeze, in through the open windows, joined its voice to the applause of the audience.

Oh! what an audience! The faces in general looked fit subjects for the gibbet; others were simply disgusting: surprise, pleasure, and fear of Equality were reflected on every physiognomy. The carpenter, Pindy, military governor of the Hôtel de Ville, was in close conversation with a girl from Philippe's. The ex-spy Clémence muttered soft speeches into the ear of a retired *chiffonnière*, who smiled awkwardly in reply. The cobbler Dereure was intently contemplating his boots; while Brilier, late coachman, hissed the singers by way of encouragement, as he would have done to his horses. They were going to recite some verses: I only waited to hear—

"PUIS, QUEL AVEUGLEMENT! QUEL NON-SENS POLITIQUE!"

an Alexandrine, doubtless, launched at the National Assembly, and made my way to the garden as quickly as I could.

There, in spite of the Venetian lamps, all was very dull and dark. The walks were almost deserted, although it was scarcely half-past nine. I took a turn beneath the trees: the evening was cold; and I soon left the gardens by the Rue de Rivoli gate. A good many people were standing there " to see the grand people come from the fête"—a fête given by lackeys in a deserted mansion!

LXXXVIII.

I was busy writing, when suddenly I heard a fearful detonation, followed by report on report. The windows rattled: I thought the house was shaking under me. The noise continued: it seemed as if cannon were roaring on all sides. I rushed down into the street; frightened people were running hither and thither, and asking questions. Some thought that the Versaillais were bombarding Paris on all sides. On the Boulevards I was told it was the fort of Vanves that had been blown up. At last I arrived on the Place de la Concorde: there the consternation was great, but nothing was known for certain. Looking up, I saw high up in the sky what looked like a dark cloud, but which was not a cloud. I tried again and again to obtain information. It appeared pretty certain that an explosion had taken place near the Ecole Militaire—doubtless at the Grenelle powder-magazine. I then turned into the Champs Elysées. A distant cracking was audible, like the noise of a formidable battery of mitrailleuses. Puffs of white smoke arose in the air and mingled with the dark cloud there. I no longer walked, I ran: I hoped to be able to see something from the Rond Point de l'Etoile. Once there, a grand and fearful sight met my eyes. Vast columns of smoke rolled over one another towards the sky. Every now and then the wind swept them a little on one side, and for an instant a portion of the city was visible beneath the rolling vapours. Then in an instant a flame burst out—only one, but that gigantic, erect, brilliant, as one that might dart forth from a volcano sud-

RAZOUA, GOVERNOR OF THE ÉCOLE MILITAIRE.*

denly opened, up through the smoke which was reddened, illumined by the eruption of the fire. At the same moment there were explosions as of a hundred waggons of powder blown up one

* Razoua served in a regiment of Spahis in Africa. Becoming acquainted with the journalists who used to frequent the Café de Madrid, he was a constant attendant there. He took up literature, and in 1867 published some violent articles in the *Pilori* of Victor Noir. He afterwards went with Delescluze to the *Réveil*, where his revolutionary principles were manifested. In the month of February, 1871, he was elected a member of the National Assembly by the people of Paris. After having sat for some time at Bordeaux, he gave his resignation, and became one of the Communal council.

Appointed governor of the École Militaire, he distinguished himself in no way in his position, except by the sumptuous dinners and déjeûners with which he regaled his friends.

after another. All this scene, in its hideous splendour, blinded and deafened me. I wanted to get nearer, to feel the heat of the burning, to rush on. I had the fire-frenzy!

Going down to the Quai de Passy, I found a dense crowd there. Some one screamed out: "Go back! go back! the fire will soon reach the cartridge-magazine." The words had scarcely been uttered, when a storm of balls fell like hail amongst us. Each person thought himself wounded, and many took to their heels. It did not enter into my head to run away. From where I was then, the sight was still more terribly beautiful, and the crowd that had withdrawn from the spot soon re-assembled again. Dreadful details were passed from mouth to mouth. Four five-storied houses had fallen; no one dared to think even of the number of the victims. Bodies had been seen to fall from the windows, horribly mutilated; arms and legs had been picked up in different places. Near the powder-magazine is a hospital, which was shaken from foundation to roof: for an instant it had trembled violently as if it were going to fall. The nurses, dressers, and even the sick had rushed from the wards, shrieking in an agony of fear; the frightened horses, too, with blood streaming down their sides, pranced madly among the fugitives, or galloped away as fast as they could from the awful scene.

As to the cause of the explosion, opinions varied much. Some said it was owing to the negligence of the overseers or the imprudence of the workwomen; others, that the fire was caused by a shell. A woman rushed up to us, screaming out that she had just seen a man arrested in a shed in the Champ de Mars, who acknowledged having blown up the powder-magazine, by order of the Versailles government. Of course this was inevitable. The Commune would not let such a good opportunity pass for accusing its enemies. A few innocent people will be arrested, tried with more or less form, and shot; when they are so many corpses, the Commune will exclaim, "You see they must have been guilty: they have been shot!"

As evening came on I turned home, thinking that the cup was

now filled to overflowing, and that the devoted city had had to suffer defeat, civil war, infamy, and death ; but that this last disaster seemed almost more than divine justice. Ever and anon I turned my head to gaze again. In the gathering gloom, the flames looked blood-red, as if the Commune had unfurled its sinister banner over that irreparable disaster.

LXXXIX.

I HAVE gazed so long on what was passing around me that my eyes are weary. I have watched the slow decline of joy, of comfort and luxury, almost without knowing how everything has been dying around me, as a man in a ball-room where the candles are put out, one by one, may not perceive at first the gathering gloom. To see Paris, as it is at the present moment, as the Commune has made it, requires an effort. Let me shut my eyes, and evoke the vision of Paris as it was, living, joyous, happy even in the midst of sadness. I have done so—I have brought it all back to me ; now I will open my eyes and look around me.

In the street that I inhabit not a vehicle of any kind is visible. Men in the uniform of National Guards pass and repass on the pavement ; a lady is talking with her *concierge* on the threshold of one of the houses. They talk low. Many of the shops are closed ; some have only the shutters up ; a few are quite open. I see a woman at the bar of the wine-shop opposite, drinking.

Some quarters still resist the encroachments of silence and apathy. Some arteries continue to beat. Some ribbons here and there brighten up the shop-windows : bare-headed shopgirls pass by with a smile on their lips ; men look after them as they trip along. At the corner of the Boulevards a sort of tumult is occasioned by a number of small boys and girls, venders of

Communal journals, who screech out the name and title of their wares at the top of their voices. But even there where the crowd is thickest, one feels as if there were a void. The two contrary ideas of multitude and solitude seem to present themselves at once in one's mind. A weird impression! Imagine a vast desert with a crowd in it.

The Boulevards look interminable. There used to be a hundred obstacles between you and the distance; now there is nothing to prevent your looking as far as you like. Here and there a cab, an omnibus or two, and that is all. The passers-by are no longer promenaders. They have come out because they were obliged: without that they would have remained at home. The distances seem enormous now, and people who used to saunter about from morning till night will tell you now that "the Madeleine is a long way off." Very few men in black coats or blouses are to be seen; only very old men dare show themselves out of uniform. In front of the cafés are seated officers of the Federal army, sometimes seven or eight around a table. When you get near enough, you generally find they are talking of the dismissal of their last commander. Here and there a lady walks rapidly by, closely veiled, mostly dressed in black, with an unpretending bonnet. The gallop of a horse is distinctly audible—in other times one would never have noticed such a thing; it is an express with despatches, a Garibaldian, or one of the *Vengeurs de Flourens*, who is hoisted on a heavy cart-horse that ploughs the earth with its ponderous forefeet. Several companies of Federals file up towards the Madeleine, their rations of bread stuck on the top of their bayonets. Look down the side-streets, to the right or the left, and you will see the side-walks deserted, and not a vehicle from one end to the other of the road. Even on the Boulevards there are times when there is no one to be seen at all. However, beneath it all there is a longing to awaken, which is crushed and kept down by the general apathy.

In the evening one's impulses burst forth; one must move about; one must live. Passengers walk backwards and forwards, talking in a loud voice. But the crowd condenses itself between the Rue Richelieu and the Rue du Faubourg Montmartre. Solitude has something terrible about it just now. People congregate together for the pleasure of elbowing each other, of trying to believe they are in great force. Quite a crowd collects round a little barefooted girl, who is singing at the corner of a street. A man seated before a low table is burning *pastilles*; another offers barley-sugar for sale; another has portraits of celebrities. Everybody tries hard to be gay; but the shops are closed, and the gas is sparingly lighted, so that broad shadows lie between the groups.

Some few persons go to the theatres; the playbills, however, are not seductive. If you go in, you will find the house nearly empty; the actors gabble their parts with as little action as possible. You see they are bored, and they bore us. Sometimes when some actor, naturally comic, says or does something funny, the audience laughs, and then suddenly leaves off and looks more serious than before. Laughter seems out of place. One does not know how to bear it; so one walks up and down the corridors, then instead of returning to the play, wanders out again on to the Boulevard. It is ten o'clock—dreadfully late. Many of the cafés are already closed for the night. At Tortoni's and the Café Anglais, not a glimmer is visible. The crowd has nearly disappeared. Only a few officers remain, who have been drinking all the evening in an *estaminet*. They call to each other to hurry on; perhaps one of them is drunk, but even he is not amusing. Let us go home. Scarcely anyone is left in the street. A bell is rung here and there, as the last of us reach our respective homes.

That, Commune de Paris, is what you have made of Paris! The Prussians came, Paris awaited them quietly with a smile; the shells fell on its houses, it ate black bread, it waited hours in the cold to obtain an ounce of horse-flesh or thirty pounds of green wood; it fought, but was vanquished; it was told to surrender, and "it was given up," as they say at the Hôtel de Ville; and yet through all, Paris had not ceased to smile. And this, they say, constitutes its greatness; it was the last protestation against unmerited misfortunes; it was the remembrance of having once been proud and happy, and the hope of becoming so again; it was, in a word, Paris declaring it was Paris still. Well, what neither defeats, nor famine, nor capitulation could do, thou hast done! And accursed be thou, O Commune; for, as Macbeth murdered sleep, thou hast murdered our smiles!

XC.

THE roaring of cannon close at hand, the whizzing of shells, volleys of musketry! I hear this in my sleep, and awake with a start. I dress and go out. I am told the troops have come in. "How? where? when?" I ask of the National Guards who come rushing down the street, crying out, "We are betrayed!" They, however, know but very little. They have come from the Trocadéro, and have seen the red trousers of the soldiers in the distance. Fighting is going on near the viaduct of Auteuil, at the Champ de Mars. Did the assault take place last night or this morning? It is quite impossible to obtain any reliable information. Some talk of a civil engineer having made signals to the Versaillais; others say a captain in the navy was the first to enter Paris.* Suddenly about thirty men

---

* It was known by this time at Versailles in what a desperate condition was the Commune, by the information of persons devoted to order, but who remained amongst the insurgents to keep watch over and restrain them as much as possible.

The Versailles authorities know that, thanks to the well-directed fire of Montretout, the bastions of the Point du Jour were no longer tenable, and that their defenders had abandoned them and had organized new works of defence; nevertheless, the operations were carried on just as systematically as if the fire of the besieged had not ceased for several days, when, on Sunday, the 21st May, about midday, an officer on duty in the trenches, in course of formation in the Bois de Boulogne, perceived a man making signs with a white handkerchief

CAFÉ LIFE UNDER THE COMMUNE.
et au hazard.

SPECTACLES DE PARIS.

rush into the streets crying, "We must make a barricade." I turn back, fearing to be pressed into the service. The cannonading appears dreadfully near. A shell whistles over my head. I hear some one say, "The batteries of Montmartre are bombarding the Arc de Triomphe;" and strange enough, in this moment of horror and uncertainty, the thought crosses my mind that now the side of the arch on which is the bas-relief of Rude will be exposed to the shells. On the Boulevard there is only here and there a passenger hurrying along. The shops are closed; even the cafés are shut up. The harsh screech of the mitrailleuse grows louder and nearer. The battle seems to be close at hand, all round me. A thousand contradictory suppositions rush

near the military post of Saint Cloud; the officer immediately approached near enough to hear the bearer of the flag of truce, say:—

"My name is Ducatel, and I belong to the service of the Engineers of Roads and Bridges, and I have been a soldier. I declare that your entrance into Paris is easy, and as a guarantee of the truth of what I say, I am about to give myself up;" so saying, he passed over the fosse by means of one of the supports of the drawbridge, in spite of several shots fired at him by Federals hidden in the houses at Auteuil, but none of which reached him.

A few resolute men now passed over the fosse, and arrived without accident on the other side. A few insurgents, who were still there, made off without loss of time, leaving the invaders to establish themselves, and wait for reinforcements.

A short time after a white flag was exhibited in the neighbouring bastion, which bore the number 62, and the fire from Montretout and Mont Valérien was stopped, the infantry of the Marine took possession of the gate, cut the telegraphic wires which were supposed to be in communication with torpedoes, while information was immediately despatched to Versailles of these important events.

The division of General Vergé, placed for the time under the orders of General Douay, entered the gate at half-past three in the afternoon, and took possession of Point du Jour, after having taken several barricades; at one of these, Ducatel was sent with a flag of truce towards the insurgents, who offered to surrender, but he received a bayonet wound, was carried off to the École Militaire, tried by court-martial and condemned to death, from which he was fortunately snatched by the arrival of the Versailles troops at the Trocadéro at two o'clock in the morning.

At the same time, the first corps d'armée (that of General L'Admirault), made its way into the city by the Portes d'Auteuil and Passy, and took up a strong position in the streets of Passy.

through my brain and hurry me along, and here on the Bou[le]vard there is no one that can tell me anything. I walk in the [di]rection of the Madeleine, drawn there by a violent desire to kn[ow] what is going on, which silences the voice of prudence. As [I] approach the Chaussée d'Antin I perceive a multitude of m[en,] women, and children running backwards and forwards, carryi[ng] paving-stones. A barricade is being thrown up; it is alrea[dy] more than three feet high. Suddenly I hear the rolling of hea[vy] wheels; I turn, and a strange sight is before me—a mass [of] women in rags, livid, horrible, and yet grand, with the Phrygi[an] cap on their heads, and the skirts of their robes tied round the[ir] waists, were harnessed to a mitrailleuse, which they dragge[d] along at full speed; other women pushing vigorously behin[d.] The whole procession, in its sombre colours, with dashes of re[d] here and there, thunders past me; I follow it as fast as I can. Th[e] mitrailleuse draws up a little in front of the barricade, and is haile[d] with wild clamours by the insurgents. The Amazons are bein[g] unharnessed as I come up. "Now," said a young *gamin*, such a[s] one used to see in the gallery of the Theatre Porte St. Martin[,] "don't you be acting the spy here, or I will break your head open as if you were a Versaillais."—"Don't waste ammunition," cried an old man with a long white beard—a patriarch of civil war— "don't waste ammunition; and as for the spy, let him help to carry paving-stones. Monsieur," said he, turning to me with much politeness, "will you be so kind as to go and fetch those stones from the corner there?"

I did as I was bid, although I thought, with anything but pleasure, that if at that moment the barricade were attacked and taken, I might be shot before I had the time to say, "Allow me to explain." But the scene which surrounds me interests me in spite of myself. Those grim hags, with their red headdresses, passing the stones I give them rapidly from hand to hand, the men who are building them up only leaving off for a moment now and then to swallow a cup of coffee, which a young girl prepares over a small tin stove; the rifles symmetrically piled; the barricade, which rises higher and higher; the solitude in which we are working—only here and there a head appears at a window, and is quickly withdrawn; the ever-increasing noise of the battle; and, over all, the brightness of a dazzling morning sun—all this has something sinister and yet horribly captivating about it. While we are at work, they talk; I listen. The Versaillais have been coming in all night.* The Porte de la Muette and the Porte Dauphine have been surrendered by the 13th and the 113th battalions of the first arrondissement. "Those two numbers 13 will bring them ill-luck," says a woman. Vinoy is established at the Trocadéro, and Douai at the Point du Jour: they continue to advance. The Champ de Mars has been taken from the Federals after two hours' fighting. A battery is erected at the Arc de Triomphe, which sweeps the Champs Élysées and bombards the Tuileries. A shell has fallen in the Rue du Marché Saint Honoré. In the Cours-la-Reine the 188th battalion stood bravely. The Tuileries is armed with guns, and shells the Arc de Triomphe. In the Avenue de Marigny the gendarmes have shot twelve Federals who had surrendered; their bodies are still lying on the pavement in front of the tobacconist's. Rue de Sèvres, the *Vengeurs de Flourens* have put to flight a whole regiment of the line: the *Vengeurs* have sworn to resist to a man. They are fighting in the Champs Élysées, around the Ministère de la Guerre, and on the Boulevard Haussman. Dom-

---

* At ten o'clock at night, the army had taken possession of the region comprised between the *ceinture*, or circular railway, and the fortifications, the streets of Auteuil to the viaduct, and the bridge of Grenelle.

At midnight, the movement which had been suspended for a time to rest the troops, was recommenced all along the line.

At two o'clock in the morning, General Douay occupied the Trocadéro; and at about four o'clock his soldiers, after a short struggle, captured the château of La Muette, making about six hundred prisoners, and then, advancing in the direction of Porte Maillot, they joined the troops of General Clinchant, who had got within the ramparts on that side.

At the break of day, the tricolour floated over the Arc de Triomphe, without the Versailles forces having sustained sensible loss. All this passed on the right bank of the Seine.

browski has been killed at the Château de la Muette. The V[er]‐
saillais have attacked the Western Saint Lazare station, and [are]
marching towards the Pépinière barracks. "We have be[en]
sold, betrayed, and surprised; but what does it matter, we w[ill]
triumph. We want no more chiefs or generals; behind t[he]
barricades every man is a marshal!"

Eight or ten men come flying down the Chaussée d'Antin; th[ey]
join, crying out, "The Versaillais have taken the barracks; th[ey]
are establishing a battery. Delescluze has been captured at t[he]
Ministère de la Guerre."—"It is false!" exclaims a vivandièr[e,]
"we have just seen him at the Hôtel de Ville."—"Yes, yes," c[ry]
out other women, "he is at the Hôtel de Ville. He gave us [a]
mitrailleuse. Jules Vallés embraced us, one after another; he [is]
a fine man, he is! He told us all was going well, that the Ve[r]‐
saillais should never have Paris, that we shall surround them, a[nd]
that it will all be over in two days."—"Vive la Commune!" [is]
the reply. The barricade is by this time finished. They expe[ct]
to be attacked every second. "You," said a sergeant, "you ha[d]
better be off, if you care for your life." I do not wait for th[e]
man to repeat his warning. I retrace my steps up the Boulevar[d,]
which is less solitary than it was. Several groups are standin[g]
at the doors. It appears quite certain that the troops of th[e]
Assembly have been pretty successful since they came in. Th[e]
Federals, surprised by the suddenness and number of the attack[,]
at first lost much ground. But the resistance is being organised[.]
They hold their own at the Place de la Concorde; at the Plac[e]
Vendôme they are very numerous, and have at their disposal [a]
formidable amount of artillery. Montmartre is shelling furiously[.]
I turn up the Rue Vivienne, where I meet several people in searc[h]
of news. They tell me that "two battalions of the Faubour[g]
Saint Germain have just gone over to the troops, with thei[r]
muskets reversed. A captain of the National Guard has been the
first in that quarter to unfurl the tricolour. A shell had set fir[e]
to the Ministère des Finances, but the firemen in the midst of th[e]
shot and shell had managed to put it out." At the Place de la

POOR PRADIER'S STATUES.

Bourse I find three or four hundred Federals constructing a barricade; having gained some experience, I hurry on to escape the trouble of being pressed into the service. The surrounding streets are almost deserted; Paris is in hiding. The cannonading is becoming more furious every minute. I cross the garden of the Palais Royal. There I see a few loiterers, a knot of children are skipping. The Rue de Rivoli is all alive with people. A battalion marches hurriedly from the Hôtel de Ville; at the head rides a young man mounted on a superb black horse. It is Dombrowski. I had been told he was dead. He is very pale. "A fragment of shell hit him in the chest at La Muette, but did not enter the flesh," says some one. The men sing the *Chant du Départ* as they march along. I see a few women carrying arms among the insurgents; one who walks just behind Dombrowski has a child in her arms. Looking in the direction of the Place de la Concorde, I see smoke arising from the terrace of the Tuileries. In front of the Ministère des Finances, this side of the barricade is a black mass of something; I think I can distinguish wheels; it is either cannon or engines. All around is confusion. I can hear the musketry distinctly, but the noise seems to come from the Champs Élysées; they are not firing at the barricade. I turn and walk towards the Hôtel de Ville: mounted expresses ride constantly past; companies of Federals are here and there lying on the ground around their piled muskets. By the Rue du Louvre there is another barricade; a little further there is another and then another.* Close to Saint Germain l'Auxerrois women

---

* The insurrectionists followed a decided and pre-conceived plan. The barricades, which intersected the streets of Paris in every direction, were arranged on a general system which showed considerable skill. Was this ensemble a conception of Cluseret? or a plan of Gaillard, or Eudes, or Rossel? No one now could say which, but at any rate we are able to deduce the plan from the facts and set it out as follows:—

Within the line of the fortifications the insurgents had formed a second line of defence, which runs on the right bank of the river, by the Trocadéro, the Triumphal Arch, the Boulevard de Courcelles, the Boulevard de Batignolles, and the Boulevard de Rochechouart;

are busy pulling down the wooden seats; children are rolling empty wine-barrels and carrying sacks of earth. As one nears the Hôtel de Ville the barricades are higher, better armed, and better manned. All the Nationals here look ardent, resolved, and fierce. They say little, and do not shout at all. Two guards seated on the pavement, are playing at picquet. I push on, and am allowed to pass. The barricades are terminated here, and I have nothing to fear from paving-stones. Looking up, I see that all the windows are closed, with the exception of one, where two old women are busy putting a mattress between the window and the shutter. A sentinel, mounting guard in front of the Café de la Compagnie du Gaz, cries out to me, "You can't pass here!" I therefore seat myself at a table in front of the café, which has doubtless been left open by order, and where several officers are talking in a most animated manner. One of them rises and advances towards me. He asks me rudely what I am doing there. I will not allow myself to be abashed by his tone, but draw out my pass from my pocket and show it him, without saying a word.

and on the left across the bridge of Jéna, the Avenue de la Bourdonnaye, the École Militaire, the Boulevard des Invalides, the Boulevard Montparnasse, and the Western Railway Station. Along the whole extent of this circuit the entrances of the streets were barricades, and the "Places" turned into redoubts.

From this double *enceinte* of fortifications the lines of defence converged along the great boulevards, the Rue Royale, by the Ministry of Marine, the terrace of the Tuileries Gardens, the Place de la Concorde, the Palace of the Corps Législatif, the Rue de Bourgogne, and the Rue de Varenne. This third *enceinte* of defence was the pride of the insurgents; they were never tired of admiring their celebrated barricade of the Rue St. Florentin, and that which intercepted the quay at the corner of the Tuileries Gardens on the Place de la Concorde.

This is not all. Supposing that the third line were forced, the insurgents would not even then be without resource. On the left bank of the Seine they fell back successively on the Rue de Grenelle, Rue Saint Dominique, and Rue de Lille, all three closed by barricades; on the right bank they could carry on the struggle by the Rue Neuve-des-Petits-Champs, the Rue de la Paix, and the Place Vendôme, and even when beaten back from these last retreats, they could still defend the Rue St. Honoré and operate a retreat by the Palace of the Tuileries, the Louvre, and the Hôtel de Ville.

"All right," says he, and then seats himself by my side, and tells me, "I know it already, that a part of the left bank of the river is occupied by the troops of the Assembly, that fighting is going on everywhere, and that the army on this side is gradually retreating.—Street fighting is our affair, you see," he continues. In such battles as that, the merest gamin from Belleville knows more about it than MacMahon. . . . It will be terrible. The enemy shoots the prisoners." (For the last two months the Commune had been saying the same thing.) "We shall give no quarter."—I ask him, "Is it Delescluze who is determined to resist?"—"Yes," he answers.* "Lean forward a little. Look at

---

* In the following proclamation, published on the 21st May, Delescluze stimulated the Communist party, which felt its power melting away on all sides:

"To the People of Paris, to the National Guard.

"Citizens,—We have had enough of militaryism; let us have no more stuffs embroidered and gilt at every seam!

"Make room for the people, the real combatants, the bare arms! The hour of the revolutionary war has struck!

"The people know nothing of scientific manœuvres, but with a rifle in hand and the pavement beneath their feet, they fear not all the strategists of the monarchical school.

"To arms, citizens! To arms! You must conquer, or, as you well know, fall again into the pitiless hands of the *réactionaires* and clericals of Versailles; those wretches who with intention delivered France up to Prussia, and now make us pay the ransom of their treason!

"If you desire the generous blood which you have shed like water during the last six weeks not to have been shed in vain, if you would see liberty and equality established in France, if you would spare your children sufferings and misery such as you have endured, you will rise as one man, and before your formidable bands the enemy who indulges the idea of bringing you again under his yoke, will reap nothing but the harvest of the useless crimes with which he has disgraced himself during the past two months.

"Citizens! your representatives will fight and die with you, if fall we must; but, in the name of our glorious France, mother of all the popular revolutions, the permanent source of ideas of justice and unity, which should be and which will be the laws of the world, march to the encounter of the enemy, and let your revolutionary energy prove

those three windows to the left of the trophy. That is the Salle de l'État-Major. Delescluze is there giving orders, signing commissions. He has not slept for three days. Just now I scarcely knew him, he was so worn out with fatigue. The Committee of Public Safety sits permanently in a room adjoining, making out proclamations and decrees."—"Ha, ha!" said I, "decrees!"— "Yes, citizen, he has just decreed heroism!"* The officer gives me several other bits of information. Tells me that "Lullier this very morning has had thirty *réfractaires* shot, and that Rigault has gone to Mazas to look after the hostages." While he is talking, I try to see what is going on in the Place de l'Hôtel de Ville. Two or three thousand Federals are there, some seated, some lying on the ground. A lively discussion is going on. Several little barrels are standing about on chairs; the men are continually getting up and crowding round the barrels, some have no glasses, but drink in the palms of their hands. Women walk up and down in bands, gesticulating wildly. The men shout, the women shriek. Mounted expresses gallop out of the Hotel, some in the direction of the Bastille, some towards the Place de la Concorde. The latter fly past us crying out, "All's well!" A man comes out on the balcony of the Hôtel de Ville and addresses the crowd. All the Federals start to their feet enthusiastically.—"That's Vallès," says my neighbour to me. I had already recognised him. I frequently saw him in the students' quarter in a little *crémerie* in the Rue Serpente. He was given to making verses, rather bad ones by-the-bye; I remember one in particular, a panegyric on a green coat. They used to say he had a situation in the *pompes*

---

to him that Paris may be sold, but can never be delivered up or conquered.

"The Commune confides in you, and you may trust the Commune!
"The civil delegate at the Ministry of War.
"(Signed)   "CH. DELESCLUZE.
"Countersigned by the Committee of Public Safety:—Antoine Arnauld, Billioray, E. Eudes, F. Gambon, G. Ranvier."

Such was the despairing cry of the insurrection at bay.

* See Appendix, No. 9.

funèbres.* His face even then wore a bitter and violent expression. He left poetry for journalism, and then journalism for politics.

JULES VALLÈS, COMMISSIONER OF PUBLIC INSTRUCTION.†

* There are no private undertakers and funeral furnishers in Paris. It is all done by a company, under the supervision of Government, a very large concern, called the *Pompes Funèbres.*

† Jules Vallès was one of the most conspicuous among the men of the 18th of March. He had been journalist, working printer, a clerk at the Hôtel de Ville, editor of a newspaper, pamphleteer, and café orator in turn, but always noisy and boastful. André Gill, the caricaturist, once drew him as an undertaker's dog, dragging a saucepan behind him, and the caricature told Vallès' story well enough. In face he was ugly, but energetic in expression, almost to ferociousness.

He was born at Puy, in 1833, and on leaving the college of Nantes, came to study law in Paris, but politics occupied him chiefly, and he soon got himself shut up in Mazas as a political prisoner. After some time spent in confinement, he obtained his liberty, and published at Nantes, a pamphlet under the title of "Money: by a literary man become a journalist;" and the pamphlet, having gained him some slight popularity, he was engaged, later, on the *Figaro*, to write the

To-day he is spouting forth at a window of the Hôtel de Vill[e]
I cannot catch a word of what he says; but as he retires he [is]
wildly applauded. Such applause pains me sadly. I feel th[at]
these men and these women are mad for blood, and will kno[w]
how to die. Alas! how many dead and dying already! neith[er]
the cannonading nor the musketry has ceased an instant. I no[w]
see a number of women walk out of the Hotel, the crowd make[s]
room for them to pass. They come our way. They are dresse[d]
in black, and have black crape tied round their arms and a re[d]
cockade in their bonnets. My friend the officer tells me tha[t]
they are the governesses who have taken the places of the nuns.
Then he walks up to them and says, "Have you succeeded?"—
"Yes," answers one of them, "here is our commission. The schoo[l]
children are to be employed in making sacks and filling them
with earth, the eldest ones to load the rifles behind the barricades.
They will receive rations like National Guards, and a pension
will be given to the mothers of those who die for the Republic.
They are mad to fight, I assure you. We have made them work
hard during the last month, this will be their holiday!" The
woman who says this is young and pretty, and speaks with a sweet

reports of the Bourse, and in the meantime he eked out his slender
salary by working as a clerk at the Hôtel de Ville. When Ernest
Feydeau brought out the *Epoque*, in 1864, Jules Vallès published
a few articles in its columns, and a little later became a writer on the
Evénement, with the magnificent salary of eighteen thousand francs
a year. A month afterwards, he was without occupation again, but he
soon re-appeared with a new journal of his own, *La Rue*. *La Rue*, in
its turn, however, only lived during a few numbers, and Jules Vallès
now took up café politics, and practised table oratory at the *Estaminet
de Madrid*, where he fostered and expounded the projects which he
has since brought to so fearful a result.

In 1869, he became one of the most inveterate speakers at election
meetings, and presented himself as a candidate for the Corps Législatif. He was not elected, but the profession of opinions that he then
made was certain to obtain him a seat in the Communal Assembly.
One of the last articles in the *Cri du Peuple* of Jules Vallès announced
the fatal resolution of defending Paris by all possible means. An
article finishing with this prophetic sentence, "M. Thiers, if he is
chemist enough will understand us."

smile on her lips. I shudder. Suddenly two staff officers appear and ride furiously up to the Hôtel de Ville; they have come from

BARRICADE DIVIDING THE RUE DE RIVOLI AND THE PLACE DE LA CONCORDE.

the Place Vendôme. An instant later and the trumpets sound. The companies form in the Place, and great agitation reigns in the Hotel. Men rush in and out. The officers who are in the café where I am get up instantly, and go to take their places at the head of their men. A rumour spreads that the Versaillais have taken the barricades on the Place de la Concorde.—"By Jove! I think you had better go home," says my neighbour to me, as he clasps his sword belt; "we shall have hot work here, and that shortly." I think it prudent to follow this advice. One glance at the Place before I go. The companies of Federals have just started off by the Rue de Rivoli and the quays at a quick march, crying "Vive la Commune!" a ferocious joy beaming in their faces. A young man, almost a lad, lags a little behind, a woman rushes up to him, and lays hold of his collar, screaming, "Well, and you, are you not going to get yourself killed with the others?"

I reach the Rue Vieille-du-Temple, where another barricade is being built up. I place a paving-stone upon it and pass on. Soon I see open shops and passengers in the streets. This tradesmen's quarter seems to have outlived the riot of Paris. Here one might almost forget the frightful civil war which wages so near, if the conversation of those around did not betray the anguish of the speakers, and if you did not hear the cannon roaring out unceasingly, "People of Paris, listen to me! I am ruining your houses. Listen to me! I am killing your children."

On the boulevards more barricades; some nearly finished, others scarcely commenced. One constructed near the Porte Saint Martin looks formidable. That spot seems destined to be the theatre of bloody scenes, of riot and revolution. In 1852, corpses laid piled up behind the railing, and all the pavement tinged with blood. I return home profoundly sad; I can scarcely think. —I feel in a dream, and am tired to death; my eyelids droop of themselves; I am like one of those houses there with closed shutters.

Near the Gymnase I meet a friend whom I thought was at Versailles. We shake hands sadly. "When did you come back?" I ask.—"To-day; I followed the troops."—Then turning back

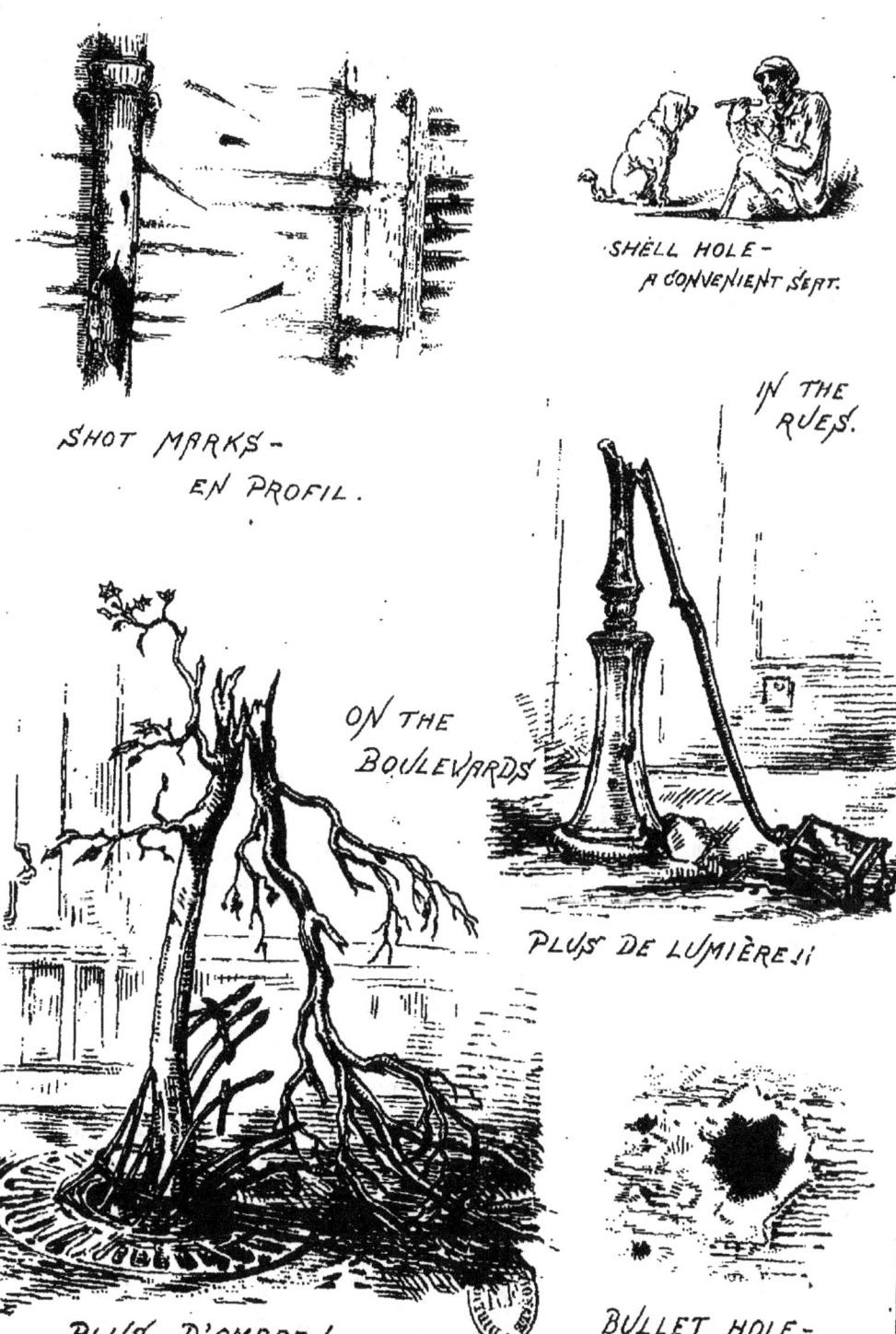

with me he tells me what he has seen. He had a pass, and walked into Paris behind the artillery and the line, as far as the Trocadéro, where the soldiers halted to take up their line of battle. Not a single man was visible along the whole length of the quays. At the Champ de Mars he did not see any insurgents. The musketry seemed very violent near Vaugirard on the Pont Royal and around the Palais de l'Industrie. Shells from Montmartre repeatedly fell on the quays. He could not see much,—however only the smoke in the distance. Not a soul did he meet. Such frightful noise in such solitude was fearful. He continued his way under shelter of the parapet. In one place he saw some gamins cutting huge pieces of flesh off the dead body of a horse that was lying in the path. There must have been fighting there. Down by the water a man fishing while two shells fell in the river, a little higher up, a yard or two from the shore. Then he thought it prudent to get nearer to the Palais de l'Industrie. The fighting was nearly over then, but not quite. The Champs Elysées was melancholy in the extreme; not a soul was there. This was only too literally true, for several corpses lay on the ground. He saw a soldier of the line lying beneath a tree, his forehead covered with blood. The man opened his mouth as if to speak as he heard the sound of footsteps, the eyelids quivered and then there was a shiver, and all was over. My friend walked slowly away. He saw trees thrown down and bronze lamp-posts broken; glass crackled under his feet as he passed near the ruined kiosques. Every now and then turning his head he saw shells from Montmartre fall on the Arc de Triomphe and break off large fragments of stone. Near the Tuileries was a confused mass of soldiery against a background of smoke. Suddenly he heard the whizzing of a ball and saw the branch of a tree fall. From one end of the avenue to the other, no one; the road glistened white in the sun. Many dead were to be seen lying about as he crossed the Champs Élysées. All the streets to the left were full of soldiery; there had been fighting there, but it was over now. The insurgents had retreated in the direction of the Madeleine. In many places tricolor flags were hanging from the windows, and women were smiling and waving their handkerchiefs to the troops. The presence of the soldiery seemed to reassure everybody. The concierges were seated before their doors with pipes in their mouths, recounting to attentive listeners the perils from which they had escaped; how balls pierced the mattresses put up at the windows, and how the Federals had got into the houses to hide. One said, "I found three of them in my court; I told a lieutenant they were there, and he had them shot. But I wish they would take them away; I cannot keep dead bodies in the house." Another was talking with some soldiers, and pointing out a house to them. Four men and a corporal went into the place indicated, and an instant afterwards my friend heard the cracking of rifles. The concierge rubbed his hands and winked at the bystanders, while another was saying, "They respect nothing those Federals; during the battle they came in to steal. They wanted to take away my clothes, my linen, everything I have, but I told them to leave that, that it was not good enough for them, that they ought to go up to the first floor, where they would find clocks and plate, and I gave them the key. Well, Messieurs, you would never believe what they have done, the rascals! They took the key and went and pillaged everything on the first floor!" My friend had heard enough, and passed on. The agitation everywhere was very great. The soldiers went hither and thither, rang the bells, went into the houses, and brought out with them pale-faced prisoners. The inhabitants continued to smile politely but grimly. Here and there dead bodies were lying in the road. A man who was pushing a truck allowed one of the wheels to pass over a corpse that was lying with its head on the curbstone. "Bah!" said he, "it won't do him any harm." The dead and wounded were, however, being carried away as quickly as possible.

The cannon had now ceased roaring, and the fight was still going on close at hand—at the Tuileries doubtless. The townspeople were tranquil and the soldiery disdainful. A strange contrast; all these good citizens smiling and chatting, and the soldiers, who had come to save them at the peril of their lives, looking down upon them with the most careless indifference. My friend reached the Boulevard Haussmann; there the corpses were in large numbers. He counted thirty in less than a hundred yards. Some were lying under the doorways; a dead woman was seated on the bottom stair of one of the houses. Near the church of "La Trinité" were two guns, the reports from which were deafening; several of the shells fell on a bathing establishment in the Rue Taitbout opposite the Boulevard. On the Boulevard itself, not a person was to be seen. Here and there dark masses, corpses doubtless. However, the moment the noise of the report of a gun had died away, and while the gunners were reloading, heads were thrust out from doors to see what damage had been done—to count the number of trees broken, benches torn up, and kiosques overturned. From some of the windows rifles were fired. My friend then reached the street he lived in and went home. He was told that during the morning they had violently bombarded the Collége Chaptal, where the Zouaves of the Commune had fortified themselves; but the engagement was not a long one, they made several prisoners and shot the rest.

My friend shut himself up at home, determined not to go out. But his impatience to see and hear what was going on forced him into the streets again. The Pépinière barracks were occupied by troops of the line; he was able to get to the New Opera without trouble, leaving the Madeleine, where dreadful fighting was going on, to the right. On the way were to be seen piled muskets, soldiers sitting and lying about, and corpses everywhere. He then managed, without incurring too much danger, to reach the Boulevards, where the insurgents, who were then very numerous, had not yet been attacked. He worked for some little time at the barricade, and then was allowed to pass on. It was thus that we had met. Just as we were about to turn up the Faubourg Montmartre a man rushed up saying that three hundred Federals had taken refuge in the church of the Madeleine, followed by gendarmes, and had gone on fighting for more than an hour. "Now," he finished up by saying, "if the *curé* were to return he would find plenty of people to bury!"

I am now at home. Evening has come at last; I am jotting down these notes just as they come into my head. I am too much fatigued both in mind and body to attempt to put my thoughts into order. The cannonading is incessant, and the fusillade also. I pity those that die, and those that kill! Oh! poor Paris, when will experience make you wiser?

XCI.

It is imprudent to go out; the night was almost peaceable, the morning is hideous. The roar of musketry is intense and without interruption. I suppose there must be fighting going on in the Rue du Faubourg Montmartre. I start back, the noise is so fearful. In the Cour Trévise not a person to be seen, the houses are closely shut and barred. On a second floor I hear a great moving of furniture, and hear quite distinctly the sound of sobbing, of female sobbing. I hear that the second floor of the house is inhabited by a member of the Commune and his family. I am about to go up and see if I can be of any help to the women in case of danger, when I see a man precipitately enter the Court. He wears a uniform of lieutenant; I recognise him, it is the porter. He stops, looks around him, and seeing that he is alone, takes his rifle in both hands and throws it with all his strength over the high wall which is on the left hand of the Court. That done, he rushes into the house. There I distinctly hear him say to his wife, "The barricade is taken, give me a *blouse*, they are at Montmartre. We are done for!" I think the porter must have made a mistake, and that the battery is not taken yet, for I hear the whistling of a shell that seems to come from Montmartre. The deafening clamour on all sides redoubles, all the separate noises seem to confound themselves in one ceaseless roar, like the working of a million of hammers on a million of anvils. I can scarcely bear it; my hands clutch the door-posts convulsively. I lean out as far as I can, but see nothing but a company of soldiers preceded by two gendarmes, who are entering the Court. They stop before the door of the house. Several of them go in, and then I hear the sound of a door suddenly opened and shut, and heavy steps on the wooden floor. I feel myself trembling; this man they have come to arrest—are they going to shoot him here, in his own apartment, before his wife? Thank God, no! The two gendarmes reappear in the street holding the prisoner between them; his hands are bound; the soldiers surround them, and they are going to march away, when the man, lifting up his arms, cries fiercely, "I have but one regret, that I did not blow up the whole of the quarter." At this instant the window above is opened, and a woman with grey hair leans out, crying, "Die in peace, I will avenge you!" At these words the soldiers arrest their steps, and the two gendarmes re-enter the house. They are going to take the wife prisoner after having taken the husband. I fall back into a chair horrified; I shut my eyes not to see, and I press my hands on my ears, not to hear the dreadful sound of the musketry, but the horrible shrill noise is triumphant, and I hear it all the same.

XCII.

OH! those that hear it not, how happy they must be; they will never understand how fearful this continuous, this dreadful noise is, and to feel that each ball is aimed at some breast, and each shell brings ruin in its train. Fear and horror wrings one's heart and maddens one's brain. Visions pass before one's eyes of corpses, of houses crushing sleeping inmates, of men falling and crying out for mercy! and one feels quite strange to go on living among the crowds that die!

I have been out a little while, a ball whistled over my shoulder, and flattened itself against an iron bar on a shop front. I heard a mass of glass shiver into fragments on the pavement. I determined to return home.

On my way back, I had to pass in front of a liqueur shop, the door of which was open, and several men were talking there. I stopped to learn the news. Montmartre is taken; the Federals had not opposed much resistance; but a great deal of firing had gone on in the side streets and lanes. Seven insurgents were surrounded. "Give yourselves up, and your lives will be saved," cried out the soldiers. They replied, "We are prisoners;" but one of them drew his revolver and shot an officer in the leg. Then the soldiers took the seven men, threw them into a large hole, and shot them from above like so many rabbits. Another man told me that he had seen a child lying dead at the corner of the Rue de Rome. "A pretty little fellow," he said, "his brains were strewed on the pavement beside him." A third, that when all the fighting was over at the Place Saint-Pierre a rifle shot was heard, and a captain of Chasseurs fell dead. The major who was there, looked up and saw a man trying to hide himself behind a chimney pot; the soldiers got into the house, seized him on the roof, and brought him down into the Place. What did the insurgent do, but walked up to the major, smiling, and hit him a blow on the cheek. The major set him up against a wall, and blew his brains out with a revolver. Another insurgent who was arrested, made an insulting grimace at the soldiers; they shot him. On the southern sides of Paris, the operations of the army have not been so fortunate as on this. In the Faubourg St. Germain it advances very slowly, if it advance at all. The Federals fight with heroic courage at the Mont-Parnasse Station, the Rue

Notre-Dame-des-Champs, and the Croix-Rouge; from the corners of the streets, from the windows, from the balconies proceed shots rarely ineffective. This sort of warfare fatigues the soldiers, particularly as the discipline prevents them from using the same measures. At Saint-Ouen, likewise, the march of the troops is stayed; the barricade of the Rue de Clichy holds out, and will hold out some time. In other quarters the advantages gained by the Versaillais are evident. Here and there some small show of resistance is offered, but the insurgents are flying. I cannot tell whether all these floating rumours are true. As I return home, I look round; in the Rue Geoffroy-Marie, near the Faubourg Montmartre, I see a National Guard alone in the middle of the street, nothing to screen him whatsoever; he loads his rifle and fires, loads and fires again; again and again! Thirty-three times! Then the rifle slips to the ground, and the man staggers and falls.

XCIII.

This morning, the 23rd, after a combat of three hours, the barricade of the Place de Clichy has not yet yielded. Yet two battalions of National Guards had, at the beginning of the fight, reversed their arms, and were fraternising with the soldiers on the Place de la Mairie, a hundred and fifty yards from the scene of the fray. The cracking of the rifles, the explosion of shells, and the sound of mitrailleuses filled the air. The smell of powder was stifling. Dreadful cries arose from the poor wounded wretches; and the whizzing projectiles from Montmartre rent the air above in their fiery course. "Beneath us," said an inhabitant of Batignolles who gave me these particulars, "beneath us the city lay like a seething caldron."

The beating of drums and the sharp trumpet-calls mixed in this monstrous din, and were every now and then lost in the tremendous noise of the firing.

About half-past one the sounds grew quieter; the barricade was taken. The insurgents were retreating to La Chapelle and Belleville in disorder; the soldiers of the line rushed like a torrent into the Avenue de Clichy, leaving a tricolour flag hoisted upon the dismantled barricade.

Here and there, in the streets, the struggle had not ceased. In the Rue Blanche a rifle-shot proceeded from a ground-floor; the man was taken and executed outside his own door. The artillery was moving up the Rue Chaptal towards Montmartre and La Chapelle. The day was very hot; pails of water were thrown over the guns to quench their burning thirst. All the young men who were found in the streets were provisionally put under arrest, for they feared everyone, even children, and horrible vengeance and thirst for blood had seized upon all. Suddenly an isolated shot would be heard, followed a minute or two after by five or six others. One knew reprisal had been done.

At about four o'clock in the afternoon, when the quarters of Belleville and Clichy were pretty well cleared of troops, two insurgents were walking, one behind the other, in the Rue Léonie. The one who walked last lifted his rifle and fired carelessly in the direction of the windows; the report sounded very loudly in the silent street, and a pane of glass fell in fragments to the ground. The insurgent who was in front did not even turn his head; these men seem to have become quite reckless and deaf to everything.

What the troops feared the most were the sharp-shooters hidden in the houses, aiming through little holes and cracks; suddenly a snap would be heard, and the officers would lift their glasses to their eyes; more often nothing was to be seen at all, but if the slightest shadow were visible behind a window curtain, the order was, "Search that house!" The executions did not take place in the apartments. Now and then an inhabitant or two were brought down into the street, and those never returned!

XCIV.

It is the middle of the night; and I awake with a terrible start. A bright red light streams through the panes. I throw open the window; the sky to the left is one mass of dark smoke and lurid streaks of light—it is a fire, Paris on fire!* I dress and go out. At the corner of the Rue de Trévise a sentinel stops me, "You can't pass." I am so bewildered that I do not think of noticing whether he is a Federal or a soldier. What am I to do, where am I to go? Although an hour ago balls were whistling around, there are now people at every window. "The Ministère des Finances is on fire! the Rue Royale! the Louvre!" The Louvre! I can scarcely avoid a cry of horror. In a minute the enormity of the disaster has broken upon me. Oh! *chefs-d'œuvre* without number! I see you devoured, consumed, reduced to ashes! I see the walls tottering, the canvases fall from the frames and shrivel up; the "Marriage of Canaan" is in flames! Raphael is struggling in the burning furnace! Leonardo da Vinci is no more! This was, indeed, an unexpected calamity! Fortune had reserved this terrible surprise for us! But I will not believe it, these rumours are false, doubtless! How should

---

* The 24th May the COMMITTEE FOR PUBLIC SAFETY issued these cold-blooded decrees:—

"Citizen Millière, at the head of one hundred and fifty fuse-bearers, is to set fire to all houses of suspicious aspect, as well as to the public monuments of the left bank of the Seine.

"Citizen Dereure, with one hundred and fifty fuse-bearers, is charged with the 1st and 2nd Arrondissement.

"Citizen Billioray, with one hundred men, is charged with the 9th, 10th, and 20th Arrondissements.

"Citizen Vésinier, with fifty men, has the Boulevards of the Madeleine and of the Bastille especially entrusted to him.

"These Citizens are to come to an understanding with the officers commanding the barricades, for the execution of these orders.

"DELESCLUZE, RÉGÈRE, RANVIER, JOHANNARD, VÉSINIER, BRUNEL, DOMBROWSKI.

"Paris, 3 Prairial, year 79."

these people who inhabit this quarter know what I am ignorant of? Yet over our heads the sky is tinged with black and red

RUINS OF THE RUE ROYALE, LOOKING TOWARDS THE PLACE DE LA CONCORDE AND ACROSS THE RUE DU FAUBOURG SAINT-HONORÉ.

A strange smell fills the air, like that of a monstrous petroleum lamp just lighted. That dreaded word, petroleum, makes me shudder. Once distinctly I hear the sound of a vast body falling

A BAY of the TUILERIES- from the PLACE du CARROUSEL

A WARM CORNER APPROACHING THE LOUVRE.

heavily. Not to be able to obtain information is terrible; not to know what is going on, while all around seems on fire; the day is beginning to break, the musketry and the cannonading commences afresh, it is a hell, with death for its girdle! In front of me I see the corner of a building lighted up by the fire, on which little spirals of smoke are reflected from the distant conflagration. I rush home, I want to hide myself, to sleep, to forget. When I am in my room, I see through the white curtains of the window a bright light. I tremble and rush to the window! It is the gilt letters of a signboard, on the opposite side of the way, that are darting forth brilliant flashes, borrowed from the distant flames.

XCV.

CERTAINLY I nursed no vain illusions. What you had done, gentlemen of the Commune, had enlightened me as to your value, and as to the purity of your intentions. Seeing you lie, steal, and kill, I had said to you, " You are liars, robbers, and murderers; " but truly, in spite of Citizen Félix Pyat, who is a coward, and Citizen Miot, who is a fool ; in spite of Millière, who shot *réfractaires*, and Philippe, whose trade shall be nameless; in spite of Dacosta, who amused himself with telling the Jesuits at the Conciergerie, " Mind, you are to be shot in an hour," and then an hour afterwards returning to say, " I have thought about it, and it is for to-morrow; " in spite of Johannard, who executed a child of fifteen guilty of selling a suppressed newspaper; in spite of Rigault, who, chucking the son of Chaudey under the chin, laughingly said to him, " To-morrow, little one, we shall shoot papa;" in spite of all the madmen and fools that constituted the Commune de Paris, who after being guilty of more extravagances than are necessary to get a man sent to the Madhouse of Charenton, and more crimes than are sufficient to shut him up in prison at Sainte-Pélagie, had managed, by means of every form of wicked-

MILLIÈRE.*

ness and excess, to make our beloved Paris a frightened slave, crouching to earth under their abominable tyranny; in

* This Millière, formerly an advocate and writer on the *Marseillaise*, was a native of St.-Etienne, and fifty-four years of age, a cool speaker, and advocate of advanced ideas, that got him several imprisonments. In March 1870 he was taken from the prison of Sainte-Pélagie to give evidence at Tours against Pierre Bonaparte for the murder of Victor Noir, where his lucid depositions told greatly against the prisoner. When regaining his liberty he became more revolutionary than ever, writing during the siege in the *Patrie en Danger*. At the peace he became one of the members for Paris, and sat at Bordeaux and Versailles, agitating social subjects and the law of lodgers. About the 10th of April he took part with the Commune, and at the entrance of the troops was taken at the Luxembourg after having fired six rounds from a revolver, was shot on the steps of the Pantheon, and died as he opened his shirt front, shouting, "*Vive la République! Vive la Liberté! Vive l'Humanité!*"

spite of everything, I could not have dreamed that even their demoniac fury could have gone so far as to try to burn Paris, after having ruined it! Nero of the gutter! Sardanapalus drunk with vitriol! So your vanity wanted such a volcano to engulf you, and you wished to die by the light of such an *auto-da-fé*. Instead of torches around your funeral car, you wished

PALAIS DE JUSTICE, PARTLY DESTROYED.
SAINTE CHAPELLE, SAVED.

the Tuileries, the library of the Louvre, and the Palace of the Legion of Honour burnt to ashes, the Rue Royale one vast conflagration, where the walls as they fell buried alive women and children, and the Rue de Lille vomiting fire and smoke like the crater of Vesuvius.

It has pleased you that thousands of families should be ruined, their savings scattered in the ashes of the vanished papers of the burnt Ministère des Finances and the *Caisse des dépôts*. In seeing that the art-galleries of the Louvre had remained intact, only its library burnt, you must have been seized with mad rage. How! Notre Dame not yet in flames? Sainte-Chapelle not on fire? Have you no more petroleum, no more flaming torches? The cry "To Arms!" is not enough, you must shout "To Fire!" Would you consume the entire city, and make of its ruins a horrible monument to your memory?

Do not say, "We have not done this; it is the people who are working out their own revenge, and we stand for nothing, we are as gentle as lambs. Ranvier would not hurt a fly." Away with all this pretence; were you not on the balcony of the Hôtel de Ville with your blood-red scarfs, uttering your commands? The populace, deceived and blinded, have but obeyed you. Do not all the circumstances leading to this stupendous catastrophe, reveal an elaborate and digested plan, determined long beforehand? Did we not read this notice, daily, in your official journal: "All those who have petroleum are requested immediately to declare the quantities in their possession?" Was there not a quick-match extinguished in the quarter of the Invalides that was to have communicated the flames to barrels of powder placed, long ago, in the great sewers? Yes, what has taken place you had decreed. If the disasters have not been more terrible, is it not, that, surprised at the sudden arrival of the troops, you had not the time to finish your preparations? Yes, you are the criminals! It was Eudes who gave out the petroleum to the *Pétroleuses;* it was Félix Pyat who laid the train of gunpowder. It is Tridon who said: "Take care that the phials be not uncorked." The public incendiary committee has well performed its duty! Wicked criminals! Execrable madmen! May Heaven bear me witness that my heart abhors revenge, is always inclined to pardon—but for these! What chastisement can be great enough to appease the wrath of justice! What vow of repentance could be offered up fervent enough to be received in Heaven, even at the moment when, struck down by balls, they offer their lives as expiation? Misguided humanity!

XCVI.

With three friends I stood upon the roof of a house near the new opera, watching what was passing around. The

FERRÉ.*

* Ferré, the friend of Raoul Rigault, and his colleague in the Commission of General Safety, like the latter, had inhabited the prisons for a considerable time for his political writings, seditious proposals, plots against the state, &c. He is a small man about five feet high, and very active. He signed with avidity the suppression of nearly all the journals of Paris, and the sentence of death of a great number of unfortunate prisoners, with the approbation of Raoul Rigault. He willingly undertook to announce to the Archbishop of Paris that his last hour had arrived. The following order, drawn up by him, was found on the body of an insurgent:—"Set fire to the Ministry of Finance immediately, and return here.

"4 Prairial, An 79.

(Signed)   TH. FERRÉ."

See Appendix, No. 10.

spectacle was such, that horror paralyses every other sentiment, even that of self-preservation. Consternation sits encircled by a blazing atmosphere of terror! The Hôtel de Ville is in flames; the smoke, at times a deep red, envelops all, so that it is impossible to distinguish more than the outlines of immense walls; the wind brings, in heavy gusts, a deadly odour—of burnt flesh, perhaps—which turns the heart sick and the brain giddy. On the other side the Tuileries, the Légion d'Honneur, the Ministère de la Guerre, and the Ministère des Finances are flaming still, like five great craters of a gigantic volcano! It is the eruption of Paris! Alone, a great black mass detaches itself from the universal conflagration, it is the Tour Saint-Jacques, standing out like a malediction.

One of the three friends, who are with me on the roof of the house, was able, about an hour ago, to get near the Hôtel de Ville. He related to me what follows:—

"At the moment of my arrival, the flames burst forth from all the windows of the Hôtel de Ville, and the most intense terror seized upon all the inhabitants blocked up in the surrounding quarters, for a terrible rumour is spread; it is said that more than fifty thousand pounds of powder is contained in the subterranean vaults. The incendiaries must have poured the demoniacal liquid in rivers through the great halls, down the great staircases, from the very garrets, to envelop even the Salle du Trône. The great fire throws a blood-red glare over the city, and on the quays of the Institute. Night is so like day that a letter may be read in the street. Is this the end of the famous capital of France? Have the infamous fiends of the committee for public safety ordered, in their cowardly death-agony, that this should be the end? Yes, it is the ruin of all that was grand, generous, radiant, and consolatory for our country that they have decided to consummate, with a chorus of hellish laughter, in which terror and ferocity struggle with brutal degradation.

"In the midst of this horror, confused rumours are circulated.

It is said that the heat will penetrate to the cellars and cause an explosion of whole quarters. Then what will become of the inhabitants, and the riches that they have accumulated? The heat is overwhelming between the Tuileries and the Hôtel de Ville—that is, over the space of about a mile. The two barricades of the Rue de Rivoli and of the Rue de la Coutellerie, near which are the offices of the municipal services—the lighting of the city, the octroi, waters, sewers, &c.,—will not be taken until too late, in spite of the energy with which the army attacks them. It is feared that the flame will reach the neighbourhood of the great warehouses, so thickly do the burning flakes fall and scatter destruction. The barricades of the quays are still intact, it will be another hour yet before they are taken. The firemen are there furiously at work, but their efforts are insufficient! It would take tons of ammonia to slake the fury of the petroleum which flows like hot lava upon the place from the Hôtel de Ville, and the horrible reflection reddens the waters of the Seine, so that the current of the river seems to flow with blood, which stains the stones as it dashes against the arches of the bridge!"

These scenes are being pictured to me as I gaze upon the terrible conflagration, and all that is told me I seem to see. An irresistible longing to be near seizes me. I am under the power of an invincible attraction. I lean forward, my arms outstretched; I run a great risk of falling, but what matters? The sight of these almost sublime horrors has burnt itself into my very brain!

XCVII.

SHE walks with a rapid step, near the shadow of the wall; she is poorly dressed; her age is between forty and fifty; her forehead is bound with a red checkered handkerchief, from which

PALACE OF THE LUXEMBOURG (GARDEN FRONT).*
Used as a Federal Ambulance Hospital.

* On the Wednesday succeeding the explosion of the powder-magazine in the garden of the Luxembourg, which unroofed a portion of the palace, and destroyed the windows, and did fearful damage to the surrounding houses, all the Communeux disappeared from the neighbourhood. The following night four men returned, bringing a quantity of petroleum with them. They gave orders that the six hundred wounded men who were then lying in the Palace should be taken away immediately. They had commenced their sinister project, and were pouring the petroleum about in the cellars, when the soldiers of the Brigade Paturel were informed of it, and arrived in time to prevent its execution. The criminals were taken and shot on the spot.

hang meshes of uncombed hair. The face is red and the eyes blurred, and she moves with her look bent down on the ground. Her right hand is in her pocket, or in the bosom of her half-unbuttoned dress; in the other hand she holds one of the high, narrow tin cans in which milk is carried in Paris, but which now, in the hands of this woman, contains the dreadful petroleum liquid. As she passes a *poste* of regulars, she smiles and nods; when they speak to her she answers, "My good Monsieur!" If the street is deserted she stops, consults a bit of dirty paper that she holds in her hand, pauses a moment before the grated opening to a cellar, then continues her way, steadily, without haste. An hour afterwards, a house is on fire in the street she has passed. Who is this woman? Paris calls her a *Pétroleuse.**

One of these *pétroleuses*, who was caught in the act in the Rue Truffault, discharged the six barrels of a revolver and killed two men before being passed over to execution. Another was seen falling in a doorway of a house in the Rue de Boulogne, pierced with balls—but this one was a young girl; a bottle filled with petroleum fell from her hand as she dropped. Sometimes one of these wretched women might be seen leading by the hand a little boy or girl; and the child probably carrying a bottle of the incendiary liquid in his pocket with his top and marbles.

* The incendiaries formed a veritable army, composed of returned convicts, the very dregs of the prisons, pale, thin lads, who looked like ghosts, and old women, that looked like horrible witches; their number amounted to eight thousand! This army had its chiefs, and each detachment was charged with the firing of a quarter.
The order for the conflagration of public edifices bore the stamp of the Commune, and of the Central Committee, and the seal of the delegate at the Ministry of War. For the private houses more expeditive means were used. Small tickets, of the size of postage stamps, were found pasted upon walls of houses in different parts of Paris, with the letters B. P. B. (*bon pour brûler*), literally, good for burning. Some of the tickets were square, others oval, with a bacchante's head in the centre. They were affixed on spots designated by the chiefs. Every *pétroleuse* was to receive ten francs for each house she fired. Sept. 5, 1871. Amongst the insurgents tried at Versailles, three pétroleuses were condemned to death, and one to imprisonment for life, a host of others being transported or otherwise punished.

XCVIII.

It is seven in the evening, the circulation has become almost impossible. The streets are lined with patrols, and the regiments of the Line camp upon the outer boulevards. They dine, smoke, and bivouac, and drink with the citizens on the doorsteps of their houses. In the distance is heard the storm of sounds which tells of the despairing resistance of Belleville, and along the foot of the houses are seen square white patches, showing the walled-up cellars, every hole and crevice being plastered up to prevent insertion of the diabolical liquid—walled up against *pétroleurs* and *pétroleuses*, strings of prisoners, among whom are furious women and poor children, their hands tied behind their backs, pass along the boulevards towards Neuilly. Night comes on, not a lamp is lighted, and the streets become deserted as by degrees the sky becomes darker. At nine o'clock the solitude is almost absolute. The sound of a musket striking the pavement is heard from time to time; a sentinel passes here and there, and the lights in the houses grow more and more rare.

XCIX.

The hours and the days pass and resemble each other horribly. To write the history of the calamities is not yet possible. Each one sees but a corner of the picture, and the narratives that are collected are vague and contradictory; it appears certain now that the insurrection is approaching the end. It is said that the fort of Montrouge is taken; but it still hurls its shells upon Paris. Several have just fallen in the quarter of the Banque. There is fighting still at the Halles, at the Luxembourg, and at the Porte Saint-Martin. Neither the cannonading nor the fusillade has ceased, and our ears have become accustomed to the continued roar. But, in spite of the barbarous heroism of the Federals, the force of their resistance is being exhausted. What has become of the chiefs?

We continue to note down the incidents as they reach us.

It is said that Assy has been taken, close to the New Opera House. He was going the nightly rounds, almost alone—"Who's there!" cried a sentinel. Assy, thinking the man was a Federal, replied, "You should have challenged me sooner." In an instant he was surrounded, disarmed, and carried off. However, it is a very unlikely tale; it is most improbable that Assy should not know that the New Opera was in the hands of the Versaillais.

They say that Delescluze has fled, that Dombrowski has died[*] in an ambulance, and that Millière is a prisoner at Saint-Denis. But these are merely rumours, and I am utterly ignorant as to their worth. The only thing certain is that the search is being carried on with vigour. Close by the smoking ruins of what was once the Hôtel de Ville they caught Citizen Ferraigu, inspector of the barricades; he confessed to having received from the Committee of Public Safety particular orders to burn down the shop of the Bon-Diable. Had one of these committee-men been an assistant there, and did he owe his former master a grudge? Ferraigu had a bottle of petroleum in his pocket; he was shot. I am told that at the

---

[*] The most reliable account of his death is given by a medical student who attended him in his last moments. "Dombrowski was passing with several members of the Commune in the Rue Myrrha, near the Rue des Poissonniers, when he was struck by a bullet, which traversed the lower part of his body. He was carried to a neighbouring chemist's, where I bandaged the wound. Before his transportation to the Lariboisière Hospital, he ordered the fire to cease, but the troops defending the barricade disobeyed the injunction. His sword was handed by me to a captain of the 45th of the Line. His last words were nearly identical with those which he uttered as he fell: 'I am no traitor!'" His worst enemies have said of him that he was a good soldier in a bad cause.

Théâtre du Châtelet a court-martial has been established on the stage. The Federals are brought up twenty at a time, judged, and condemned; they are then marched out on to the Place, with their hands tied behind their backs. A mitrailleuse, standing a hundred yards off, mows them down like grass. It is an expeditious contrivance. In a yard, in the Rue Saint-Denis, is a stable filled with corpses; I have myself seen them there. The Porte Saint-Martin Theatre is quite destroyed, a guard is stationed near. This morning three *pétroleuses* were shot there, the bodies are still lying on the boulevards. I have just seen two insurgents walking between four soldiers; one an old man, the other almost a lad. I heard the elder one say to the younger, "All our misery comes of our having arms. In '48 we had none, so we took those of the soldiers, and then they were without. Now there is more killing and less business done." A few minutes after the little procession passed up the Rue d'Hauteville, and I heard the reports of two rifles. Oh! what horrible days! I feel a prey to the deepest dejection—if it were but over! The town looks wretched; even where the fighting is not going on, the houses are closed and the streets deserted, except here and there a lonely passenger hurrying along, or a wretched prisoner marching between four soldiers. It is all very dreadful! In the streets where the battle is still raging the shutters are not closed; as soon as the soldiers get into a new quarter of the town they cry out, "Shut the windows, open the shutters." The reason for this is, that the open barred outer shutters, or *persiennes*, form a capital screen through which aim may be taken with a gun. As for me, in the midst of this horror and sadness, I feel like a madman in the night. The rumour that the hostages have been shot at Mazas gains ground.* I am told that the Archbishop, the

---

* At the prison of Sainte-Pélagie, on Tuesday, the 23rd of May, the unfortunate gendarmes, who had been made prisoners on the 18th, were shot, together with M. Chaudey, a writer on the *Siècle*, arrested at the office of the journal, and conducted, first to Mazas and afterwards to Sainte-Pélagie. (Appendix 11).

According to the *Siècle*, the "Procureur" of the Commune, Raoul

THEATRE PORTE ST MARTIN.

SENSATION DRAMA
OUT SENSATIONED.

Abbé Deguerry, and Chaudey have all been assassinated. It

CELL OF THE ARCHBISHOP IN THE PRISON OF LA ROQUETTE.

Rigault, presented himself, at the office at about eleven at night, and having sent for M. Chaudey, said to him, without any preamble:
"I am here to tell you that you have not an hour to live."

was Rigault who ordered these executions. He has since been

COURT-YARD OF PRISON OF LA ROQUETTE, WHERE THE HOSTAGES WERE SHOT.

"You mean to say that I am to be assassinated," replied Chaudey.
"You are to be shot, and that directly," was the other's rejoinder.
But, on reaching the prison, the National Guards who had been summoned refused to do the odious work, and the Procureur went himself to find others more docile. Chaudey was led before them, Raoul Rigault drew his sword to give the signal, the muskets were

taken, and fell, crying "Down with murderers!" This reminds one of Dumollard, the assassin, calling the jurymen "Canaille!"

levelled and fired, and Chaudey fell, but wounded only. A sergeant gave him the death blow by discharging his pistol at his head. The next day, a hundred and fifty hostages of the Commune, confined at the Prefecture of Police, amongst whom were Prince Galitzin and Andreoli, a journalist, were about to be shot by an order of Ferré, when the incendiary fires broke out and prevented the execution of the order. At eleven o'clock, Raoul Rigault commanded the prisoners to be released, and enjoined them to fight for the Commune; upon their refusal, a shower of balls was discharged at them. The prisoners rushed for refuge into the Rue du Harlay, which was in flames, and were afterwards rescued by a detachment of the line.

That same day was fatal to Raoul Rigault. He was perceived by a party of infantry at the moment when he was ringing at the door of a house in the Rue Gay Lussac. His colonel's uniform instantly made him a mark for the soldiers; he had time to enter the house, however, but was soon discovered, gave his name, and allowed himself to be taken off towards the Luxembourg, but before reaching it, he began to shout, "Vive la Commune!" "Down with the assassins!" and made an effort to escape. The soldiers thrust him against a wall and shot him down.

The next day, the 24th, marked the fate of the hostages, who, in expectation of an attack of the Versaillais, had been transferred from Mazas to La Roquette. "Monseigneur Darboy," writes an eye-witness (Monsieur Dubutte, miraculously saved by an error of name), "occupied cell No. 21 of the 4th division, and I was at a short distance from him, in No. 26. The cell in which the venerable prelate was confined had been the office of one of the gaolers; it was somewhat larger than the rest, and Monseigneur's companions in captivity had succeeded in obtaining for him a chair and a table. On Wednesday, the 24th, at half-past seven in the evening, the director of the prison—a certain Lefrançais, who had been a prisoner in the hulks for the space of six years—went up, at the head of fifty Federals, into the gallery, near which the most important prisoners were incarcerated. Here they ranged themselves along the walls, and a few moments later one of the head-gaolers opened the door of the archbishop's cell, and called him out. The prelate answered, 'I am here!' Then the gaoler passed on to M. le President Bonjean's cell (Appendix 12), then to that of Abbé Allard, member of the International Society in Aid of the Wounded; of Père du Coudray, Superior of the School of Ste.-Geneviève; and Père Clère, of the Brotherhood of Jesus; the last called being the Abbé Deguerry, curé of the Madeleine. As the names were called, each prisoner was led out into the gallery and down the staircase to the courtyard; each side, as far as I could judge, was lined with Federal guards, who insulted the prisoners in

Millière is said to have been shot in the Place du Panthéon. When they told him to kneel down he drew himself up to his full height, his eyes flashing defiance. Strange caprice of nature, to make these scoundrels brave.

In the meantime, the Commune is in its death throes. Like the dragon of fairy lore, it dies, vomiting flames. La Villette is on fire, houses are burning at Belleville and on the Buttes-Chaumont. The resistance is concentrated on one side at Père la Chaise, and on the other at the Mont-Parnasse cemetery. The insurrection was mistress of the whole of Paris, and then the army came stretching its long arms from the Arc de Triomphe to Belleville, from the Champ-de-Mars to the Panthéon. Trying hard to burst these bonds, tightly surrounded, now resisting, now flying, the *émeute* has at last retreated. It is over there now, in two cemeteries; it watches from behind tombstones; it rests the barrels of its rifles on marble crosses, and erects a battery on a sepulchre. The shells of the Versaillais fall in the sacred enclosure, plough up the earth, and unbury the dead. Something round rolled along a pathway, the combatants thought it was a shell; it was a skull! What must these men feel who are killing and being killed in the cemetery! To die among the dead

language that I cannot repeat. Amid the hues and cries of these wretches my unfortunate companions were conducted across the courtyard to the infirmary, before which a file of soldiers were drawn up for the execution. Monseigneur Darboy advanced and addressed his murderers—addressed them words of pardon: then two of the men approached the prelate, and falling on their knees implored his pardon. The rest of the Federals threw themselves upon them, and thrust them aside with oaths, then, turning to the prisoners, they heaped fresh insults upon them. The chief officer of the detachment, however, imposed silence on the men, and uttering an oath, said, 'You are here to shoot these men, not to insult them.' The Federals were silenced, and upon the command of their lieutenant, they loaded their muskets.

"Père Allard was placed against the wall, and was the first who was struck; then Monseigneur Darboy fell, and the six prisoners were thus shot in turn, showing, at this supreme moment, a saintly dignity and a noble courage."

My NEIGHBOUR 'EN FACE' _
BUSINESS CARRIED ON
AS USUAL —

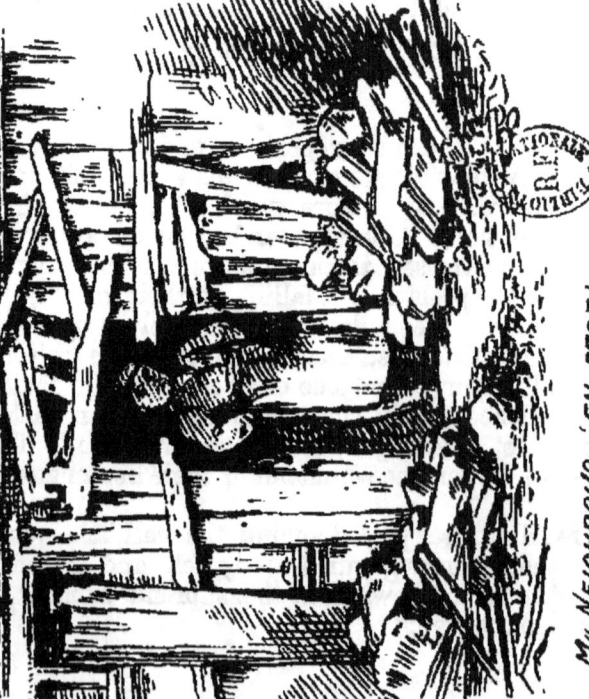

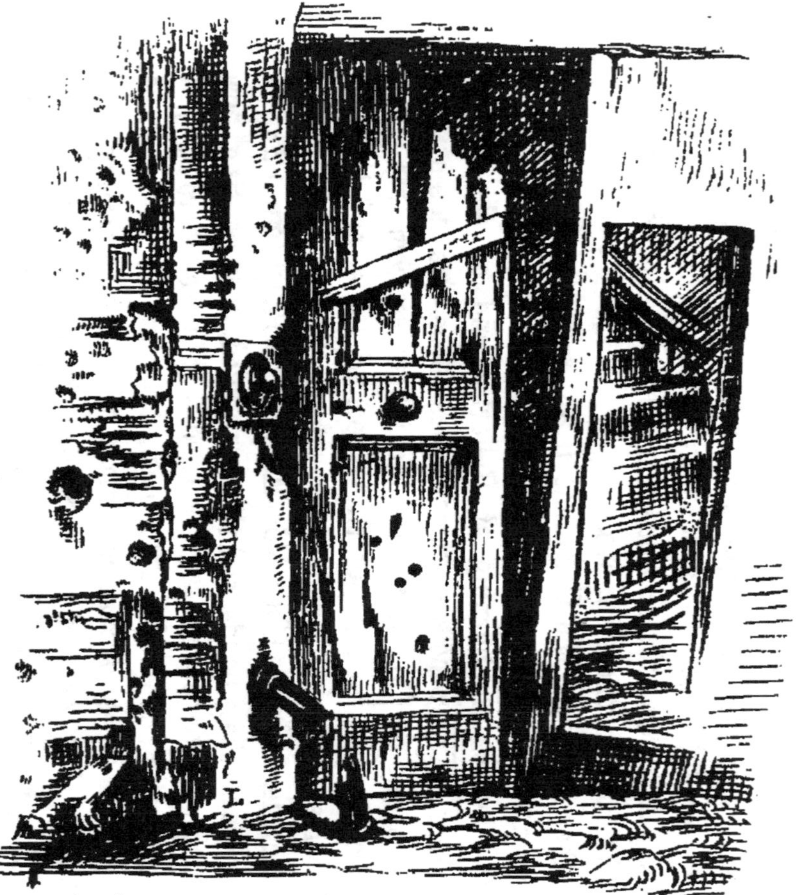

MY NEIGHBOUR NEXT DOOR -
WHO THINKS HIMSELF
FORTUNATE

seems horrible. But they never give it a thought; the bloody thirst for destruction which possesses them allows them only to think of one thing, of killing! Some of them are gay, they are brave, these men. That makes it only the more dreadful; these wretches are heroic! Behind the barricades there have been instances of the most splendid valour. A man at the Porte Saint-Martin, holding a red flag in his hand, was standing, heedless of danger, on a pile of stones. The balls showered around him, while he leant carelessly against an empty barrel which stood behind.—"Lazy fellow," cried a comrade.—"No," said he, "I am only leaning that I may not fall when I die." Such are these men; they are robbers, incendiaries, assassins, but they are fearless of death. They have only that one good quality. They smile and they die. The vivandières allow themselves to be kissed behind the tombstones; the wounded men drink with their comrades, and throw wine on their wounds, saying, "Let us drink to the last." And yet, in an hour perhaps, the soldiers will fight their way into the cemeteries, which their balls reach already, they too mad with rage; then the horrible bayonet fighting will commence, man against man among the tombs, flying over the mounds, desecrating the monuments, everything that imagination can conjure up of most profane and terrible—a battle in a cemetery!

C.

WHERE are these men going with hurried steps, and with lanterns in their hands? Their uniform is that of the National Guard, and consequently of Federals, but the tricolour band which they wear on the arm would seem to indicate that they belong to the Party of Order. They are making their way by one of the entries of the sewers, and preceded by an officer are disappearing beneath the sombre vaults. Calling to mind the sinister expression of a Communal artillery commander—"The reactionary quarters will all be blown up; not one shall be spared," it is impossible to avoid feeling a shudder of terror. What if the incendiaries all wearing the badge of the Party of Order, be about

PARIS UNDERGROUND.

to set fire to mines prepared beforehand, or to barrels of petroleum ready to be staved in! The wild demons of the Commune are capable of everything; an invention of incendiary firemen is quoted as an example of the diabolical genius which presided over the work of destruction; individuals wearing the fireman's

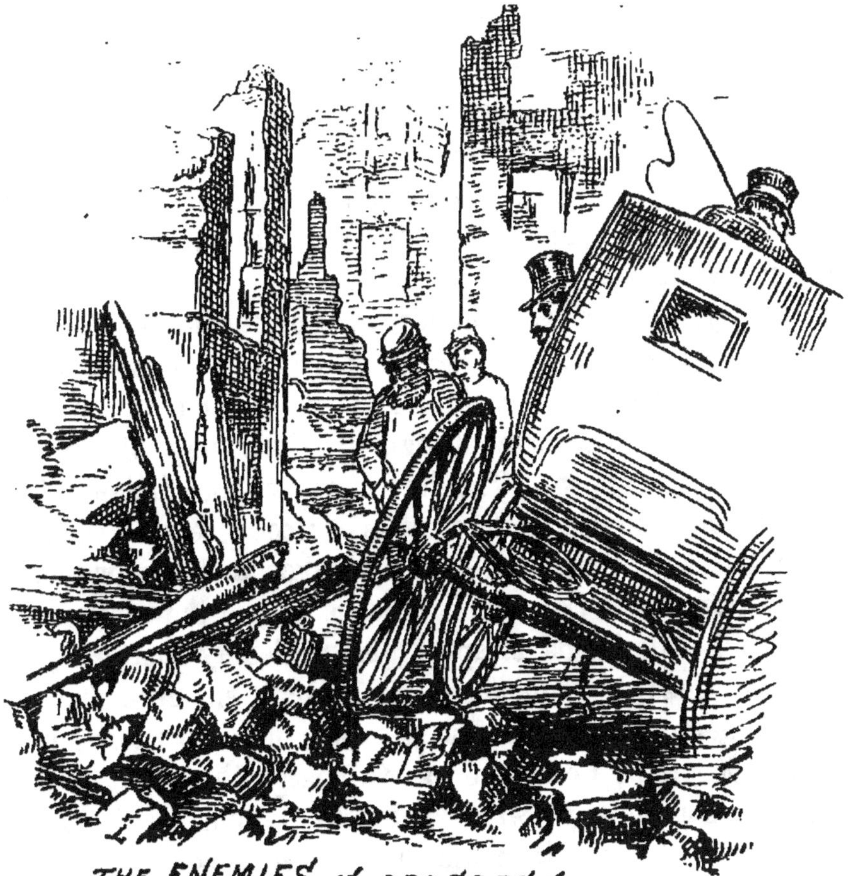

THE ENEMIES of PROGRESS.

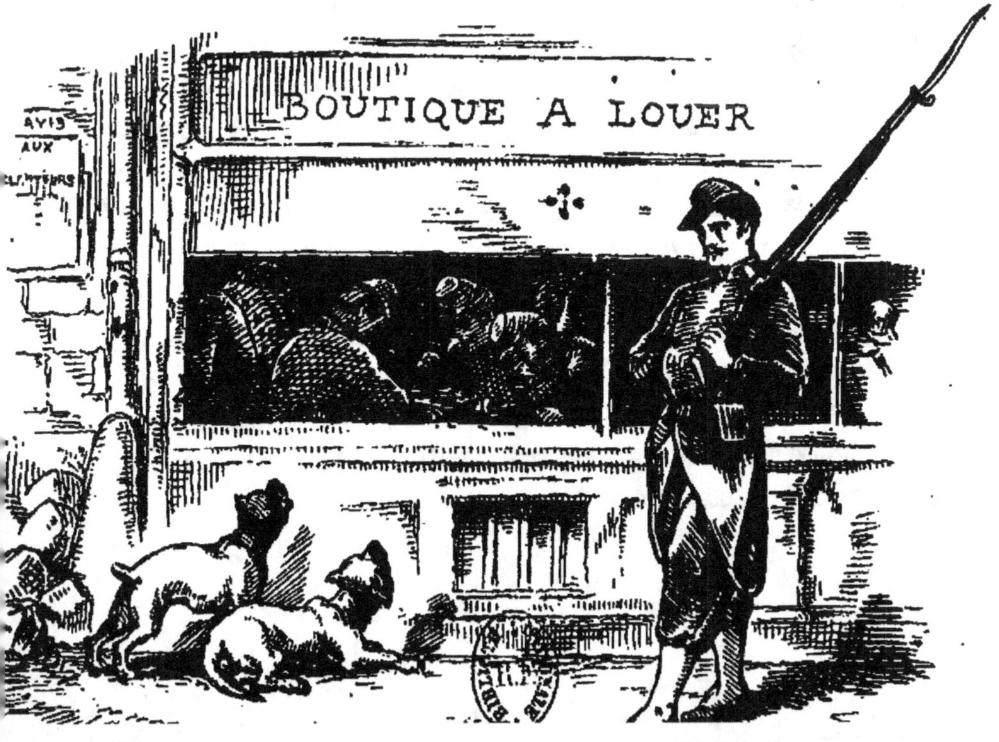
AVIS
AUX
BOUTIQUE A LOUER

uniform were seen to throw combustible liquids by means of pumps and pails on the burning houses, instead of aiding to extinguish the flames.

Fortunately, the fear is unfounded, the object of these men, on the contrary, is to cut the wires which connect all parts with inflammable materials, torpedoes, and other atrocious machines. They have already passed several nights in destroying this underground telegraphic system. The duty is not without danger; for not only are they exposed to the terrible consequences of a sudden explosion, but also to the risk of being taken and shot without trial, as traitors to the Commune. That is, should they chance to fall in with hostile bands, or appear in unfriendly quarters. It appears that these determined and devoted citizens have already lost two of their companions in the execution of this perilous duty. The intention of the Commune was to charge the whole of the main sewers and subways with combustibles; but luckily they had not time to mature their schemes, the advance of the Versailles troops being too quick for them. The Catacombs were included in the arrangement; for did not the able Assy direct his agent Fossé to keep them open as a means of escape? Alas! these subterranean passages that underlie so large a portion of ancient Paris, what stories could they not tell of starved fugitives and maimed culprits dragging their weary limbs into the darkness of these gloomy caverns, only that they might die there in peace! Men and women, whose forms will in a few short weeks be unrecognisable, whose whitened bones will be crushed and kicked aside by the future explorer, who may perchance penetrate the labyrinths, and whose dust will finally be mixed up and undistinguishable from that of the bones and skulls taken from ancient cemeteries and graveyards with which this terrible Golgotha is decorated in Mosaic.

CI.

The fire is out, let us contemplate the ruins.* The Commune is vanquished. Look at Paris, sad, motionless, laid waste. This is what we have come to! Consternation is in every breast, solitude is in every street. We feel no longer either anger or pity; we are resigned, broken by emotion; we see processions of prisoners pass on their way to Versailles, and we scarcely look at them; no one thinks of saying either, "Wretches!" or "Poor fellows!" The soldiers themselves are very silent. Although they are the victors they are sad; they do not drink, they do not sing. Paris might be a town that had been assaulted and taken by dumb enemies; the irritation has worn itself off, and the tears have not yet come. The tricolour flags which float from all the windows surprise us; there does not seem any reason for rejoicing. Yet, of late especially, the triumph of the Versaillais has been ardently wished for by the greater portion of the population; but all are so tired that they have not the energy to rejoice. Let us look back for a moment. First the siege, with famine, separation and poverty; then the insurrection of Montmartre, surprises, hesitations, cannonading night and day, ceaseless musketry, mothers in tears, sons pursued, every calamity has fallen on this miserable city. It has been like Rome under Tiberius, then like Rome after the barbarians had overrun it. The cannon balls have fallen upon Sybaris. So much emotion, so many horrors have worn out the city; and then all this blood, this dreadful blood. Corpses in the streets, corpses within the houses, corpses everywhere! Of course they were terribly guilty, these men that were taken, that were killed; they were horrible criminals, those women who poured brandy into the glasses and petroleum on the houses! But, in the first moment of victory, were there no mistakes? Were those that were shot all guilty? Then

* See Appendix 15, 16, 17, and 18.

the sight of these executions, however merited, was cruelly

PALACE OF THE LUXEMBOURG (STREET FRONT). NOW THE SEAT OF THE PREFECTURE OF PARIS.

painful. The innocent shuddered at the doom of justice. True, Paris is quiet now, but it is the quiet of the battle-field on the morrow of a victory; quiet as night, and as the tomb! An unsupportable uneasiness oppresses us; shall we ever be able to shake off this apathy, to pierce through this gloom? Paris, rent and bleeding, turns with sadness from the past, and dares not yet raise her eyes to the future!

POOR PARIS!

On August 15th, the *Times* reporter gave the number awaiting trial at Versailles at 30,000. On the 7th September they had reached 39,000, daily arrests adding to the number; out of these, 35,000 only had their charges made out, of which 13,900 had been examined, 2,800 writs of release having been issued, though only a few hundreds have been set at liberty. There are only 94 reporting officers: 20 attached to the Council of War, 6 to the Orangerie, 4 to Satory, 3 to the Prison des Femmes, and 16 to the Western Ports: 17 more are to be added shortly.

MARSHAL MACMAHON,
Duc de Magenta.

Commander-in-Chief of the Army of Versailles.

APPENDIX.

CHRONOLOGY OF THE PARISIAN INSURRECTION,

FROM THE 18th OF MARCH TO THE 29th MAY, 1871.

The dash (—) in each day after the commencement of military operations divides the civil from the military.

Saturday, 18th March: Early in the morning troops take possession of the Buttes Montmartre and Belleville. The soldiers charged with the recovery of the pieces of artillery fraternise with the people and the National Guard. Arrest of Generals Lecomte and Clément Thomas: they are shot at Montmartre without trial. National Guards take possession of the Hôtel de Ville. The Prefecture of Police is invaded by Raoul Rigault, Duval, and others.

Sunday, 19th March: The Central Committee of the National Guard take possession of the offices of the *Journal Officiel*. Arrest of General Chanzy. Gustave Flourens, imprisoned at Mazas, is set at liberty by the new masters of Paris. M. Thiers addresses a circular to the country enjoining obedience to the only authority, that of the Assembly.

Tuesday, 21st March: Manifestation of the "Friends of Order." Procession for public demonstration. Sitting of the Assembly at Versailles. M. Jules Favre advises prompt measures. Appeal to the people and army.

Wednesday, 22nd March: Friends of Order shot in the Rue de la Paix. Lullier arrested by order of the Central Committee.

Thursday, 23rd March: Vice-Admiral Saisset is appointed by the Assembly Commander-in-Chief of the National Guard.

Friday, 24th March: The delegates Brunel, Eudes, Duval, are promoted to the rank of generals by the Central Committee. Vice-Admiral Saisset's proclamation.

Saturday, 29th March: Occupation of the Mairie of the 1st Arrondissement by the Federals. First placard of the Committee of Conciliation. Rumour of the arrest of Lullier reproached for moderation. Vice-Admiral Saisset retires to Versailles.

Sunday, 26th March: Municipal elections to constitute the Commune of Paris.

Tuesday, 28th March: 4 p.m., names of the elect proclaimed at the Hôtel de Ville. Arrival of General Chanzy at Versailles.

Wednesday, 29th March: Conscription abolished—all citizens to be National Guards. Pawnbroking decree. Organisation of commissions: executive, financial, military, etc. Ministers to be called delegates.

Saturday, 1st April: The Executive Committee issues a decree to suppress the rank and functions of General-in-Chief. General Eudes appointed Delegate of War; Bergeret to the staff of the National Guard, in place of Brunel; Duval to the military command of the ex-Prefecture of Police, where Raoul Rigault was civil delegate.

Sunday, 2nd April: Military operations commence 9 a.m. Action at Courbevoie. Flourens marches his troops to Versailles, viâ Rueil.

Monday, 3rd April: The corps d'armée of General Bergeret at the Rond Point near Neuilly, is stopped by the artillery of Mont Valérien. Exchange of shot between Fort Issy and Fort Vanves, occupied by insurgents, and Meudon.—The separation of Church and State decreed.

Tuesday, 4th April: General Duval made prisoner in the engagement at Châtillon and shot. Death of Flourens at Rueil.—Delescluze, Cournet, and Vermorel succeed Generals Bergeret, Eudes, and Duval on the Executive Commission. Cluseret Delegate of War, and Bergeret commandant of Paris forces.

Wednesday, 5th April: General Cluseret commences active operations. Military service compulsory for all citizens under forty. Abbé Deguerry, and Archbishop of Paris arrested.

Thursday, 6th April: Extension of action to Neuilly and Courbevoie. Versailles army decreed by executive authority. Obsequies of Flourens at Versailles.—Decree concerning the complicity with Versailles, and arrest of hostages. The rank of general suppressed by the Commune. Dombrowski succeeds Bergeret as Commandant of Paris.

Friday, 7th April: Decree for disarming the Réfractaires. The guillotine is burnt on the Place Voltaire.

Saturday, 8th April: Federals abandon Neuilly.—Commission of barricades created and presided over by Gaillard Senior. Military occupation of the railway termini by the insurgents.

Sunday, 9th April: Insurgents attempt to retake Châtillon, but are repulsed. Forts Vanves and Montrouge disabled. Mont Valérien shells the Avenue des Ternes.—Assy and Bergeret arrested by order of the Commune.

Tuesday, 11th April: Marshal MacMahon, Commander-in-Chief, distributes his forces. Commences the investment of fort Issy.

Wednesday, 12th April: Versailles batteries established on Châtillon. The Orleans railway and telegraph cut. Communications of the insurgents with the south intercepted.—Decree ordering the fall of the Column Vendôme. Decree concerning the complementary elections.

Thursday, 13th April: Courbet presides at a meeting of artists at the École de Médecine. Publication of the reports of the sittings of the Commune.

Friday, 14th April: The redoubt of Gennevilliers taken. The troops of Versailles make advances to the Château de Bécon, a post of importance.—Lullier takes the command of the flotilla on the Seine.

Sunday, 16th April: Complementary elections. Organisation of a court-martial under the presidence of Rossel, chief officer of the staff.

Monday, 17th April: Capture and fortification of the Château de Bécon.

Tuesday, 18th April: Station and houses at Asnières taken by the army of Versailles.

Thursday, 20th April: The village of Bagneux is occupied by the Versaillais.—Reorganisation of commissions. Eudes appointed inspector-general of the southern forts. Transfers his quarters from Montrouge to the Palace of the Legion of Honour.

Saturday, 22nd April: Deputation from the Freemasons to Versailles.

Monday, 24th April: Raoul Rigault takes the office of public prosecutor, resigning the Prefecture of Police to Cournet.

Tuesday, 25th April: The Versailles batteries at Breteuil, Brimorion, Meudon, and Moulin de Pierre trouble the Federal Fort Issy, and battery between Bagneux and Châtillon shells Fort Vanves. Truce at Neuilly from 9 a.m. to 5 p.m. The inhabitants of Neuilly enter Paris by the Porte des Ternes.

Wednesday, 26th April: Capture of Les Moulineaux, outpost of the insurgents, by the troops, who strongly fortify themselves on the 27th and 28th.

Saturday, 29th April: Cemetery and park of Issy taken by the Versaillais in the night.—Freemasons make a new attempt at conciliation. The Commune levies a sum of two millions of francs from the railway companies.

Sunday, 30th April: A flag of truce sent to Fort Issy by the Versaillais, calling upon the Federals to surrender. General Eudes puts fresh troops in the fort, and takes the command himself.—Cluseret imprisoned at Mazas by order of the Commune. Rossel appointed Provisional Delegate of War.

Monday, 1st May: The Versaillais take the station of Clamart and the Château of Issy.—Creation of the Committee of Public Safety. Members: Antoine Arnauld, Léo Meillet, Ranvier, Félix Pyat, Charles Gérardin.

Wednesday, 3rd May: The troops of General Lacretelle carry the redoubt of Moulin Saquet.

Friday, 5th May: Colonel Rossel appointed to the direction of military affairs. He defines the military quarters: General Dombrowski, Place Vendôme; General La Cécilia, at the Ecole Militaire; General Wroblewski, at the Elysée; General Bergeret, at the Corps Législatif; General Eudes at the Palace of the Legion of Honour. The Central

Committee of the National Guard charged with Administration of War under the supervision of the military commission. The Chapelle Expiatoire condemned to destruction—the materials to be sold by auction.

Saturday, 6th May: Concert at the Tuileries in aid of the ambulances. Suppression of newspapers.

Monday, 8th May: Battery of Montretout (70 marine guns) opens fire.

Tuesday, 9th May: Morning, insurgents evacuate the Fort Issy.—The Committee of Public Safety renewed. Members: Ranvier, Antoine Arnauld, Gambon, Eudes, Delescluze. Rossel resigns; his letter to the Commune.

Wednesday, 10th May: Cannon from the Fort Issy taken to Versailles.—Decree for the demolition of M. Thiers' house. Delescluze appointed Delegate of War.

Friday, 12th May: Troops take possession of the Couvent des Oiseaux at Issy, and the Lyceum at Vanves.

Saturday, 13th May: Triumphal entry of the troops into Versailles with flags and cannon taken from the Convent. The evacuation of the village of Issy completed. Fort Vanves taken by the troops.

Sunday, 14th May: Vigorous cannonade from the batteries of Courbevoie, Bécon, Asnières on Levallois and Clichy: both villages evacuated. Commencement of the demolition of house of M. Thiers.

Monday, 15th May: Report of the rearmament of Montmartre.

Tuesday, 16th May: The Column Vendôme falls.

Wednesday, 17th May: Powder magazine and cartridge factory near the Champ de Mars blown up.

Sunday, 21st May: 2 p.m. the troops enter Paris.—Rochefort arrives at Versailles. Raoul Rigault and Régère charged with the hostage decree.

Monday, 22nd May: Noon, explosion of the powder magazine of the Manége d'Etat-Major (staff riding-school). The hostages transferred from Mazas to La Roquette. Assy arrested in Paris by the Versaillais. The Assembly votes the re-erection of the Column Vendôme.

Tuesday, 23rd May: Montmartre taken. Death of Dombrowski. Morning, Assy arrives at Versailles. Execution of gendarmes and Gustave Chaudey at the prison of Sainte-Pélagie. Night, the Tuileries are set on fire. Delescluze and the Committee of Public Safety hold permanent sittings at the Hôtel de Ville.

Wednesday, 24th May: One p.m., the powder magazine at the Palais du Luxembourg blown up. The Committee of Public Safety organise detachments of fusee-bearers. Raoul Rigault shot in the afternoon by the soldiers. In the evening, execution in the Prison of La Roquette of the Archbishop, Abbé Deguerry, etc.

Thursday, 25th May: The forts Montrouge, Hautes-Bruyères, Bicêtre evacuated by the insurgents. The death of Delescluze is reported to have taken place this day. Executions in the Avenue d'Italie of the Pères Dominicains of Arcueil.

Friday, 26th May: Sixteen priests shot in the Cemetery of Père Lachaise by the insurgents.

Saturday, 27th May: The Buttes Chaumont, the heights of Belleville, and the Cemetery of Père Lachaise carried by the troops. Taking of the prison La Roquette by the Marines. Deliverance of 169 hostages.

Sunday, 28th May: The investment of Belleville complete.

Monday, 29th May: Six p.m., the Federal garrison of the fortress of Vincennes surrendered at discretion.

I. (Page 2.)

HENRI ROCHEFORT.

Henri Rochefort, personal enemy of the Empire, republican humourist of the *Marseillaise*, and the lukewarm socialist of the *Mot d'Ordre*, who could answer to the judge who demanded his name, "I am Henri Rochefort, Comte de Lucey," has been reproached by some with his titles of nobility, and with the childish pleasure that he takes in affecting the plebeian. It is said of him that he aspires but to descend, but who would condemn him for spurning the petrifactions of the Faubourg Saint-Germain? A man must march with the times.

Rochefort has distinguished himself among the young men by the marvellous tact that he has shown in discovering the way to popular favour. If I were allowed to compare a marquis to one of the canine species, I should say that he has a keen scent for popularity; but one must respect rank in a period like ours, when we may go to sleep to the shouts of the *canaille*, and awake to the melodious sounds of "*Vive Henri V!*" "Long live the King!"

Born in January, 1830, Henri Rochefort was the son of a marquis, although his father, lately dead, was a *vaudevilliste* and his mother a *pâtissière*. From such a fusion might have emanated odd tastes, such as preferring truffles to potatoes, but putting the knife into requisition whilst eating green peas. But in his case Mother Nature had intermingled elements so cleverly that Rochefort could be republican and royalist, catholic and atheist, without being accused for all that of being a political weathercock.

As a writer of drollery and scandal in the *Charivari*, would it have been well if he had used his title as a badge? Later, when contributing to the *Nain Jaune*, the *Soleil*, the *Evénement*, and the *Figaro*, when everyone would have been enchanted to call him *mon cher Comte*, he never displayed his rank, except when on the ground, face to face with the sword or pistol of Prince Achille Murat or Paul de Cassagnac.

A frequenter of *cafés*, living fast, bitter with journalists, hail-fellow with comedians, he lavished his wit for the benefit of minor theatres, and expended the exuberance of his patrician blood in comic odes.

Dispensing thus some of his strength in such pieces as the *Vieillesse de Brididi*, the *Foire aux Grotesques*, and *Un Monsieur Bien-Mis*, in 1868 he founded the *Lanterne*, and thenceforth became the most ardent champion of the revolutionary party; and in the brilliant articles we all know, he cast its light on the follies of others under the pretext that they were his own. This satirical production reached the eleventh number, when its author, overstepping all bounds, took Napoleon by the horns and the gendarmes by the nose, and committed other extravagances, until the Government fined him to the amount of ten thousand francs penalties, and ordered him a short repose in the prison of Sainte-Pélagie. The notoriety attaching to his name dates from that period, and the events which accompanied the violent death of Victor Noir tended to augment his popularity and to convert him into the leader of a party, or the bearer of a flag, around which rallied all the elements of the struggle against established authority. He escaped to Belgium, and studied socialism, which he expounded later to an admiring audience of seventeen to eighteen thousand electors at Belleville. Elected deputy by the 20th Arrondissement, M. de Rochefort became, in 1869, a favourite representative of that class of the Parisian population whose bad instincts he had flattered and whose tendencies to revolt against authority he had encouraged, and in virtue of these claims he was chosen to form part of the Government of the National Defence. As President of the Commission of Barricades, after the 4th of September, during the siege of Paris, in the midst of the difficulties of all sorts caused to the Government of the National Defence by the investment of the capital, M. De Rochefort, making more and more common cause with the revolutionary party, separated himself from his colleagues in the Government who refused to permit the establishment of a second Government, the Commune, within a besieged city. By this act he openly declared himself a partisan of the Commune, and immediately after the acceptance of the preliminaries of peace he resigned his position as a deputy, alleging that his commission was at an end, and retired to Arcachon.

His wildly sanguinary articles in the *Marseillaise*, and the compacts sealed with blood, with Flourens and his associates, now had so exhausted our poor Rochefort that at the moment of flourishing his handkerchief as the standard of the *canaille*, he dropped pale and fainting to the ground, attacked by a severe illness. He was hardly convalescent when the events of the 18th of March occurred. But early in April, he exerted himself to assume the direction of the *Mot d'Ordre*, which, after having been suppressed by order of General Vinoy, the military commandant of Paris, had reappeared immediately upon the establishment of the Commune. He arrived on the scene of contest about the 8th or 10th of April. The daily report of military operations states the movements of the enemy, and points out what should be done to meet and resist him most advantageously (12th, 13th, and 14th of April; 10th, 16th, and 20th of May). Imaginary successes, the inaccuracy of which must in most instances have been known to the chief editor of the *Mot d'Ordre*, encouraged the hopes of the insurgents, while the announcement of unsuccessful combats was delayed with evident intention; the most ridiculous stories, the falsity of which was evident to the plainest common sense, and which could not escape the intelligence of M. Rochefort, were published in his journal, and kept up the popular excitement (12th, 15th, 19th, 26th, 27th, and 28th of April; 6th and 7th of May). It was in this manner that the pretended Pontifical Zouaves were brought upon the scene, with emblazoned banners, which were seized by the soldiers of the Commune (18th and 19th of April, 8th and 10th of May); that the Government of Versailles was furnished with war material given by, or purchased from the Prussians (27th and 28th of April, 6th and 17th of May); that it was again accused of making use of explosive bullets (18th and 19th of May), and of petroleum bombs (20th of April, and 2nd, 5th, 17th, and 19th of May); and that the best-known and most respected generals had been guilty of the grossest acts of cruelty and barbarity. Incitement to civil war (2nd and 26th of April and 14th and 24th of May) followed, as did also the oft-repeated accusation against the Government of wishing to reduce Paris by famine; indescribable calumnies directed against the Chief of the Executive Power (2nd, 16th, 20th, and 30th of April, and 8th of May), against the minister, the Chambers (16th of April and 14th of May), and the generals (12th, 15th, and 26th of April). The director of the *Mot d'Ordre* then finding that men's minds were prepared for all kinds of excesses, started the idea of the demolition of M. Thiers's house by way of reprisal (6th of April); he mentioned the artistic wealth which it contained. He also referred to the dwellings of other ministers. He returned persistently to this idea, and on the 17th of May he invited the people, in the name of justice, to burn off-hand that other humiliating monument which is styled the History of the Consulate and of the Empire—in short, he insists on the execution of these acts of Vandalism. He did not call for the destruction of the Column Vendôme, but approved of the decree. He demands the destruction of the Expiatory Chapel of Louis XVI. (20th of April), and suggests the seizure of the crown jewels, which were in the possession of the bank (14th of April). In short, M. Rochefort, having entered upon a road which must naturally lead to extremes, finally arrives at a proposition for assassination. In the same way as he pointed out to the demolishers the house of M. Thiers, and to the bandits released by the Commune the treasures of the Church, so he points out to the assassins the unfortunate hostages.

A few days before the end of the reign of the Commune he judged it prudent, "seeing the gravity of events," to suspend the publication of his journal and to quit Paris.

He was arrested at Meaux. It was the "*Meaux de la fin,*"* said a friend and fellow-writer.

* "*Le mot de la fin,*" the final word—the finale.

He arrived at Versailles on the twenty-first of May, at two o'clock, the same day on which the troops entered Paris. On Sept. 20 Rochefort was tried with the Communists before the military tribunal of Versailles. Physically he seemed to have suffered much during his three months of incarceration. He is reported to have made anything but a brilliant defence, and to have restricted himself to pleading past actions and good services. He said that he suppressed *The Marseillaise* at a loss of 20,000 francs per month, when he had no other private means of support, because he thought the effect of its articles would weaken the plan of Trochu for the defence of Paris, and that when he (M. Rochefort) held the *forces populaires*, and had an *occasion unique*, he chose to play a subordinate part. He stated himself a journalist *under* the reign of the Commune, and not an active power *in* the Commune from which in the end he had to fly. Rochefort owned that his articles in the *Mot d'Ordre* had been more or less violent, but he pleaded the cause his "*façon plus ou moins nerveuse à écrire*," and that from illness he did not sometimes see his own journal. When pandering to a vulgar audience, Rochefort seemed to have lost his rich vein of satire, and to have lost himself in vile abuse. On the 21st he was sentenced to transportation for life within the enceinte of a French fortress.

II. (Page 27.)

THE EIGHTEENTH OF MARCH.

It was on the day of the 18th of March, exactly six months after the appearance of Prussians beneath the walls of Paris, that the Government had chosen for the repression of the rebellion. At four o'clock in the morning, the troops of the army of Paris received orders to occupy the positions that had been assigned to them. All were to take part in the action, but it is just to add here that the most arduous and fatiguing part fell to the share of the Lustielle division, composed of the Paturel brigade (17th battalion of Chasseurs), and of the Lecomte brigade (18th battalion of Chasseurs). Three regiments of infantry were entrusted with the guard of the Hôtel de Ville; another, the 89th, mounted guard at the Tuileries. The Place de la Bastille was occupied by a battalion of the 64th, and two companies of the 24th. Three other battalions remained confined to barracks on the Boulevard du Prince Eugène. The Rue de Flandre, the Rue de Puebla, and the Rue de Crimée were filled with strong detachments of infantry; a battalion of the Republican Guard and the 35th Regiment of Infantry were drawn up in the neighbourhood of the Buttes Chaumont. The whole quarter around the Place Clichy was occupied by the Republican Guard, foot Chasseurs, mounted gendarmes, Chasseurs d'Afrique, and a half battery of artillery. Other troops, starting from this base-line of operation, were led up the heights of Montmartre, together with companies of Gardiens de la Paix (the former Sergents-de-Ville converted into soldiers). At six o'clock in the morning the first orders were executed; the Gardiens de la Paix surrounded a hundred and fifty or two hundred insurgents appointed to guard the park of artillery, and the troops made themselves masters of all the most important points. The success was complete. Nothing remained to be done but to carry off the guns. Unhappily, the horses which had been ordered for this purpose did not arrive at the right moment. The cause of this fatal delay remains still unknown, but it is certain that they were still on the Place de la Concorde at the time when they ought to have been harnessed to the guns at Montmartre. Before they arrived, agitation had broken out and spread all over the quarter. The turbulent population, complaining in indignant tones of circulation being stopped, insulted the sentinels placed at the entrances of the streets, and threatened the artillerymen who were watching them. At the same time, the Central Committee caused the rappel to be beaten, and towards seven o'clock in the morning ten or twelve thousand National Guards from the arrondissements of Batignolles, Montmartre, La Villette, and Belleville poured into the streets. Crowds of lookers-on surrounded the soldiers who were mounting guard by the recaptured pieces, the women and children asking them pleadingly if they would have the heart to fire upon their brothers.

Meanwhile, about a dozen tumbrils, with their horses, had arrived on the heights of the Buttes, the guns were dragged off, and were quietly proceeding down hill, when, at the corner of the Rue Lepic and the Rue des Abbesses, they were stopped by a concourse of several hundred people of the quarter, principally women and children. The foot soldiers, who were escorting the guns, forgetting their duty, allowed themselves to be dispersed by the crowd, and giving way to perfidious persuasion, ended by throwing up the butt ends of their guns. These soldiers belonged to the 88th Battalion of the Lecomte brigade. The immediate effect of their disaffection was to abandon the artillerymen to the power of the crowd that was increasing every moment, rendering it utterly impossible for them either to retreat or to advance. And the result was, that at nine o'clock in the morning the pieces fell once more into the hands of the National Guards.

Judging that the enterprise had no chance of succeeding by a return to the offensive, Général Vinoy ordered a retreat, and retired to the quarter of Les Ternes. This movement had been, moreover, determined by the bad news arriving from other parts of Paris. The operations at Belleville had succeeded no better than those at Montmartre. A detachment of the 35th had, it is true, attacked and taken the Buttes Chaumont, defended only by about twenty National Guards; but as soon as the news of the capture had spread in the quarter, the drums beat to arms, and in a short time the troops were found fraternising with the National Guards of Belleville, who got possession again of the

Buttes Chaumont, and not only retook their own guns, but also those which the artillery had brought up to support the manœuvre of the infantry of the line. At the same time, the 120th shamefully allowed themselves to be disarmed by the people, and the insurgents became masters of the barracks of the Prince Eugène.

At about four o'clock in the afternoon, two columns of National Guards, each composed of three battalions, made their way towards the Hôtel de Ville, where they were joined by a dozen other battalions from the left bank of the river; at the same hour, the insurgent guards of Belleville took and occupied the Imprimerie Nationale, the Napoleon Barracks, the staff-quarters of the Place Vendôme, and the railway stations; the arrest of Général Chanzy completed the work of the day, which had been put to profitable account by the insurgents.—" *Guerre des Communeux de Paris.*"

III. (Page 77.)

THE PRUSSIANS AND THE COMMUNE.

The enemies of yesterday, the Prussians, did not disdain to enter into communication with the Central Committee on the 22nd of March. This was an additional reason for the new masters of Paris to regard their position as established, and the *Official Journal* took care to make known to the public the following despatch received from Prussian head-quarters:—

" To the actual Commandant of Paris, the Commander-in-Chief of the third corps d'armée.

" Head-quarters, Compiègne,
" 21st March, 1871.

" The undersigned Commander-in-Chief takes the liberty of informing you that the German troops that occupy the forts on the north and east of Paris, as well as the neighbourhood of the right bank of the Seine, have received orders to maintain a pacific and friendly attitude, so long as the events of which the interior of Paris is the theatre, do not assume towards the German forces a hostile character, or such as to endanger them, but keep within the terms settled by the treaty of peace.

" But should these events assume a hostile character, the city of Paris will be treated as an enemy.

" For the Commandant of the third corps of the Imperial armies,
" (Signed) Chief of the Staff, VON SCHLOSHEIM,
" Major-General."

Paschal Grousset, the delegate of the Central Committee for Foreign Affairs, who had succeeded Monsieur Jules Favre, but who instead of minister was called delegate, which was much more democratic, replied as follows :—

"Paris, 22nd March, 1871.
"To the Commandant-in-Chief of the Imperial Prussian Armies.
"The undersigned, delegate of the Central Committee for Foreign Affairs, in reply to your despatch dated from Compiègne the 21st instant, informs you that the revolution, accomplished in Paris by the Central Committee, having an essentially municipal character, has no aggressive views whatever against the German armies.
"We have no authority to discuss the preliminaries of peace voted by the Assembly at Bordeaux.
"The member of the Central Committee, Delegate for Foreign Affairs.
"(Signed) PASCHAL GROUSSET."

It was very logical of you, Monsieur Grousset, to avow that you had no authority to discuss the preliminaries of peace voted by the Assembly. What right had you then to substitute yourselves for it? He did not, however, thus remain midway in his diplomatic career, for after the election of the Commune he thought it his duty to address the following letter to the German authorities :—

"COMMUNE OF PARIS.
"To the Commander-in-Chief of the 3rd Corps.
"GENERAL,
"The delegate of the Commune of Paris for Foreign Affairs has the honour to address to you the following observations :—
"The city of Paris, like the rest of France, is interested in the observance of the conditions of peace concluded with Prussia; she has therefore a right to know how the treaty will be executed. I beg you, in consequence, to have the goodness to inform me if the Government of Versailles has made the first payment of five hundred millions, and if in consequence of such payment the chiefs of the German army have fixed the date for the evacuation of the part of the territory of the department of the Seine, and also of the forts which form an integral portion of the territory of the Commune of Paris.
"I shall be much obliged, General, if you will be good enough to enlighten me in this respect.
"The Delegate for Foreign Affairs,
"(Signed) PASCHAL GROUSSET."

The German general did not think fit, as far as we know, to send any answer to the above.

IV. (Page 88.)

GAMBON.

There are certain legendary names which when spoken or remembered evoke a second image and raise a double personality. Castor implies Pollux; Ninos, Euryalus; Damon, Pythias. An inferior species of union connects Saint Anthony with his pig, Roland with his mare, and the infinitely more modern Gambon with his historic cow. He was "the village Hampden" of the Empire. By withstanding the tyranny of Cæsar's tax-gatherer and refusing to pay the imperial rates, he obtained a popularity upon which he existed until the Commune gave him power. His history is brief. About a year before the fall of the Second Empire, he declared that he would pay no more taxes imposed by the Government. Thereupon, all his realizable property, consisting of one cow, was seized by the authorities and sold for the benefit of the State. This procured him the commiseration of the entire party of *irréconciliables*. A subscription was opened in the columns of the *Marseillaise* to replace the sequestrated animal, and "La vache à Gambon" — "Gambon's cow" — became a derisive party cry. Gambon had been a deputy in 1848, and when the Commune came into power took a constant though not remarkable part in its deliberations. He was appointed member of the Delegation of Justice on the twentieth of April.

V. (Page 120.)

LULLIER.

Charles Ernest Lullier was born in 1838, admitted into the Naval School in 1854, and appointed cadet of the second class in 1856. He was expelled the Naval School for want of obedience and for his irascible character. When on board the Austerlitz he was noted for his quarrelsome disposition and his violent behaviour to his superiors as well as his equals, which led to his removal from the ship and to his detention for a month on board the Admiral's ship at Brest. He was first brought into notoriety by his quarrel with Paul de Cassagnac, the editor of the *Pays*, whom he challenged, and who refused his cartel. Lullier is celebrated for several acts of the most violent audacity. He struck one of the Government counsel in the Palais de Justice, and openly threatened the Minister of Marine. He was condemned several times for political offences and breaches of discipline. On the fourth of September he left Sainte-Pélagie at the same time as Rochefort. He attacked the new government in every possible way; and when the events of the 18th March occurred, M. Lullier—the man of action, the man recommended by Flourens—seized the opportunity to justify the hopes formed of him by his political associates, who had not lost sight of him, and who elected him military chief of the insurrection. As General of the National Guard, he has given us the history of his deeds during the 18th, 19th, 20th, 21st, and 22nd March. He has since complacently described the energy with which he executed his command, has explained the means he used, and the points occupied by the insurgents; and has described in the same style the occupation of the Paris forts by the National Guard.

When, on the 18th of March, the Central Committee offered him the command in chief of the National Guard, he would only accept it on the following conditions:—

1. The raising of the state of siege.
2. The election by the National Guard of all its officers, including the general.
3. Municipal franchises for Paris—that is to say, the right of the citizens to meet—to appoint magistrates for the city, and to tax themselves by their representatives.

On being appointed he made it a condition that the initiative should rest with him, and then he began to execute his duties with a zeal which never relaxed till his arrest on the 22nd March. By his orders barricades were erected in the Rue de Rivoli, where he massed the insurgent forces. He ordered the occupation of the Hôtel de Ville and the Napoleon Barracks by Brunel, the commander of the insurgents. At midnight he took possession of the Prefecture of Police, at one o'clock of the Tuileries, at two o'clock of the Place du Palais Royal, and at four o'clock he was informed that the Ministry were to meet at the Foreign Office.—" I would have surrounded them," he said, " but Jules Favre's presence withheld me. I contented myself therefore with occupying the Place Vendôme, the Hôtel de Ville, and ordering strategical points on the right bank of the river and four on the left."

He was subsequently accused of having sold Mont Valérien to the Versailles authorities, arrested, and thrown into the Conciergerie. He reappeared, however, on the 14th April as commander of the flotilla of the Commune. Furious with the Central Committee and the Commune he opposed them and was arrested, but contrived to escape from Mazas. From that moment the general of the Commune put himself in communication with Versailles through the mediation of M. Camus and Baron Dathiel de la Tuque, who agreed with him to organise a counter revolution. Lullier was now busily employed in endeavouring to make people forget the part he had taken in the insurrection of the 18th March. He had made it a condition that neither he nor his accomplices, Gomez d'Absin and Bisson, should be prosecuted. The expenses were calculated at 30,000 francs; of which M. Camus gave 2000 francs to Lullier, but the scheme did not succeed. Lullier undertook to have all the members of the Commune arrested, and to send the hostages to Versailles. Lullier is a man of courage, foolhardy even, who never hesitated to fight, and if at the end of the Commune he tried to serve the legitimate government, it was from a spirit of revenge against the men who had refused his dictation, and in his own interest.

VI. (Page 220.)

PROTOT.

Citizen Protot, appointed Delegate of Justice by a decree of the twentieth of April, 1871, was born in 1839.

As an advocate, he defended Mégy, the famous Communist general of the fort of Issy, when he was accused of the assassination of a police agent on the eleventh of April, 1870. This trial, and the ability he displayed, drew public attention for a moment upon him. Compromised as a member of secret societies, he managed to escape the police, but was condemned in his absence to fines and imprisonment. Having been himself a victim of the law, his attention was first given to the drawing up of a decree, thus worded:—

"The notaries and public officers in general shall draw up legal documents which fall within their duty without charge."

In the discussion on the subject of the confiscation of the property of M. Thiers, he proposed that all the plate and other objects in his possession bearing the image of the Orleans family should be sent to the mint.

VII. (Page 229.)

" And now he thinks : 'The Empire is tottering,
  There's little chance of victory.'
Then, creeping furtively backwards, he tries to slink away.
  Remain, renegade, in the building !

" 'The ceiling falls,' you say ; 'if they see me
  They will seize and stop me as I go,'
Daring neither to rest nor fly, you miserably watch the roof
  And then the door,

" And shiveringly you put your hand upon the bolt.
  Back into the dismal ranks !
Back ! Justice, whom they have thrust into a pit,
  Is there in the darkness.

" Back ! She is there, her sides bleeding from their knives,
  Prostrate ; and on her grave
They have placed a slab. The skirt of your cloak
  Is caught beneath the stone.

"Thou shalt not go! What! Quit their house!
  And fly from their fate!
What! Would you betray even treachery itself,
  And make even it indignant?
"What! Did you not hold the ladder to these tricksters
  In open daylight?
Say, was the sack for these robbers' booty
  Not made by you beforehand?
"Falsehood, Hate, with its cold and venomous fang,
  Crouch in this den.
And thou wouldst leave it? Thou! more cunning than Falsehood,
  More viperous than Hate."

VIII. (Page 231.)

JOURDE.

Jourde certainly occupied one of the most difficult offices of the Commune, for he had to find the means to maintain the situation, but as the Ministry of Finances is burnt, no documents can be found to show the employment he made of the funds which passed through his hands. On the 30th of May, when he was arrested, disguised as an artizan, with his friend Dubois, he had about him a sum of 8070 francs in bank notes, and Dubois 3100 francs; making a total sum of 11,170 francs between the two. A part of Jourde's cash was hidden in the lining of his waistcoat; he declared that it was the only sum taken by him out of the moneys belonging to the state, thus clearly proving that he had been guilty of embezzlement.

The amounts declared to have been received by Jourde form a total of 43,891,000 francs, but as the expenses amount to 47,000,000 francs, it is clear there is a deficiency of 3,309,000. Notwithstanding this fact, all the payments were made up to the 29th of May. It is, then, certain that other moneys were received by Jourde, and as he says that cash has been refused from some unknown persons who offered to lend 50,000,000 francs on the guarantee of the picture gallery of the Louvre, the suggestion comes naturally to the mind that the 3,309,000 francs may have been produced by the sale of valuables in the Tuileries. Jourde was sentenced by the tribunal of Versailles to transportation beyond the seas.

IX. (Page 316.)

These are the last proclamations from the Hôtel de Ville. They refer immediately to the burning of the capital.

In the evening of the thirty-first of May, when Delescluze denied with vehemence that the regular army had made its entry, he wrote to Dombrowski:—

"CITIZEN,—I learn that the orders given for the construction of barricades are contradictory.

"See that this be not repeated.

"Blow up or burn the houses which interfere with your plans for the defence. The barricades ought to be unattackable from the houses.

"The defenders of the Commune must be removed above want: give to the necessitous that which is contained in the houses about to be destroyed.

"Moreover, make all necessary requisitions.

"DELESCLUZE, A. BILLIORAY."

"Paris, 2nd Prairial, an 79.

On the 22nd appeared the following proclamation:—

"CITIZENS,—The gate of Saint-Cloud, attacked from four directions at once, was forcibly taken by the Versaillais, who have become masters of a considerable portion of Paris.

"This reverse, far from discouraging us, should prove a stimulus to our exertions. A people who have dethroned kings, destroyed Bastilles, and established a Republic, can not lose in a day the fruits of the emancipation of the 18th of March.

"Parisians, the struggle we have commenced cannot be abandoned, for it is a struggle between the past and the future, between liberty and despotism, equality and monopoly, fraternity and servitude, the unity of nations and the egotism of oppressors.

"AUX ARMES!

"Yes, to arms! Let Paris bristle with barricades, and from behind these improvised ramparts let her shout to her enemies the cry of war, its cry of fierce pride of defiance, and of victory; for Paris with her barricades is invincible.

"Let the pavements of the streets be torn up; firstly, because the projectiles coming from the enemy are less dangerous falling on soft ground; secondly, because these paving-stones, serving as a new means of defence, can be carried to the higher floors where there are balconies.

"Let revolutionary Paris, the Paris of great deeds, do her duty; the Commune and the Committee for Public Safety will do theirs.

"Hôtel de Ville, 2nd Prairial, an 79.

"The Committee for Public Safety,

"ANTOINE ARNAULT, E. EUDES, F. GAMBON, G. RANVIER."

These are the commentaries made by Citizen Delescluze:—

"Citoyen Jacquet is authorised to find men and materials for the construction of barricades in the Rue du Château d'Eau and in the Rue d'Albany.

"The citoyens and citoyennes who refuse their aid will be shot on the spot.

"The citoyens, chiefs of barricades, are entrusted with the care of assuring tranquillity each in his own quarter.

"They are to inspect all houses bearing a suspicious appearance &c., &c.

"The houses suspected are to be set light to at the first signal given.

"DELESCLUZE."

X. (Page 335.)

FERRÉ.

At half-past nine on the morning of the 18th of March Ferré was at No. 6, Rue des Rosiers, opposing the departure of the prisoners of the Republican Guard, by obtaining from the Commander Bardelle the revocation of the order for their dismissal, which was known to have been issued. He went to the council of the Château Rouge, whither General Lecomte was about to be taken, and made himself conspicuous by the persistency with which he called for the death of that general. On the morning of Monday, the 24th May, a witness residing at the Prefecture of Police saw Ferré and five others going up the stairs of the Prefecture of Police. Ferré said to him, "Be off as quick as you can. We are going to set fire to the place. In a quarter of an hour it will be in flames." Half an hour afterwards the witness saw the flames burst forth from two windows of the office of the Procureur-Général. When Raoul Rigault was installed during the insurrection, a woman saw some persons washing the walls of the Prefecture of Police with petroleum. Seeing them going out by the court of the St. Chapelle, she noticed among them one smaller than the rest, wearing a grey paletot with a black velvet collar, and black striped trousers. On the same day a police agent went to La Roquette to order the shooting of Mgr. Darboy and the other prisoners—the President Bonjean, the Abbé Allard, the Père Ducoudray, and the Abbé Deguerry. On Saturday, the 27th, Ferré installed himself in the clerk's office of the prison, and ordered the release of certain of the criminals and gave them arms and ammunition. Upon this they proceeded to massacre a great number of the prisoners, among whom were 66 gendarmes. Several witnesses saw Ferré that day at the prison.

XI. (Page 342.)

At the trial of Ferré, August 10, Dr. Puymoyen, physician to the prison for juvenile offenders, opposite La Roquette, gave the following graphic evidence:—

"Immediately after the insurgents, driven back by the troops, had occupied La Roquette, they installed a court-martial at the children's prison opposite, where I live. It was from thence I saw the poor wretches whom they feigned to release, ushered in to the square, where they encountered an ignoble mob, that ill-treated them in the most brutal manner. I was told that Ferré presided over this court-martial. Its proceedings were singular. I saw an unfortunate gendarme taken to the prison; he had been arrested near the Grenier d'Abondance, on a denunciation. He wore a blouse, blue trousers, and an apron, and was charged with having stolen them. The mob wanted to enter the prison along with him, but the keepers, who behaved very well, prevented the invasion of the courtyard. The escort was commanded by a young woman carrying a Chassepot, and wearing a chignon. I entered the registrar's office with this unfortunate gendarme. One Briand, who was charged to question the prisoners summarily, asked him where his clothes came from. The man was very cool and courageous, and his perfect self-possession disconcerted this *juge d'instruction*. He was asked if he were married, and had a family. He replied, 'Yes, I have a wife and eight children.' He was then shown into the back office, where the 'judges' were. These judges were mere boys, who seemed quite proud of the part they were playing, and gave themselves no end of airs. I asked the governor of the gaol soon afterwards what had been done with the gendarme. He told me that they were going to shoot him. I replied, 'Surely it can't be true. I must see the president—we can't allow a married man with eight children to be murdered in this way.' I tried to get into the room where the court-martial was sitting, but was prevented. One of the National Guards on duty at the door told me 'Don't go in there, or you're done for (*N'y entrez pas, ou vous êtes f—*).' I made immediately further inquiries about M. Grudnemel, and was told he was in 'a provisional cell.' I trembled for him, for I knew that meant he would be given up to the mob, which would tear him to pieces. When they said, 'This man is to be taken to a cell,' that meant that he was to be shot. When they said, 'Put him in a provisional cell,' it meant that he should be delivered over to the mob for butchery. I continued to plead the gendarme's cause with the National Guard, dwelling on the fact of his having eight children. Thereon, the woman above referred to, who appeared to be in command of the detachment, exclaimed, 'Why does this fellow go in for the gendarme?' One of her acolytes replied, 'Smash his jaw.' This woman seemed to understand her business. She minutely inspected the men's pouches to ascertain that they had plenty of ammunition. She would not hear of the gendarme being reprieved, and she had her way. I understood that I had better follow the governor's advice and keep quiet. A mere boy was placed as sentry at the door of the court-martial. He told me, 'You know I sha'n't let you in.' When I saw the poor gendarme leave the room he looked at me imploringly; he had probably detected in my eyes a look of sympathy. And when he was told that he might go out—hearing the yells of the mob—he turned towards me and said, 'But I shall be stoned to death;' and, in fact, it was perfectly fearful to hear the shouts of the crowd outside. I could not withstand the impulse, and I took my place by his side, and tried to address the crowd. 'Think on what you are going to do—surely you won't murder the father of eight children.' The words were hardly out of my mouth when a kind of signal was given. I was shoved back against the wall, and one National Guard, clapping his hand on his musket, ejaculated, 'You know, you old rascal, there is something for you here,' and he drove his bayonet through my whiskers. The unfortunate gendarme was taken across the place, close to the shop where they sell funeral wreaths, but there was no firing party in attendance. He then took to his heels, but was pursued, captured, and put to death. I began to feel rather bewildered, and some one urged me to return to the prison, which I did. A young linesman was then brought in. He was quite a young fellow, barely twenty; his hands were tied behind his back. They decided to kill him within the prison. They set upon him, beat him, tore his clothes, so that he had hardly a shred of covering left; they made him kneel, then made him stand up, blindfolded him, then uncovered his eyes; finally they put an end to his long agony by shooting him, and flung the body into a costermonger's cart close to the gate. Several priests had got out of the prison of La Roquette. The Abbé Surat, on passing over a barricade, was so imprudent as to state who he was, and showed some articles of value he had about him. He had got as far as about the middle of the Boulevard du Prince Eugène, when he was arrested and taken back to the prison, where they prepared to shoot him. But the young woman whom I have before mentioned, with a revolver in one hand and a dagger in the other, rushed at him exclaiming, 'I must have the honour of giving him the first blow.' The abbé instinctively put his hands out to protect himself, crying, '*Grâce! grâce!*' Whereon this fury shouted, '*Grâce! grâce! en voilà un maigre,*' and she discharged her revolver at him. His body was not searched, but his shoes were removed. Afterwards his pastoral cross and 300 francs were found about him. The boys detained in the prison were set at liberty. The smaller ones were made to carry pails of petroleum, the others had muskets given them, and were sent to fight. Six of them were killed; the remainder came back that night, and on the following day. About a hundred boys were taken to Belleville by a member of the Commune, quite a young man; they were wanted to make sand-bags, to be filled with earth to form barricades."

XII. (Page 345.)

Regarding the death of President Bonjean, the Abbé de Marsay said—"That gentleman carried his scruples so far that he would not avail himself of forty-eight hours' leave on *parole*, fearing he could not get back in time; thus did not see his family."

The Abbé Perni, a venerable man with a white beard, who had been a missionary in China, and who had been at Mazas with Archbishop Darboy, said—

"On Wednesday, the 24th of May, we were ordered back to our cells at La Roquette at an earlier hour than usual, and at about four o'clock in the afternoon a battalion of federates noisily occupied the passage into which our cells opened. They spoke at the topmost pitch of their voices. One of them said, 'We must get rid of these Versailles banditti.' Another replied, 'Yes; let us bowl them over, put them to bed.' I understood what this meant, and prepared for death. Soon after the door next mine was opened, and I heard a man asking if M. Darboy was there. The prisoner replied in the negative. The man passed before my door without stopping, and I soon heard the mild voice of the archbishop answering to his name. The hostages were then dragged out of the lobby; ten minutes later I saw the mournful *cortège* pass in front of my windows; the federates were walking along in a confused way, making a noise to cover the voice of their victims, but I could hear Father Allard exhorting his companions to prepare for death. A little after I heard the report of the muskets, and understood that all was over. On Thursday (the 25th) the day passed off quietly, but on Friday shells began to fall on the prison, and at about half-past four in the afternoon a corporal, named Romain, came up, and with a joyful face told us we would soon be free. He said answer to your names; I must have 15. He had a list in his hand, and I must confess a feeling of terror came over us all. Ten hostages answered to their names. One of them, a father of the order of Picpus, asked if he could take his hat. Romain replied, 'Oh, it's no use; you are only going to the registrar's.' None of these unfortunate men ever returned. On Saturday (the 27th) we learnt that several of the prisoners had been armed with hammers, files, &c. They threw us some of these in at the windows. We were then informed that several members of the Commune had arrived at La Roquette. I cannot say whether Ferré was among them. We were taken back to our cellars, where we expected to be put to death every minute. At about four o'clock the cells of the common prisoners were opened, and they escaped, shouting 'Vive la Commune!' Our keeper himself had disappeared, and a turnkey presently opened our cells, and recommended us to run away. We were afraid this was a trap, but as it might afford a chance we determined to avail ourselves of it. Those amongst us who had plain clothes hurried them on, and I must say the gaolers behaved admirably in this emergency; they lent clothes to such of us as had none, and we were thus all enabled to escape. As for myself, after wandering for about an hour in the streets about the prison, and being unable to find shelter anywhere, and afraid of being murdered in the streets, I determined to return to La Roquette. As I reached it I met the archbishop's secretary, two priests, and two gendarmes, who, like myself, had been driven to return to the prison. One of the keepers told us that the safest for us was the sick ward. We dressed up in the hospital uniform and hid in bed. At eight in the evening the federates, who were not aware that we had escaped, came back and called on the gaolers to produce us. They were told we had gone; fortunately they believed it. On Sunday the troops came in, and I left La Roquette for good this time. In reply to a further question the witness said that as the hostages marched past his windows, on their way to execution, he saw President Bonjean raising his hands, and heard him say, 'Mon Dieu, mon Dieu !'

XIII. (Page 82.)

URBAIN.

Urbain, formerly head master of an academy, was elected to the Commune, and became, in virtue of his former office of teacher, a member of the Committee of Instruction, retaining at the same time his office of mayor. He finally installed himself in his mayoralty about the middle of April, with his sister and young son, and gave protection there to his mistress, Leroy, who had great influence over him, and who used to frequent the committees and clubs. At the mayoralty of the 7th Arrondissement this woman, in the absence of the mayor, took the direction and management of affairs. During the administration of Urbain searches were made in private and in religious houses, this woman, Leroy, sometimes taking part in the proceedings; on these occasions seizures were made of letters and articles of value, which were sent to the mayoralty and from thence to the police-office. Urbain and the woman Leroy are accused of having appropriated to themselves money and jewellery. At the mayoralty of the 7th Arrondissement there were deposits for public instruction to the amount of 8000 francs, which had dwindled down to 2900 francs. Urbain confesses having employed this money in helping persons compromised like himself. It is certain that during the residence of the woman Leroy at the mayoralty the expenses exceeded the sum allowed to Urbain. According to the evidence of a domestic everybody had recourse to this unfortunate deposit, and it is stated in the instructions that the accused had left by will to his son a sum of 4000 francs in bank notes and gold, deposited in the hands of his aunt, Madame Danelair, while there is clear proof that before the days of the Commune he did not possess a sou. Madame Leroy herself, who came to the mayoralty without a penny, was found in possession of 1000 francs, which she said were the results of her savings. It appears from the statement of M. Laudon, inspector of police, that the search made at his house resulted in the subtraction of a sum of 5000 francs, and that he has seen a ring which belonged to his wife on the finger of the woman Leroy. Though not taking a conspicuous share in the military operations, Urbain played an important part. His duty was to visit the military stations and to take possession of the Fort d'Issy, which had been abandoned. He admits that he thus visited the barracks and the ramparts. He ordered the construction of barricades, and says that, on the occasion of the repulse of the 22nd May, he resisted the entreaties of the woman Leroy, who wished him to give up the struggle and to betake himself to the Hôtel de Ville, with the view of remaining at his post. As a politician, Urbain, in the discussions of the Commune, was very zealous and spoke frequently. By his vote he gave his sanction to all the violent decrees relating to the hostages, the demolition of the Column, the destruction of M. Thiers' house, and the Committee of Public Safety, of which he was one of the most ardent supporters. To him is to be attributed in particular the demand for the carrying into execution the decree relating to the hostages. On this point here is Urbain's proposal, copied from the *Official Journal* of the 18th May:—"I demand that either the Commune or the Committee of Public Safety should decree that the ten hostages in our custody should be shot within twenty-four hours, in retaliation for the murders of our cantinière and of the bearer of our flag of truce, who were shot in defiance of the law of nations. I demand that five of the hostages should be executed solemnly in the centre of Paris, in presence of deputations from all the battalions, and that the rest should be shot at the advanced posts in presence of the soldiers who witnessed the murders. I trust my proposal will be agreed to." By this proposal Urbain has linked his name to the horrible crime committed on the hostages. Latterly he was a member of the military committee, and his ability served well the cause of the insurgents. He was condemned by the court-martial of Versailles to hard labour for life, September 2, 1871.

XIV.

THE DEVASTATIONS OF PARIS.

The following is the way in which the fires were prepared:—In some instances a number of men, acting as *avant-courriers*, went first, telling the inhabitants that the Quarter was about to be delivered to the flames, and urging them to fly for their lives; in other cases, the unfortunate people were told that the whole city would be burnt, and that they might as well meet death where they were as run to seek it elsewhere. In some places—in the Rue de Vaugirard, for instance—it is asserted that sentinels were placed in the streets and ordered to fire upon everyone who attempted to escape. One incendiary, who was arrested in the Rue de Poitiers, declared that he received ten francs for each house which he set on fire. Another system consisted in throwing through the cellar doors or traps tin cans or bottles filled with petroleum, phosphorus, nitro-glycerine, or other combustibles, with a long sulphur match attached to the neck of the vessel, the match being lighted at the moment of throwing the explosives into the cellar. Finally, the batteries at Belleville and the cemetery of Père la Chaise sent destruction into many quarters by means of petroleum shells.

Eudes, a general of the Commune, sent the following order to one of his officers :—

"Fire on the Bourse, the Bank, the Post Office, the Place des Victoires, the Place Vendôme, the Garden of the Tuileries, the Babylone Barracks; leave the Hôtel de Ville to Commandant Pindy and the Delegate of War, and the Committee of Public Safety and of the Commune will assemble at the *mairie* of the eleventh Arrondissement, where you are established; there we will organize the defence of the popular quarters of the city. We will send you cannon and ammunitions from the Parc Basfroi. We will hold out to the last, happen what may.

"(Signed)   E. EUDES."

The insurgents had collected a considerable quantity of powder in the Pantheon, and when the Versailles troops obtained possession of the building the officer in command at once searched for the slow match, and cut it off when it had not more than a yard to burn!

Instructions were given to the firemen not to extinguish the fires, but to retire to the Champ de Mars with the pumps and other apparatus. Whenever a man attempted to do anything to arrest the conflagration he was fired at. The firemen, who had arrived from all parts, even from Belgium, and honest citizens who joined them, worked to extinguish the fires amid showers of bullets. At the Treasury the labours of these men were four times interrupted by the violent cannonading of the insurgents.

The fire broke out at the TUILERIES on Tuesday evening. When the battalions at the Arc de Triomphe and at the Corps Législatif had silenced the guns ranged before the Palace, the insurgents set fire to it, and threw out men *en tirailleur* to prevent anyone from approaching to subdue the flames.

At the same moment an attempt was made to set fire to the MINISTRY OF MARINE, in obedience to an order given to Commandant Brunel, which was thus worded:—"In a quarter of an hour the Tuileries will be in flames; as soon as our wounded are removed, you will cause the explosion of the Ministry." It was Admiral Pothuau, the minister himself, who, at the head of a handful of sailors, set the incendiaries to flight, Brunel along with them. They also arrived in time to prevent any damage being done to the BIBLIOTHÈQUE NATIONALE.

The struggle was terrific during the night; the insurgents, who had sought refuge in the Ministry of Finance, after the taking of the barricade in the Rue Saint-Florentin, increased the fury of the flames by firing from the windows, and discharging jets of petroleum at the soldiers.

On Wednesday morning the battle had become fearful. Towards ten o'clock columns of smoke rose above Paris, forming a thick cloud, which the sun's rays could not penetrate. Then, simultaneously, all the fires burst forth: at the CONSEIL D'ÉTAT, at the LEGION OF HONOUR, at the CAISSE DES DÉPÔTS ET CONSIGNATIONS. at the HÔTEL DE VILLE, at the PALAIS ROYAL, at the MINISTRY OF FINANCE, at the PREFECTURE OF POLICE, at the PALAIS DE JUSTICE, at the THÉÂTRE LYRIQUE, in the Rue du Bac, the Rue de Lille, the Rue de la Croix-Rouge, Rue Notre-Dame-des-Champs, in a great number of houses in the Faubourgs Saint-Germain and Saint-Honoré, in the Rue Royale, and in the Rue Boissy d'Anglas. Not many hours later, flames were seen to arise from the Avenue Victoria, Boulevard Sébastopol, Rue Saint-Martin, at the Château d'Eau, in the Rue Saint-Antoine, and the Rue de Rivoli.

During the night of Friday, the docks of LA VILLETTE, and the warehouses of the DOUANE, the GRENIER D'ABONDANCE and the GOBELINS were all burning! So great was the glare that small print could be read as far off as Versailles, even on that side of the town towards Meudon and Ville d'Avray.

THE DOME OF THE INVALIDES.—This was placed in imminent danger. Mines were laid on all sides, but their positions were discovered, and the electric wires cut which were to have communicated the spark.

THE PLACE DE LA CONCORDE.—When the noise of the fusillade and cannonading ceased, the Place de la Concorde was a scene of absolute desolation. On all sides lay broken pieces of candelabra, balustrades, paving-stones, asphalte, and heaps of earth. The water-nymphs and Tritons of the fountains were much mutilated, and the statue of the town of Lille—one of the eight gigantic, seated figures of the principal towns of France, which form a prominent ornament to the Place, the work of Pradier, and a likeness of one of the Orleans princesses—lay shivered on the ground.

THE ARC DE L'ETOILE.—The triumphal arch bears many scars, but none of them of much importance. On the façade looking towards Courbevoie, the great bas-relief by Etex, representing "War," was struck by three shells; the group of "Peace" received only the fragment of one. Here and there, in the bas-relief representing the "Passage of the Bridge of Arcole," and the "Taking of Alexandra," some traces of balls are visible. On the whole, no irremediable harm is done here. Rude's masterpiece, "The Marseillaise," is untouched.

THE PALACE OF INDUSTRY.—Rumour says Courbet had, among other projects, formed an idea of demolishing the Palace of Industry. The painted windows of the great nave have received no serious injury. The bas-relief of the main façade, picturing Industry and the Arts offering their products to the universal exhibitions, has several of its figures mutilated. The same has happened to the colossal group by Diebolt—France offering laurel crowns to Art and Industry.

THE TUILERIES.—Felix Pyat, in the *Vengeur*, proposed converting the Palace of the Tuileries into a school for the children of soldiers. He says:—" They have taken possession by the work and activity that reign there; a whole floor is filled with tools and activity, and converted into workshops for the construction of messenger balloons. King Labour is enthroned there. I recognised there among the workmen an exile of the revolutionary Commune of London. The workmen and the proscribed at the Tuileries! From the prison of London to the palace of the Tuileries. It is well!" But in the heart of the Commune the soul of the *Vengeur* underwent a change, and insisted on the complete destruction of the "infamous pile."

The portion of the building overlooking the river was alone preserved. The roofing is destroyed, but the façade is but little injured, the only work of art damaged here being a pediment by M. Carrier-Belleuse, representing "Agriculture." Fortunately the Government of the Fourth of September had sent all the most precious things to the Garde-Meuble (Stores); but how can the magnificent Gobelins tapestry, the fine ceilings, the works of Charles Lebrun, of Pierre Mignard, of Coypel, of Francisque Meillet, of Coysevox, of Girardon, and of many others, and the exquisite Salon des Roses be replaced?

The Tuileries burnt for three days, and ten days afterwards the ruins blazed forth anew near the Pavillon de Flore. Not only did the devouring fire threaten to destroy inestimable treasures, but on Monday a number of men carrying slow matches, and led by a man named Napias-Piquet, made all their preparations to set fire to several points of the museum of the Louvre, and two of the guardians were shot. This Napias-Piquet threatened to make of the whole quarter of the Louvre one great conflagration. He was taken and shot, and in his pocket was found a note of his breakfast of the preceding day, amounting to 57 francs 80 centimes.

THE LOUVRE.—The preservation of the museum was due to the strong masonry, and the thick walls of the new portion of the building, on which the raging flames could make no impression. But it ran other risks: when the troops entered the building, they planted the tricolour on the clock pavilion, which served as an object for the insurgents' aim. It was immediately removed, however, when this was perceived. It was generally believed that the galleries of the Louvre contained all their art treasures. This was not the case; prior to the first siege the most precious of the contents had been carefully packed and conveyed to the arsenal of Brest, where they safely reposed, but many very admirable works remained.

MINISTRY OF FINANCE (Treasury).—On the 22nd of May, the official journal of the Commune published a note declaring that the certificates of stock and the stock books (*grand livre*) would be burnt within forty-eight hours. The Commune was annoyed at the publicity given to this note, and a violent debate took place in its council in consequence. On this occasion Paschal Grousset uttered the following:—

"I blame those who inserted the note in question, but I demand

COURT OF THE LOUVRE, FROM THE PLACE DU CARROUSEL. More than 90,000 volumes are burnt. Rare editions, Elzevirs, precious MSS., coins, and unique collections, priceless treasures, are irrevocably lost. The Library is completely destroyed.

that measures may be taken for the destruction of all such documents belonging to those at Versailles, the day that they shall enter Paris."

The building forms one of the most striking ruins in Paris. Citizen Lucas, appointed by Ferré to set the Ministry on fire, did his task well. The conflagration, which lasted several days, began in the night of the 23rd of May. Not only was every part soaked with petroleum, but shells had also been placed about the building, and burst successively as the fire extended. Scarcely anything remains of the huge pile but the offices of the Administration of Forest Lands, which are almost intact. A considerable number of valuable documents were saved, but the quantity was very small in comparison with the immense collection accumulated since the beginning of the century. Four times was the work of salvage interrupted by the insurgents. Not a single book in the library has escaped; and this library contained almost the whole of the enormous correspondence of Colbert, the minister, forming no less than two thousand volumes.

PALAIS ROYAL.

The PALAIS ROYAL.—The palace itself alone is destroyed; the galleries of the THÉÂTRE FRANÇAIS are preserved. The *Constitutionnel* published the following account of the conflagration:—

"It was at three o'clock that this fearful fire burst forth. A shopkeeper of the PALAIS ROYAL, M. Emile Le Saché, came forward in all haste to offer his services. A Communist captain, or lieutenant, threatened to fire on him if he did not retire on the instant; he added that the whole quarter was going to be blown up and burned. In the teeth of this threat, however, two fire-engines were brought to the Place, and were worked by the people of the neighbourhood. It was four o'clock. No water in the Cour des Fontaines. But some was procured by a line of people being placed along the passage leading from the Cour d'Honneur, who passed full buckets of water from hand to hand.

"A ladder was placed against the wall for the purpose of reaching the terrace of the Rue de Valois. The insurgents proved so true to their word that the people were forced to renounce the attempt at saving the entire pavilion. Fire and smoke burst forth from three windows just above the terrace. In the midst of the balls showered from the barricade at the corner of the Rue de Rivoli, they succeeded in extinguishing the fire on that side. At five o'clock M. C. Sauve, captain in the commercial service, with a handful of brave workmen, got a fire engine into the Cour d'Honneur, and thus saved a great quantity of pictures, precious marbles, furniture, hangings, &c. Here another line of people was formed for the carrying of buckets, but unfortunately water ran short: the pipes had been cut, the wretches had planned that the destruction should be complete. At seven o'clock M. Bessignet, jun., hastened there with four Paris firemen, but already the Pavilion, where the flames were first apparent, was entirely consumed.

"On the arrival of the firemen they used every effort to prevent the fire communicating itself to the apartments of the Princess Clothilde; it had already reached the façade on the side of the Place. Here, too, all the fittings and ornaments of the chapel were saved.

"At last, at seven o'clock, the soldiers of the line arrive. 'Long live the line!' is shouted on all sides. 'Long live France!' Signals are made with the ambulance flags. Help is come at last!

"Those present now regard their position with more coolness, and use every effort to combat the fire, pumping from the roofs and upper storeys of the neighbouring houses. The fire continues, however, increasing and spreading on the theatre side. Here is the greatest danger. If the theatre catch light, all the quarter will most probably be destroyed. They then determine to avail themselves of the water appliances of the theatre to stay the progress of the flames. This is rendered more difficult and dangerous by the continuous firing from the Communists installed in the upper story of the Hôtel du Louvre. M. Le Saché mounts on the roofs, with the principal engineer, to conduct this movement. They are compelled to hide out of the way of the shower of balls coming from the Communists.

"At ten o'clock the companies from the quarter of the Banque, the 12th battalion of National Guards, arrive. The Federals are put to flight. Thereupon thirty *sapeurs-pompiers* of Paris came at full speed and succeed in mastering the remaining fire. An hour sooner and all could have been saved."

THE HÔTEL DE VILLE.—The Hôtel de Ville was set on fire by order of the Committee of Public Safety at the moment when the entry of the troops caused them to fly to the École des Chartes, which was thus saved, and whence they fled to the Mairie of Belleville. Five battalions of National Guards—the 57th, 156th, 178th, 184th, and the 187th—remained to prevent any attempt being made to extinguish the fire. Petroleum had been poured about the *Salle du Trône*, and the *Salle du Zodiaque*, which were decorated by Jean Goujon and Cogniet;

in the *Galerie de Pierre*, in which were paintings by Lecomte, Baudin,

HÔTEL DE VILLE.

Desgoffes, Hédouin, and Bellel; in the *Salon des Arcades*, in the *Salon Napoléon*, in the *Galerie des Fêtes*, and in the *Salon de la Paix*, which contained works of Schopin, Picot, Vauchelet, Jadin, Girard, Ingres, Delacroix, Landelle, Riesener, Lehmann, Gosse, Benouville and Cabanel. It is not only as a fine specimen of architecture that the Hôtel

FOREIGN OFFICE.

de Ville is to be regretted, but as the cradle of the municipal and revolutionary history of Paris, as well as for the vast collection of archives of the city, duplicates of which were at the same moment a prey to the flames at the Palais de Justice.

APPENDIX.

The Prefecture of Police was set fire to by the Communal delegate Ferré and a band of drunken National Guards.

The Palais de Justice, thanks to the prompt arrival of the soldiers, has been partially spared. The damage done, however, is very great. In the Salle des Pas-Perdus several of the grand arches that support the roof have fallen in, and many of the columns are lying in ruins on the pavement. The Cour de Cassation and the Cour d'Assises are entirely destroyed. The conflagration was stopped when it reached the Cour d'Appel and the Tribunal de Première Instance.

Palace of the Quai d'Orsay.—This vast building, in which the Conseil d'État and the Cour des Comptes held their sittings, has suffered seriously, though the walls are not destroyed; but what is irreparable is the loss of the many precious documents belonging to the financial and legislative history of France. The most famous artists of our time have contributed to the decoration of the interior. Jeanron painted the twelve allegorical subjects for the vaulted ceiling of the *Salle des Pas-Perdus;* Isabey, the Port of Marseilles in the Committee-room. The Death of President de Renty, in the *Salle du Contentieux*, was by Paul Delaroche; the fine portrait of Napoleon I., as legislator, in the great Council Chamber, by Flandrin; and in another apartment the portrait of Justinien by Delacroix. These, and many other treasures, are lost; for the work of destruction was complete.

Ministry of Foreign Affairs.—The façade has been seriously injured. It was fired upon from the terrace of the Tuileries, and from a gunboat lying under cover of the Pont-Royal. The Doric and Ionic columns are partly broken, as well as the fifteen medallions in white marble, which bore the arms of the principal powers. The apartments in front have been greatly damaged, and especially the *salon* of the ambassadors, where the Congress of Paris was held in 1856.

The Palace of the Legion of Honour.—This is a specimen of French architecture, unique of its kind. Happily, drawings and plans have been preserved, and the members of the Legion of Honour have offered a subscription for its re-instatement.

The Gobelins.—The public gallery, the school of tapestry, and the painters' studios have been destroyed. The incendiaries would have burned all, works, frames and materials, if the people of the quarter, with the Gobelins weavers, had not defended them at the peril of their lives. An irreparable loss is that of a valuable collection of tapestry dating from the time of Louis XIV.

The military hospital of the Val de Grâce, the Asylum for the Deaf and Dumb, the Mint, the façade of the annex of the École-des-Beaux-Arts, have been riddled with balls. At the Luxembourg the magnificent camellia-house and conservatories exist no longer, and the graceful Medici fountain has been injured.

The Bank had most fortunately been placed in charge of the

delegate Beslay, who, during the whole time he was there, made every effort to prevent the pillage of the valuables. He was ably seconded by all the officials and *employés*, who had before been armed and incorporated into a battalion.

PALACE OF THE LÉGION D'HONNEUR.

Post Office.—The Communal delegate, Theiz, prevented the incendiaries from setting fire to this important establishment.

The Triumphal Arch of the Porte-St.-Denis.—The bas-relief

containing an emblematical figure of the Rhine resting on a rudder has been mutilated, a shell having carried the arm and its support entirely away. The other bas-relief of Holland vanquished and in tears, has been struck by balls, as have also the figures of Fame in the tympans of the arcades.

The Triumphal Arch of the Porte-St.-Martin.—The sculptures, which represent the taking of Limbourg and the defeat of the Germans, have suffered considerably. They are the works of Le Hongre and the elder Legros.

A tragic incident marked the burning of the Theatre of the Porte St. Martin (see sketch). After having massacred the proprietor and people of the *restaurant* Ronceray, the Federals set fire to the house and the theatre which is adjoining. At eight o'clock in the evening, on beholding the first flames arise, the inhabitants of the quarter united in endeavouring to extinguish the fire, notwithstanding that the projectiles fell thickly in the Boulevard Saint-Martin and in the Rue de Bondy. The Federals from behind their barricades at the corner of the Rue Bouchardon, fired upon everyone who attempted to enter the theatre.

The Archives (Record Office), the Imprimerie Nationale, and the Bibliothèque Mazarine were all preserved through the strenuous endeavours of MM. Alfred Maury, Haureau, and Charles Asselineau, who had all managed to keep their places in spite of the Commune.

At the Docks of La Villette, and at the warehouses of the Douane, the destruction of property has been enormous. Many millions' worth of goods were consumed there.

In the great buildings belonging to the Magasins Réunis (Co-operative Stores) an ambulance had been established, and this was in the utmost danger during two days. It was only owing to the wonderful energy of M. Jahyer that the fire was mastered while the poor wounded men were transported to a place of safety.

THE CHURCHES.

Notre-Dame.—In the interior of Notre-Dame the insurgents set fire to three huge piles of chairs and wood-work. Fortunately the fact was discovered before much mischief had happened.

The Sainte-Chapelle.—This incomparable gem of Gothic art, by some marvellous good fortune was neither touched by fire nor shells. It will still be an object for the pilgrimages of the erudite and the curious.

The Madeleine.—The balls have somewhat damaged the double colonnade of the peristyle, but the sculptured pediment by Lemaire is all but untouched.

The Trinité.—The façade has been seriously injured. The Federals, from their barricades at the entrance of the Chaussée-d'Antin, bombarded it for several hours. The painted windows by Oudinot had been removed before the siege—like those of the ancient

Cathedral of St. Denis, and the Chapel of St. Ferdinand, by Ingres, they repose in safety.

Of all the churches of Paris ST. EUSTACHE has suffered the most. At one time the fire had reached the roof, but it was fortunately discovered in time.

The paintings at NOTRE-DAME-DE-LORETTE, at SAINT-GERMAIN-L'AUXERROIS, and at SAINT-GERMAIN-DES-PRÉS have been spared.

It is curious that the churches suffered so little, whilst several theatres were burned, including the Porte St. Martin, Théâtre du Châtelet, Lyrique, Délassements Comiques, &c.

The windows of the church of SAINT-JACQUES-DU-HAUT-PAS are destroyed.

It has been estimated that the value of the houses and other property destroyed in Paris amounts to twenty millions sterling. In addition to this, it is said that twelve millions' worth of works of art, furniture, &c., have disappeared, and that more than two and a half millions' worth of merchandise was burnt, making a total of nearly thirty-five millions. It has been said that the value of the window-glass alone destroyed during the reign of the Commune approaches a million sterling. The demand for glass was at one time so great that the supply was quite insufficient, and at the present moment the price is 20 per cent. higher than usual.

XV.

The following order of the day of General de Ladmirault, commanding the first army corps of Versailles, sums up the principal episodes of this eight days' battle:—

"Officers and soldiers of the First Corps d'Armée,—

"The defences of the lines of Neuilly, Courbevoie, Bécon and Asnières served you by way of apprenticeship. Your energy and courage were formed amid the greatest works and perils. Every one in his grade has given an example of the most complete abnegation and devotion. Artillery, engineers, troops of the line, cavalry, volunteers of the Seine-et-Oise, you rivalled each other in zeal and ardour. Thus prepared, on the 22nd of the month you attacked the insurgents, whose guilty designs and criminal undertakings you knew and despised. You devoted yourselves nobly to save from destruction the monuments of our old national glory, as well as the property of the citizens menaced by savage rage.

"On the 23rd of the month, the formidable position of the Buttes Montmartre could no longer resist your efforts, in spite of all the forces with which they were covered.

"This task was confided to the first and second division and the volunteers of the Seine and Seine-et-Oise, and the heads of the various columns arrived simultaneously at the summit of the position.

"On the 24th, the third division, which alone had been charged with the task of driving the insurgents out of Neuilly, Levallois-Perret, and Saint-Ouen, joined the other divisions, and took possession of the terminus of the Eastern Railway, while the first division seized that of the Northern line by force of arms.

"On the 26th, the third division occupied the *rotonde*—circular place —of La Villette.

"On the 27th, the first and second division, with the volunteers of the Seine-et-Oise, by means of a combined movement, took the Buttes Chaumont and the heights of Belleville by assault, the artillery having by its able firing prepared the way for the occupation.

"Finally, on the 28th, the defences of Belleville yielded, and the first corps achieved brilliantly the task which had been confided to them.

"During the days of the struggle and fighting you rendered the greatest service to civilization, and have acquired a claim to the gratitude of the country. Accept then all the praise which is due to you.

"Paris, 29th May, 1871.

"The General commanding the First Corps d'Armée,
(Signed) "LADMIRAULT."

During the day of the 28th of May Marshal MacMahon caused the following proclamation to be posted in the streets of Paris:—

"Inhabitants of Paris,—

"The army of France is come to save you. Paris is relieved. The last positions of the insurgents were taken by our soldiers at four o'clock. To-day the struggle is at an end; order, labour, and security are springing up again.

"Paris, Quartier Général, the 28th May, 1871.
(Signed) "MACMAHON, Duc de Magenta, Marshal of France, Commander-in-Chief."

On the 28th of May the war of the Communists was at an end, but the fort of Vincennes was still occupied by three hundred National Guards, with eighteen of their superior officers and fifteen of the high functionaries of the Commune. They made an appeal to the commander of the Prussian forces in front of the fort, in the hope of obtaining passports for Switzerland. General Vinoy, hearing of this, took at once the most energetic measures, and at six o'clock on the 29th of May the last defenders of Vincennes surrendered at discretion.

XVI.

The amount of the extraordinary expenses of the army of Versailles was, at the rate of three millions of francs a day, 216 millions from the 18th March to the 28th May. The list of artillery implements

APPENDIX.

removed from the arsenals of Douai, Lyon, Besançon, Toulon, and Cherbourg, and forwarded to Versailles from the 18th March to the 21st May, comprise—

    30 cannons of $0^m \cdot 16$ (6 in. $\frac{299}{1000}$ diameter) from the War Arsenal.
    60 ,, ,, ,, from the Marine Arsenal.
    10 ,, of $0^m \cdot 22$ (8 in. $\frac{661}{1000}$ diameter) Marine.
    110 Rifled long 24-pounders.
    30 Rifled short 24-pounders.
    80 Rifled siege 12-pounders.
    3 Mortars of $0^m \cdot 32$ (12 in. $\frac{598}{1000}$ diameter).
    15 Mortars of $0^m \cdot 27$ (10 in. $\frac{629}{1000}$ diameter).
    15 Mortars of $0^m \cdot 22$ (8 in. $\frac{661}{1000}$ diameter).
    40 Mortars of $0^m \cdot 15$ (5 in. $\frac{905}{1000}$ diameter).

Total 393 artillery siege pieces.

Ammunition received at Versailles—
    Shells of $0^m \cdot 16$ (marine) 73,000
    ,, $0^m \cdot 22$,, ... 10,000
    ,, $0^m \cdot 24$ (rifled) 140,000
    ,,   for 12-pounder (rifled) . . 80,000
    Bombs of $0^m \cdot 32$ 1,000
    ,, $0^m \cdot 27$ 7,000
    ,, $0^m \cdot 22$ 7,000
    ,, $0^m \cdot 15$ 30,000
                                    Total 348,000

The stock of gunpowder amounted to 400 tons.

Up to the 21st of May, the artillery received 20 tons a day, and on that day 50 tons were forwarded to the besieging army.

Up to the 21st of May the field ordnance consisted of—
    36 batteries of 4-pounders.
    18 ,, 12-pounders.
    4 ,, 7-pounders (breech-loaders).
    12 ,, of mitrailleuses.

Total 70 batteries, 63 of which were provided with horses (7 being in store).

The ammunition service consisted of—
    80 tumbrels (calibre 12), each containing 54 charges.
    30 ,, (calibre 7) ,, 90 ,,
    120 ,, (calibre 4) ,, 120 ,,
    55 ,, of mitrailleuses ,, 243 ,,
    5000 cases of ammunition (for calibre 12), containing 49,000 charges.
    600 ,, (for calibre 4), ,, 12,000 ,,
    2000 ,, (for calibre 7), ,, 20,000 ,,
    1000 ,, for mitrailleuses ,, 30,000 ,,
    16 millions of Chassepot cartridges, and
    2 millions of Remington cartridges.

On the evening of the 23rd of May the army of Versailles expended—
26,000 discharges (calibre $0^m\cdot 16$), marine guns.
  2,000   ,,   ,, $0^m\cdot 22$),   ,,
60,000   ,,   ,, $0^m\cdot 24$), rifled guns.
30,000   ,,   ,, $0^m\cdot 12$), rifled siege guns.
12,000   ,,   (calibre of 7), used as a siege gun.
   150 bombs of $0^m\cdot 32$
   350   ,, $0^m\cdot 27$
  2500   ,, $0^m\cdot 22$
  5500   ,, $0^m\cdot 15$

Total 138,500 discharges of siege guns and mortars.—"*Guerre des Communeux*," p. 321.

The great feature of the second siege of Paris was the prudence exercised in manœuvring the men so as to protect them from needless exposure, practical experience in German encounters having taught the line a severe lesson. From the report of Marshal MacMahon we learn that the lost amounted to 83 officers killed, and 430 wounded; 794 soldiers killed, and 6,024 wounded, and 183 missing in all.

XVII.

LIST OF PUBLIC BUILDINGS, MONUMENTS, CHURCHES, AND HOUSES, DAMAGED OR DESTROYED BY THE COMMUNISTS OF PARIS, MAY 24—29, 1871.

Fire commenced in the houses marked thus (*).

Palais des Tuileries (Emperor's Paris residence). *Burnt.*
Musée du Louvre. *Library totally destroyed.*
Palais Royal (Prince Napoleon's Paris residence). *Burnt.*
Palais de la Légion d'Honneur (records all gone). *Burnt.*
Conseil d'Etat. *Burnt.*
Corps Législatif. *Damaged.*
Cour des Comptes (Exchequer). *Burnt.*
Ministère d'Etat (Minister of State). *Fired, but saved.*
Ministère des Finances (Treasury). *Burnt.*
Hôtel de Ville. (Town Hall of Paris.) *Burnt.*
Palais de Justice (Law courts). *Burnt.*
Préfecture de Police. *Burnt.*
The Conciergerie (House of Detention). *Partly burnt.*
Mairie of the 1st Arrondissement. *Dam.*
Mairie of the 4th Arrondissement. *Partially burnt.*
Mairie of the 11th Arrondissement. *Partially.*
Mairie of the 12th Arrondissement. *Burnt.*
Mairie of the 13th Arrondissement. *Damaged.*
Imprimerie Nationale. (National Printing office). *Damaged.*
Polytechnic School. *Damaged.*

Manufacture des Gobelins (National tapestry manufactory). *Partially burnt.*
Grenier d'Abondance (Enormous corn and other stores). *Burnt.*
Colonne Vendôme. *Overthrown on the 16th of May.*
Colonne de Juillet, on the Place de la Bastille. *Greatly damaged.*
Porte Saint-Denis. *Damaged.*
Porte Saint-Martin. *Damaged.*
Cathedral of Notre Dame. *Very slightly damaged.*
Panthéon. *Very slightly damaged.*
Church of Belleville. *Damaged.*
Church of Bercy. *Burnt.*
Church of La Madeleine. *Slightly dam.*
Church of St. Augustin. *Damaged.*
Church of Saint Eustache (used as a club). *Fired and much damaged.*
Church of Saint Gervais (used as a club). *Damaged.*
Church of St. Laurent. *Damaged.*
Church of Saint Leu. *Damaged.*
Church of Reuilly. *Fired but not burnt.*
Church of the Trinité. *Damaged.*
Church of La Villette. *Damaged.*
Sainte-Chapelle. *Slightly, if at all, dam.*
Théâtre du Châtelet. *Fired, but saved.*
Théâtre Lyrique. *Burnt.*
Ba-ta-clan Music Hall. *Fired, but not burnt.*
Théâtre des Délassements-Comiques. *Burnt.*
Théâtre de la Porte Saint-Martin. *Totally destroyed.*
Théâtre Cluny. *Only damaged.*
Théâtre Odéon. *Damaged.*
Abattoir de Grenelle. *Damaged.*
Assistance Publique (offices of public charity). *Burnt.*
Caisse des Dépôts et Consignations (Bank of Deposit). *Burnt.*
Caisse de Poissy (Bank of Deposit). *Burnt.*
Service des Ponts et Chaussées of the 13th Arrondissement (Civil engineer's office). *Partially.*
Arsenal. *Partly burnt.*
Caserne du Château-d'Eau (barracks). *Damaged.*
Caserne Mouffetard. *Damaged.*
Caserne Napoléon. *Damaged.*
Caserne Quai d'Orsay. *Burnt.*
Caserne de Reuilly. *Burnt.*
Docks, Bonded Warehouses and Storehouses at La Villette. *Burnt.*
Les Halles Centrales (Great general market). *Damaged.*
Marché du Temple (General market). *Damaged.*
Marché Voltaire (General market). *Dam.*
Bridge over the Canal de l'Ourcq. *Dam.*
Passerelle de la Villette (Foot-bridge). *Burnt.*
Pont d'Austerlitz, with restaurant Trousseau and sluice-keeper's house. *All burnt.*
Rotonde de la Villette. *Damaged.*
Hospice de l'Enfant Jesus. *Damaged.*
Hospital Lariboisière. *Damaged.*
Hospital Salpétrière: (House of refuge and lunatic-asylum for women). *Burnt.*
Prison of la Roquette. *Damaged.*
Gare de Lyon (Lyons railway terminus). *Fired and damaged.*
Gare d'Orléans (Orleans railway terminus.) *Damaged.*
Gare Montparnasse (Western railway terminus). *Damaged.*
Gare de Strasbourg (Eastern railway terminus). *Damaged.*
Gare de Vincennes (Vincennes railway terminus). *Damaged.*
House of M. Thiers (Place St. Georges). *Pulled down (previously).*
Cimetière du Père-Lachaise (cemetery). *Damaged.*
Barrière Charenton. *Damaged.*

APPENDIX.

Luxembourg : Powder Magazine in rear of Palace *blown up*, some subsidiary buildings *burnt*, and whole quarter *damaged*.

Avenue des Amandiers : Nos. 1, 2, 4. *Burnt*.
No. 69. *Damaged*.
Avenue de Choisy : Nos. 202, 221. *Dam*.
Avenue de Clichy : Nos. 2, 4, 22. *Dam*.
Avenue d'Italie : Nos. 1, 2, 3, 5, 78, 88. *Damaged*.
Avenue d'Orléans : Nos. 79, 81, 83. *Dam*.
Avenue Victoria : Nos. 2, 3, 4, 5. *Burnt*.
No. 6. *Damaged*.
Avenue de Vincennes : Nos. 2, 4, 10. *Damaged*.
Boulevard Beaumarchais : No. 1. *Burnt*.
Nos. 2, 13, 15, 26, 28, 30, 109. *Dam*.
Boulevard de Bercy : No. 4, 8. *Dam*.
Boulevard Bonne-Nouvelle : Nos. 11, 15. *Damaged*.
Boulevard Bourdon : Nos. 7, 17. *Dam*.
Boulevard des Capucines : No. 11 ; Maison Giroux, Nos. 43, 58, 60. *Damaged*.
Boulevard de la Chapelle : Nos. 10, 12, 14, 18, 20, coach houses and stables, 22, 30, 34, 40, 62, 86, 90, 94, 100, 122, 141, 143, 145, 147, "Aux Buttes Chaumont," 157, 163, 165, 169, 208, "Au Cadran Bleu," 216, 218. *Damaged*.
Boulevard de Charonne : Nos. 50, 52, 74. *Damaged*.
Boulevard de Clichy : No. 77 ; Convent and Church ; Nos. 79, 81, 84, 86. *Dam*.
Boulevard Contrescarpe : Nos. 2, 4. *Burnt*.
Nos. 42, 46. *Damaged*.
Boulevard de la Gare : No. 131. *Dam*.
Boulevard Haussmann : Nos. 23, 72. *Damaged*.
Boulevard d'Italie : Nos. 7, 69. *Dam*.

Boulevard de la Madeleine : No. 1. *Dam*.
Boulevard Magenta : Nos. 1, 3, 5, 6, 15, 48, 70, 73, 98, 114, "Au Méridien," 118, 143, 151, 153, 156. *Damaged*.
Boulevard Malesherbes : Nos. 9, 33. *Damaged*.
Boulevard Mazas : Nos. 1, 2, 3, 4, 5. *Burnt*.
Nos. 22, 26, 28 bis, 30, 60. *Dam*.
Boulevard Montmartre : No. 1. *Dam*.
Boulevard du Montparnasse : Nos. 9 bis, 41, 70, 100, 120, 150. *Damaged*.
Nos. 25, three shops, 110, 112. *Burnt*.
Boulevard Ornano : No. 56. *Burnt*.
Nos. 1, 4, 7, 9, 22, 27, 32. *Dam*.
Boulevard Poissonnière : No. 15. *Dam*.
Boulevard du Port-Royal : Nos. 16, 18, 20. *Damaged*.
Boulevard du Prince Eugène : Magazins-Réunis (co-operative store). *Dam*.
Boulevard Richard-Lenoir : Nos. 20, 82. *Burnt*.
Nos. 1, 5, 7, 9, 31, 36, 50, 69, 76, 87, 93, 107, 109, 116, 118, 136, 140. *Damaged*.
Boulevard Saint-Denis : Nos. 6, 13, Café Magny. *Damaged*.
Boulevard St. Jacques : Nos. 69. *Dam*.
Boulevard Saint-Marcel : No. 21. *Dam*.
Boulevard Saint Martin : Nos. 14, 16, 18, 20. *Damaged*.
Boulevard Saint Michel : No. 20 ; Café du Musée, 25 ; Café Miller, 65 ; Restaurant Molière, 73 ; Dreher Beer House, 99 ; School of Mines. *Dam*.
Boulevard Sébastopol : Nos. 9, 11, 13, 15. *Burnt*.
Nos. 42, 65, 83. *Damaged*.
Boulevard du Temple : Nos. 52, 54. *Burnt*.
Nos. 2, 19, 20, 22, 24, 26, 30, 32, 34, 35, 38, 40, 44, 50. *Damaged*.

APPENDIX.

Boulevard de la Villette: Nos. 85, 87, 117, Usine Falk. *Burnt.*
Nos. 97, 128, 134, 136, 138, 140, 162. *Damaged.*
Boulevard Voltaire: Nos. 2, 3, 4, 5, 6, 20, 22, 28, 60. *Burnt.*
Nos. 38, 53, 55, 60, 78, 94, 97, 98, 141, 166. *Damaged.*
Carrefour de l'Observatoire: No. 11. *Damaged.*
Chaussée Clignancourt: "Château-Rouge" (a public dancing-room). *Damaged.*
Chaussée du Maine: No. 164. *Dam.*
Chaussée de Ménilmontant: Nos. 56, 58, 81, 98. *Damaged.*
Croix-Rouge (crossway): Nos. 2, 4. *Burnt.*
Faubourg Montmartre: No. 50, 64. *Dam.*
Faubourg Poissonnière: Nos. 39, 168. *Damaged.*
Faubourg Saint-Antoine: No. 2. *Burnt.*
Nos. 1, 3, 4, 5, 6, 7, 22, 141, 154, 156, 158, 162. *Damaged.*
Faubourg Saint-Denis: Nos. 68, 77, 114, 208 bis, 214. *Damaged.*
Faubourg Saint-Honoré: Nos. 1, 2, 3. *Burnt.*
Nos. 4, 29, 30, 33, 35. *Damaged.*
Faubourg Saint-Martin: Nos. *55, 65, 67, 69, 71, "Tapis Rouge." *Burnt.*
Nos. 147, 184, 221, 234, 267. *Dam.*
Faubourg du Temple: No. 30. *Burnt.*
Nos. 9, 16, 17, 19, 20, 25, 29, 32, 33, 35, 41, 47, 48, 49, 53, 64, 66, 73, 81, 82, 93, 94, 106, 117. *Dam.*
Impasse Constantine: No. 2. *Damaged.*
Impasse Saint-Sauveur: No. 2. *Dam.*
Passage du Saumon. *Damaged.*
Place de la Bastille: Nos. 8, 10, 12, Poste de l'Ecluse. *Burnt.*
Nos. 4, 5, 6, 14. *Damaged.*
Place Blanche: Nos. 2, 3. *Damaged.*
Place Cambronne: No. 8. *Damaged.*
Place du Château-d'Eau: Nos. 7, 15. *Burnt.*
*9, 13, "Pauvres Jacques;" Nos. 17, 19, 21, 23, Café du Château-d'Eau. *Damaged.*
Place de la Concorde (Fountain). *Dam.*
Place de la Concorde (Statue of Lille). *Destroyed.*
Place de l'Hôtel de Ville: Nos. 1, 3, 7, 9, 11. *Burnt.*
Place de Jessaint: No. 4. *Damaged.*
Place du Louvre: No. 1. *Burnt.*
Place de la Madeleine: No. 31. *Dam.*
Place de l'Odéon: No. 8; Café de Bruxelles. *Damaged.*
Place de l'Opera: No. 3. *Damaged.*
Place Pigalle: No. 1. *Damaged.*
Place de la Sorbonne: No. 8. *Dam.*
Place Valhubert: "Châlet du Jardin." *Damaged.*
Place des Victoires: No. 2. *Damaged.*
Place de Vintimille: Nos. 1, 27. *Dam.*
Place Voltaire: No. 7. *Burnt.*
No. 9. *Damaged.*
Quai d'Anjou: Nos. 5, 11, 19, 23, 27, 43; "Au Petit Matelot." *Damaged.*
Quai de Bercy: No. 12, 13. *Burnt.*
Nos. 3, 5, 10. *Damaged.*
Quai de Béthune: Nos. 12, 20. *Dam.*
Quai Bourbon: No. 3. *Damaged.*
Quai des Célestins: No. 6. *Damaged.*
Quai de Gèvres: No. 2. *Burnt.*
Quai de l'Hôtel-de-Ville: Nos. 28, 58, 72, 78, 82. *Damaged.*
Quai de Jemappes: Nos. 18, 30, 34, 42. *Damaged.*
No. 32. *Burnt.*
Quai de la Loire: Nos. 10, 84, 86, 88. *Burnt.*
No. 60. *Damaged.*
Quai du Louvre: Nos. 2, 4, 6. *Dam.*
Quai de la Mégisserie: No. 22; "Belle Jardinière." *Damaged.*
Quai d'Orsay (a Club). *Damaged.*
Quai de la Rapée: No. 92, 94, 96, 98, 100. *Burnt.*

Quai de Valmy: Nos. 27, 29. *Burnt.*
Nos. 31, 39, 43, 71, 73, 79. *Dam.*
Quai Voltaire : No. 9, 13, 17. *Dam.*
Rue d'Alibert : Nos. 1, 2. *Damaged.*
Rue d'Allemagne: Nos. 2, 10. *Dam.*
Rue d'Alsace: Nos. 31, 33, 39. *Dam.*
Rue des Amandiers : Nos. 3, 4, 20, 65, 85, 87. *Damaged.*
Rue Amelot : Nos. 2, 21, 25, 104, 106, 139. *Damaged.*
Rue de l'Ancienne Comédie : No. 2 : "À Mazarin" (drapers). *Damaged.*
Rue d'Angoulême : Nos. 2, 28, 31, 43, 72 bis. *Damaged.*
Rue d'Anjou : No. 23. *Damaged.*
Rue de l'Arcade : No. 2. *Damaged.*
Rue de l'Arsenal: No. 8. *Burnt.*
Rue d'Assas : Nos. 30, *78, 86, 90, 96, 98, 106, 112, 118, 124. *Dam.*
Rue d'Aubervilliers: No. 138. *Burnt.*
Nos. 2, 24, 38, 92, 96. *Damaged.*
Rue Audran : No. 1. *Damaged.*
Rue d'Aval : No. 11. *Damaged.*
No. 17. *Burnt.*
Rue du Bac : Nos. 3, 4, 6, 7, 9, 11, 13. *Burnt.*
Nos. 54, 55, 56, Leborgne House, 58, 62, 64. *Damaged.*
Rue Barrault: Nos. 3, 31. *Damaged.*
Rue de Belleville : Nos. 1, 2, 66, 70, 89, 91, 133. *Damaged.*
Rue de Bercy : No. 257. *Damaged.*
Rue Bichat : No. 67. *Damaged.*
Rue Bisson: No. 49. *Damaged.*
Rue Blanche : Nos. 97, 99. *Damaged.*
Rue Boissy-d'Anglas : No. 31. *Burnt.*
Nos. 33, 35, 37. *Damaged.*
Rue de Bondy : Nos. 15, 17, 19, 21. *Burnt.*
Nos. *22, *32; 24, 26, Grand Café Parisien, 28, 30, 40, 44. *Dam.*
Rue Bréa : Nos. 1. *Burnt.*
No. 3. *Damaged.*
Rue de Bruxelles : No. 29. *Damaged.*
Rue de Buffon : Nos. 1, 8. *Damaged.*
Rue de la Butte-aux-Cailles : Nos. 1, 16. *Damaged.*
Rue de la Butte-Chaumont: No. 1. *Burnt.*
Rue Cail : No. 25. *Damaged.*
Rue Castex : No. 20. *Damaged.*
Rue de la Cerisaie : Nos. 20, 41, 45, 47. *Damaged.*
Rue de la Chapelle : Nos. 5, 16, 19, 35, 37, 75, 77. *Damaged.*
Rue de la Charbonnière : Nos. 32, 42. *Damaged.*
Rue de Charenton : No. 1. *Burnt.*
Nos. 2, 3, 4, 5, 6, 7, 8, 9, 11, 13, 100, 102, 187, 214, 230. *Dam.*
Rue de Charonne: Nos. 61, 79, 155. *Dam.*
Rue du Château : Nos. 169, 180. *Dam.*
Rue du Château-d'Eau : Nos. 1, 3, 73. *Burnt.*
Nos. 32, 55, 71, 75, 79, 81. *Dam.*
Rue de la Chaussée-d'Antin : Nos. 58, 64, 68. *Damaged.*
Rue du Chemin-Vert: Nos. 46, 54. *Dam.*
Rue Clavel : No. 3. *Damaged.*
Rue de Clignancourt : Nos. 9, 39, 43, 45, 49, 59. *Damaged.*
Rue Conti : No. 2. *Damaged.*
Rue de Cotte : No. 8. *Damaged.*
Rue de la Coutellerie: No. 2. *Burnt.*
Rue de Crimée : Nos. 156, 158. *Burnt.*
Nos. 81, 83, 155, 163. *Damaged.*
Rue du Croissant: (Saint Joseph's Market). *Damaged.*
Rue Curial : No. 134. *Damaged.*
Rue Damesne : No. 1. *Damaged.*
Rue Delambre : Nos. 2, 4. *Burnt.*
Rue Descartes : No. 6. *Damaged.*
Rue Domat : No. 24. *Damaged.*
Rue Dombasle : No. 61. *Damaged.*
Rue Durantin : No. 7. *Damaged.*
Rue des Écoles : No. 25. *Damaged.*
Rue d'Elzévir: Nos. 4, 7, 11, 12; "Auberge de la Bouteille" (inn). *Dam.*
Rue de l'Espérance: Nos. 7, 11. *Dam.*

Rue Fléchier: No. 2. *Damaged.*
Rue Folies-Méricourt: Nos. 51, 64, 75. *Damaged.* No. 115. *Burnt.*
Rue des Francs-Bourgeois: No. 38, Hotel Carnavalet. *Damaged.*
Rue Geoffroy-Saint-Hilaire: No. 18. *Dam.*
Rue de la Glacière: Nos. 36, 75. *Dam.*
Rue Grange-aux-Belles: No. 20. *Dam.*
Rue de Grenelle: Nos. 1, 3. *Burnt.* No. 34. *Damaged.*
Rue Guy-Patin: No. 3. *Damaged.*
Rue des Halles: No. 28. *Damaged.*
Rue Jacques-Cœur: No. 31. *Dam.*
Rue Joquelet: No. 12. *Damaged.*
Rue Julien-Lacroix: No. 2. *Damaged.*
Rue de Jussieu: No. 41. *Damaged.*
Rue de Lafayette: No. 107, 127. *Dam.* Nos. 195, Aubin (fireworks), 208, 213, 215. *Damaged.*
Rue Lacuée: Nos. 2, 4, 6. *Burnt.*
Rue de Lappe: No. 2. *Damaged.*
Rue Lepelletier: No. 26. *Damaged.*
Rue Lesdiguières: No. 2. *Damaged.*
Rue Levert: No. 12. *Damaged.*
Rue de Lille: Nos. 27, 37, 39, 43, 45, *47, 48, 49, 50, 51, Museum of M. Gatteaux, bequeathed to nation, 53, 55, 57, 61, 63, 65, 67, 69, 81, 83. *Burnt.*
Rue Louis-le-Grand: Nos. 32, 84. *Dam.*
Rue du Louvre: Nos. 6, 8. *Burnt.*
Rue de la Lune: No. 1. *Damaged.*
Rue de Lyon: No. 16. *Damaged.*
Rue des Marais: No. 68. *Damaged.*
Rue du Maroc: No. 38. *Damaged.*
Rue de Meaux: Nos. 2, 14. *Damaged.*
Rue Ménars: No. 8. *Damaged.*
Rue Meslay: No. 2. *Burnt.*
Rue Montmartre: Nos. 49, 53, 55. *Dam.*
Rue Montorgueil: Nos. 1, 29, 31, 33, 65. *Damaged.*
Rue Mouffetard: Nos. 132, 134, 136, 138, 139, 150; Church of St. Médard. *Damaged.*

Rue du Moulin-des-Prés: Nos. 83, 85. *Damaged.*
Rue Neuve-des-Petits-Champs: No. 105, Piver's. *Damaged.*
Rue Notre Dame-des-Champs: Nos. 52, 54. Studio of M. John Leighton. *Burnt.* Nos. 55, 57. *Damaged.*
Rue Notre-Dame-de-Nazareth: Nos. 16, 31. *Damaged.*
Rue Oberkampf: No. 4; À la Ville d'Alençon, No. 11, 12, 13, 15, 25, 36, 37, 41, 49, 50, 53, 57, 60, 67. *Damaged.*
Rue aux Ours: Nos. 47, 48, 49, 55. *Dam.*
Rue des Petites-Ecuries: Nos. 2, 4. *Damaged.*
Rue du Petit-Musc: No. 21. *Damaged.*
Rue Pierre Lescot: No. 16. *Damaged.*
Rue Popincourt: No. 2. *Damaged.*
Rue du Pressoir: No. 54. *Damaged.*
Rue de Provence: No. *20. No. 28. *Damaged.*
Rue de Puebla: Nos. 2, 3, 4, 17, 30, 292. *Damaged.*
Rue Racine: No. 2. *Damaged.*
Rue Rambuteau: Nos. 32, 58, 60, 102. "Aux Fabriques de France:" No. 124. *Damaged.* No. 16, "Colosse de Rhodes;" No. 19, Café du Marais; Nos. 26, 28, 30, 34, 62, 65, 72; Mr. Leforestier's house, "À l'Alliance," Nos. 49, 61, 63, 66, 69, 71. *Damaged.*
Rue Ramey: Nos. 41, 43. *Damaged.*
Rue Rampon: No. 18. *Damaged.*
Rue Réaumur: Nos. 14, 25, 43. *Dam.*
Rue de Rennes: No. 2; Café de Rennes, 151. *Damaged.*
Rue de Reuilly: No. 68. *Damaged.*
Rue du Rhin: No. 6. *Damaged.*
Rue Riquet: Nos. 63, 64. *Damaged.*
Rue de Rivoli: Nos. 33, 35, 37, 39, 79, 80, 82, 84, 86, 91, 98, 100; "À Pygmalion." *Burnt.*

Nos. 41, 88, 126, 210, 226, 236, 238. *Damaged.*
Rue Rollin: No. 18. *Damaged.*
Rue de la Roquette: Nos. 1, 3, 5, 7, 9, 11, 13, 18, 19, 20, 22, 24, 26. *Burnt.*
Nos. 4, 8, 15, 17, 34, 37, 38, 78. *Dam.*
Rue Royale: Nos. 15, 16, 17, 19, 21, 23, 25. *Burnt.*
Nos. 24, 27. *Damaged.*
Rue Saint André-des-Arts: Nos. 26, 42. *Damaged.*
Rue Saint-Antoine: Nos. 3, 7, 9, 114, 142, 150, 152, 160, 176, 178, 182, 192, 194, 198, 199, 201, 202, 203, 204, 205, 207, 212; "À la Fiancée," No. 213; "Phares de la Bastille," 214, 216, 218, 220, 222, 224, 226, 228, 232, 234, 236; Protestant Church. *Dam.*
Petite rue Saint Antoine: Nos. 3, 7, 9. *Damaged.*
Nos. 11, 13. *Burnt.*
Rue Saint-Denis: No. 223; Église Saint Leu. *Damaged.*
Rue Saint-Fiacre: No. 15. *Damaged.*
Rue Saint-Honoré: No. 422. *Burnt.*
No. 132. *Dam.*
Rue Saint-Jacques: Nos. 26, 146, 164, Café de l'École de Droit, 186, 196, 198, 216. *Damaged.*
Rue Saint-Lazare: No. 46. *Damaged.*
Rue Sainte-Marguerite: No. 22. *Dam.*
Rue Saint-Martin: Nos. 8, 10; "The Bon-Diable." Nos. 12, 14. *Burnt.*
Nos. *16, 248. *Damaged.*
Rue Saint-Maur: Nos. 151, 184, 225, 227. *Damaged.*
Rue des Saints-Pères: Nos. 46, 48. *Dam.*
Rue Saint-Sabin: Nos. 2, 4, 6. *Burnt.*
Nos. 3, 10, 12, 14. *Damaged.*
Rue Saint Sébastien: Nos. 42, 43, 44. *Damaged.*

Rue Sauval: No. 13. *Damaged.*
Rue de la Santé: No. 63. *Damaged.*
Rue Sedaine: No. 1. *Burnt.*
Nos. 5, 6, 8, 10, 11, 12, 14, 15, 16, 18, 19, 20. *Damaged.*
Rue du Sentier: No. 22. *Damaged.*
Rue du 4 Septembre: No. 13. *Dam.*
Rue de Sèvres: No. 2. *Burnt.*
Nos. 14, 16 (reservoir); Nos. 91, 92, 141. *Damaged.*
Rue de Sully: No. 11. *Damaged.*
Rue de Suresnes: Nos. 1, 9, 15, 17, 19. *Damaged.*
Rue de la Tacherie: Nos. 1, 2, 3, 4. *Burnt.*
Rue Taitbout: Nos. 22, 26. *Damaged.*
Rue Taranne: No. 10. *Damaged.*
Rue du Temple: Nos. 7, 10, 39, 201. *Damaged.*
No. 207. *Burnt.*
Rue Toquelet: No. 12. *Damaged.*
Rue Traversière: No. 53. *Damaged.*
Rue de Turbigo: Nos. 1, 3; "Au Grand Parisien," Nos. 5, 8, 11, 19, 21, 47; Church of Saint-Nicholas-des-Champs, Nos. 51, 53, 56, 63, 74. *Damaged.*
Rue De Vaugirard: Nos. 50, 63, 69, 70, Couvent des Carmes, 82, School for Girls, 92, School for Boys. *Dam.*
Rue Vavin: Nos. 2, *18, 20, 22. *Burnt.*
Nos. 16, 34, 36, 39. *Damaged.* 54 (Collection of M. Reiber, Architect). *Destroyed.*
Rue de la Victoire: No. 61. *Damaged.*
Rue du Vieux-Colombier: No. 31. *Dam.*
Rue Vilin: No. 2. *Damaged.*
Rue de la Villette: Nos. 20, 25, 26, 70. *Damaged.*
Rue de la Ville l'Évêque: Nos. 7, 18. *Damaged.*
Rue Volta: No. 33. *Damaged.*
Rue de Wiarmes: No. 1. *Damaged.*

The barricades of Paris numbered about 600—from a slight breast-work to a

INDEX TO PLAN.

B. Burnt.   P. B. Partly Burnt.   D. Damaged.   S. Damaged by Shot and Shell.

NORTH OF THE RIVER SEINE.

	Div. of Map.
1 Palace of the Tuileries, B.	8
2 Museum of the Louvre, P. B.	8
3 Palais Royal, B.	8
4 The Bourse (Exchange)	8
5 The New Opera-House	8
6 The Church of the Madeleine, D.	8
7 The Column Vendôme (overthrown)	8
8 The Palace of the Elysée	7
9 The Triumphal Arch, D.	7
10 Palais de l'Industrie, D.	7
11 Church of St. Augustin, D.	8
12 ,, of the Trinity, D.	8
13 ,, Notre Dame de Lorette	8
14 Ministère of Marine	8
15 Bibliothèque Nationale	8
16 Halles Centrales, S.	8
17 Church of Saint Eustache, D.	8
18 Opéra Comique	8
19 Church of St. Vincent de Paul	8
20 Hospital of Lariboisière, D.	8
21 Barracks of Prince Eugène, D.	9
22 Hospital of St. Louis	9
23 Prison of La Roquette, D.	14
24 Statue of Prince Eugène (removed)	14
25 Hôtel de Ville, B.	13
26 Tower of St. Jacques, D.	13
27 Prison of Mazas	14
28 Barracks Napoléon, D.	14
29 Conservatoire of Arts and Métiers	9
30 Hospital of St. Eugénie	15
31 Cattle Market and Slaughter H.	5
32 Magasins of Bercy (sacked)	20
33 Ministère des Finances, B.	8
34 Place de la Concorde, D.	8
35 Porte St. Denis, D.	8
36 Porte St. Martin, D.	9
37 Theatre of Porte St. Martin, B.	9
38 Church of St. Laurent, D.	9
39 Mairie Ist Arrondissement, D.	8
40 Théâtre du Châtelet, P. B.	13
41 Théâtre Lyrique, B.	13
42 Caisse Municipale, B.	13
43 Assistance Publique, B.	13
44 Mairie IVth Arrondissement, P. B.	14
45 Magasins-Réunis, D.	9
46 Théâtre des Del. Comiques, B.	9
47 Mairie XIth Arrondissement, P. B.	14
48 Column of July, D.	14
49 The Arsenal, B.	14
50 Hospital of Salpétrière, B.	19
51 Granary of Abundance, B.	14
52 Lyons Railway Station, P. B.	14
53 Mairie of XIIth Arrondissement and Church of Bercy, B.	14

SOUTH OF THE RIVER SEINE.

	Div. of Map.
1 Foreign Office, D.	7
2 Military School	12
3 Les Invalides and Tomb of Napoléon I.	12
4 Corps Législatif	7
5 Barracks d'Orsay, P. B.	8
6 Palace of the Institute	13
7 The Mint	13
8 Church of St. Sulpice	13
9 Palace of the Luxembourg, D.	13
10 Odéon Theatre, D.	13
11 Museum of Cluny	13
12 Palais de Justice, B.	13
13 Cathedral of Notre Dame	13
14 Church of the Pantheon, D.	18
15 Church of Val de Grâce	18
16 The Observatory	18
17 Wine Market (sacked)	14
18 Palace of Légion d'Honneur, B.	8
19 Conseil d'Etat and Exchequer, B.	8
20 Bank of Deposit, B.	8
21 Western Railway Station, B.	13
22 Gobelins Tapestry Manufactory, P. B.	18
23 Orleans Railway Station, P. B.	14

See western side of Plan for the fire and devastation caused by shot and shell during the engagements between the Federal troops and the army of Versailles:— Point du Jour, Auteuil, Passy, Porte Maillot, Avenue de la Grande Armée (Arc de Triomphe, much injured), Neuilly, Villiers, Levallois, &c.

BRADBURY, EVANS, AND CO., PRINTERS, WHITEFRIARS.

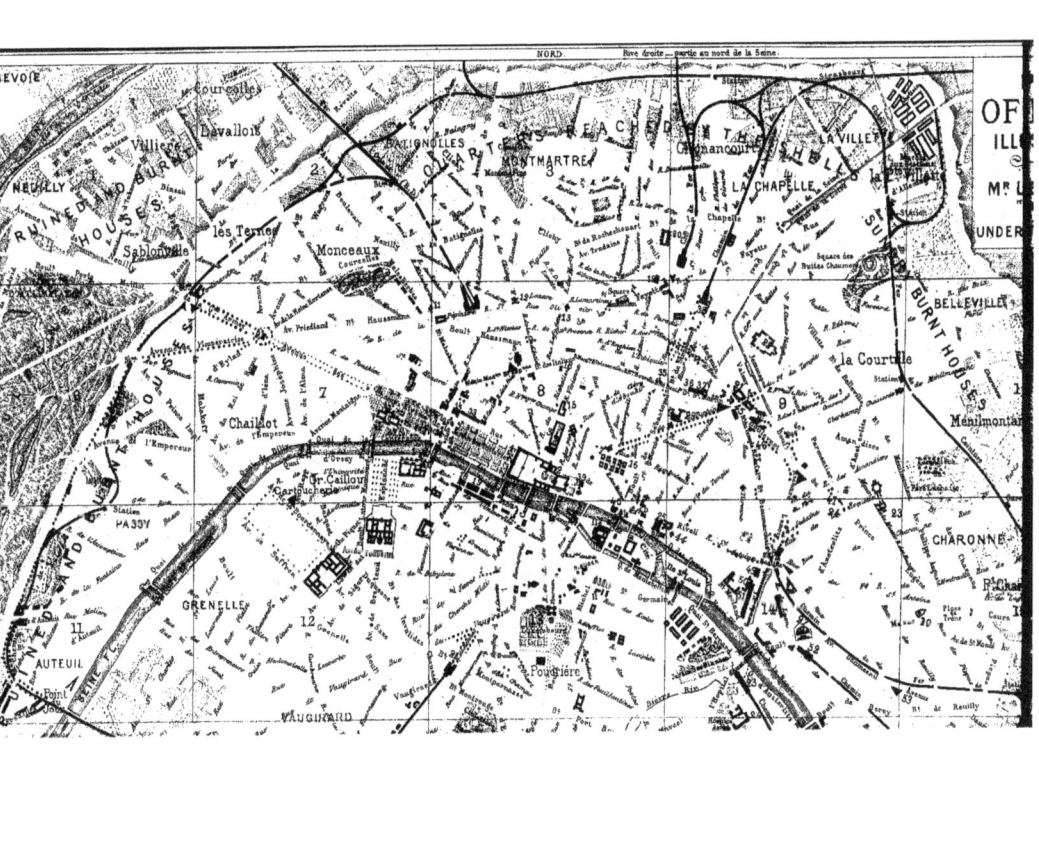

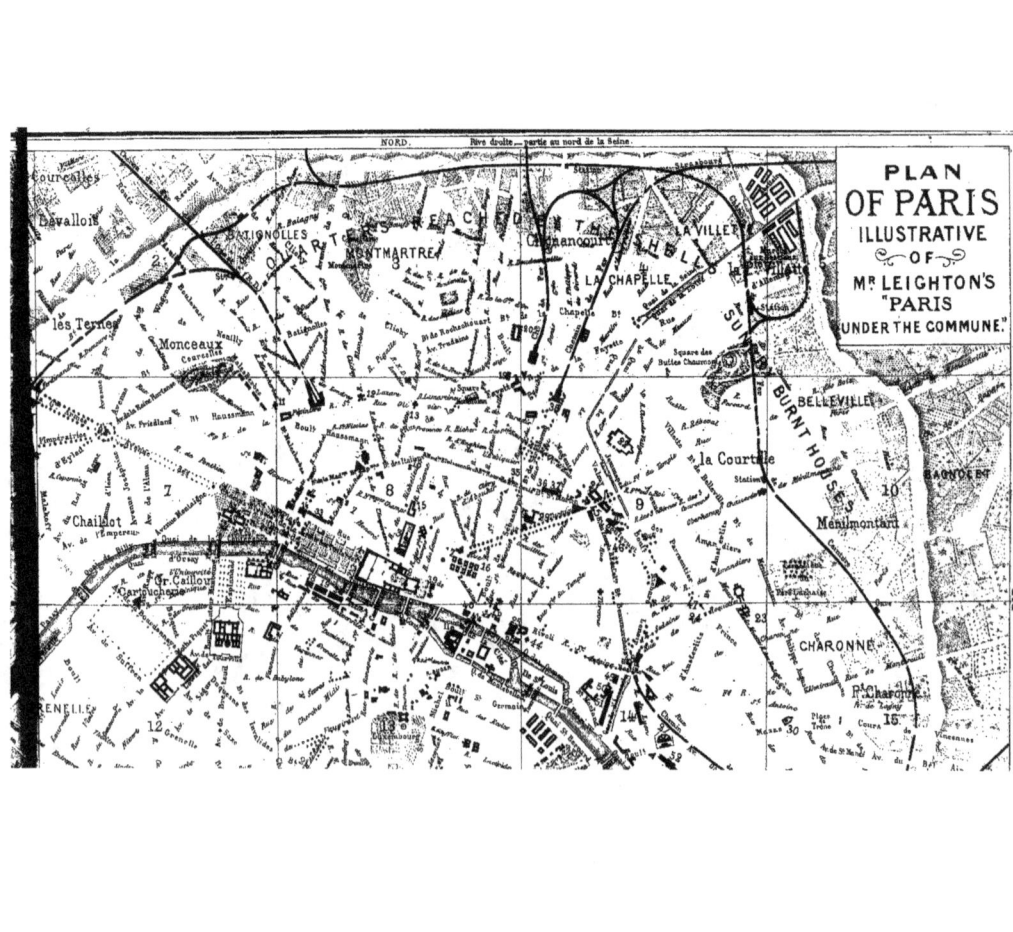

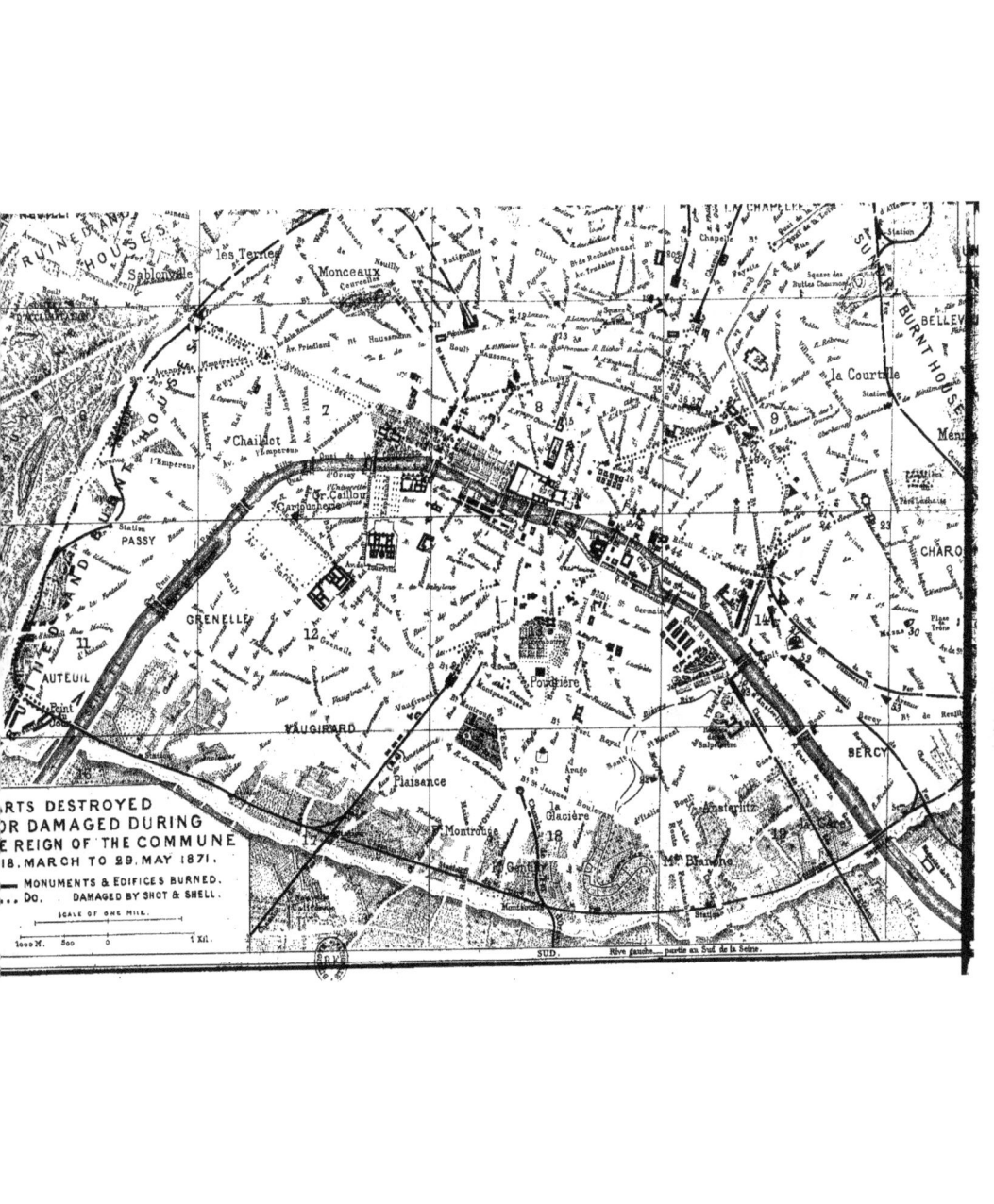

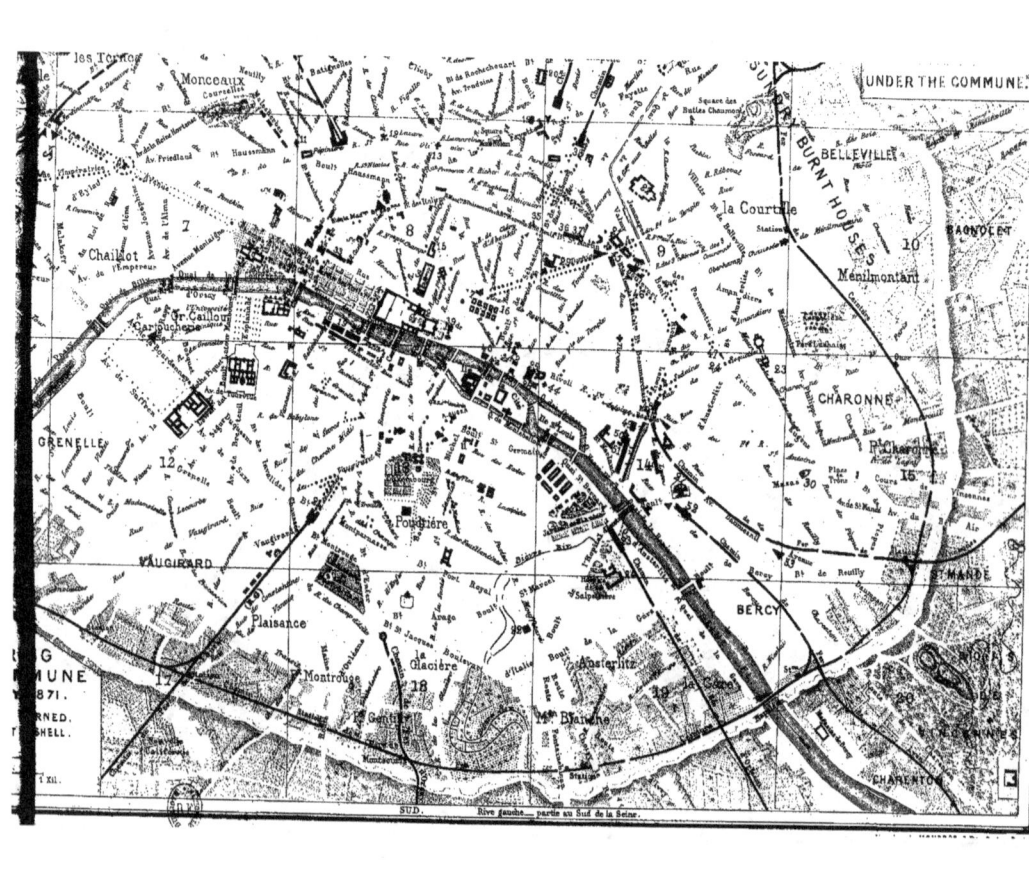

NEW WORKS

PUBLISHED BY

BRADBURY, EVANS, & CO.

SECOND EDITION, with additional Illustrations of The Louvre, The Tuileries, The Palais Royal, The Luxembourg, &c.

In post 8vo, price 10s. 6d., with Illustrations.

MEMORIES OF FRENCH PALACES.

By A. E. CHALLICE.

"All that is most romantic and touching in the history of the Palaces of French Monarchs is here told, simply, but very effectively."—*Standard*.

"This is a very pleasant book, treating of an interesting subject in an agreeable but not pretentious style. Giving an account of all the French palaces from Versailles to Fontainebleau which have been known to fame, it really presents an excellent and graphic summary of French history. That history, more, perhaps, than the history of any other European country, as we know, centres round the palace life. Then we have the beauty and the glory and the death of Marie Antoinette, the pomposity and the splendour of Louis XIV., the orgies of his drunken successor, the ecstasies and the miseries of the first Bonaparte, and the amiability and fidelity of the Empress Eugénie. A book of this sort it is almost impossible to criticise generally; we might almost as well attempt to give a *précis* of a portrait gallery. Our simple duty, and we can most conscientiously perform it, is to advise our readers to buy the book. We know no volume of the size that gives more simply, and yet more pleasantly, an account of that portion of French history which is worth knowing. It is due to the publishers to say that the engravings of the palaces enhance the value of the work."—*Edinburgh Courant*.

A book which deserves to be read for the striking picture that it presents of the most important episode of the war.

In large 8vo, cloth, price 18s.

THE FALL OF METZ.

By G. T. ROBINSON.

WITH MAP SHOWING THE FRENCH AND GERMAN POSITIONS.

"A valuable contribution to the history of this lamentable war."—*Standard*.
"An unquestionably valuable contribution to the history of the war."—*Spectator*.
"A book that deserves to be read for the striking pictures that it presents of the most important episode of the war. His narrative is, in our view, the most important single contribution to the history of the campaign yet published, if we except the ex-Emperor's late memoir. Indeed, we might possibly have dispensed with the latter the better of the two; for the weight of what comes from a merely neutral observer of such events as those that lately passed within Metz it is difficult to overrate."—*Saturday Review*.

BRADBURY, EVANS, & CO., 10, BOUVERIE STREET, E.C.

THE DAILY LIFE OF OUR FARM.

By the Rev. W. HOLT BEEVER, M.A., Oxon.,
Author of "Successful Farming," &c. &c.

In crown 8vo, price 5s.

By the Author of "RAVENSHOE," "GEOFFREY HAMLYN," &c.

HETTY.

By HENRY KINGSLEY.
Author of "Geoffrey Hamlyn," "Ravenshoe," &c.

In crown 8vo, cloth, with Frontispiece and Vignette, price 5s.

Mr. TROLLOPE'S LATEST STORY OF CLERICAL LIFE.

In crown 8vo, extra cloth, price 6s.

THE VICAR OF BULLHAMPTON.

By ANTHONY TROLLOPE.

With 12 Illustrations by HENRY WOODS.

CHEAP EDITION of VICTOR HUGO'S "L'HOMME QUI RIT."

In crown 8vo, extra cloth, price 5s.

BY ORDER OF THE KING.

By VICTOR HUGO.

With 12 Illustrations by S. L. FILDES.

A NEW VOLUME OF HAPPY THOUGHTS.

MORE HAPPY THOUGHTS.

By F. C. BURNAND.

In small crown 8vo, cloth, price 2s. 6d.

BRADBURY, EVANS, & CO., 10, BOUVERIE STREET, E.C.

In large quarto, price 21s.

MR. TENNIEL'S CARTOONS FROM PUNCH.

A SECOND SERIES, WITH PORTRAIT OF MR. TENNIEL.

"All the world is familiar with the pathos and sublimity of many of these cartoons, with the exquisite figure and portrait drawing of all, with their political insight so rarely falsified by events. Taken together, they are a pictorial history of the times they embrace, an acquisition to any Library, an ornament and a resource in any Drawing Room."

"The volume will be hailed with delight at many a fireside, and it will be appealed to in after-ages as illustrating the history of the times in which we live."—*Daily News.*

"We should prefer this volume to any other book of the season."—*Daily Telegraph.*

On many a hundred bookshelves, and in many a thousand hands.

DOUGLAS JERROLD'S WORKS.

"The fanciful wit again which flavours the writings of Mr. Jerrold carries us back to Fuller or Cowley, and is of a far rarer growth than the men of past times would have expected in a paper professedly comic and polemic."—*Quarterly Review.*

THE COLLECTED WORKS of DOUGLAS JERROLD. With a Memoir by his Son, and Frontispieces by the late JOHN LEECH. In 4 vols., cloth, price 6s. each; or bound in half calf, price 36s.

THE LIFE OF DOUGLAS JERROLD. By W. Blanchard Jerrold. Forming a Fifth Volume. New and Revised Edition. Price 6s. cloth; or half calf, price 9s.

THE COMEDIES AND DRAMAS OF DOUGLAS JERROLD. In 2 vols., small 8vo, cloth, price 4s. each.

POPULAR CHEAP EDITIONS.

MRS. CAUDLE'S CURTAIN LECTURES	Price 1s.
PUNCH'S LETTERS TO HIS SON	Price 1s. 6d.
SKETCHES OF THE ENGLISH	Price 1s. 6d.
THE LESSON OF LIFE, &c.	Price 1s. 6d.
THE STORY OF A FEATHER	Price 1s. 6d.

G. A. A'BECKETT'S WORKS.

THE COMIC HISTORY OF ENGLAND. Illustrated with Woodcuts and Coloured Etchings by the late JOHN LEECH. Demy 8vo, cloth gilt, price 12s.; half calf extra, price 16s.

THE COMIC HISTORY OF ROME. Uniform with the Comic History of England. Illustrated by the late JOHN LEECH. Demy 8vo, cloth gilt, price 7s. 6d.; half calf extra, price 11s.

THE COMIC BLACKSTONE. Illustrated by George Cruikshank. Small 8vo, price 2s.

BRADBURY, EVANS, & CO., 10, BOUVERIE STREET, E.C.

National University for Industrial and Technical Training.
Demy 8vo, cloth, price 9s.

TECHNICAL EDUCATION.

By J. SCOTT RUSSELL, M.A., F.R.S.

"Mr. Scott Russell has rendered no common service by bringing together in this volume a quantity of what, for want of a better word, may be called 'floating' information, and has added to this the results of his own painstaking investigations. * * * The book comprises all the facts and figures requisite for a knowledge of the subject; and at the same time is the original research of an able author, who puts his whole heart into the matter about which he writes. Henceforth every one who wishes for information upon 'Technical Education' will be compelled to resort to Mr. Scott Russell's comprehensive volume."—*Daily News.*

"The author deserves the gratitude of his country for the manner in which he has taken up and advocated this important subject; and it is to be earnestly hoped that the work will attract the serious attention of our legislators, and that once fairly started it will not be allowed to rest until the English people receive what they have a right to demand—an education equal to the best that any foreign government bestows upon its people."—*Standard.*

"We regard the book before us as a very timely and bold venture, into an arena few have dared to enter. Its boldness is a great merit,—its comprehensiveness a greater; * * * we thank its author for giving us a whole scheme; it is a substantial thing about which discussions may take place, and forms a present basis for practical action and suggestion."—*Manchester Guardian.*

"The work, of which the above is the title, is a very noble exposition of what is needed, what has been done, and what should be done, towards giving a scientific education to the people of England. * * * The necessity for such an education by the advances made by the peoples of other countries by means of the same, is demonstrated in the pages of Mr. Scott Russell's work—an authority which should be consulted before any steps are taken."—*Birmingham Daily Post.*

"Mr. Scott Russell has produced a book which ought to be read, talked over, and discussed by every skilled workman, overman, and master, in this busy mining, metal-working, and pottery-manufacturing county; and it should be read at this time, while the education question is on the carpet. * * * Let Staffordshire read this book, and answer in the next session of Parliament."—*Staffordshire Advertiser.*

A Standard History which should be on the shelves of all Libraries.

CHARLES KNIGHT'S
HISTORY OF ENGLAND.

ILLUSTRATED
WITH 1000 STEEL PLATES AND WOODCUTS.

In Eight Volumes, cloth, price £3 16s.
  "   "   *half calf extra, gilt, price £5 5s.*

"So observes Mr. Charles Knight in his admirably comprehensive Popular History of England, from which no topic that concerns the history of the English people—not even this question of the history of parish registers—has been omitted; that book of Mr. Knight's being, let us say here, by the way, the best history extant, not only for, but also of, the people."—*Charles Dickens's All the Year Round.*

BRADBURY, EVANS, & CO., 10, BOUVERIE STREET, E.C.

www.ingramcontent.com/pod-product-compliance
Lightning Source LLC
Chambersburg PA
CBHW060931230426
43665CB00015B/1905